# ESSAYS
# CATHOLIC AND CRITICAL

# ESSAYS
# CATHOLIC & CRITICAL

## BY MEMBERS OF
## THE ANGLICAN COMMUNION

EDITED BY

EDWARD GORDON SELWYN

LONDON
## SOCIETY FOR PROMOTING
## CHRISTIAN KNOWLEDGE
NEW YORK AND TORONTO: THE MACMILLAN CO.

*Printed in Great Britain*

1926

# PREFACE

THE contributors to this volume have been drawn together by a common desire to attempt a fresh exposition and defence of the Catholic faith. They have nearly all been engaged in University teaching during recent years, and have thus been brought into close touch with the vigorous currents and cross-currents of thought and feeling amid which Christianity has to render its own life and truth explicit ; and they have been compelled, both for themselves and for others, to think out afresh the content and the grounds of their religion. This book is the result of their endeavour.

Among precursors in the same field, the essayists owe pre-eminent acknowledgment to the authors of " Lux Mundi," a book which exercised upon many of them a formative influence and still has a living message. But by two forces especially, both of them operating with great intensity, theology has been constrained both to lengthen its cords and to strengthen its stakes during the generation which has elapsed since that work was first published. On the one hand many thoughtful men have been led by the spectacle of a disordered and impoverished Christendom to a keener discernment of the supernatural element in religion, and to a renewed interest in the expressions of it which are seen in Catholic unity and authority, in whatever form these come ; so that solidarity has taken its true rank at the side of continuity, as a necessary " note " of the Church. On the other hand, the critical movement, which was already in " Lux Mundi " allowed to effect a significant lodgment in the citadel of faith, has continued with unabated vigour to analyse and bring to light the origins and foundations of the Gospel. As the title of this volume implies, it is the writers' belief that these two movements can be and must be brought into synthesis ; and we believe further that, in the task of effecting it, in thought, in devotion, and finally in the visible achievement of the Church's unity, the Anglican

Communion and its theologians have a part of peculiar importance to play.

For the two terms Catholic and critical represent principles, habits, and tempers of the religious mind which only reach their maturity in combination. To the first belongs everything in us that acknowledges and adores the one abiding, transcendent, and supremely given Reality, God ; believes in Jesus Christ, as the unique revelation in true personal form of His mystery ; and recognises His Spirit embodied in the Church as the authoritative and ever-living witness of His will, word, and work. To the second belongs the exercise of that divinely implanted gift of reason by which we measure, sift, examine, and judge whatever is proposed for our belief, whether it be a theological doctrine or a statement of historical fact, and so establish, deepen, and purify our understanding of the truth of the Gospel. The proportion in which these two activities are blended will vary in different individuals and in relation to different parts of our subject-matter : but there is no point at which they do not interact, and we are convinced that this interaction is necessary to any presentment of Christianity which is to claim the allegiance of the world to-day.

The scope and arrangement of the essays call for little explanation. The first three essays are concerned with the presuppositions of faith—with its rudimentary origins and development, with its justification in reason and experience, and with the claims of the Catholic Church to provide for it a rational basis of authority ; though there is a sense in which no doctrine of authority can claim to be more than a kind of torso, so long as the divisions of Christendom hinder its concrete expression and operation. The second and central section of the book aims at unfolding the revelation of God and the redemption of man which centre in, and derive from, the Person of Christ, incarnate, crucified, and risen ; and the historical evidence for these facts is considered with some fulness in face of modern criticism. The concluding section embraces the institutional expression and vital application of the redemptive resources of Christianity in the Church and the sacraments, particular heed being given to certain aspects of these which are much in men's minds at the present time. It will be clear that many problems have had to be left untouched ; but some omissions were necessary, if the book were not to assume an inconvenient bulk. Our purpose, however, has not been to be exhaustive, but rather to bear witness to the faith we have received and commend it, so far as may be, to others.

In a work of this kind the measure of collective responsibility is not easy to define. Nor perhaps is it necessary. Domiciled as we are in different places, and not all of us even in England, we have found it impossible to meet together for discussion. On the other hand, each author has seen and been encouraged to criticise every essay, and all criticisms have been considered before any essay assumed its final form. In some cases care has been taken by the use of the first person to show that an expression of opinion is markedly the writer's own. These cases, however, though not unimportant, are few ; and while none of the authors should be held responsible for more than his own contribution, it may be legitimately said that the volume represents a common faith, temper, and desire.

E. G. S.

*Eastertide*, 1926.

# CONTENTS

# THE EMERGENCE OF RELIGION
## BY EDWIN OLIVER JAMES

# CONTENTS

# I

## Introductory

THE progress of scientific research in recent years has not only changed our view of the universe, but it has also materially altered our conception of human and religious origins. In the old days when it was thought that the world was brought into being in a short space of time by a series of special creative acts culminating in man, the whole scheme of creation and redemption seemed to fit together into one composite whole. Now, for those who are acquainted with contemporary thought, religion, like all other attributes of the universe, is known to be a product of evolution, inasmuch as it has proceeded from simple beginnings to complex conceptions of man and his relation to the supernatural order. But since this fact was first demonstrated in the latter part of the nineteenth century, further evidence has thrown much new light on the early history of religion. Nevertheless, anthropology is still a young and somewhat speculative science, and it becomes anthropologists to be very modest in their assertions. At present we know only in part, and with the completion of knowledge (if indeed such is attainable) doubtless many of our provisional hypotheses will have to be abandoned or at least modified. Therefore, in venturing upon an account of the emergence of religion, it should be made clear to the general reader at the outset that we are dealing with tentative propositions based upon evidence that is in process of accumulation. But provisional formulation according to the data available at a given time and the use of the scientific imagination are part of the scientific method and not to be despised in the great quest of truth. Moreover, it is impossible for a writer who is himself engaged in specialised research to be entirely free from a mental bias resulting from his own investigations. It is the business of the scientist to collect and classify the data at his disposal and to form judgments upon the basis of this classification, but always claiming the right, of course, to adjust his conclusions, or, if need be, change them, in the light of new and additional evidence    Therefore, while he is concerned primarily with facts, he cannot altogether escape from theories.

It is now becoming clear that the view concerning the origin of religion which the late Sir Edward Tylor put forth in 1872 in his great work, " Primitive Culture," is too specialised to be a "minimum definition," as he described it.   Religion, he thought, originated in animism, a term used to signify a " belief in the existence of spiritual beings," [1] that is to say, of " spirits " in the wide sense that includes " souls."   Man is supposed to have arrived at this conception by the realisation that within him dwells a kind of phantasm or ghost which is capable of leaving the body during sleep, trance, or sickness, and finally going away altogether at death.   This doctrine is thought to have been extended to the rest of creation, so that the entire scene of his existence was pervaded by these " spiritual beings."   That such a view is held to-day by many people living in a primitive state of culture is beyond dispute ;  but does it follow, therefore, that this was the case when man first emerged from his mammalian forbears ?

## II

### Life, Death, and Immortality in Early Cult

#### 1. *Beliefs in Survival after Death*

When we turn from modern native races to the evidence revealed by the pick and spade of the archæologist—and after all it is this that is of supreme importance, since the savage can never be anything but a " modern man," however arrested his development may be—the first indication of religion occurs in what is known as the Middle Palæolithic period (the Old Stone Age), when, shivering under the effects of the great Ice Age, man was driven to seek shelter and warmth in the caves of France and Spain.   The inference is based upon the manner of burial adopted by the prehistoric race named *Neanderthal* (after the place where the first example of the type was found), which inhabited these caves and rock-shelters perhaps a quarter of a million years ago.   Though brutish-looking fellows, the Neanderthalers not only made beautifully worked flint tools, but also laid their dead to

---

[1] *Primitive Culture* (London, 1891), 3rd ed., i. 424.

rest with great care and ceremony. Thus at Le Moustier the skeleton of a youth about sixteen years of age was found carefully placed in the attitude of sleep, with the right forearm under the head. A bed of flint chips formed his pillow, and close by the hand was a splendid implement. Other flints of the pattern characteristic of this period were discovered in the grave, together with the bones of the wild ox. Since the latter were charred and split, it is generally thought that they were the relics of a funeral feast. Similar ceremonial burials have been found elsewhere, notably at La Chapelle-aux-Saints.[1]

These interments prove beyond doubt that Neanderthal man had some conception of a life after death. Professor Macalister, in his recent "Text-Book of European Archæology," has summed up the situation by saying that Neanderthal man, degenerate though he may have been, " was conscious of something more than merely animal within him : already he had begun to look forward to a life beyond the grave—a life like that to which he was accustomed, for he could conceive of none other, where he would need food and clothing, and the instruments for procuring them. As his comrades passed, each in his turn, into the silent land, he laid beside their bodies such things as he imagined would minister to their necessities in the mysterious otherworld." [2]

Neanderthal man, however, does not represent the earliest stages of human development. At least one example of a much older and probably far superior type of man has been found, taking us back to a very remote period, before the Ice Age, perhaps half a million years ago. This remarkable discovery was made in 1912 in a narrow stratum of river-gravel on Piltdown Common, near Uckfield, in Sussex. Although the precise date of the skull is a matter of dispute among scholars, all are agreed that the lady of Piltdown—for the skeleton was apparently that of a woman— is the oldest inhabitant of Great Britain, if not of the world, so far discovered.[3] Contemporary with, or perhaps rather earlier than, *Eoanthropus*, as the Piltdown woman is called, " a being human in stature, human in gait, human in all its parts, save its brain," and therefore named *Pithecanthropus erectus* (the ape-man

[1] *Arch. für Anthrop.* (1909), vii. 287 ff. ; *L'Anthropologie* (1913), xxiv., 609–634 ; H. Obermaier, *Fossil Man in Spain* (New Haven, 1924), pp. 95 ff., 132 ff.

[2] (Cambridge, 1921), p. 343.

[3] *Quart. Journal Geol. Soc.*, March 1913, xix. 117.

who stands erect), was found in Java in 1894.[1]    While some authorities regard the Javan fossil as the most primitive member of the human family, others think that it is most satisfactorily explained as a degeneration on lines of its own.    The size of a man's head, of course, is no precise criterion of his intellectual powers, but nevertheless a brain must reach a certain weight— 950 grammes, or 1000 cubic centimetres in volume—before it can become the seat of human intelligence.    *Pithecanthropus*, with a cranial capacity of 850 cubic centimetres, is therefore well below the human level, whereas his contemporary (or successor) in Sussex had a thoroughly human-shaped skull with a large capacity variously estimated at from 1100 to 1397 cubic centimetres, and resembling in many ways the head-form of modern man.    Moreover, as Professor Keith has shown, the front part of the brain—the pre-frontal region, as it is called—with which all the higher mental faculties are associated, was well developed. This suggests that the ancient lady was a person of some intelligence, infinitely superior intellectually either to *Pithecanthropus* or to Neanderthal man.[2]    Therefore, if the Cave people had some conception of religion, although we have no direct evidence that the same is true of the earlier Piltdown race, yet there is certainly no adequate reason to deny it.    On the contrary, if we are compelled to grant a religious sense to Neanderthal man, it would be illogical to suppose that his intellectually superior predecessor was inferior in this respect.    It is, therefore, not improbable, if the Piltdown remains are at all typical of the earliest human beings, that religion emerged at a very early period in the history of mankind.

Can we go a step further, and determine the nature of the earliest strivings after things unseen ?    With regard to the theological doctrine of a primitive revelation and a state of original righteousness having at one time prevailed, the anthropological evidence, of course, is silent, the question being one for the theologian to decide and not for the scientist.    Since we are here concerned primarily with the scientific evidence, suffice it to say that there is no *prima facie* reason for rejecting the possibility

[1] Keith, *Antiquity of Man* (London, 1916), pp. 257 ff.

[2] The pre-frontal region of Neanderthal man is by no means fully developed, and has a protuberance as in the brain of the anthropoid apes. *Cf.* Elliot Smith, *Evolution of Man* (Oxford, 1924), p. 41.

of a primitive revelation having been vouchsafed to man, since a person with a head like that of the Piltdown woman would not have been incapable of conscious communion with the Deity, but on the other hand there is nothing in the available evidence to suggest this having occurred. Again, there is no innate tendency in man to be progressive,[1] and apparently degeneration manifested itself in prehistoric times in the Cave period. These facts are certainly not inconsistent with the view that man started his career in a higher state than that in which he is to-day known to the archæologist. But, so far as the anthropological evidence is concerned, nothing is known of religion, if it existed, before the middle of the Palæolithic period, when the Neanderthal folk apparently asked the eternal question, " If a man die shall he live again ? "

To the primitive mind death doubtless appeared as a sleep that knows no waking, and therefore the Cave men laid their dead in a position of rest surrounded by implements, shells,[2] etc., in the belief that the grave was not the ultimate and absolute end of human existence. It is scarcely likely that his eschatological speculations went beyond this, though it has been suggested that burial in the contracted position had reference to the idea of rebirth—a conclusion presupposing a degree of anatomical and embryological knowledge, to say nothing of mystical interpretation, which early man could hardly have possessed. There is reason to think, however, that he may have been led by his observations as a hunter to associate the heart with the centre of vitality, since this organ figures prominently in some of the hunting scenes depicted on the walls of the later Palæolithic caves in France and Spain.[3] Life and death were facts of experience, and the obvious inference to be drawn from a dead body is that something has left it. Moreover, hunters would know that loss of blood produced loss of vitality, faintness, and death. It would therefore not require much speculation to associate the blood with the life ; and their experience in the chase again would lead them to the knowledge that the heart was the vital spot, as is proved by the

---

[1] *Cf.* Elliot Smith, *op. cit.*, p. 118.

[2] It is possible that these shells were used as amulets to give life to the dead. *Cf.* J. W. Jackson, *Shells as Evidence of the Migration of Early Culture* (Manchester, 1917), pp. 135 ff.

[3] E. A. Parkyn, *Prehistoric Art* (London, 1915), pp. 89, 107 ff. ; Sollas, *Ancient Hunters*, 2nd ed. (London, 1915), pp. 326, 333, 361.

Palæolithic drawings of animals in which this organ is represented with arrows in it.[1]

This belief in the blood as the vitalising essence doubtless led to the heart being regarded as the seat of the vital principle, and the blood as a vital fluid. Thus arose also the practice of painting the bones of the dead red, as in the case of the skeleton found in a Palæolithic cave at Paviland in Wales,[2] and in the later kurgans or Neolithic (New Stone Age) and Bronze Age tumuli of Russia.[3] The purpose of the rite is clear, for, as Macalister says, " red is the colour of living health. The dead man was to live again in his own body, of which the bones were the framework. To paint it with the colour of life was the nearest thing to mummification that the Palæolithic people knew ; it was an attempt to make the body again serviceable for its owner's use."[4]

## 2. *Response to the Mystery of Nature and Life*

Although it is not in the least likely that the primitive mind was concerned with problems of theology, yet it is not unreasonable to surmise, that when the knowledge of natural law was so limited, the overpowering awesomeness of Nature found a religious expression at a very early period. As the lightning shivered the trees, and the thunder crashed amid torrential rains, the cave-dwellers may have felt themselves in the presence of a Power that they did not understand, and which therefore terrified and mystified them. In all ages the sense of wonder in the presence of Nature has been one of the primary impulses of religion, and it may well be that it played a prominent part in the earliest stages of religious evolution. Thus Otto says, " all ostensible explanations of the origin of religion in terms of animism or magic or folk psychology are doomed from the outset to wander astray and miss the real goal of their inquiry, unless they recognise this fact of our nature— primary, unique, underivable from anything else—to be the basic factor and the basic impulse underlying the entire process of religious evolution." [5] This is more or less the view put forth by Marett. In his opinion, religion manifested itself on its emotional side when ideation was vague, as an attitude of mind

---

[1] *Op. cit.*          [2] *Journ. Anthrop. Institute*, xlviii. (1913), p. 325.
[3] *K. Russ. Arch. Gesellschaft*, xi. 1.
[4] *Text-book of Europ. Archæol.*, p. 502.
[5] *The Idea of the Holy* (Oxford, 1923), p. 15.

dictated by awe of the mysterious, which provided religion with its raw material apart from animism.[1] This " pre-animistic " phase at the threshold of religion he terms *animatism*, and connects it with a mystic impersonal force, called by the Melanesians *mana*, which " works to effect everything which is beyond the power of men, outside the common process of nature." [2] It should be remembered, however, that while *mana* is largely impersonal in the Banks and Torres Islands, elsewhere in the Pacific its ultimate source is personal beings, and is " out and out spiritualistic." [3]

Nevertheless, apart from the precise significance of the Melanesian conception of *mana*, it would seem that something akin to the idea of " power " at a very early period was attached to objects that showed signs of " activity," life and mystery— " a primal numinous awe "[4]—which may represent " the beginning of the notion, however vague, of a transcendent Something, a real operative entity of a numinous kind, which later, as the development proceeds, assumes concrete form as a ' numen loci,' a dæmon, an 'El, a Baal, or the like." [5] It is this which lies behind the notion of " sacredness," tabu, and worship, producing that attitude of mind which finds expression in the cry, " How dreadful is this place ! " Thus the concept of the eerie and awful passes into that of the " numen," a divine power associated with an object or place. " This is none other than the house of Elohim." On this hypothesis, the religious attitude of early man may not have been far removed from that of the author of the 29th Psalm to whom the thunderstorm that passed over the country was a revelation of God.

But if Neanderthal man felt himself in the presence of powers that mystified and terrified him, his successors the *Aurignacians*, as they are called, sought their god in the mysterious life-giving power that appears to animate Nature. The two great interests of primitive people everywhere and at all times are food and children. " To live and to cause to live, to eat food and to beget children, these were the primary wants of man in the past, and they will be the primary wants of man in the future so

[1] *Threshold of Religion* (London, 1914), pp. 3 ff.
[2] Codrington, *The Melanesians* (Oxford, 1891), pp. 119 ff.
[3] Hocart, *Man* (1914), p. 46.
[4] Otto coins the word " numinous " to express the apprehension of supernatural power producing the idea of non-moral holiness.
[5] *Idea of the Holy*, p. 130.

long as the world lasts." [1]  They have been described as the foundation-stones of magic and religion,[2] and as early as the Aurignacian culture phase, Palæolithic man made female figures with the maternal organs grossly emphasised, identical with the statues found in Crete, the Ægean, Malta, Egypt and Western Asia, known to have been associated with the cult of the Mother Goddess.[3]  To the Aurignacians the Great Mother may have been little more than a life-giving amulet—the " push of life " from within and the struggle for existence from without directing the religious impulse to the conservation and promotion of life by magical devices.  But as life-giving amulets developed, the " numinous consciousness " was doubtless stirred, and gradually there arose the conception of the Great Mother, the giver of life and health.  Elliot Smith thinks that " this Great Mother, at first with only vaguely defined traits, was probably the first deity that the wit of man devised to console him with her watchful care over his welfare in this life, and to give him assurance as to his fate in the future." [4]  This perhaps is true, inasmuch as the religious sense in man was awakened largely through the practical problems of life and death calling forth the " numinous quality " of religious awe.  Ideas invariably originate not in speculation but in facts, and in the case of religions, it would seem that God led man on to a knowledge of Himself chiefly through natural means.  Nature proved a stern school in early days, and when man reached the end of his ordinary practical and emotional tether, he became conscious of his own limitations and of the vastness and mysteriousness of the world.  Thus the fear of Nature led him to the fear of the Lord, just as to-day the religious impulse is stimulated when a person reaches the limit of his own resources.  While, on the one hand, this may have led him to the notion of a " transcendent Something " akin to an external Creator, a real operative entity of a numinous kind, a personification of the concept of *mana* ;  on the other, the purely practical side, it is not improbable that the Great Mother represents the earliest expression of the creative principle in terms of deity, and therefore she may be the first concrete deity the wit of man devised.  Be

---

[1] *Golden Bough,* 3rd ed., pt. iv. ("Adonis, etc," I.), p. 5.

[2] J. Harrison, *Epilegomena to the Study of Greek Religion* (Cambridge, 1921), p. 1.

[3] Déchelette, *Manuel d'archéologie* (Paris, 1908), pp. 217, 428 ff., 584, 594.

[4] *Evolution of the Dragon* (Manchester, 1919), pp. 151, 143, 150.

this as it may, there can be little doubt that it was through the practical problems of life, coupled with an emotional attitude towards natural phenomena, that man was first made to seek God and feel after Him if haply he might find Him.

### 3. Ideas of Body and Soul

From these simple beginnings the history of religion pursues an even course for thousands of years along the lines indicated above until revolutionary and far-reaching changes appear in the Eastern Mediterranean about the middle of the fourth millennium B.C. In Mesopotamia the existence of a Sumerian civilisation has been revealed preceding the first Semitic kingdom founded in that region by Sargon of Akkad (c. 2800 B.C.), while at Anau in Russian Turkestan, and at Susa in Elam, the remains of an early copper culture occur having affinities with the 6th "city" at Hissarlik (Troy).[1] In the Ægean, the ancient civilisation of Crete has been divided into an early, middle, and late Minoan age, each in its turn split up into three sub-periods. Evans places the beginning of the Minoan age at 3400 B.C., and considers that the Neolithic deposits in Crete probably go back to 8000 B.C.[2] In Egypt the Dynastic period begins about the same time (3400 B.C.), and it has lying behind it a pre-Dynastic period, certainly going back to 8000 B.C., divided into early, middle, and late, according to the age of the graves found in prehistoric cemeteries scattered over Egypt and Nubia.[3] Thus the close of the Palæolithic age in Europe serves as the pedestal for the beginning of the history of the oldest civilisations.

While the majority of scholars look to Babylonia for the cradle land of civilisation, Elliot Smith argues in favour of the original broadcasting of culture from the Nile Valley.[4] The discovery that the bodies of the dead were desiccated by natural forces as a result of their having been deposited in the hot desert sand, turned the thoughts of the pre-dynastic Egyptians, he thinks, to the preservation of the body to eternal life. Around the

---

[1] R. Pumpelly, *Explorations in Turkestan* (Washington, 1908); De Morgan, *Délégation en Perse*, Mémoires xiii.; *Prehistoric Man* (London, 1924), pp. 105, 208 ff.; H. Frankfort, *Royal Anthrop. Inst. Occas. Papers*, No. 6, 1924, pp. 78 ff.

[2] *Palace of Minos* (London, 1921), i. 25, 35.

[3] Petrie, *Journal Anthrop. Institute*, xxix. 295.

[4] *Ancient Egyptians* (London, 1923).

practice of mummification there grew up, on this hypothesis, the complex system of ritual and belief which contributed to a considerable degree to the wonderful civilisation that subsequently developed in Egypt and Western Asia and finally spread throughout the world.[1] Apart from this theory of the initiative of Egypt in the creation of civilisation, it is beyond dispute that in the Nile Valley at the beginning of the Dynastic period there arose a complex idea of immortality centred in the literal restoration to life of the dead body.[2] Having freed themselves from the precarious and absorbing life of the chase by the discovery of agriculture, men turned their attention to the problem of the essential nature and destiny of man. The notion of a vital principle in the body was elaborated in the doctrine of the *ka* or guardian genius, which was born with the man, and resided in his body during the whole of his terrestrial life except when it went on a journey during sleep. It gave all the attributes of life to the human organism, but the actual personality consisted of the visible body and the invisible intelligence (*khu*), which was situated in the heart (*ab*) or abdomen. The breath, as distinct from the intelligence, was the actual vital essence, and after the Twelfth Dynasty the two were symbolised by the *ba*, or human-headed bird with human arms, hovering over the mummy, extending to its nostrils in the one hand the figure of a swelling sail, the hieroglyph for wind or breath, and in the other the *crux ansata*, or symbol of life.[3] The *ba* was the disembodied soul or ghost which came into existence for the first time at death. It was represented as flying down the tomb-shaft to the mummy in the chamber below, and wandering about the cemetery. The *ba* was therefore connected with the mummy (*sahu*), just as the *ka* was associated with the *khat* or body. The *ka* was said to go to Osiris, the god of the dead, or to the boat of the Sun, or to the company of the gods who gave it, and it was separated from its protégé by more than the mere distance of the cemetery, for in one passage in the Pyramid Texts the deceased "goes to his *ka*, to the sky." [4] It was always the protecting genius, and seems to have combined the function of a guardian spirit and an animating essence. But it was always distinct from the conception of the soul (*i.e.* the ghost)

---

[1] *Proc. Royal Philos. Soc.* (Glasgow, 1910), xli. pp. 59 ff.

[2] Breasted, *Development of Religion and Thought in Ancient Egypt* (London, 1912), p. 56.

[3] Breasted, *op. cit.*, 52 ff.      [4] *Op. cit.*, p. 55.

as expressed in the doctrine of the *ba*. To ensure physical restoration to the dead the personality had to be reconstituted, and if the corpse was to be resuscitated, the missing " substance " or vitality must be restored. To this end elaborate ceremonies were devised which aimed at reconstituting the individual by processes external to him, under the control of the survivors and the mortuary priest. First the body had to be resuscitated, and the faculties were restored one by one, till at length the deceased became a " living soul " (*ba*), in which capacity he again existed as a person, possessing all the powers that would enable him to survive hereafter. A human being therefore did not become a *ba* merely by dying, but through the renewal of his vitality and personality. First the tissues of the physical body had to be preserved, and the individual features and natural form. maintained so far as possible in the mummy itself. Then it had to be animated. But the technical difficulties in the way of making the mummy the *simulacrum* of the deceased were so great that, notwithstanding the measure of success achieved by the Egyptians of the Pyramid Age, the practice was never wholly successful, and the custom of making images of the dead in stone and wood and transferring the *ka* to them was adopted at an early period. These portrait statues seem to have been regarded not merely as abodes or vehicles of the life of the deceased, but as the man himself in his entire nature—that is to say, they were in all respects identical with the resuscitated mummy. Thus the sculptor was called " he who makes to live " (*s'nh*), and the ceremony of the animation of the statue—" opening the mouth," as it was termed— was looked upon as a creative act.[1] In Mexico and elsewhere images of the dead were brought into physical contact with the actual body, or a life-giving substance, to transform them into live men. Either the ashes of the cremated remains were transferred to the effigy, or blood (identified with the life) of human or animal victims was smeared upon them, a practice that very probably represents the beginning of sacrifice.[2]

This transference of the life of man to his portrait statue or effigy tended, however, to magnify the importance of the vital principle at the expense of the body ; and although the Egyptians

---

[1] Breasted, *op. cit.,* pp. 52 ff. ; A. H. Gardner, *Encycl. Rel. and Ethics,* viii. 23.

[2] Oviedo, *Historia General de las Indias* (Madrid, 1855), iv. 48 ff. Cf. *American Anthropologist* (1914), p. 61.

never dissociated a person from the body, elsewhere the external
embodiment—be it either the mortal remains or their surrogate—
gradually lost its significance in the process of securing immortality for the soul. In Egypt, however, since the conception of the continuation of life beyond the grave was
bound up with the imperishability of the body, cremation was
never adopted. Nevertheless, as will be explained later, from
the Fifth Dynasty onwards the Pharaohs began to turn their
gaze skywards as the solar theology became predominant. In
consequence the ritual of mummification gradually became celes-
tialised, the mummy eventually being conveyed to the sky by
Hathor, the divine cow, and other vehicles.

The Egyptian conception of the soul, while in many respects
clearly an extension of the prehistoric notion of the indwelling
vital principle concentrated in certain parts or attributes of the
body, is a very specialised doctrine, in which all the various theories
found elsewhere are contained. Thus in many parts of the
world—*e.g.* Indonesia, China, New Guinea, the Pacific, North
America, etc.—the belief that man has two souls is widespread.[1]
The life or vital principle is invariably (but not always) distinguished from the kind of double of the deceased (the ghost) that
came into existence at the moment of death as a new and independent entity. Even when the life was thought to become
the ghost instead of returning to the sky whence it proceeded,
it took over a rather different guise after death.

In Babylonia the spiritual double corresponding to the Egyptian
*ka* was designated the *Zi* or "life," and was symbolised in the
cuneiform script by a flowering plant. It was the *Zi* that made
man a living soul in this world, and beyond the grave it continued
to represent his personality. But in addition to this at death man
became an *edimmu* or *lila, i.e.* a ghost.[2] The body was not essential
to the attainment of immortality, as no attempt was made to
preserve it, and cremation seems to have been practised in certain
parts of Sumer and Akkad from very early times.[3] In the
Ægean, on the other hand, great care was taken in the disposal of
the body. The kings of Knossos and Mycenæ were buried in

---

[1] *Encycl. Rel. and Ethics*, vii. 233 ff. ; De Groot, *The Religious System of
China*, iv. bk. ii. (Leiden, 1901), pp. 3, 57, 396 ; *Folk-lore*, xxxi. (1920), pp. 53 ff.
[2] Sayce, *Religion of Ancient Egypt and Babylonia* (ed. 1903), pp. 276 ff.
[3] Koldeway, *Zeitschrift für Assyriologie*, ii. (1887), pp. 403 ff.

elaborately furnished, chambered and domed tombs,[1] and although
the dwellings of the dead passed through many changes of form
during the Minoan age, they all agreed in testifying that soul and
body were not dissociated, till, in the Homeric period, there arose
a new conception of the soul as the last breath distinct from the
vital principle. While relics of preservation of the body remained
in the preparation of the corpse immediately after death, cremation
was adopted as the means of freeing the soul from its fleshly
entanglement.[2] The doctrine of transmigration added later by
the Orphics to the Dionysiac cult, and taught by Pythagoras,
developed this conception of the soul as an immaterial entity.

Thus in the great religions of antiquity in the Near East we
can observe the gradual dissociation of body and soul, which,
outside Egypt, found expression in such practices as cremation,
and possibly in the doctrine of reincarnation and transmigration.
From crude notions concerning the revivification of the physical
body with all its attributes, there arose apparently a belief in the
life of the spirit as a new entity carrying on the life of the individual
either in another body or in the disembodied state, but independent
of the mortal remains. Moreover, the same tendency may be
observed in the phenomena of nature as in man. The whole
universe, according to primitive philosophy, belongs to one great
system of interrelated and inherent life—probably the unconscious
expression of the religious emotion itself. But as the individual
object becomes associated with the religious emotion it takes on
an individuality of its own, and the inherent vitality becomes more
and more specialised and independent of its external embodiment.
By some such process as this the belief in spiritual beings, phantasms,
and all that is comprised by the term animism, used in its Tylorian
sense, may have arisen. Thus in North America, the Iroquois
of the Eastern States suppose that in every object there is an
inherent power called *orenda*, analogous to will and intelligence
rather than to purely mechanical force.[3] This is the equivalent
of the Melanesian concept of *mana*. On the Plains to the west
of the Iroquois, the Omaha address prayers and ascribe certain
anthropomorphic attributes to a kind of vital essence called *wakonda*

---

[1] A. Evans, *Prehistoric Tombs of Knossos* (London, 1906), p. 5 ; cf. *Journal of Hellenic Studies*, xxii. 393 ; cf. Ridgeway, *Early Age of Greece* (Camb., 1901), i. 7.
[2] *Iliad*, xxii. 151, xiii. 763, xviii. 345 ff., 315 ff., xxiii. 106.
[3] Hewitt, *Handbook of Amer. Indians* (Washington, 1907–10), ii. 147.

("the power that moves ").[1] It would seem that here we have the impersonal energy on its way to becoming a separate spiritual being with a cult of its own. To the north, the Eastern Algonquins apply the term *manitu* to any spirit or *genius loci*, but these spirits were not necessarily definite in shape. An arrow, for example, was *manitu* because a spirit had either transformed itself into the arrow, or dwelt in it.[2]

## III

### EARLY DEVELOPMENTS OF THEISM

#### 1. *The Divine King and Culture-hero*

Once the doctrine of spirits became established their form and number were limitless. They appeared as human beings, animals, " mythological " creatures, rocks, trees, phantasies, etc., according to the predominance of the image in the mind of the individual. Some spirits were indeterminate in shape because the object with which they were associated had no definite form, as in the case of such spirits as wind, fire, water, etc. As spirits of definitely circumscribed type developed, one of the first and most natural reactions seems to have been that the people elevated to the supernatural order those chiefs and heroes so dear to the popular mind. Thus Seligman has shown that the Shilluk of the White Nile reverence their king because they regard him as a reincarnation of the spirit of Nyakang, the semi-divine hero who founded the Dynasty and settled the tribe in their present territory. The pedigree of the kings from Nyakang to the present day has been preserved. These monarchs number twenty, distributed over twelve generations, though probably many more have reigned.[3] The natives think of Nyakang as having been a real man in appearance and physical qualities, though, unlike his royal descendants of more recent times, he did not die but simply disappeared. His holiness is manifested especially by his relation to Juok, the Supreme Creator of the Shilluk who sends down rain at the intercession of Nyakang. The latter appears to have been a real man who led the tribe to their present home on the Nile, and he is therefore regarded by Frazer as the modern counterpart of the

---

[1] *27th Report Bureau Amer. Ethnol.* (1911), pp. 134, 597.

[2] *Journal Amer. Folk-lore*, xxvii. (1914), pp. 349 f.

[3] *Cult of Nyakang and the Divine Kings of the Shilluk* (Khartoum, 1911), pp. 216 ff.

ancient Egyptian Osiris whom Elliot Smith describes as "the prototype of all gods."[1]

The origin of Osiris is still a matter of controversy. Petrie thinks that he was a civilising king of Egypt who was murdered by his brother Set and seventy-two conspirators,[2] and Frazer concludes that "though in the main a god of vegetation and of the dead," originally Osiris was a real man who "by his personal qualities excited a larger measure of devotion than usual during his life and was remembered with fond affection and deeper reverence after his death ; till in time his beloved memory, dimmed, transfigured, and encircled with a halo of glory by the mists of time, grew into the dominant religion of his people."[3] Further he suggests the possibility " that Osiris was no other than the historical king Khent of the First Dynasty, that the skull found in the tomb is the skull of Osiris himself."[4] But what Frazer fails to show is how Osiris the divine king and Osiris the vegetation god are to be reconciled.

An examination of the early Texts reveals scanty evidence of Osiris as the source of all vegetable life, for in the Old Kingdom it is his royal character that is emphasised, especially in the sculptures and hieroglyphs. Furthermore, " it is always as a dead king that he appears, the rôle of the living king being invariably played by Horus, his son and heir."[5] Thus in the Sed festival, which appears to have been normally celebrated every thirty years, and is usually supposed to have been on the occasion of the king being deified as Osiris,[6] Gardiner has given reasons for believing that the king there played the part of Horus and not of Osiris, and that " it is only in death that the monarch's transformation from Horus to Osiris was effected,"[7] on the twenty-fifth day of the fourth month during the embalmment ceremonies. In this case a complete identity existed between the king and the gods both in life and after death.

---

[1] *Golden Bough*, pt. iv. (" Adonis," etc., II.), pp. 160 ff. ; Elliot Smith, *Evolution of the Dragon*, p. 32. While it cannot be maintained, as the philosopher Euhemeros supposed, that all myths are of historical origin, and all gods merely deified men, it is nevertheless true that historical facts have been preserved in tribal traditions, and some culture-heroes have been deified after death.

[2] *Religion of Ancient Egypt* (London, 1906), pp. 38 f.

[3] *Golden Bough, op cit.*, p. 160.    [4] *Op. cit.*, p. 198.

[5] *Journal of Egyptian Archæology*, ii. (1915), p. 122.

[6] Petrie, *Researches in Sinai* (London, 1906), p. 185.

[7] *Journal Egypt. Archæol., op. cit.*, p. 124.

Nevertheless, that Osiris was connected with vegetation is shown by the unmistakable relation which exists between the dates of the Osirian festivals and the seasons of the agricultural year. The representation of a king on a very early mace using a hoe to inaugurate the making of an irrigation canal [1] has led Elliot Smith to conclude that there was a close connection between the earliest kings and irrigation. Civilisation, he thinks, began when the Egyptians first devised methods of agriculture and invented a system of irrigation. The irrigation engineer, on this hypothesis, became the ruler of the whole community—the king—whose beneficence was apotheosised after his death, so that he became the god Osiris, who was identified with the river, the life-giving powers of which he controlled. Thus he was at once a dead king and connected with agriculture, and regarded as the controller of life-giving powers to the dead as well as to the living.[2]    But as the originator of civilisation he was also, it is claimed, the prototype of all gods ; " his ritual was the basis of all religious ceremonial ; his priests who conducted the animating ceremonies were the pioneers of a long series of ministers who for more than fifty centuries, in spite of endless variety of details of their ritual and the character of their temples, have continued to perform ceremonies that have undergone remarkably little essential change." [3]

On this hypothesis the creative function of sky-gods is explained as the result of the deification of the Sun in the Fifth Dynasty when the king regarded himself as the physical son of Re, the Sun-god. Henceforth every Pharaoh ascended to the sky at death, and all life-giving powers were attributed to the sky-gods. The Sun was the source of life to the earth, and the realm whence life proceeded and whither it returned. Thus the Sun and the sky-beings came to be regarded as Creators.[4]    It is undoubtedly true that in the Pyramid texts and funerary literature in Egypt the sky-god is represented as the source of life and death, of rain and heavenly fire. Among his names that of Horu (symbolised by the hawk) has given rise to the so-called " hawk names " which appear among the most ancient forms of royal names—those of the Thinite period of the First and Second Dynasties. These show, when set in order, that the king was regarded as an

---

[1] Quibell, *Hierakonpolis* (London, 1900), i. pl. xxvi. chap. 4. *Cf.* p. 9.
[2] *Evolution of the Dragon*, pp. 29 f.        [3] *Op. cit.*, p. 32.
[4] W. J. Perry, *The Children of the Sun* (London, 1923), pp. 201 ff., 440 ff.

emanation upon the earth of the Supreme Being. Thus in Egypt the conception of the monarch appears to have been based solely upon the assimilation of the king to the gods. But did the notion of a heavenly Creator arise as the result of the elaboration of the Sun-cult in the valley of the Nile at the beginning of the Dynastic period ?

The gods associated with creation in Egyptian theology are many. The genesis of the sun (Re) is variously attributed to Seb and Nuit, the First Dynasty sky-goddess who produced the earth, and gave the king the name of " Son of Nuit." This prepared the way for the assimilation of the king to Re and Osiris, according as these successive theologies connected these deities with Nuit. The Sun-god therefore was not the first sky deity to be assigned creative functions, and the conception of an external Supreme Creator is probably independent in origin of that of the divine culture-hero, the fusion of the two cults having been effected perhaps from the king being regarded as either the incarnation or the son of the Creator. Thus in Babylonia the Sumerian city-kings claimed to have been begotten by the gods and born of the goddesses, but they were not deified,[1] while in Greece the Homeric king was descended from gods (*diotrephes*) and had *supernatural* powers.[2] It is even possible that such phrases as " the Spirit of the Lord came upon him," used of Othniel, Jephthah, and Samson (Jud. iii. 10, xi. 29, xiii. 25) may have had originally a similar significance. The story of the birth of Samson is singularly like that of the birth of the solar deity Mithra,[3] and, as in the case of the other judges, he was certainly a vicar of God.

## 2. *The Beneficent Creator*

It would seem, then, that the divinity of kings was intimately related with the early developments of theism, and one of the germs of monotheism may lie in this doctrine of divine kingship. If Osiris was the first king of Egypt, and if the Dynastic period in the Nile Valley predated the rise of other ancient monarchies, he may be regarded as a prototype of the gods who began life as

---

[1] Langdon, *The Museum Journal*, viii. (Philadelphia, 1917), p. 166.
[2] *Golden Bough*, 3rd ed., pt. i. p. 366. *Cf.* Hocart, *Man*, xxv. (February 2, 1925), pp. 31 f. *Cf. Od.* iv. 692 ; ii. 409; xix. 109-114. *Il.* ii. 335; xvii. 464.
[3] Cumont, *Mysteries of Mithra* (1913), pp. 124, 130.

chiefs, kings, or popular heroes. Thus may be explained the striking resemblances between Nyakang and Osiris. Both died violent deaths, the graves of both were pointed out in various parts of the country ; both were deemed great sources of fertility, and both were associated with certain sacred trees and animals, especially with bulls. Moreover, just as Egyptian kings identified themselves both in life and death with Osiris, so Shilluk kings are still believed to be animated by the spirit of Nyakang and to share his divinity. But behind the figure of Nyakang there stands the shadowy form of the High God Juok, and although his worship has been eclipsed by that of the divine king and ancestor, yet he remains the Creator and Supreme God.

This is typical of the All-Father belief among primitive people. Beside the culture-hero there is the Creator, beneficent and ethical, who dwells in the heavens in dignified seclusion from the affairs of man. The Uitoto of Colombia, South America, for example, in addition to the deified ancestors, recognise Nainema, " He-who-is-appearance only," as the Creator,[1] while among the Dakota in North America the Supreme Deity is comprehended as Wakan Tanka, the Great Mystery, made up of four eternal essences to be regarded as one—the Chief God, the Great Spirit, the Creator, and the Executive.[2] In Australia the All-Fathers seem to be a combination of deified culture-heroes and beneficent Creators, since they are usually regarded as highly ethical gods who have had their abode on earth like Osiris, and retired to their present abode in the sky, whence they sent down "everything that the blackfellow has." [3] Therefore primitive monotheism is apparently a dual concept, one aspect of which is based on a custom which may be traced as far back as early Egypt and Sumer—the custom of worshipping kings in their own name—the other, the notion of the beneficent Creator, going back probably to a much earlier period of religious development.

In the determination of the evolution of theism it is important to remember the part played by these two concepts in the origin of the idea of God. It has often been suggested that ethical

---

[1] K. T. Preuss, *Rel. und Mythologie der Uitoto*, i. 166 ff.

[2] J. R. Walker, *Anthrop. Papers Mus. Nat. Hist.*, vol. xvi. pt. ii. pp. 78 ff., 152 ff.

[3] Spencer and Gillen, *Northern Tribes of Central Australia* (London, 1904), pp. 498 ff. ; Howitt, *Native Tribes of S.E. Australia* (London, 1904), p. 488 ; A. Lang, *Making of Religion* (London, 1898), pp. 187 ff.

monotheism is the result of successive transformations of some particular deity or lesser being. Thus while the religion of the Semites consisted of a complex system of polytheism and dæmonism,[1] there arose in Babylonia about 2000 B.C. a tendency towards henotheistic monolatry (belief in and worship of one God together with the recognition of other gods and spirits) when Marduk, the personification of the Sun and the early city god of Babylon, became the principal god of Babylonia and the head of the pantheon, when Babylon was made the capital, and all the attributes of the other gods were absorbed by him.[2] Again, in Egypt in the Eighteenth Dynasty (*c.* 1400 B.C., Amenhotep III and IV) the elaboration of the Sun-cult led to a belief in the universal and life-giving power of the Sun-god, who was the author of his own being as well as the Creator of all things visible and invisible. The Aton or solar disk was worshipped as the living manifestation of the one God behind the Sun. At Akhetaton (horizon of Aton), now called Tell-el-Amarna, between Thebes and the sea, Amenhotep, the brother or half-brother of Tutankhamen, who had changed his name to Ikhnaton, built a new capital which was evidently intended as a centre of the dissemination of solar monotheism, since the name of the Sun-god is the only divine name found there.[3] Here several sanctuaries of Aton were erected, and similar cities were founded in Nubia, and probably another in Asia. The recognition of the fatherly solicitude of Aton above all creatures—" thou art the father and mother of all that thou hast made "—raised this remarkable development of monotheism above anything that had been attained before in Egypt or elsewhere. The beauty of the eternal and universal light was identified with love as the visible evidence of the presence of God who is the author of the beneficence of the natural order.[4]

But why should the Sun-god become an ethical, intelligent, and benevolent Creator ? The magic word evolution does not really explain such a development of monotheism because there is no obvious reason why there should be one god rather than many, and such an intelligent people as the Greeks found that polytheism

---

[1] W. R. Smith, *Religion of the Semites* (London, 1907), pp. 84 ff.

[2] Jastrow, *Religious Belief and Practice in Babylonia and Assyria* (New York, 1911), pp. 100 ff.

[3] Breasted, *Development of Religion and Thought in Ancient Egypt*, pp. 322 ff.

[4] Weigall, *Akhnaton, Pharaoh of Egypt* (Edinburgh and London), pp. 115 ff.

solved their theological problems more easily than monotheism.[1]
It is by no means clear why a centralised government or the
political predominance of one city over another should cause the
gods of a nation to become one.   Thus in Babylonia henotheism
which centred in Marduk passed into polytheism again because the
people failed to regard each and every god as the highest deity,
without conflicting with the claims of any other god, just as in
Egypt a reaction in favour of the traditional gods took effect after
the death of Amenhotep IV, and swept away the short-lived cult
of Aton.

Once man had come to believe in gods, polytheism fitted in
with the primitive conception of the universe much better than
monotheism.   Having no conception of the universality and continuity of natural causation, early man attributed every event
which arrested his attention or demanded an explanation to supernatural agencies.   Cause and effect, and even agent and act, were
not clearly differentiated.   Any extraordinary event that called
for the help of an intervening agent provided an impetus to penetrate more deeply into the nature of the supernatural powers and
to establish a more intimate alliance with them.   But as knowledge of cause and effect in nature increased, it became apparent
that the hitherto inexplicable events depended upon natural causes
rather than on the intervention of departmental deities.   Thus in
the sixth century B.C., Thales, the earliest of the Greek philosophers,
explained the universe as the result of a " primitive substance "
which he identified with water, out of which all things were
evolved ;  but Socrates inferred from the presence of design
in the world that a benevolent Creator existed behind the
universe, to whom alone the term God is applicable.[2]   Therefore
the monotheism of the Greek philosophers defined God as the
source and guiding principle of the world.   But this is a very
different conception both of the Deity and of the universe from that
which found expression in the earlier developments of monotheism.

---

[1] The few passages in Homeric literature that seem to assert the principle
of monotheism, as, for example, the use of θεός in the abstract as the equivalent
of Zeus [*Il.* xiii. 730 ;  *Od.* iv. 236], are more easily explained as the expressions
of a special kind of religious thought and emotion than as a general trend
towards monotheism, since the doctrine never affected the popular religion.
*Cf.* Farnell, *The Cult of the Greek States* (Oxford, 1896), i. p. 84 ff.

[2] Aristotle, *Met.* i. 3, 983B.   *Cf.* Burnet, *Early Greek Philosophy* (London,
1908), pp. 47 ff., 141, 314.

The benevolent Creators among primitive peoples are certainly not the product of philosophical thinking, nor the triumph of the unifying principle over the disruptive, of abstract over concrete thought. They would seem rather to represent the purposive functioning of an inherent type of thought and emotion,[1] rather than the elaboration of a certain kind of knowledge concerning the universe. Hence the recurrence of monotheism in all states of culture and in every stage of religious development. There is reason to think, as has been explained above, that in Palæolithic times there arose a notion akin to the idea of God as a " transcendent Something, a real operative entity of a numinous kind." The concept of supernatural power (*i.e. mana*) and the belief in Supreme Beings represent psychological tendencies rather than stages in an evolutionary system. The remote High God or beneficent Creator, as distinct from the deified culture-hero, is apparently the climax of primitive religious thought. Although the savage has hardly any relations with this All-Father in practice, yet he attaches to him a value superior to that of all other mythological beings, a value which may well accord with the divine in the highest sense.[2] Men probably did not search for this conception of the Deity in the beginning, since when the primitive mind did reflect upon the universe it was invariably led to a polytheistic interpretation of nature. But certain individuals were led to it spontaneously. In every community there are always a few people to whom religion makes a ready appeal, but in the case of the majority it is only at certain times—at crises such as birth, marriage, death, harvest, etc.—that the religious emotion is aroused to any appreciable extent.[3] To the intermittently and indifferently religious ethical monotheism seldom makes an appeal, and therefore it is the lesser deities, spirits, totems, or ancestors that men of this type usually approach. The High God thus tends to become remote unless he is brought into relation with a popular culture-hero or spirit. This doubtless explains why monotheism invariably gave place to polytheism in the religions of antiquity. Nevertheless, the recurrence of monotheistic notions in Babylonia and Egypt, to say nothing of savage Supreme Beings, and the ease with

[1] P. Radin. Cf. *Monotheism among Primitive Peoples* (London, 1924), p. 67.

[2] Otto, *op. cit.*, p. 134.

[3] Cf. *Journal of American Folk-lore*, xxvii. (1914), pp. 338 f. *Cf.* Farnell, *Cults of the Greek States* (Oxford, 1896), i. p. 86.

which primitive people identify the Christian idea of God with their own, show that this aspect of theism is an innate disposition rather than a later product of evolution or a mere survival of a primitive revelation.

### 3. *Towards Monotheism in Greece and Israel*

The emergence of this " instinct for unification," as James Adam called it, is clearly discernible in the literature of ancient Greece as well as in that of Israel. It runs there in two streams, the one poetical and popular, the other philosophical, which find their confluence in the mind of Plato, at once philosopher and poet, and derives from him through Aristotle to Cleanthes and the Stoics. It would be rash, perhaps, as we have seen, to trace it back to Homer's notion of the supremacy of Zeus as the father of the Olympian divinities. Pindar represents an advance upon the Homeric notion in that he abjures all idea of struggles and conflicts among the gods, as also does Sophocles ; yet in both the current polytheism is accepted rather than renounced. Aeschylus, on the contrary, marks a real step forward. It is true that he recognises a number of gods. But apart from particular phrases, like that poignant utterance of the Chorus in the *Agamemnon* [1]— Ζεὺς, ὅστις ποτ' ἐστὶν, κ.τ.λ.—there are whole passages, like the choric odes in the *Suppliants,* and at least one whole play, the *Prometheus,* which presuppose a belief that has crossed the border of monotheism. In these cases, if other gods are named, they are little more than such " principalities and powers " as St. Paul was to speak of later : the central issue lies between God and man.

But a far more serious inroad on popular polytheism had already been made a generation earlier by Xenophanes, who wrote with all the dogmatic certainty, the moral ardour, and even the poetical form of a Hebrew prophet. Aristotle says of him that " he throws his glance upon the whole heaven and says that God is unity ! " [2] Despite occasional dissent, as from Gomperz, modern scholarship has not tended to revise that verdict. For Xenophanes God is one, uncreated, righteous, and without resemblance to man : the only prayer which we may address to Him is for " power to do what is right." In this he is nearer to the theism of Jew

[1] Aesch., *Ag.* 160, cf. Eur., *H.F.* 1263.    [2] Aristotle, *Metaph.* I. v.

and Christian than is Heraclitus ; for, though like Heraclitus he conceives of God as wholly immanent in the universe, he does not follow the logic of Pantheism to the point of denying the ultimate validity of ethical distinctions. For Heraclitus, on the contrary, God is beyond good and evil ; " to God all things are beautiful and good and right, but men consider some things wrong and others right." [1] The truth is that Xenophanes came to far closer grips with popular religion than either Aeschylus among the poets or Heraclitus among the philosophers ; and his protest against the traditional conceptions of deity was to receive classical expression a century later in the *Republic* of Plato.

Meanwhile philosophy was pursuing a path which more and more prepared the way for the break-up of polytheism as a possible belief for thoughtful men. The material unity—water, air, fire —proclaimed by the Ionian scientists, the logical unity asserted by Parmenides the pupil of Xenophanes, the deistic unity asserted by Anaxagoras all alike attest an instinct or innate disposition which could not rest content with pluralism, and either ignored the evidence of the Many or else relegated it to the sphere of unreality and opinion. In this atmosphere we are of course far removed from the theology proper to the Olympian deities : the problem of Being has ousted the problem of the gods : even in Anaxagoras the Mind which ordered Chaos in the beginning has no other rôle in things to play. Nevertheless we cannot regard this development as without significance for Greek theology. The abrupt dogmatic form which marks the surviving fragments of these philosophers points to its having some other source in the mind than either observation or dialectic, and suggests that human reason carries somehow within it the affirmation of unity.

It was reserved for the genius of Plato to give expression, first in the *Republic* and its correlative dialogues, later and with greater precision and critical analysis in the *Timaeus* and the *Laws*, to a thoroughly Greek monotheism, and to gather up into it all that the poetical imagination, moral earnestness, and metaphysical subtlety of his predecessors had portended. Into the Platonic conception of God it is impossible here to enter ; nor can we trace the criticism of it through which Aristotle passed to his pregnant conception of the Unmoved Mover. It will be clear from the next essay in this volume how much Western theology owes to

[1] Ritter and Preller, 436.

these two great lamps of antiquity. But if evidence be needed that the monotheism of ancient Hellas was not only a philosophical, but a religious belief, it may be found in a few lines of the Hymn of Cleanthes, the Stoic :

> O King of kings,
> Through ceaseless ages, God, whose purpose brings
> To birth, whate'er on land or in the sea
> Is wrought, or in high heaven's immensity ;
> Save what the sinner works infatuate.
> Nay, but thou knowest to make crooked straight :
> Chaos to thee is order : in thine eyes
> The unloved is lovely, who didst harmonise
> Things evil with things good, that there should be
> One Word through all things everlastingly.[1]

There are few believers in revelation who would not say that we hear its accents in these lines.

But of course it is in Israel that the note of revelation sounds most clearly. The Hebrew prophets certainly did not arrive at their remarkable conception of ethical monotheism through a process of observation and reflection upon causation, as they held in company with the rest of Israel that supernatural beings intervened in natural events. But they saw behind all the phenomena of nature one creative and sustaining, omniscient and omnipotent will—that of Yahweh, the righteous Ruler of the universe, the Doer of justice, whose law is holy and whose power is infinite. That such a Deity should intervene in the course of nature from time to time was not to them extraordinary, since He sends forth the wind, the ice, and the snow, and speaks in the thunder, and smites His enemies in the hinder parts. The prophets, therefore, combined a primitive theory of the universe and of causation with a pure ethical monotheism.[2] Thus they constitute a unique development in the history of revelation.

Whence did they obtain this knowledge ? Clearly they did not derive it from the observation of the facts of nature, especially as righteousness and not mere benevolence was for them the characteristic feature of Yahweh. They give no evidence of

---

[1] James Adam's translation in *The Vitality of Platonism*, Essay IV.
[2] H. F. Hamilton, *Discovery and Revelation* (London, 1915), pp. 98 ff.

possessing a knowledge superior to that of their age and environment, as in the case of the ancient philosophers. They were just ordinary men distinguished only by their religious experience and spiritual insight (Amos vii. 14). They were conscious, in fact, of the contrast between their own feelings and ideas, on the one hand, and of the purpose and mind of God who constrained them, on the other (Amos vii. 2 ff., 15 ; Is. vi. 5 ff.). They spoke that they did know and testified that they had seen and heard ; in other words, they were the recipients of a self-revelation given directly by God and not mediated through reflection on the natural universe. Each prophet's message bears the stamp of originality, of opposition to contemporary thought, of a word of God forcing itself to find expression through the human instrument. Surely here we may reasonably claim to have a revelation from God to man independent of human reflection and discovery—" a down-rush from the super-conscious," rather than " an uprush from the sub-conscious." [1]

That truly religious men from the beginning by reason of their innate disposition were made to " seek God and feel after Him if haply they might find Him," seems clear. In this way He was not left without witnesses in any age or community, but, nevertheless, it was in Israel that the purest form of monotheism developed to the exclusion of all other theistic and animistic systems. If the view here advanced concerning the emergence of religion is correct, there is no adequate reason to deny the existence of Hebrew monotheists prior to the rise of the prophets in the eighth century B.C. In fact, it would be remarkable if believers in a Supreme Deity did not arise from time to time as elsewhere. There is nothing improbable, for example, in supposing that Abraham, who is generally thought to have lived at Ur of the Chaldees about 2000 B.C., developed the monolatrous and heno-theistic tendency in Babylonian cult at this time in a monotheistic direction by assigning to one God all those attributes which hitherto had been distributed among many deities. The traditional history of Israel as it is set forth in the Old Testament represents a prolonged struggle between a mono-Yahwist minority of religious leaders against a polytheistic majority ending in the final triumph of the monotheists. This seems to be a very likely situation in view of the evidence from other sources which we have here

[1] Gore, *Belief in God* (London, 1921), pp. 102 ff.

briefly examined.   Thus while there is no reason to suppose with Renan that the Semites, more than any other people, had a racial tendency to monotheism, they unquestionably produced men who were capable of transforming a system of nature-worship and polytheism into the lofty ethical monotheistic ideals of Amos, Hosea, and Isaiah, and thereby prepared the way for our Lord and His Church.   The ethical teaching of the prophets emphasised the moral purity of God ;   their Messianic expectations became more spiritualised and complex, until the supreme manifestation was vouchsafed in Him in whom dwelt the fulness of God.   The main light thus shone more purely and powerfully till all shadows of lesser deities had fled away, and the conceptions of Israel were fulfilled by Him who was at once the light to lighten the Gentiles and the glory of His people Israel.   By the Eternal Son assuming conditions of time the religious impulse was satisfied that led primitive man to bring himself into union with the Divine by sacrifice and prayer to lesser supernatural beings.   Thus Catholic Christianity, with its doctrine of the Trinity in unity of the Godhead, and its sacramental system, meets the entire need of man and thereby supplies that which was wanting in the earlier conceptions both of monotheism and polytheism.   The Incarnation and its extension in the Church, therefore, fulfilled the dumb, dim expectations of mankind throughout the ages.

# THE VINDICATION OF RELIGION
## BY ALFRED EDWARD TAYLOR

# CONTENTS

*" Tres sunt qui testimonium dant . . . et tres unum sunt."*

## Introductory

" Being ready always to give answer to every man that asketh you
a reason concerning the hope that is in you, yet with meekness
and fear."—1 Peter iii. 15.

It might fairly be said that these few words, written in the infancy
of the Christian Church, sufficiently indicate for all time the
scope of Christian " apologetics " and the temper in which they
should be conducted. The Christian is eminently a hopeful
being ; he has hopes for himself and for his kind which surprise
the non-Christian society around him. Since, as his neighbours
can readily satisfy themselves, he is not a mere lunatic, he presumably has good grounds for his hopefulness which he can make
intelligible to others, and it is his duty to produce them when they
are asked for. But he is to do so courteously and carefully.
His faith is not to be a blind faith for which he can give no better
reason than that it makes him comfortable to hold it, or that he
has been ordered to hold it by some authority into whose trustworthiness it is forbidden to inquire. Those who ask the reason
of his hope are asking a fair question and are entitled to a candid
and mannerly answer. They are not to be met, as they too often
have been by imperfect Christians, with revilings and anger
at their presumption in daring to put the question. The answer
is to be given not merely courteously but " with fear," with
a scrupulous anxiety not to exaggerate the strength of his case,
to push an argument further than it will legitimately reach, or
to cover up the difficulties of his position. Above all, there
is no suggestion that the Christian believer should expect to
be able to demonstrate the truth of his convictions as one may
demonstrate a proposition in the mathematics. No doubt we
should all like to show that *it would* be as absurd in a rational
being to deny the truths upon which we base our highest hopes
for ourselves and for the world as it would be to deny the statements of the multiplication table, or of an accurately calculated set
of logarithms. But just in so far as a man could succeed in doing

this he would be converting " faith " into knowledge and hope into vision.[1] The apostolic writer makes no such demand as this on the believers whom he is addressing.  It may be that none of the considerations on which their hopes are founded can be proved to demonstration, in a way which must compel the assent of every rational man ;  it is certain that not all of them can be so demonstrated.  If they could be, faith would have lost all its value as a test of a man's spiritual condition ;  as the theologians put it, faith would no longer be a response of the soul called out by " grace " and could consequently have no " merit " towards salvation. Where demonstration is forthcoming, assent, just so far as a man is reasonable, is not free but necessitated ;  the worth of a faith in anything at all as a revelation of a man's inmost self depends on the fact that it is a free assent to the drawings of a dimly descried high and noble object which cannot be *demonstrated* not to be an illusion.  It is because this logical possibility of illusion is never simply closed, where faith is in question, as it is in matters of demonstration, that the exercise of faith ennobles the man who has it—in fact, that faith " justifies."  We can readily see that this is so when we compare the attitude of the religious man who lives by his faith in God with similar attitudes to which we give the same name.  We speak of a man's " noble " confidence in the loyalty of his friend, or the fidelity of his wife, in the face of all appearances to the contrary ;  there would be nothing " noble " in being convinced of your wife's fidelity, if you had locked her up in a high tower and carried the key away in your pocket.  The moral nobility of trust is only possible when a man is trusting where he cannot demonstrate, or, at any rate, has not demonstrated and does not know that he ever will.  (The Vatican Council, it is true, decreed that " the existence of God can be demonstrated by natural reason."  But its decree was not meant to legitimate suspense of assent until the demonstration has been produced and found satisfactory.)

It may even be worth while to remark that this attitude of trust and faith, where demonstration is impossible, is just as characteristic of science, as the word is commonly understood, as it is of religion.  Outside the sphere of mathematics how far can we say that any of the propositions which make up the

---

[1] In medieval language, he would be exchanging the *lumen gratiae* for the *lumen gloriae*, a thing impossible, except by a miracle, for Christians still in the tate of " pilgrimage."

" scientific view of the world " are strictly and rigidly proved ?
It is at least certain that most of them have never received and
do not seem capable of receiving anything like demonstration.
Thus it is a commonplace that all natural science is bound up with
a belief in the principle that " nature " is in some way " uniform."
Without this conviction it would be quite impossible to argue
from the handful of facts we have learned, by observation or active
experiment, about the little region of space and time open for our
direct examination to the structural laws of events in vastly remote
spaces and distant times.  Yet it is quite certain both that this
fundamental principle cannot be demonstrated, since all reasoning
in the sciences depends on assuming it, and that it cannot even be
definitely expressed by any formula which does not appear highly
questionable.[1]  Or, to take a rather different instance, no scientific
man to-day doubts that the enormous variety of vegetable and
animal species have been developed in the course of a long history
from a few simpler types, perhaps a single simpler type.  The
precise factors which have contributed to this development, the
precise steps in the process, may be and are the subjects of controversy, but the general conception seems to have established itself
permanently.  But if we are to speak of proof or demonstration
in the matter, it is plain that we are using the words in a very lax
sense.  It has been said of Darwin that the actual basis of fact
on which his gigantic edifice of speculation was raised amounts to
little more than the experiences of a small number of breeders
of animals, and it might equally well be said of the later formidable
theory which directly contravenes the peculiar Darwinian conception of the process of " evolution " as due to the accumulation
in successive generations of imperceptible differences, that it too
has for its foundation in observed fact only a relatively few experiences of gardeners and observational botanists.  In both cases
the superstructure of theory is quite incommensurable with the
narrow basis of fact on which it is reared.  Little indeed would be
left of " evolutionary science " if we cut away everything which
a cautious logician would pronounce not proved by the evidence.
To take a third illustration.  The late Philip Gosse was at once
a keen naturalist and a firm believer in the literal inerrancy of the
Book of Genesis.  As a naturalist he could not deny the genuineness

[1] See particularly the thorough discussion by Professor C. D. Broad,
" Relation between Induction and Probability," in MIND, N.S., Nos. 108, 113
(October 1918, January 1920).

of the discoveries of fossil remains which suggest that life on our planet had its beginnings at an era immensely more remote than any honest interpretation of the Book of Genesis will allow. As an amateur theologian he felt unable to deny the inerrancy of Genesis. Accordingly, he reconciled his theology with his natural science by the theory that the earth was indeed created out of nothing a few thousand years ago, but created with fossil deposits ready-made under its surface. It is not surprising that the men of science would have nothing to say to Mr. Gosse's theory ; yet it is equally clear that there is not and cannot be any means of demonstrating its falsity. What led to the ignoring of the speculation was not, as would be the case with a claim to have "squared the circle," knowledge of its falsity, but sound scientific instinct.

Speaking quite generally, I suppose we may say that no great and far-reaching scientific theory is ever adopted because it has been demonstrated. It is not believed because it can be shown by stringent logic that all other accounts of facts involve self-contradiction. The real reason for belief is that the theory provides a key for the interpretation of the facts on which it is said to be founded, that on further investigation it is found also to provide a key to the interpretation of numerous groups of often very dissimilar facts, which were either uninterpretable or actually unknown when the theory was first put forward, and that even where at first sight there are facts which seem refractory to the proposed interpretation, the general theory can be made to fit them by some modification which does not interfere with its continued use for the interpretation of the facts by which it was first suggested. In this respect the interpretation of the " book of Nature " is exactly similar to the process of deciphering a cryptogram or an inscription in a hitherto unknown language. The decipherer has first to be in possession of a " key " of promising make. Thus, the inscription may be bilingual and one language may be a known one ; there may be good reasons for believing that the cipher message is in English, and this enables the reader to make a probable conjecture from the relative frequency of certain signs alone or in combination. The original identifications will usually be in part erroneous, but even where they are so, if enough of them are correct, the partial decipherment will make the words of the text sufficiently intelligible to lead to subsequent correction of initial mistakes, though when all our ingenuity has been expended, it may still remain the case that some of the signs we are trying to decipher have to be left uninterpreted owing to the insufficiency of our data. If our inscription were interminable, we might readily have to acknowledge that, though successive scrutiny made each new reading more nearly correct than those which went before, a final and definitive transcription was beyond our reach, and that all we could do was to make the tentative and provisional element in our readings steadily smaller. It is hardly necessary to mention the way in which this tentative process of decipherment of symbols, applied to the hieroglyphs of Egypt and the cuneiform of Babylon, has already enriched our historical knowledge of the early civilisations by making real to us the politics and social life of people who, a few generations ago, were little but names to us, or the still greater flood of light on the past of our race which may yet come from the successful reading of Cretan and Hittite records.

Consider for a moment the assumption which lies behind such an attempt at the reading of a cipher. It is taken for granted that the marks we are examining convey a message or statement which someone was meant to understand. They must have been read and understood by someone and therefore presumably may be read and understood by us, if we will have patience. Commonly, no doubt, we should say that the very fact that an intelligible statement has been extracted from the marks proves both that this general assumption was correct and that the meaning the decipherer has extracted is the meaning intended by the composer. But, strictly speaking, we have no right to call this demonstration. If the series of marks is a very short one it is quite a reasonable suggestion that there is *no* meaning behind them. There is a fair chance that in some cases they were not made by man at all, and that in others they were made in mere idleness and are quite insignificant. Even if the series is a tolerably long one, there is an appreciable chance that the various symbols may succeed one another in the very order which would yield an intelligible sense without any such sense being in the mind of the inscriber. Yet if a proposed decipherment yields a satisfactory sense, a sound instinct will lead to its acceptance long before the point is reached at which the probability that it was unintended becomes mathematically negligible. We may make the same point in a rather different way. Why do sober scholars refuse to believe in the existence of a " Baconian " cipher in the works of Shakespeare ? Not because the thing is an impossibility. Indeed, it might be argued that the very fact that an ingenious "Baconian," by applying his " key " to such an enormous mass of writing, can extract a narrative with any sort of coherence supplies a high mathematical probability that there really is a narrative to be extracted and that the " Baconian " is, at any rate, largely right in his proposed reading of the " cipher." The real reason why sober scholars refuse to believe in such a cipher, and would still refuse were the " Baconians " more able than they are to make the " key " work, without a host of subsidiary hypotheses to explain its apparent failures, is their unproved and unprovable conviction of the inherent craziness of the whole thing. It is " not in human nature " that a sane man should have conceived the idea of embodying a secret narrative in a series of plays produced over an interval of many years for the entertainment of the public, nor, if he had done so, that the seventeenth-century printers of a posthumous volume of such magnitude should have been so scrupulously exact in their typography as to leave the key to the narrative unobliterated. These are convictions which we cannot demonstrate by an appeal to the mathematical calculus of Probability ; they rest simply on our conviction of the sanity of the parties concerned. " Men do not do such things."

Now, let us apply these considerations to the closely parallel case of the whole body of scientific workers who are engaged in the decipherment of the book of Nature. Here too we shall find that the whole interpretation presupposes convictions which are neither self-evident nor *demonstrably* true. No great scientific theory is accepted because it accounts for all the facts of Nature without a remainder. There always are facts which are recalcitrant to explanation by the theory and remain over as " difficulties," and, for this very reason, it is idle to reject a great scientific theory, as a certain type of apologist often proposes to do, because there are difficulties which it cannot explain. It would, for example, be silly to reject the theory of " evolution "—I mean here the theory of the derivation of living species from a smaller number of original types—on the plea that the theory has its unexplained " difficulties," or that there are grave differences between eminent men of science about the particular process which leads to the appearance of a new permanent " kind." Even the greatest of all modern scientific theories, the Newtonian gravitational astronomy, all along had its difficulties, as Newton himself was well aware. To mention only the most far-reaching and obvious of these difficulties, in the gravitational astronomy it appears as an outstanding and unexplained oddity that we have to assume the " law of gravity " side by side with the general laws of motion : the " laws " of themselves indicate no reason why there should be this universal attraction between material particles or why it should follow the law of the " inverse square " rather than any other. This was the reason why Newton himself was careful to hint that there must be some as yet undiscovered " cause of gravity," and one principal attraction offered by the Theory of Relativity is that it removes this particular difficulty by making gravitation itself a direct consequence of its revised version of the laws of motion. Yet it is notorious that the Theory of Relativity has its own difficulties too, and that at present some of these are so grave as to prevent many eminent physicists from accepting it.

Perhaps I may be pardoned if I take still a third illustration. One of the first principles of the science of Thermodynamics is the so-called " principle of Carnot " or " law of the dissipation of energy." In virtue of this principle, heat always tends to pass from a body of higher temperature to bodies of lower. The hotter body tends to impart heat to colder bodies in its vicinity, so that it becomes cooler and they warmer. It follows that at the end of a period of time which, however long, must be finite, the heat of our stellar universe must ultimately be distributed uniformly over its whole extent ; change, variety, and life must thus be lost in one dreary monotony. But if we ask why these dismal consequences have not as yet occurred, we are driven to assume that at a remote, but still finite, distance of past time the distribution of heat through the stellar universe must have been one which, on mathematical principles, is infinitely improbable. The difficulty is a recognised one, and attempts have been made to meet it, though apparently without success. In fact, there seems to be ample justification for the thesis of a brilliant writer on the philosophy of science, that all a scientific theory ever does in the way of explanation is to remove the inexplicable a few steps farther back.[1]

---

[1] E. Meyerson, *L'explication dans les sciences* (1921). For the particular difficulty here specified see bk. ii. chap. 6 (vol. i. pp. 181–225) and appendix iv. (vol. ii. p. 405).

Yet, in face of all the difficulties which beset every great scientific theory and are much more familiar to the scientific man himself than they can be to outsiders, there is one attitude towards Nature which no scientific man ever thinks of taking up.      He never says, as the pessimistic man of letters sometimes does, " since all scientific theory of Nature whatever has its difficulties, we may infer that the whole attempt at the construction of a scientific theory of Nature has been a mistake.      Nature is radically unknowable and irrational ; there is no sort of coherence between our notions of intelligibility and the reality in which we are immersed.      Let us have done with this secular nightmare and interest ourselves in something else."      No one who has the scientific spirit in him ever dreams of the possibility that Nature is like one of those riddles to which there is no answer.      The progress of science absolutely depends on the conviction that our difficulties arise from the fragmentary character of our knowledge, not from the inherent incoherence of Nature.      Even as concerns our acquaintance with what we call the " bare facts," it holds good that what we are looking for determines what we see.      If men ever convinced themselves that Nature is in her own structure incoherent, not only should we have no more scientific " theories," we should cease, except occasionally and accidentally, to discover the " facts " which suggest theories.      Yet it is not demonstrable that Nature is not incoherent, and it is not self-evident that the sceptic's assertion that we have no right to expect her to conform to our " human " standards of coherence is absurd.      Scientific progress is only made possible by an act of faith—faith that there really is coherence in Nature and that the more we look for it, the more of it we shall find.      The words in which Newman describes his own attitude to the " difficulties " of theology might equally well be used by men of science with reference to the no less real " difficulties " of natural science : " ten thousand difficulties do not make one doubt." [1]

If all this is so, we cannot be fairly asked to justify religion by producing a different kind of vindication, or a fuller degree of vindication, of the " religious view " of the world than the man of science would think adequate if he were called on to " vindicate "

[1] *Apologia*, Pt. VII.  The parallel would not apply in the case of a theologian who regards the whole of theological knowledge, or at any rate of its principal propositions, as revealed together once for all in a definitive form.  It holds of Newman precisely in virtue of his doctrine of " development."

the " scientific view " of the world.   In either case the most that
can be demanded of us is to show that there are real and undeniable facts which call for explanation and must not be explained
*away* ;   that the interpretation supplied brings coherence and
" sense " into them, where they would, without it, be an un-
intelligible puzzle ;   that the more steadily and systematically the
principles we fall back on are employed, the less puzzling does the
reality we are trying to interpret become.   In a word, we need to
show that there is the same solid ground for holding that religion
cannot be dismissed as a passing illusion incident to a particular
stage in the mental growth of humanity as there is for holding the
same view about science.   If we cannot *demonstrate* that religion
is not temporary illusion, neither can we *demonstrate* that science
is in any better position.   And it may be worth while to observe
in express words that the real weight of the " evidence " which is
accepted as sufficient ground for assurance can only be judged by
a mind of the right kind and with the right training.   This holds
good without exception in all branches of " secular " learning.
An experiment which the trained chemist or physicist sees to be
" crucial " as deciding for or against a speculation will often seem
of no particular significance to a layman ;   it requires another and
a different type of mind and a different training to appreciate
the sort of considerations which a trained palæographer will
regard as decisive for the authenticity of a document, the soundness
of a reading, the worth of a speculation about the relations between
the various extant manuscripts of an ancient author.[1]

[1] This is why even men of high intellectual power so often make themselves
merely ridiculous when they venture into fields of knowledge where they are
amateurs.   Their training has not prepared them to be sound judges of the
kind of considerations which are decisive in dealing with the unfamiliar
matter.   It is notorious that some of the very worst Biblical and Shakespearian
" criticism " has been produced by lawyers who are very sound judges of evidence within their own sphere.   The trouble is that their training disposes
them to assume that what cannot be " proved " under the rules of the English
or some other law of evidence cannot be adequately established in history or
in literary criticism, or that what would be regarded as sufficient evidence for
a British jury must always be sufficient evidence for the historian or the critic.
Both assumptions are mistaken.   Thus a " lawyer turned apologist " will
argue that the critical analysis of the Pentateuch must be rejected because no
one can " produce to the court " copies of the earlier documents into which it is
analysed, or again that he has proved the correctness of the traditional ascription
of a work like the Fourth Gospel to a particular author by merely showing that
the tradition is ancient, as though some sort of law of " prescription " held good
in questions of authorship.

In secular matters men of sound sense are pretty quick to recognise the truth of this principle. No one would think of regarding the verdict of an archæologist or a chemist on a moot point in law as deriving any particular value from the eminence of the archæologist or the chemist in his own subject ; no one would attach any weight to a Lord Chancellor's opinion about the genuineness of an alleged Rembrandt, or a disputed fragment of Simonides, because the opinion was that of the best Lord Chancellor the country had ever possessed. We all understand that the sort of consensus of " authorities " which makes it proper for the man who is not an " authority " to dispense with his own private judgment is the consensus of " authorities " in a particular subject, who derive their claim to authority from native aptitude and long training. But we ought to be equally ready to recognise that in the same way the only consensus which is of weight in matters of religion is the consensus of deeply religious men. Religion is not shown to be an " illusion " because worldly-minded men, who have never felt the sense of personal sin or the need of adoration, can see nothing in it, any more than, for example, the Theory of Relativity is shown to be " moonshine," because it seems un-intelligible to the type of man whom R. L. S. used to speak of as " the common banker," or disinterested devotion to be an illusion, because a clever cynical diplomatist assures one that he has never felt such devotion himself and sees no evidence of it in the behaviour of others. If the diplomatist sees no disinterested-ness in human life, it is because he is not looking for it, and the reason why he does not look for it in other men is probably that he has never felt it within himself. The evidence which a Talleyrand finds non-existent may be overwhelming to a plain man who has friendliness in his own heart and consequently finds it in his fellows, just because he goes half-way to meet them by showing that he expects it. In the same way the " evidences of religion," whatever they may turn out to be, must not be expected to produce much conviction in the man of thoroughly irreligious temper who has done nothing to counteract that temper, the merely sensual or ambitious or proud or inquisitive ; it is sufficient that they should be found adequate by those who have within them at least the making of " holy and humble men of heart," who feel the need of something they can love and adore without any of the reservations which clear insight sets to all our devotion to friend or wife or child or country, the need of deliverance from their own ingrained sinfulness and self-centredness, support and guidance in their own creaturely helplessness and ignorance, abiding peace in a world where things are mutable. If, among all their differences, such men are agreed that what they are seeking with their whole hearts is really to be found, it is no detraction from the weight of such evidence to say that others who are looking for nothing of the kind have, very naturally, not found what they never troubled to seek. It is as though one should say that there can be no gold in a certain district because I, who know little or nothing of the signs of the presence of this metal, and care less, have traversed the district from end to end, without discovering what I made no attempt to find.[1]

So far we have been speaking of the similarity of the religious man's quest with that of the student of science, a similarity which may be briefly expressed by saying that both are seeking a clearer and more coherent explanation of something which they find obscurely and confusedly "given" as part of our human experience, or, if you prefer to put it so, "suggested" by that experience. The common problem of both is to find the presuppositions of the facts of life. But it may be necessary to add a remark on an important difference in the kind of facts with which the two quests deal. Perhaps we do not commonly recognise as clearly as is desirable that " science " in the current sense of the

[1] These considerations ought to make us careful in not being too eager to get the blessing of scientific men on our religion. If both our religion and our science rest on truth, they cannot, of course, come into conflict. And it is our duty as religious men to see that we do not confuse religion with science by asserting or denying, *e.g.*, biological theories on grounds which have nothing to do with the kind of evidence which is available and relevant in biology. But equally there is the same obligation on the men of science not to judge of matters which belong to religion on irrelevant evidence. I incline to think that though both theologians and students of natural science have sinned in this way in the past, at the present moment it is the men of science who have the greater sin. In every branch of the Christian Church theologians are at present only too eager to snatch at what they take to be the " latest results " in the natural sciences and work them into the fabric of their creed. Usually they commit the two inevitable errors of the amateur : they misunderstand the precise meaning of the scientific speculation and they often take a brilliant but disputed hypothesis, which a few years may see abandoned or gravely modified in the light of newer knowledge, for a fully established theory. But the " man of science " is often as bad if not worse, (worse, I mean, because his vaunted intellectual training ought to have borne fruit in the production of the judicious mind).

word is not the whole of knowledge but a special kind of knowledge which makes up by its one-sidedness and limitation of scope for the precision and exactitude of its vision, just as the field of view under the microscope compensates its definition and wealth of detail by the narrowness of its limits. The natural sciences, in the first place, if we take the view of their range which is perhaps commonest among their votaries, are exclusively concerned with physical reality, what is outside and around us. Of ourselves as movers and agents they have nothing to say. They can indeed tell us much about the human brain, but always about the human brain as it is for the physiological or anatomical observer who is looking at it from the outside. Even if we take, as I for one think we must, a rather more generous view and admit that psychology has established its right to count as an independent natural science, and that anthropology, in its various branches, is at least a natural science *in fieri*, the case remains in principle the same. The rigidly " scientific " psychologist—and this is precisely what creates the special difficulty of his science— treats the mind of which he discourses exactly as the geologist might treat a rock, or the biologist a frog. The mind of which he speaks is a " typical " human mind not his own, at which he is looking on, (and at times interfering to see what the result of his interference will be). The anthropologist, in like fashion, discourses of the religious cultus, the superstitions, the marriage customs, the moral codes, of groups of his fellow-creatures as they look to an outside observer who does not follow the cult, share the terrors and hopes, or practise the customs of which he treats. So long as we keep strictly to the methods of the natural sciences, we never penetrate, so to say, within our own skins. We deal with human practice in all its forms and with the convictions it expresses simply as " objects presented to our notice," as they might equally be presented to the notice of a being who shared none of the convictions and shaped his life by none of them. It is this attitude of detachment which makes it possible to introduce into our study the quantitative and numerical precision which is the peculiar glory of science. But it ought to be clear to us that our acquaintance with our own inmost self and character, however come by, is not originally got by observation of an " object presented to our notice." Our loves, our hates, our hopes, our despondencies, our pleasures, our pains are not revealed to us by inspection of them as presented objects but by living through the experience of loving, hating, hoping, despairing and the like. It is only after we have learned by living through them what these experiences are that we can artificially, if we like, contrive to put ourselves in the position of the observer with a microscope and look on at the expressions of personal mental life in another, or even in ourselves, *as if* it were a presented object. If it were only that, the " experimental psychologist " would be attempting an impossible task, because he would be without any key to the real significance of his observation of the behaviour of himself or of any one else. This, as it seems to me, is the real reason why all that gives human action its significance for the poet, the biographer, the historian, falls, and must fall, wholly outside the purview of the scientific psychologist and the anthropologist. The " trick," if I may call it so, on which these sciences depend for their special success, lies just in treating human doings and thoughts as though they were " events " forming part of the great event which is Nature. But in truth the thoughts and deeds of men are not mere " events " but something more : they are personal acts. Hence, I submit, the information of the psychologist and the anthropologist is true and valuable so far as it goes, but it does not go very far. The knowledge of man which makes the great biographer or historian or dramatic poet, the knowledge of the self, its strength and weakness, won by meditation and prayer go infinitely deeper ; that is knowledge of self from within, and this explains why such knowledge brings wisdom where the knowledge of the other kind amounts at best to science. A life spent in the psychological laboratory, or in anthropological research, may leave a man no more than a learned fool, but a fool will never be a great historian, whatever his learning. In fact, the confusion of knowledge with the sub-species of it which we call natural science would lead directly to the conclusion that there can be no history of a human society, except in the loose sense in which we might talk of the history of an ant-heap or even of a lump of sandstone.[1] If any of my readers are acquainted, as I hope some of them may be, with the writings of St. Bonaventura on practical religion, they will remember that consideration of what is around

[1] For a fuller discussion of the difference between scientific and historical knowledge I may perhaps refer to a short essay by myself in MIND, N.S., No. 124, where some rival views on the matter are also expressed by Dr. Schiller.

us, consideration of what is within, consideration of what is above us, are with him three successive well-marked stages of the intellectual ascent to knowledge of God. The restriction of the facts to which we look for the vindication of religion to facts which fall within the purview of the natural sciences and no others would, of course, cut off at one stroke all material for the higher stages of this contemplative ascent.

They are, however, not rightfully excluded from our survey. Even if no one fact or group of facts which can be dealt with by the methods of the museum and the laboratory of itself points Godward, it may well be that when we attempt to take a philosophic, or, as Plato says, a " synoptical " view of physical Nature as a whole, when we ask after the ultimate presuppositions of natural science, we shall find that Nature " as a whole " exhibits unmistakable indications of being after all not a " whole," but something incomplete and dependent, hints at least at the existence of a reality beyond itself which is at once its source and its completion. When we further take into view the aspirations of man as a moral person, we may find that they carry us further. They may be found not only to point to the existence of a reality above and beyond Nature but to indicate, however dimly, something of the character of that reality. And when we further come to consider the specific experiences which are the supports of personal religion, and, so far as we can see, must have been the origin of the different religions known to us from history, we may have reason to think that here we are actually in the presence of a genuine self-disclosure, always imperfect but none the less real, of this " super-nature " itself. If this can be maintained, we shall have a justification for following Bonaventura's line of thought. There will be a witness of Nature to God, a witness of Ethics to God, and a witness of Religion itself to God, none of which can be disregarded without mutilating the rich content of human experience, and the three witnesses will be at one in pointing to the same reality. On each of these three lines of thought I propose to offer a few remarks.

(It may be thought strange that I have so far said nothing about a topic which bulks very large in most philosophical discussions of religious problems, the *metaphysical* way to God. The omission has been made of set purpose. So far as we can

draw any distinction between metaphysics and science, the difference seems to be little more than that metaphysics is, as it has been
called by someone, "an unusually hard effort to think clearly."
Or, to put it in a different way, any attempt to discover the most
*ultimate* presuppositions on which any branch of knowledge falls
back is the metaphysic of that particular branch of knowledge, and,
since we cannot be said to have mastered any subject until we have
discovered what its most ultimate presuppositions are, the study of
any organised body of knowledge, scientific or historical, must
finally culminate in metaphysics. This is, so far as I can see,
the meaning of the old definition of metaphysics as "the science
of first principles," or "the science of being as such." From this
point of view there is no real distinction between a peculiar metaphysical way to God and the ways we have just enumerated. In
studying them we are from start to finish within the region of
metaphysics and there is no fourth special "way of metaphysics"
to follow. It will be the object of the remainder of this essay to
urge that, no matter which of the three "ways" we may choose
to follow, we are conducted from similar starting-points along
similar lines to the same goal, the difference being only that the
character of the route and the goal is clearer if we follow the second
route than if we confine ourselves to the first, and again if we
follow the third than if we confine ourselves to the first two.
Thus we shall agree with Bonaventura that in truth there are not
three different routes, but three distinguishable stages on the same
route.[1])

---

[1] The references to Bonaventura are primarily to the well-known *Itinerarium
Mentis in Deum* and the *Soliloquium de quatuor mentalibus exercitiis* (in *S. Bona-
venturae opuscula decem*, Edit. Minor, Quaracchi, 1900).

Among modern works I may specially mention, as illustrative largely of the
first "way," Professor James Ward's *Naturalism and Agnosticism* and *Realm
of Ends*, and Professor A. S. Pringle-Pattison's *The Idea of God* ; as illustrative of the second, Professor Sorley's *Moral Values and the Idea of God* ; as
illustrative of the third, such a work as Otto's now famous *Das Heilige* (English
tr., *The Idea of the Holy*, Oxford University Press, 1923).

See further the note appended at the end of the essay. Naturally one or
other of these "ways" will appeal to us with special force according to our
individual interests and education. But it leads to mental one-sidedness, and
religious one-sidedness too, to disregard any of them. Thomism suffers from
exclusive devotion to the first, Kant from his undue concentration on the
second. Excessive preoccupation with the third leads to a blind Fideism and
leaves us at the mercy of our own personal uncriticised fancies and feelings.

## I. From Nature to God

(1) The argument " from Nature up to Nature's God " can be presented in very different forms and with very different degrees of persuasiveness, corresponding with the more or less definite and accurate knowledge of different ages about the detailed facts of Nature and the greater or less degree of articulation attained by Logic. But the main thought underlying these very different variations is throughout the same, that the incomplete points to the complete, the dependent to the independent, the temporal to the eternal. Nature, in the sense of the complex of " objects presented to our notice," the bodies animate and inanimate around us, and our own bodies which interact with them and each other, is, in the first place, always something incomplete ; it has no limits or bounds ; the horizon in space and time endlessly recedes as we carry our adventure of exploration further ; " still beyond the sea, there is more sea." What is more, Nature is always dependent ; no part of it contains its complete explanation in itself ; to explain why any part is what it is, we have always to take into account the relations of that part with some other, which in turn requires for explanation its relation to a third, and so on without end. And the fuller and richer our knowledge of the content of Nature becomes, the more, not the less, imperative do we find the necessity of explaining everything by reference to other things which, in their turn, call for explanation in the same way. Again, mutability is stamped on the face of every part of Nature. " All things pass and nothing abides." What was here in the past is now here no more, and what is here now will some day no longer be here. " There stood the rock where rolls the sea." Even what looks at first like permanence turns out on closer examination to be only slower birth and decay. Even the Christian Middle Ages thought of the " heavens " as persisting unchanged from the day of their creation to that of their coming dissolution in fiery heat and new creation ; modern astronomy tells us of the gradual production and dissolution of whole " stellar systems." Thoughts like these suggested to the Greek mind from the very infancy of science the conclusion that Nature is no self-contained system which is its own *raison d'être*. Behind all temporality and change there must be something unchanging and eternal which is the source of all things mutable and the explanation why they are as they

are.   In the first instance this sense of mutability gave rise only
to a desire to know what is the permanent stuff of which what
we call " things " are only passing phases ;  is it water, or vapour,
or fire, or perhaps something different from them all ?   The one
question which was primary for the earliest men of science was
just this question about the stuff of which everything is made.
To us it seems a very different thing to say " all things are water,"
or to say " I believe in God," but at bottom the quest after the
stuff of which things are made is a first uncertain and half-blind
step in the same direction as Aristotle's famous argument, adopted
by St. Thomas, for the existence of an " unmoved Mover " (who,
remaining *immotus in se,* is the source of all the movement and life
of this lower world), and as all the since familiar *a posteriori* proofs
of the existence of God.

(2) It is but a further step in the same direction, which was
soon taken by the early founders of science, when it is perceived
that the persistence of an unchanged " stuff " is no complete
explanation of the apparent facts of Nature, and that we have
further to ask where the " motion " which is the life of all natural
processes comes from.   This is the form in which the problem
presented itself to Aristotle and his great follower St. Thomas.
They believed that " Nature is uniform " in the sense that all the
apparently irregular and lawless movements and changes with
which life makes us familiar in the world around us issue from,
and are the effects of, other movements (those of the " heavens "),
which are absolutely regular and uniform.   On this view, the
supreme dominant uniform movement in Nature is naturally
identified with the apparently absolutely regular diurnal revolution
of the whole stellar heavens round the earth.   But Aristotle
could not be content to accept the mere fact of this supposed
revolution as an ultimate fact needing no further explanation.
No motion explains itself, and we have therefore to ask the
" cause " or reason why the heavens should display this uniform
continuous movement.   That reason Aristotle and his followers
could only explain in the language of imaginative myth.   Since
nothing can set itself going, the movement which pervades the
whole universe of Nature must be set going by something which is
not itself set going by anything else ;  not mutable and changeable
therefore, but eternally selfsame and perfect, because it already is
all that it can be, and so neither needs nor permits of development

of any kind. "From such a principle depends the whole heaven." [1]    And it follows from certain other presuppositions of Aristotle's philosophy that this "principle" must be thought of as a perfect and living intelligence.    Thus in Aristotle's formulation of the principles of natural science we reach the explicit result that Nature is in its inmost structure only explicable as something which depends on a perfect and eternal source of life, and this source is not itself Nature nor any part of Nature ; the "transcendence of God" has at last been explicitly affirmed as a truth suggested (Aristotle and St. Thomas would say demonstrated) by the rational analysis of Nature herself.    In principle their argument is that of every later form of the "cosmological proof."

Meanwhile with the transference of interest from the question about the stuff of which things are made to the question of the source of their movement and life, another line of thought had become prominent.    The connection between organ and function is one which naturally struck the far-away founders of the science of biology.    For living things show adaptation to their environment, and the various organs of living beings show adaptation to the discharge of specific functions conducing to the maintenance of the individual or the kind.    And again, the living creature is not equally adapted at all stages of its existence for the full discharge of these functions.    We can see it adapting itself to one of the most important of these as we watch the series of changes it undergoes from infancy to puberty, and we see the same process more elaborately if we widen our horizon and study the pre-natal history of the embryo.    From such considerations derives the further suggestion which ultimately becomes the "argument from design."    Aristotle is convinced that the biological analogy may be applied to all processes of the organic or inorganic world.    Every process has a final stage or "end" in which it culminates, as the whole process of conception, birth, post-natal growth culminates in the existence of the physically adult animal ; and it is always the "end" to which a process is relative that determines the character of the earlier stages of the process.    One seed grows into an apple-tree, another into a pear-tree, not because the two have been differently pulled or pushed, heated or cooled, wetted or dried, but because from the first the one was the sort of thing which was going, if not interfered with, to become an apple, the other the sort

[1] Aristotle, *Metaphysics*, 1072b, 14.

of thing which was going to become a pear. In the same way, there is definite order or plan everywhere in the structure of Nature, though Aristotle, unlike his master Plato, will not account for this orderliness by appeal to the conscious will and beneficent intention of his supreme Intelligence, but regards it rather, in the fashion of many modern biologists, as due to an unconscious and instinctive " quasi-purposiveness " in Nature herself.[1]

Let us look back at this line of thought, out of which the familiar " proofs of the existence of God " brought forward in popular works on Natural Theology have been developed, and ask ourselves what permanent value it retains for us to-day and how far it goes towards suggesting the real existence of a God whom a religious man can worship " in spirit and in truth." We must not suppose that the thought itself is necessarily anti-quated because the language in which it is clothed strikes us as old-fashioned, or because those who gave it its first expression held certain views about the details of Nature's structure (notably the geocentric conception in astronomy) which are now obsolete. It may very well be that the substitution of contemporary for antiquated views about the structure of the " stellar universe " or the fixity of animal species will leave the force of the argument, whatever that force may be, unaffected. There are two criticisms in particular which it is as well to dispose of at once, since both sound plausible, and both, unless I am badly mistaken, go wide of the mark.

(*a*) The point of the argument about the necessity of an " unmoving source of motion " must not be missed. We shall grasp it better if we remember that " motion " in the vocabulary of Aristotle means change of every kind, so that what is being asserted is that there must be an unchanging cause or source of change. Also, we must not fancy that we have disposed of the argument by saying that there is no scientific presumption that the series of changes which make up the life of Nature may not have been without a beginning and destined to have no end. St. Thomas, whose famous five proofs of the existence of God are all of them variations on the argument from " motion,"

[1] For an excellent summary account of the early Greek science referred to above see Burnet, *Greek Philosophy : Thales to Plato*, pp. 1–101 ; and for what has been said of Aristotle, W. D. Ross, *Aristotle*, chap. iii. pp. 62–111, chap. iv. pp. 112–128, and chap. vi. pp. 179–186 ; or, for a briefer summary, A. E. Taylor, *Aristotle* (Nelson & Sons, 1919), chaps. iii.–iv. pp. 49–98.

or, as we might say, the appeal to the principle of causality, was also the philosopher who created a sensation among the Christian thinkers of his day by insisting stiffly that, apart from the revelation given in Scripture, no reasons can be produced for holding that the world had a beginning or need have an end, as indeed Aristotle maintained that it has neither. The dependence meant in the argument has nothing to do with succession in time. What is really meant is that our knowledge of any event in Nature is not complete until we know the full reason for the event. So long as you only know that A is so because B is so, but cannot tell why B is so, your knowledge is incomplete. It only becomes complete when you are in a position to say that ultimately A is so because Z is so, Z being something which is its own *raison d'être*, and therefore such that it would be senseless to ask *why* Z is so. This at once leads to the conclusion that since we always have the right to ask about any event in Nature why that event is so, what are its conditions, the Z which is its own *raison d'être* cannot itself belong to Nature. The point of the reasoning is precisely that it is an argument from the fact that there is a " Nature " to the reality of a " Supernature," and this point is unaffected by the question whether there ever was a beginning of time, or a time when there were no " events."

Again, we must not be led off the track by the plausible but shallow remark that the whole problem about the " cause of motion " arose from the unnecessary assumption that things were once at rest and afterwards began to move, so that you have only to start, as the modern physicist does, with a plurality of moving particles, or atoms, or electrons to get rid of the whole question. Nor would it be relevant to remark that modern physics knows of no such absolutely uniform motions as those which Aristotle ascribes to "the heavens," but only of more or less stable motions. If you start, for example, with a system of " particles " all in uniform motion, you have still to account for the rise of " differential " motions. If you start, as Epicurus tried to do, with a rain of particles all moving in the same direction and with the same relative velocities, you cannot explain why these particles ever came together to form complexes. If you prefer, with Herbert Spencer, to start with a strictly " homogeneous " nebula, you have to explain, as Spencer does not, how " heterogeneity " ever got in. You must have individual variety, as well as " uniformity," in whatever you choose to take as your postulated original data if you are to get out of the data a world like ours, which, as Mill truly says, is not only uniform but also infinitely various. *Ex nihilo, nihil fit*, and equally out of blank uniformity nothing *fit* but a uniformity equally blank. Even if, *per impossibile*, you could exclude all individual variety from the initial data of a system of natural science, you might properly be asked to account for this singular absence of variety, and a naturalistic account of it could only take the form of deriving it from some more ultimate state of things which was not marked by absolute " uniformity." Neither uniformity nor variety is self-explanatory ; whichever you start with, you are faced by the old dilemma. Either the initial data must simply be taken as brute " fact," for which there is no reason at all, or if there is a reason, it must be found outside Nature, in the " supernatural."

(*b*) Similarly, it does not dispose of the conception of natural processes as tending to an " end " and being at least " quasi-purposive " to say that the thought originated with men who knew nothing of " evolution" and falsely believed in the fixity of natural kinds. In point of fact the notion of the gradual development of existing natural species made its appearance at the very dawn of Greek science and was quite familiar to the great philosophers who gave the Greek tradition its definitive form, though they rejected it because, so far as they knew, the evidence of facts seemed against it. The admission of the reality of the " evolution " of fresh species has, however, no direct bearing on the question of " ends in Nature " : it actually suggests the raising of that very question in a new form. Is there, or is there not, in organic evolution a general trend to the successive emergence of beings of increasing intelligence ? And if so, must the process be supposed to have reached its culmination, so far as our planet is concerned, in man, or must man be regarded as a mere stage in the production of something better, a *Pfeil der Sehnsucht nach dem Uebermenschen* ? These are questions which we are still asking ourselves to-day, and though the strict positivists among our scientific men may insist that they probably cannot be answered and that it is certainly not the business of natural science to answer them, it is at least curious that the scientific man not infrequently unconsciously betrays the fact that he has privately answered them to his own satisfaction by the very fact that he talks of " evolution "

as " progress," a phrase which has no meaning except in relation
to a goal or an end, or even, on occasion, permits himself to assume
that what is " more fully evolved," *i.e.* comes later in the course
of a development, must obviously be brighter and better than
whatever went before it.    Thus the old problem is still with us
and we cannot take it for granted that the old answers have lost
their meaning or value.

We may, for example, consider how the old-fashioned argument from " motion " to the " unmoving " source of motion,
when stated in its most general form, might still be urged even
to-day.    As we have seen, the argument is simply from the
temporal, conditioned and mutable to something eternal, unconditioned and immutable as its source.    The nerve of the whole
reasoning is that every explanation of given facts or events involves
bringing in reference to further unexplained facts ;  a complete
explanation of anything, if we could obtain one, would therefore
require that we should trace the fact explained back to something
which contains its own explanation within itself, a something which
is and is what it is in its own right ;  such a something plainly is
not an event or mere fact and therefore not included in " Nature,"
the complex of all events and facts, but " above " Nature.    Any
man has a right to say, if he pleases, that he personally does not care
to spend his time in exercising this mode of thinking, but would
rather occupy himself in discovering fresh facts or fresh and
hitherto unsuspected relations between facts.    We need not blame
him for that ;  but we are entitled to ask those who are alive to the
meaning of the old problem how they propose to deal with it, if
they reject the inference from the unfinished and conditioned to
the perfect and unconditioned.    For my own part I can see only
two alternatives.

(i) One is to say, as Hume [1] did in his " Dialogues on Natural
Religion," that, though every " part " of Nature may be dependent
on other parts for its explanation, the *whole* system of facts or
events which we call Nature may as a whole be self-explanatory ;
the " world " itself may be that " necessary being " of which
philosophers and divines have spoken.    In other words, a complex
system in which every member, taken singly, is temporal, may
as a complex be eternal ;  every member may be incomplete, but

[1] Or rather, the sceptical critic in the *Dialogues*.    We cannot be sure of
Hume's own agreement with the suggestion.

the whole may be complete ; every member mutable, but the whole unchanging. Thus, as many philosophers of yesterday and to-day have said, the " eternal " would just be the temporal fully understood ; there would be no contrast between Nature and " supernature," but only between " Nature apprehended as a whole " and Nature as we have to apprehend her fragmentarily. The thought is a pretty one, but I cannot believe that it will stand criticism. The very first question suggested by the sort of formula I have just quoted is whether it is not actually self-contradictory to call Nature a " whole " at all ; if it is, there can clearly be no apprehending of Nature as something which she is not. And I think it quite clear that Nature, in the sense of the complex of events, is, in virtue of her very structure, something incomplete and not a true whole. I can explain the point best, perhaps, by an absurdly simplified example. Let us suppose that Nature consists of just four constituents, A, B, C, D. We are supposed to " explain " the behaviour of A by the structure of B, C, and D, and the interaction of B, C, and D with A, and similarly with each of the other three constituents. Obviously enough, with a set of " general laws " of some kind we can " explain " why A behaves as it does, if we know all about its structure and the structures of B, C, and D. But it still remains entirely unexplained why A should be there at all, or why, if it is there, it should have B, C, and D as its neighbours rather than others with a totally different structure of their own. That this is so has to be accepted as a " brute " fact which is not explained nor yet self-explanatory. Thus no amount of knowledge of " natural laws " will explain the present actual state of Nature unless we also assume it as a brute fact that the distribution of " matter " and " energy " (or whatever else we take as the ultimates of our system of physics) a hundred millions of years ago was such and such. With the same " laws " and a different " initial " distribution the actual state of the world to-day would be very different. " Collocations," to use Mill's terminology, as well as " laws of causation " have to enter into all our scientific explanations. And though it is true that as our knowledge grows, we are continually learning to assign causes for particular " collocations " originally accepted as bare facts, we only succeed in doing so by falling back on other anterior " collocations " which we have equally to take as unexplained bare facts. As M. Meyerson puts it, we only get rid of the

" inexplicable " at one point at the price of introducing it again somewhere else. Now any attempt to treat the complex of facts we call Nature as something which will be found to be more nearly self-explanatory the more of them we know, and would become quite self-explanatory if we only knew them all, amounts to an attempt to eliminate " bare fact " altogether, and reduce Nature simply to a complex of " laws." In other words, it is an attempt to manufacture particular existents out of mere universals, and therefore must end in failure. And the actual progress of science bears witness to this. The more we advance to the reduction of the visible face of Nature to " law," the more, not the less, complex and baffling become the mass of characters which we have to attribute as bare unexplained fact to our ultimate constituents. An electron is a much stiffer dose of " brute " fact than one of Newton's hard impenetrable corpuscles.

Thus we may fairly say that to surrender ourselves to the suggestion that Nature, if we only knew enough, would be seen to be a self-explanatory whole is to follow a will-of-the-wisp. The duality of " law " and " fact " cannot be eliminated from natural science, and this means that in the end either Nature is not explicable at all, or, if she is, the explanation has to be sought in something " outside " on which Nature depends.

(ii) Hence it is not surprising that both among men of science and among philosophers there is just now a strong tendency to give up the attempt to " explain " Nature completely and to fall back on an " ultimate pluralism." This means that we resign ourselves to the admission of the duality of " law " and " fact." We assume that there are a plurality of ultimately different constituents of Nature, each with its own specific character and way of behaving, and our business in explanation is simply to show how to account for the world as we find it by the fewest and simplest laws of interaction between these different constituents. In other words we give up altogether the attempt to " explain Nature " ; we are content to " explain " lesser " parts " of Nature in terms of their specific character and their relations to other " parts." This is clearly a completely justified mode of procedure for a man of science who is aiming at the solution of some particular problem such as, *e.g.*, the discovery of the conditions under which a permanent new " species " originates and maintains itself. But it is quite another question whether " ultimate pluralism " can be

# From Nature to God 55

the last word of a " philosophy of Nature." If you take it so, it really means that in the end you have no reason to assign why there should be just so many ultimate constituents of " Nature " as you say there are, or why they should have the particular characters you say they have, except that " it happens to be the case." You are acquiescing in unexplained brute fact, not because in the present state of knowledge you do not see your way to do better, but on the plea that there is and can be no explanation. You are putting unintelligible mystery at the very heart of reality.

Perhaps it may be rejoined, " And why should we not acknowledge this, seeing that, whether we like it or not, we must come to this in the end ? " Well, at least it may be retorted that to acquiesce in such a " final inexplicability " as final means that you have denied the validity of the very assumption on which all science is built. All through the history of scientific advance it has been taken for granted that we are not to acquiesce in inexplicable brute fact ; whenever we come across what, with our present light, has to be accepted as merely fact, we have a right to ask for further explanation, and should be false to the spirit of science if we did not. Thus we inevitably reach the conclusion that either the very principles which inspire and guide scientific inquiry itself are an illusion, or Nature itself must be dependent on some reality which is self-explanatory, and therefore not Nature nor any part of Nature, but, in the strict sense of the words, " supernatural " or " transcendent "—transcendent, that is, in the sense that in it there is overcome that duality of " law " and " fact " which is characteristic of Nature and every part of Nature. It is not " brute " fact, and yet it is not an abstract universal law or complex of such laws, but a really existing self-luminous Being, such that you could see, if you only apprehended its true character, that to have that character and to be are the same thing. This is the way in which Nature, as it seems to me, inevitably points beyond itself as the temporal and mutable to an " other " which is eternal and immutable.

The " argument from design," rightly stated, seems to me to have a similar force. In our small region of the universe, at any rate, we can see for ourselves that the course of development has taken a very remarkable direction. It has led up, through a line of species which have had to adapt themselves to their " environment," to the emergence of an intelligent and moral creature who adapts his environment to himself and even to his ideals of what he is not yet but ought to be and hopes to be, and the environment of the species he " domesticates " to his own purposes.     It is increasingly true as we pass from savagery to civilisation that men make their own environment and are not made by it.   On the face of it, it at least looks as though, so far as our own region of Nature is concerned, this emergence of creatures who, being intelligent and moral, freely shape their own environment, is the culminating stage beyond which the development of new species cannot go, and that the whole anterior history of the inorganic and prehuman organic development of our planet has been controlled throughout by the requirements of this " end."   I know it will be said that we have no proof that the same thing has happened anywhere else in the " universe " ;   our planet may, for all we know, not be a fair " average sample."     Again, it may be urged that there are reasons for thinking that the history of our planet will end in its unfitness first to contain intelligent human life, and then to contain any form of life ;   consequently man and all his works cannot be the " end of evolution " even on this earth, but must be a mere passing phase in a process which is controlled by no " ends," and is therefore in no true sense of the term a " history."   One would not wish to shirk any of these objections, and yet it is, I think, not too much to say that, to anyone but a fanatical atheist, it will always appear preposterous to regard the production of moral and intelligent masters of Nature as a mere by-product or accident of " evolution on this planet," or indeed as anything but the " end " which has all along determined the process.   " Nature," we might say, really does show a " trend " or " bias " to the production of intelligence surpassing her own. And further, we must remember that if there is such a " trend," it will be necessary to include under the head of the processes it determines, not only the emergence of the various forms of prehuman life on our earth, but the " geological " preparation of the earth itself to be the scene of the ensuing development and the pre-preparation during the still remoter astronomical period of the formation of our solar system.   Thus to recognise so-called " quasi-purposiveness " even in the course development has followed on " one tiny planet " inevitably involves finding the same quasi-purposiveness on a vaster scale, throughout the whole indefinite

range of natural events.[1]  The more we are alive to this simple
consideration that " *de facto* determination by ends," once admitted
anywhere in Nature, cannot be confined to any single region or
part of Nature but inevitably penetrates everywhere, the more
impossible it becomes to be satisfied with such expressions as
" quasi-purposive" or " *de facto* " teleology and the like.

The vaster the dominating " plan," the more vividly must it
suggest a planning and guiding intelligence.   Nature herself, we
may suppose (if we allow ourselves to use the miserably misleading
personification at all), may, as has been said, be like a sleep-walker
who executes trains of purposive acts without knowing that he does
so.   But the plan itself cannot have originated without a wakeful
and alert intelligence.   (Even the sleep-walker, as we know, only
performs trains of acts adjusted to ends in his sleep because he has
first learnt consciously to adjust means to ends in his waking life.)
Let " Nature " be as unconscious as you please : the stronger is
the suggestion that the marvellous, and often comical, " adapta-
tions " of a highly complex character which pervade " Nature "
are the " artifices " of one who neither slumbers nor sleeps.   What
look like " accidents " may very well be deliberate designs of a
master artist, or, as Plato says, contrary to the proverbial expression,
it may be Nature which " imitates " Art.   I will not attempt to
estimate the amount of probative force which ought to be ascribed
to these suggestions.   It is enough for my purpose that they are
there, and that their drawing has notoriously been felt with special

---

[1] This is not to say that man is the sole or chief end of Creation, a proposition
which, in fact, no orthodox Christian theologian would make ;  at least not
without very careful explanations and reservations.   But it is worth while to
remind ourselves that there is nothing in itself absurd in the view of the Middle
Ages that human history is the central interest, the main plot, of the drama
of the universe.   For all we *know*, our planet may be the only home of
beings " with immortal souls to be saved."   If it is, then the fact that it is
"*tiny*" is obviously irrelevant as a reason for denying its central importance.
When I reflect on the capacities of a man for good and evil, I see nothing
ludicrous in the supposition, which, however, I am not making, that it might
have been the chief purpose of a wise Creator in making the solar system that
the sun should give us men light and warmth.
All I seriously wish to insist on, however, is that to let in " purpose "
*anywhere* into natural fact means letting it in *everywhere*.   Give it an inch
and it will rightly take infinite room.   (This as a reply to the arguments based
on the allegation that we cannot regard the part of things with which we are
acquainted as a " fair average sample."   What we are acquainted with is not
a definite isolated " part " or " region," but has ramifications which extend
indefinitely far.)

intensity by so many of those who are best acquainted with the facts, even where their metaphysical bias has led them to withhold assent.

The spectacle of movement and change which we call " Nature " thus at least suggests the presence of some " transcendent " source of movement and change which is strictly eternal, being above all mutability and having no succession of phases within itself, and is omnipotent, since it is itself the source of *all* " becoming." The orderliness and apparent purposive " trend towards intelligence " in Nature similarly at least suggest that this omnipotent and eternal " supernatural " is a wholly intelligent Will. The force of the suggestion seems to have been felt by man in every stage of his history so far as that history is accessible to us. It is noteworthy that the more intimate our inquiries become with the " savages " who by our estimate stand nearest to a pre-civilised condition, the clearer it becomes that even those of them who have been set down on first acquaintance as wholly " godless " turn out, on better knowledge, to have their traditions of a " maker of life " and the like. And at the same time we are not dealing with anything which can be set aside as a " relic of primitive savagery." *Our* conception of " One God the Father Almighty, Creator of heaven and earth," has come to us from two immediate sources, Greek science and philosophy and Hebrew prophecy, and both science and prophecy, as cannot be too often repeated, began by a complete break with the " primitive superstition " of the past. Belief in God as the source of Nature is thus a " survival of primitive superstition " only in the same sense in which the same could be said of belief in causality [1] or, if you prefer it, in " laws of uniform sequence."

So far, however, our attention has been confined to what Bonaventura calls the " things around and below us," and they clearly have taken us a very little way indeed in the direction of suggesting the reality of a God who is God in the religious man's sense, a being who can be loved and trusted utterly and without qualification. In the creatures we may have discerned the " footprints " of a Creator, but we have seen no token of his " likeness." Perhaps, if we turn our attention to " what is

[1] It is significant that Witgenstein's penetrating though unbalanced *Tractatus logico-philosophicus* definitely *identifies* " superstition " with the belief in causality. *Op. cit.* 5, 1361.

within us," we may find in our own moral being the suggestion of something further. We may get at any rate a hint that the creative intelligence we divine behind all things has also the character which makes adoration, love, and trust, as distinguished from mere wonder, possible. In man's moral being we may discern not the mere " footprints " but the " image " of God.

## II. FROM MAN TO GOD

With the line of thought we have now to consider we can deal more briefly. If meditation on the creatures in general leads us by a circuitous route and an obscure light to the thought of their Maker, meditation on the moral being of man suggests God more directly and much less obscurely. For we are now starting a fresh stage of the " ascent " from a higher level, and it is with the road to God as with Dante's purgatorial mountain : the higher you have mounted, the easier it is to rise higher still. In Nature we at best see God under a disguise so heavy that it allows us to discern little more than that someone is there ; within our own moral life we see Him with the mask, so to say, half fallen off.

Once more the general character of the ascent is the same ; we begin with the temporal, and in a certain sense the natural, to end in the eternal and supernatural. But the line of thought, though kindred to the first, is independent, so that Nature and Man are like two witnesses who have had no opportunity of collusion. The clearer and more emphatic testimony of the latter to what was testified less unambiguously by the former affords a further confirmation of our hope that we have read the suggestions of Nature, so ambiguous in their purport, aright.

A single sentence will be enough to show both the analogy of the argument from Man to God with the argument from Nature and the real independence of the two lines of testimony. Nature, we have urged, on inspection points to the " supernatural " beyond itself as its own presupposition ; if we look within ourselves we shall see that in man " Nature " and " supernature " meet ; he has both within his own heart, and is a denizen at once of the temporal and of the eternal. He has not, like the animals, so far as we can judge of their inner life, one " environment " to which he must adapt himself but two,

a secular and an eternal.    Because he is designed ultimately to be
at home with God in the eternal, he can never be really at home
in this world, but at best is, like Abraham, a pilgrim to a promised
but unseen land ;    at worst, like Cain, an aimless fugitive and
wanderer on the face of the earth.    The very "image" of his
Maker which has been stamped on him is not only a sign of his
rightful domination over the creatures ;    it is also "the mark of
Cain" from which all creatures shrink.    Hence among all the
creatures, many of whom are comic enough, man is alone in being
tragic.    His life, at the very best, is a tragi-comedy ;    at the worst,
it is stark tragedy.    And naturally enough this is so ;    for, if man
has only the "environment" which is common to him with the
beasts of the field, his whole life is no more than a perpetual
attempt to find a rational solution of an equation all whose roots
are surds.    He can only achieve adjustment to one of his two
"environments" by sacrifices of adjustment to the other ;    he can
no more be equally in tune with the eternal and the secular at
once than a piano can be exactly in tune for all keys.    In practice
we know how the difficulty is apparently solved in the best human
lives ;    it is solved by cultivating our earthly attachments and yet
also practising a high detachment, not "setting our hearts" too
much on the best of temporal goods, since "the best in this kind
are but shadows," "using" the creatures, but always in the
remembrance that the time will come when we can use them
no more, loving them but loving them *ordinate*, with care not to
lose our hearts to any of them,    Wise men do not need to be
reminded that the deliberate voluntary refusal of real good things
is necessary, as a protection against the over-valuation of the
secular, in any life they count worth living.    And yet wise men
know also that the renunciation of real good which they recommend is not recommended for the mere sake of being without
"good."    Good is always renounced for the sake of some "better
good."    But the "better good" plainly cannot be any of the good
things of this secular existence.    For there is none of them whatever which it may not be a duty to renounce for some man and at
some time.

I do not mean merely that occasions demand the sacrifice
of the sort of thing the "average sensual man" calls good—
comfort, wealth, influence, rank and the like.    For no serious
moralist would dream of regarding any of these as more, at best,

than very inferior goods. I mean that the same thing holds true of the very things to which men of nobler mould are ready to sacrifice these obvious and secondary goods. For example, there are few, if any, earthly goods to compare with our personal affections. Yet a man must be prepared to sacrifice all his personal affections in the service of his country, or for what he honestly believes to be the one Church of God. But there are things to which the greatest lover of his country or his Church must be prepared in turn to sacrifice what lies so near his heart. I may die for my country, I may, as so many a fighting man does, leave wife and young children to run the extreme hazards of fortune, but I must not purchase peace and safety for this country I love so much by procuring the privy murder of a dangerous and remorseless enemy. I may give my body to be burned for my faith, I may leave my little ones to beg their bread for its sake, but I must not help it in its need by a fraud or a forgery. It may be argued that for the good of the human race I ought to be prepared to sacrifice the very independence of my native land, but for no advantage to the whole body of mankind may I insult justice by knowingly giving sentence or verdict against the innocent. If these things are not true, the whole foundation of our morality is dissolved ; if they are true, the greatest good, to which I must at need be prepared to sacrifice everything else, must be something which cannot even be appraised in the terms of a secular arithmetic, something incommensurable with the " welfare " of Church and State or even of the whole human race. If it is to be had in fruition at all, it must be had where the secular environment has finally and for ever fallen away, " yonder " as the Neo-Platonist would say, " in heaven " as the ordinary Christian says. If this world of time and passage were really our home and our only home, I own I should find it impossible to justify such a complete surrender of all temporal good as that I have spoken of ; yet it is certain that the sacrifice is no more than what is demanded, when the need arises, by the most familiar principles of morality. Whoever says " ought," meaning " ought," is in the act bearing witness to the supernatural and supra-temporal as the destined home of man. No doubt we should all admit that there are very many rules of our conventional morality which are not of unconditional and universal obligation ; we " ought " to conform to them under certain specified and understood

conditions.   I ought to be generous only when I have first satisfied the just claims of my creditors, just as I ought to abstain
from redressing grievances with the high hand when society
supplies me with the machinery for getting them redressed by
the law.   But whoever says " ought " at all, must mean that at
least *when* the requisite conditions are fulfilled the obligation is
absolute.   There may be occasions when it is not binding on me
to speak the truth to a questioner, but if there is one single occasion on which I ought to speak the truth, I ought to speak it
then, " though the sky should fall."

Now, if there ever is a single occasion on which we ought to
speak the truth, or to do anything else, " at all costs " as we say,
what is the good in the name of which this unconditional demand is made of me ?   It cannot be any secular good that can
be named, my own health or prosperity or life, nor even the
prosperity and pleasurable existence of mankind.   For I can
never, since the consequences of my act are endless and un-
foreseeable, be sure that I may not be endangering these very
goods by my act, and yet I am sure that the act is one which I ought
to do.   No doubt, you may fall back upon probability as the guide
of life and say, " I ought to do this act because it seems to me most
likely to conduce to the temporal well-being of myself, my family,
my nation, or my kind."   And in practice these are, no doubt,
the sort of considerations by which we are constantly influenced.
But it should be clear that they cannot be the ultimate grounds
of obligation, unless all morality is to be reduced to the status of
a convenient illusion.   To say that the ultimate ground of an
obligation is the mere fact that a man thinks he would further such
a concrete tangible end by his act involves the consequence that
no man is bound to do any act unless he thinks it will have these
results, and that he may do anything he pleases so long as he thinks
it will have them.   At heart, I believe, even the writers who
go furthest in professing to accept these conclusions do themselves
a moral injustice.   I am convinced that there is not one of them,
whatever he may hold in theory, who would not in practice " draw
the line " somewhere and say, " This thing I will not do, whatever the cost may be to myself or to anyone else or to everyone."
Now an obligation wholly independent of all temporal " consequences " clearly cannot have its justification in the temporal, nor
oblige any creature constructed to find his good wholly in the

temporal. Only to a being who has in his structure the adaptation to the eternal can you significantly say " You ought." [1]

It will be seen that the thought on which we have dwelt in the last paragraph is one of the underlying fundamental themes of Kant's principal ethical treatise, the " Critique of Practical Reason." It is characteristic of Kant that, wrongly as I think, he wholly distrusted the suggestions of the " supernatural " to be derived from the contemplation of Nature itself, and that, from an exaggerated dread of unregulated fanaticism and superstition, characteristic of his century, he was all but blind to the third source of suggestion of which we have yet to speak. Hence with him it is our knowledge of our own moral being, as creatures who have unconditional obligations, which has to bear the whole weight of the argument. Here, I own, he seems to me to be definitely wrong. The full force of the vindication of religion cannot be felt unless we recognise that its weight is supported not by one strand only but by a cord of three intertwined strands ; we need to integrate Bonaventura and Thomas and Butler with Kant to appreciate the real strength of the believer's position. Yet Kant seems to me unquestionably right as far as this. Even were there nothing else to suggest to us that we are denizens at once of a natural and temporal and of a supernatural and eternal world, the revelation of our own inner division against ourselves afforded by Conscience, duly meditated, is enough to bear the strain. Or, to make my point rather differently, I would urge that of all the philosophical thinkers who have concerned themselves with the life of man as a moral being, the two who stand out, even in the estimation of those who dissent from them, as the great undying moralists of literature, Plato and Kant, are just the two who have insisted most vigorously on what the secularly-minded call, by way of depreciation, the " dualism " of " this world " and the " other world," or, in Kantian language, of " man as (natural) phenomenon " and " man as (supernatural) reality." To deny the reality of this antithesis is to eviscerate morality.

We see this at once if we compare Kant, for example, with Hume, or Plato with Aristotle. It is so obvious that Plato and Kant really " care " about moral practice and Aristotle and Hume do not care, or do not care as much as they ought. In Hume's

---

[1] I owe the expression to a report of a recent utterance of some Roman Catholic divine. I regret that I cannot give the precise reference.

hands moral goodness is put so completely on a level with mere respectability that our approval of virtue and disapproval of vice is said in so many words to be at bottom one in kind with our preference of a well-dressed man to a badly-dressed.   Aristotle cares more than this.   He reduces moral goodness to the discharge of the duties of a good citizen, family man, and neighbour in this secular life, and is careful to insist that these obligations are not to be shirked.   But when he comes to speak of the true happiness of man and the kind of life which he lives " as a being with something divine in him," we find that the life of this " divine " part means nothing more than the promotion of science.   To live near to God means to him not justice, mercy, and humility, as it does to Plato and the Hebrew prophets, but to be a metaphysician, a physicist, and an astronomer.   Justice, mercy, and humility are to be practised, but only for a secular purpose, in order that the man of science may have an orderly and quiet social " environment " and so be free, as he would not be if he had to contend with disorderly passions in himself or his neighbours, to give the maximum of time and interest to the things which really matter.   We cannot say of Hume, nor of Aristotle, nor indeed of any moralist who makes morality merely a matter of right social adjustments in this temporal world, what you can say of Plato or Kant, *beati qui esuriunt et sitiunt justitiam.*   " Otherworldliness " is as characteristic of the greatest theoretical moralists as it is of all the noblest livers, whatever their professed theories may be.

The point is again strikingly illustrated by a difficulty raised by a moralist who was also a noble liver in our own times, T. H. Green.   He rightly makes it a fatal objection to the current utilitarianism of his day that pleasure or gratified feeling, which according to the utilitarian theorists is the only good, is not a *moral* good—*i.e.* their view is that the end for which the good man acts is the same as that for which the bad man acts.   The difference between the good and the bad man is made a mere difference of the manner by which each pursues an end which is common to him with the other ; the object sought by both is the same.   To escape this reduction of virtue to prudent calculation of means Green goes on to say that true good means " moral good," " what satisfies a moral nature as such."   This seems at first sight to leave us with a vicious circle.   A moral agent is one who aims at " true " good, but " true " good again can only be defined as

" the sort of thing a moral agent as such aims at." Green's way of escape from this circle is to add that we do not know in its fulness what this true good is, but we can see at any rate that the belief that it really *is* has been the source and impulse of all attempts to obtain it, and we can learn from the history of the past along what lines progress towards its attainment has been made.[1]

Now these observations, so far as they go, are manifestly sound. It is plain that moral progress would be arrested if it were not at every stage inspired by an aspiration towards what has not yet been attained, as Herbert Spencer frankly stated that the very notion of " ought " would vanish from a " fully evolved " society— that is, that such a society would have ceased to be a moral community. It is equally plain that none of us has a " clear and distinct idea " of what it would be like to be a just man made perfect. We all walk by faith, not by sight. The conclusion which Green clearly ought to have drawn from his premises is that, since the goal of the moral life cannot by any possibility be attained under temporal conditions, and yet its reality (which, in the case of an ideal which ought to inspire and regulate all our conduct, must mean its real attainability by *us*) is the necessary condition that the inspiration to progress shall not fail, our final destiny must lie in the non-temporal. But when Green comes to face this issue, his fear of incurring the reproach of " other-worldliness " is so great that he merely equivocates about the " last things," and proves false to what was clearly his own inmost faith.[2]

Of course we could put the thought I am labouring in many other ways. We might, for example, say that it cannot be insignificant that man alone of all creatures of whom we know has a sense of sin. Animals, in a wild state, seem to show nothing of

[1] T. H. Green's *Prolegomena to Ethics*, bk. iii. chap. i. §§. 171–179.

[2] See the shuffling language, *op. cit.*, bk. iii. chap. ii. §§. 187–189, where Green simply runs away under a cloud of words from his own emphatic statement (§ 185) that moral progress can only mean progress *of* personal character *to* personal character. The same terror of being thought " otherworldly " by secularists is much more marked in Green's illustrious disciple, the late Professor Bosanquet. To my own mind it absolutely ruins his philosophy on its ethical side, besides making him a very unsafe guide as an interpreter of Plato. A Christian, or even a Platonist philosopher, should make light of the charge of "otherworldliness"; "Let us therefore go forth unto him without the camp, bearing his reproach. For here we have no continuing city, but we seek one to come." One might have a worse motto as a moralist than ἔξω τῆς παρεμβολῆς.

the kind. Mr. Bradley, it is true, once suggested that you might find the beginnings of moral self-condemnation in the sulky brooding of a tiger which has missed its spring. But I think there is here a confusion which was long ago exposed by Butler in his distinction between the feelings of a man who has been disappointed of an expectation and one who knows he has deservedly suffered for his own misdoing. " In the one case, what our thoughts fix upon is our condition : in the other, our conduct." [1] Dogs which have been well brought up are thought by some observers to be capable of " knowing they are doing wrong " and to feel ashamed of it. I cannot pronounce any opinion on the soundness of this as psychology, but supposing the fact to be so, it is important to remember that these dogs have been brought up by man, and that any approach they make to a sense of wrongdoing, as distinct from a shrinking from expected unpleasant consequences, is presumably an effect of their domestication by a being who is already moral. The alleged fact proves nothing as to the presence of a rudimentary sense of sin in an animal in the " state of nature," any more than the shameless sexual irregularities of our domesticated animals prove that before their domestication they had not their special pairing seasons. In any case the human sense of sin has peculiarities of its own which no sound psychologist can afford to neglect. There is, first of all, its special poignancy and indelibility. As to the poignancy, any one who has felt the sword-point of guilt knows, without my telling him, how it pierces to the very marrow. The indelibility, too, must not be overlooked. The dog which has disgraced itself does, perhaps, for the time being, feel shame, as well as fear of an impending unpleasant consequence. But when the temporary disgrace is once fairly over, there is no indication that the dog which has disgraced itself and been punished is troubled again about its past " misdoings." Its past self is dead and buried. Not so with us. If a man has a high standard and a sensitive conscience, it is not enough for him that he is honestly repentant for his past misdoings and has long honourably striven, perhaps with full success, to " make good," but the remembrance loses little, if anything, of its bitterness. A sincere Christian may be satisfied that he has received the remission of his sins and may trust with assurance that he will be preserved by grace from falling back to them, but he does not forget them ; the remembrance and

[1] *Dissertation upon the Nature of Virtue* (ed. W. R. Matthews, § 6).

the shame remain, like disfiguring and aching scars which testify
to ancient wounds. For us, the past may be dead, but it is not yet
the dead and buried past it seems to be for the animals. There is
the keen sense of "pollution" by our wrongdoing, testified to
by the world-wide practice of trying to get rid of the pollution
by ablution, sprinkling with the blood of sacrificial victims and
similar rites, exactly as we might try to get rid of a bodily defilement
or infection. Even where we cannot point to any member of
human society who has suffered hurt or infringement of rights by
the sinful act, the feeling still persists that a sin is a wrong done
to a person of infinite sanctity, a personal affront, an act of
*lèse-majesté*. We may no longer be convinced by the old argument that it is just that the least sin should be visited with un-
ending torments, because, as an act of treason against an infinite
Deity, it is always an infinite treason. But I believe that we do
still feel about what a third human party might call our *peccadilloes*
that, trivial as they look, they are infinitely polluting. It is the
"saint" not the "notorious evil-doer" to whom it most readily
occurs to cry "Woe is me, for I am unclean." Kant expresses
the same thought in a different way, which is all the more remarkable from his violent prejudice against "anthropomorphic" conceptions. According to him the one and only specific moral
feeling is reverence for the sanctity of the moral law as such.
He will not say reverence for a divine Author of the moral law ;
that would be "anthropomorphism." Yet when he is trying to
make it quite clear what this feeling of reverence for the majesty
of the law is, he observes that reverence is, properly speaking,
a feeling which is only evoked by moral character, and compares it
with the feeling of constraint an ordinary man would have if he
were suddenly called on to enter the presence of a "superior,"
the sort of feeling you or I might have if we were informed that
in an hour or two we should have to dine with the King or the
Pope. The natural inference, as Professor Clement Webb has
remarked, is that the reverence we feel for the moral law really is
an attitude towards an unseen being of transcendent purity and
holiness of character.[1]

Or the whole argument may be once more put in the form in
which we find it in the great scholastic thinkers, a form which
goes back in the end to Plato and Augustine. Man, like all living

[1] *Divine Personality and Human Life*, Lecture V, especially pp. 125–126.

creatures, is first and last a conative and striving being. He has a " good " which he can consciously enjoy and without the fruition of which he is discontented and unhappy. So too with his animal congeners. But the good which secures content to them is one for which the conditions of secular existence, when favourable, make adequate provision. An animal wants food, shelter, warmth, movement, repose, the gratification of its pairing or parental instincts when they are aroused ; it usually also wants to be " let alone," to be left unthwarted in its movements, and when these wants are gratified it is content and as happy as an animal can be. Man has all these wants and many more created by his possession of intelligence. He wants, for instance, to secure himself against the uncertainties of to-morrow, hence his desire of wealth, power, command of the forces of Nature. He wants to provide himself with sources of interest and excitement, one chief reason for the attractiveness of the curious game of politics. He wants to know in order to satisfy his curiosity, to surround himself with things of beauty or to make them for himself, he wants to feel himself beloved and so forth. Yet the singular thing is that none of these satisfactions, singly or together, really satisfy him. He is unhappy in deprivation and wearied in fruition by satiety. And even where there is neither deprivation nor satiety he is discontented with the best things time has to give him, because they will not last.

Most of us would perhaps say that the purest content and happiness earth has to give us is that which comes from the known possession of the life-long personal affection of a friend or a wife or a son. Yet there is something which forbids us to be really content and at peace even in such possession. However well we may love and be loved, there is always some barrier between the self and the second self in another. A man always knows at once too much and too little of the wife of his bosom and she of him. Again in these dearest intimacies we are never really assured against the changes and estrangements time brings with it. I may change subtly and imperceptibly or my other self may change, and by and by one awakens with a heartache to the perception that the old confidence and love are a thing of the past. And finally, if none of these things happen, we all know that when hands have been joined in wedlock or in friendship, they will be unjoined again by death. " One shall be taken and the other shall be left " is the irrevocable sentence on the dearest of all earthly ties. There is thus a drop of poison in the chalice of the fullest secular happiness—a poison infused, a Christian would say, by the heavenly Lover of all souls to prevent us from finding abiding and complete happiness outside Himself. Nothing seems plainer than this, that if true peace and content are to be found by man at all, they cannot be found in anything temporal or secular. They must spring from a conscious intimate possession of personal union of heart and will with a being who knows us through and through as no man knows another, or even himself, who contains within Him an inexhaustible wealth of being which excludes all risk of satiety, who is utterly eternal and abiding and therefore can never change or fail. The final peace of man, if it is to be found at all, can only be found in a God who is eternal by nature and imparts by His grace a " participated " eternity of perseverance to the other party to the relation. Our true, final good thus lies not in the world of Nature, but in that " other-world " of the supernatural which everywhere interpenetrates and sustains Nature and yet absolutely transcends her.

" If found at all," we said. But possibly the " final good " is simply not to be found. It may be an illusion, like the horizon which seems to be the end of the visible world, but recedes as we approach it. But at least the facts about human aspirations of which we have spoken are real facts, as the whole of the great literature of the world testifies. Any philosophy has to give some coherent and rational-seeming explanation of the fact that the " illusion " is there. We cannot say that it is an inevitable consequence of the fact that man is finite and perishable. We have all heard of

> " Infinite passion and the pain
> Of finite hearts that yearn."

But the finitude of the hearts does not explain the infinity of the passion ; it makes it a paradox. The animals, too, are finite, yet their finitude causes them no unrest. But man is not only finite ; he *knows* that he is finite ! There you come to the heart of the mystery. How is a creature who is merely finite to know that he is finite ? Is this any more possible than it would be, for example, that a dog should know that he is " only a dog " ? This is the real crux which a simple " this-world " philosophy persists in ignoring. Or how it comes that a race of beings shaped *by* purely temporal conditions to maintain their existence by adaptation *to* temporal conditions so obstinately insists on demanding something more ?　How obstinate is the insistence is shown by the reluctance of the very thinkers who hold in theory that man is just one of the " products of natural evolution " to advise him to behave himself accordingly.　Of the many who repeat glibly enough that man is just an animal, who would say to a son setting out on life for himself, " Be an animal " ?　Yet if any of us would count it wiser and better advice to his son to say " Live like a creature destined for eternity," is he not virtually confessing that the instinct, or whatever we may prefer to call it, for eternity, however questionable the forms in which it sometimes expresses itself, is at bottom a sound one ?

We see that the general character of the argument from Nature and from our moral being to God is the same in both cases.　In both we reason from the temporal to the eternal.　But there is this difference, that the elusive being to which we reason is, in the second case, something richer.　Reflexion on what is below and around us suggested only an eternal intelligent designer and source of Nature.　Reflexion on the moral nature of man suggests a being who is more, the eternal something before whom we must not only bow in amazement, like Job, but kneel in reverence as the source and support of all moral goodness.　This is as it should be, since in the one case we are attempting to see the cause in the effect, in the other to see the features of the father in his child. If Nature shows us only the footsteps of God, in man as a moral being we see His image.

### III. From God to God

The apparently paradoxical heading I have given to this section of my essay has been purposely chosen.　We have considered already the suggestiveness of what Bonaventura calls reflexion on what is beneath us and within us, and have now to take into account his " reflexion on what is above us."　Here, if the phrase stands for anything real, we have clearly done with mere suggestions ; we are dealing with the interpretation of a direct manifestation of the divine and super-temporal, within the limits imposed by the finitude and temporality of the human recipient.　To use phraseology which is more familiar to us of to-day, we have to consider the worth of the so-called "religious experience" as testimony to the reality of its own object, and there is no line of argument which lends itself more readily to abuse. Every kind of faddist and fanatic will appeal as readily to "experience" for testimony to his own pet fancies as the credulous appeal to the "evidence of their senses" for proof of the existence of ghosts or the reality of sorcery. We seriously need to remember, as the Bishop of Manchester has recently reminded us, that just as the "artist's experience" means the way in which the *whole* natural realm is experienced by the man who is an artist, so "religious experience" means not some isolated group of bizarre experiences but the special way in which the whole of life is experienced by the "religious" man. And yet, true as this is, the very statement implies that there are some experiences which stand out in the life of the religious man as characteristically predominant and determining the colouring of his whole experience of the world. This is equally true of the artist. A man with the artist's eye, we very rightly say, "sees beauty" everywhere, while a man without it goes through life not seeing beauty anywhere, or at best seeing it only occasionally, where it is too prominent to be missed. Still no one doubts that even a man highly endowed with the gifts of the artist has to develop his sense for the beautiful. If he comes to find it present where the rest of us would never suspect it at all but for the teaching we may get from his work, this must be because he began by being specially alive to and interested in its presence where it is more visibly displayed. This again means that, however truly beauty may pervade the whole of things, there are special regions where its presence is most manifest and obvious. What is characteristic of the artist is that he makes just these elements of experience a key to unlock the meaning of the rest. So the religious man, no doubt, means the man who sees the whole of reality under the light of a specific illumination, but he has come to see all things in that light by taking certain arresting pieces or phases of his experience as the key to the meaning of the rest. In this sense we may properly speak of specifically religious experiences, as we may speak of a man's experience in the presence of a wonderful picture or musical composition, or at a moment when a weighty decision which will colour the whole tenour of his future conduct has to be made, as specifically æsthetic or moral experiences. The question is whether there really are such specific experiences or whether what have been supposed to be so are only illusions, misinterpretations of experiences which contain nothing unique.

This question is not settled by the admission that some experiences which have been reckoned by those who have had them as religious are illusory.    All experience is liable to misinterpretation. We must not argue that sense-perception does not reveal a world of really existing bodies, which are no illusions of our imagination, on the ground that there are such things as dreams and hallucinations, any more than we may argue from the general reality of the things perceived by sense to the reality of dream-figures or ghosts. So again we may neither argue that there is no real beauty in the visible world because the best of us are capable of sometimes finding it where it is not, nor that because there is real beauty, every supposed beauty detected by any man must be real.    In a sense, " everything is given."    If there were no arresting perception of beauty in the region of colour or tone, we should never come to be on the look out for it where it is less manifest.    On the other hand, every man's immediate verdict on beauty is not to be trusted.    We have to learn how to interpret our experience in the light of the judgment of the artist who is specially endowed with a fine discrimination of beauty and has cultivated his eye or ear by long and careful attention to the æsthetic aspects of the sensible world before we can trust our own immediate " taste " for colour or line or tone.    So, too, in matters or morality, if a man has no direct perception of what " ought " means, it is impossible to convey that meaning to him ;  but a man would be led sadly astray in his morality if he assumed that his own first judgments of right and wrong are infallible.    He needs to learn " sound judgment in all things " by a training which puts him in possession of the moral tradition of a high-minded society, and by comparing his own judgment in cases of perplexity with that of men of high character, ripe reflexion, and rich knowledge of life. (This is why, though without conscientiousness there can be no true moral goodness, the faddist, who insists on treating his own " private " conscience as infallible, is a mere moral nuisance.)

We may readily admit, then, that much which the experiencer is inclined to take for " religious " experience is illusion.    He may mistake the vague stirrings and impulses of sex, or æsthetic sensibility, or even pure illusions of sense or perception, for the self-

revelation of the divine, just as any of us may, in favourable conditions, mistake what he has merely dreamed of for an event of
waking life.   And such confusions may very well lie at the bottom
of widespread aberrations ;  they may account very largely for the
puerility of many of the " religious " beliefs of mankind, and the
lewd or bloody practices which defile so many of our ritual cults.
And we must insist that if there are specific and unique religious
experiences, they must not all be taken "at their face-value " ;
like all other alleged experiences they stand in need of " interpretation " in the light of the judgment of the " expert " who is at once
keenly sensible of the actual " experience," and has brought a tried
and sane judgment to bear upon it.[1]   We thus find ourselves face
to face with a second question, and we have to ask (*a*) are there
specific *data* which furnish the basis for a " religious " interpretation of life, (*b*) and if there are, who are the " experts " whose
interpretation of the *data* should guide the interpretation ?

(*a*) As to the first question.   It has, as we all know, been
denied that there are any specific data to furnish such an interpretation with its starting-point.   The supposed *data* have been explained away, now as ordinary physical facts misunderstood by the
curious but ignorant savage, now as emotional reactions to dreams,
fear of the dark or of lonely places, now as vague emotional
reactions attendant on the different sexual modifications characteristic of adolescence, and in other ways.   The question is
whether *all* the known facts can be disposed of without remainder
in this fashion.   *A priori* we have no right to assume that this can
be done.   It may be true, for example, that " conversions "
are more common at or shortly after the reaching of puberty
than at any other time of life.   It is equally true that the same
period is often marked by the sudden appearance of other new
interests or the sudden intensification of old ones.   Thus a boy
often suddenly develops a vivid interest in literature, or a new sensi-
tiveness to art, in the years of dawning manhood.   Clearly this does

---

[1] This sort of interpretation is needed even for sense-perception.   Any one
who has, *e.g.*, ever used a microscope must remember how he had at first to
learn to " see " with it.   At first the beginner does not " see " what his teacher
says is there to be seen, or (*experto crede*) he " sees " a great deal that is not
there.   I can vividly recollect the trouble I had in this matter when first shown
sections of the spinal medulla under the microscope.   Cp. again the sharp
disputes of astronomers about many of the markings which some of them claim
to have " seen " on the disc of Mars.

not prove that the qualities we admire in literary style or in painting or music are not really there, but only supposed to be there in
virtue of an illusion of sexuality.   *A priori* it is just as likely that
the effect of a crisis which affects our whole bodily and mental life
should be to awaken a heightened perception of a reality previously
veiled from our eyes, as to create the " illusion " of a reality which
is not there.   The experiences of adolescence may be, as a matter
of my private history, the occasion of my first discovery of beauties
in Keats or Chopin which I do not find in the ordinary rhymester
or manufacturer of " music " for the piano.   But how does this
prove that in reality the poetry of Keats does not differ from that of
writers for the provincial newspaper, or the music of Chopin from
the average waltz or polka?   The problem is not how I came
to make a certain " find," but what the worth of the " find "
may be.

So with the part played by fear of the dark or of desert solitudes
in creating beliefs in gods.   The real question is not whether
emotions of this kind may not have influenced men's religious
emotions and beliefs, but whether the emotions and beliefs, however they may have been developed, *contain* nothing more than
such fears or contain something else which is quite specific, just as
musical perception may be prompted or quickened by adolescence
but certainly, *when once it is there*, contains a quite specific core
or kernel of its own.   However our sensibility to music began,
it is quite certain that what we perceive when we appreciate it is
nothing sexual.   There are, I honestly believe, men who only
respond to the appeal of music so far as it, crudely or subtly, is made
to sexual feeling, but such men are the typically " unmusical."
What they value is not musical beauty itself, but a mass of suggestions which have to be got rid of before one can begin to
appreciate " pure " music at all, exactly as one has to get rid of the
tendency to demand that a picture shall " tell a story " before one
can begin to understand the values of colour, line, disposal of
light and shade.   We have also to be on our guard against the
standing " psychologist's fallacy " which no one has done more to
expose than Dr. Otto in the work to which reference has already
been made.   It is too often assumed that because there is an
*analogy* between our mental attitude towards an object of our
adoration and our attitude towards something we fear, or something which attracts us sexually, the two attitudes must be the

same. Thus our reverence for the God we worship is in some ways like our dread of a strange and powerful natural object; our love for God is in some ways like the feelings of a devoted human lover, as the language of religious devotion is enough to prove. But it does not in the least follow that the likeness is more than a likeness; it is still perfectly possible that even the rudest savage's attitude in the presence of that which he "worships" has a character of its own quite distinct, *e.g.*, from his mere fear of a formidable beast or of the dangers of the dark. Since language has been primarily adapted to express our attitude towards "things of this world," when we want to speak of our attitude in the presence of our *numina* we have to make shift, as best we can, with words which properly designate an analogous but different attitude. The psychologist and anthropologist are only too apt to take these makeshift expressions *au pied de la lettre*; because we have to say that we "fear" or "love" God, they assume that we mean no more than when we say that we are afraid of an angry bull or that we love a young lady. Thus the specifically "religious" character of certain experiences, if it is really there, eludes them because they have not taken Bacon's warning against the *idola fori* which arises from excessive belief in the adequacy of language. They have not understood that the name of GOD is necessarily the "ineffable" name.

That civilised men, in the presence of anything they take as divine, have this sense of being face to face with the "ineffable" is quite certain, and we can see by reading the cruder utterances of the uncivilised in the light of what has grown out of them that they too must have it. It is the great service of Dr. Otto to the philosophy of religion that he has worked out this line of thought in full detail in his careful analysis of the meanings of "holy" and corresponding words, as revealed by the historical study of language and literature. The main point to be made is that, as far back as we can trace the beginnings of religion, the "holy," even if it is no more than an oddly shaped stone, does not simply mean the strange or the formidable; it means, at the lowest, the "uncanny," and the "uncanny" is precisely that which does not simply belong to "this" everyday world, but directly impresses us as manifesting in some special way the presence of "the other" world. As such, it repels and attracts at once, is at once the awful and the worshipful, but above all in both aspects the absolutely transcendent and

" *other*-worldly." At different levels of spiritual development the object which awakens this special sense of being in the presence of the " absolutely transcendent " may be very different. A low savage may feel it in the presence of what to us is simply a quaintly shaped stone or a queer-looking hill ; the prophet feels it, and is crushed by the sense of its transcendent " otherness," in his vision of the Lord of hosts ; the disciples of Christ feel it in the presence of a living man, who is also their friend and teacher, when we read of Him that " he was going before them on the road and they were *astounded* (ἐθαμβοῦντο), and as they followed they were *terrified* (ἐφοβοῦντο)" (Mark x. 32). It is precisely the same feeling which has prompted, *e.g.*, the utterance of the words of institution in the Eucharist *sotto voce*, and inspired the old Eucharistic hymn σιγησάτω πᾶσα σάρξ βροτεία,[1] as well as the modern saying that if Shakespeare came into the room we should all stand up, but if Jesus Christ came into the room we should all kneel down. It is equally the same sense of being in the presence of the wholly " other-worldly " which finds expression in such an exclamation as the prophet's " Woe is me for I am unclean, for mine eyes have seen the Lord of hosts," or St. Peter's " Depart from me, for I am a sinful man." We should quite misunderstand such language if we read it as a confession of any special wrongdoing on the part of prophet or apostle. It is the universal voice of the mutable and temporal brought face to face with the absolutely eternal ; hence in Scripture even the sinless seraphim are said to " veil their faces " as they stand before their Lord. This, again, is why it has been the belief of all peoples that he who sees a god dies.

As nearly as we can express our attitude towards that which awakens this sense of being immediately in the presence of the " other-worldly " by any one word, we may say that it is the attitude of " worship." But even here we need to remember the inadequacy of language. In our own Marriage Office the bridegroom speaks of " worshipping " the bride ; a mayor or a police magistrate is to this day officially " his worship." The word *worship*, like all other words, is really hopelessly inadequate to express the attitude a man experiences in the presence of what he feels to be the " absolutely other " made directly manifest. (We

[1] See the working out of this thought in Otto, *op. cit.* (English tr.), chap. xiv. pp. 159 ff.

do not say anything, we are simply silent when we kneel at the
INCARNATUS EST.) Yet it is hard to believe that the most sceptical
among us does not know the experience. There are those to
whom it is present as a constant experience during their lives, and
those to whom it comes but seldom ; there are those who bestow
their "worship" on inadequate objects, like the man who
"worships" his money or his mistress. But it is as doubtful
whether there is really any man who has never worshipped anything as it is doubtful whether there is any man who has never
feared or never loved. The experience moreover seems to be
specially characteristic of man ; as the Greeks said, "Man is the
only animal who has gods." (Possibly indeed, the attitude of some
dogs to their masters may offer a remote analogy, but we must
remember that these are dogs who have been brought up by man
and become at any rate distantly humanised by the process. There
is no reason to think that "Yellow Dog Dingo" could ever have
developed in this way.)

And again, there can be little doubt that the men in whom the
spirit of true worship has been most constantly present are they
who show us human nature at its best. It is the "brutalised"
man who is marked by the temper of habitual irreverence. Even
if we judge of men solely by what they have effected in the way of
"social reform," history seems to show that the men who have
achieved most for the service of man in this world are men whose
hearts have been set on something which is not of this world ;
"the advance of civilisation is in truth a sort of by-product of
Christianity, not its chief aim." [1] We may reasonably draw the
conclusion that religion is just as much a unique characteristic
and interest of humanity as love of truth, love of beauty, love of
country, and that the saint's "experience" is no more to be
dismissed as an illusion than the thinker's, the artist's, or the
patriot's.

(*b*) Of course, like all other immediate experiences, the
peculiar experience of the immediate presence of the divine
requires interpretation and criticism. A man may be moved to
adoration by an unworthy and inadequate object, like the heathen

---

[1] W. R. Inge, *Personal Religion and the Life of Devotion*, p. 84 ; cf. *ibid.*
pp. 59–60. A careful study of the debt of "civilisation" to St. Francis would
afford an admirable illustration. No one in the course of many centuries has
done more for "civilisation"; no one, probably, ever thought less about it.

who " in his blindness, bows down to wood and stone," or the lover who lavishes his spiritual treasure on a light woman.    Religion is not proved to be an illusion by its aberrations, any more than science by the labour wasted on squaring the circle or seeking the elixir and the philosopher's stone, or love by the havoc it makes of life when it is foolishly bestowed.    The sane judgment of reflexion is required to direct and correct all our human activities.    We are neither to suppose that there is no way to God because some ways which have been found promising at first have led astray, nor yet that because there is a way, any way that mankind have tried must be as good a road to the goal as any other.    We may freely assert that even the most puerile and odious " religions " have had their value ;  they have this much at least of worth about them that those who have practised them have been right in their conviction that the " other-world " is really there to be sought for.    But to draw the conclusion that " all religions are equally good," or even, like the " Theosophists," that at any rate every religion is the best for those who practise it, and that we are not to carry the Gospel to the heathen because they are not at a level to appreciate it, is like arguing that all supposed " science " is equally good, or that we ought to abstain from teaching the elements of natural science to a Hindu because his own traditional notions about astronomy and geography are " the best he is capable of."    Views of this kind rest in the end on an absurd personal self-conceit, and a denial of our common humanity.    A true religion, like a true science, is not the monopoly of a little aristocracy of superior persons ;  it is for everyone.    We may not be able to teach the mass, even of our own fellow-countrymen, more than the first elements of any science, but we must see to it that what we do teach them is as true as we can make it.    And so even more with religion, because of its direct relation with the whole conduct of life.    A savage may be capable only of very elementary notions about God and the unseen world, but at least we can see to it that the ideas he has are not defiled by cruelty or lewdness.    Not to say that you never know how far the capacity of *any* mind for receiving true ideas extends, until you have tried it.    The " Theosophist " usually claims to show a broad-minded humanity, which he contrasts complacently with the " narrowness " of the Christian who wishes all mankind to share his faith.    But he belies his own profession the moment he begins his habitual disparagement of the missionary. To say that in religion, or in any other department of life, the vile or foolish is good enough for your neighbour is the arrogance of the half-educated. The neighbour whom we are to love as ourselves deserves at our hands the best we can possibly bring him.

The point I chiefly want to make, however, is that the specific experience of contact with the divine not only needs interpretation, like all other direct experience, but that, though it is the directest way of access to the " wholly other," it is not the only way. If we are to reach God in this life, so far as it is permitted, we need to integrate the " religious experience " with the suggestions conveyed to us by the knowledge of Nature and of our own being. It seems clear that in its crudest manifestations the experience of this direct contact is not specifically connected with superiority in knowledge or in moral character. At a sufficiently low level of intelligence we find the idiot regarded as God-possessed in virtue of his very idiocy. (He is supposed to be in touch with the transcendent " other " because he is so manifestly out of touch with our " this-world " daily life.) [1] And the " holy men " of barbaric peoples are very seldom men who show anything we should call moral superiority over their neighbours. Even among ourselves it is often the simple and ignorant who make on us the impression of spending their lives most in the sense of God's presence, and again the men who show themselves most keenly sensitive to " religious impressions " are by no means always among the most faultless. Indeed, " moral excellence " itself, without humility, seems only too often to close the soul's eye to the eternal. A self-absorbed prig is in deeper spiritual blindness than many an open sinner. But if we would look at the Lord " all at once," we must of course integrate the glimpses we get in our moments of direct adoring contact with all that Nature and Morality suggest of the abiding source of them both. In particular, we need to have the conception of the " holy," as the object of adoration, transformed in such a way that it is fragrant with moral import before " Be ye holy because I am holy " can become the supreme directing note for the conduct of life. In principle this work of integrating our experience has been already accomplished for us by Christianity, with its double inheritance from the Jewish

---

[1] *Cf.* Wordsworth's application to idiots of the words " Their life is hid with Christ in God."

prophets and the Greek philosophers who freed their " reasonable worship " from entanglement in the follies and foulnesses of the old " nature-religions."　But the root of the old errors is in every one of us ; we cannot enter into the highest religious experience available to us except by a perpetual fresh interpretation of the given for ourselves.　We may have Moses and the prophets and Paul and the evangelists, and yet, without personal watching unto prayer, all this will not avail to ensure that we shall think Christianly of the unseen, or that our sense of its reality will of itself lead us to a noble life rich in good works.　And this answers for us the question " Who are the experts ? "　The true " expert critic " of the constructions and hypotheses of science is the man who has already learned what the men of science have to teach him.　The true expert critic of the painter or the musician must first have learned to see with the painter's eye and hear with the musician's ear.　Without this qualification, mere acuteness and ingenuity are wasted.　In the end, all effectual criticism must be of what a man has first seen and felt for himself.　So the verdict on the religious life if it is to count must come from the men who have first made it their own by living it.　Only they can tell " how much there is in it."

I have urged that the suggestions of an eternal above and behind the temporal are derived from three independent sources, and that the agreement of the three in their common suggestion gives it a force which ought to be invincible.　But I would end by a word of warning against a possible dangerous mistake.　The fullest recognition of the reality of the transcendental and eternal " other " world does not mean that eternity and time are simply disconnected or that a man is set the impossible task of living in two *absolutely* disparate environments at once.　The two worlds are not in the end isolated from one another, since the one shines, here more, there less, transparently through the other.　In man, in particular, they are everywhere interdependent, as Kant held that the real (or moral) and the apparent (or natural) realms are. We are not to spend half our time in the service of the eternal and the other half in the service of the secular.　If we try to do this we shall merely incur the usual fate of the man with two masters. We are not called to be *pukka* saints half the week and " worldlings " for the other half.　Strictly speaking, we cannot divide a man's occupations and duties into the " religious " and the " secular."

The true difference between the religious man and the worldly is that the religious man discharges the same duties as the other, but in a different spirit. He discharges them " to the glory of God," with God as his chief intention, that is, with his eye on an end the attainment of which lies beyond the bounds of the temporal and secular. The truest detachment is not retreat to the desert, but a life lived in the world in this spirit. Thus, for example, a man discharges the duty of a husband and a parent in a secular spirit if he has no aim beyond giving his wife a "happy time of it" and bringing up his children to enjoy a lucrative or honourable or comfortable existence from youth to old age. Marriage and parenthood become charged with a sacramental spirit and the discharge of their obligations a *Christian* duty when the "principal" intention of parents is to set forward a family in the way to know and love God and to be spiritual temples for His indwelling. It may be that the temporal will never cease to be part of our environment ; what is important is that it should become an increasingly subordinate feature in the environment, that we should cease to be at its mercy, because our hearts are set elsewhere. Christianity has always set its face against the false treatment of the eternal and the temporal as though they were simply disconnected " worlds." In the beginning, it tells us, the same God created heaven and earth, and its vision of the end of history has always included the " resurrection of the flesh " to a glorified existence in which it will no longer thwart but answer wholly to the " spirit." If we are told on the one hand that a man who is in Christ is a " new creation," we are also told by the great Christian theologians that " grace " does not destroy " nature " but perfects and transfigures it.

*Bibliographical Note.*—Besides the books referred to or quoted in the text I would specially recommend to the reader the following. Of course they are only a selection out of a much larger number. Perhaps I may also mention, as further illustrating some points touched on in the first part of this essay, an essay by myself in the volume on *Evolution in the Light of Modern Science* (Blackie, 1925).

HÜGEL, F. VON. *Eternal Life.* T. & T. Clark. 1912.
—— —— *Essays and Addresses on the Philosophy of Religion.* Dent & Sons. 1921.
SOLOVIEV, V. *The Justification of the Good.* Eng. Tr. Constable. 1918.
WARD, J. *Naturalism and Agnosticism.* A. & C. Black. First published 1899.
—— —— *The Realm of Ends.* Cambridge University Press. 1911.

# AUTHORITY

BY ALFRED EDWARD JOHN RAWLINSON

AND

WILFRED L. KNOX

# CONTENTS

# I

## AUTHORITY AS A GROUND OF BELIEF

### BY A. E. J. RAWLINSON

### 1. *The Authoritative Character of Christianity*

THE Christianity of history is a definite, historical, and positive religion. It is not (in the phrase of Harnack) " Religion itself," neither is it true to say that " the Gospel is in no wise a positive religion like the rest." [1]  On the contrary, the Gospel is in such wise " a positive religion," that it came originally into the world in a particular context, and as the result of a particular historical process. It has ever claimed to be the divinely intended culmination and fulfilment of an even earlier historical and positive religion, that of the Jews. It has been characterised, in the course of its persistence through the centuries, by a specific and definite system of religious beliefs, as well as by what has been, in the main, a specific and definite tradition of spiritual discipline and *cultus*— a system of beliefs and a type of *cultus* and discipline, which have been discovered in experience to have the property of mediating (in proportion as they are taken seriously) a spiritual life of a highly characteristic and definite kind. From all of which it follows that Christianity is not anything which could be discovered or invented for himself by any person, however intellectually or spiritually gifted, in independence of historical tradition. The term " Christian " is not an *epitheton ornans*, applicable in the spheres of religion and ethics to whatever in the way of doctrine, ideal, or aspiration may happen to commend itself to the judgment of this or that individual who is vaguely familiar with the Christian tradition as the result of having been born and brought up in a country ostensibly Christian. It is a term which to the historian possesses a definite content, discoverable from history. And because Christianity is thus an historical and positive religion, it is impossible, in the first instance, for the individual to know any-

---

[1] The statements controverted are quoted from Harnack's *What is Christianity ?* (E.T.), p. 63.

thing about it at first hand.   He must be content to derive his
knowledge of it from authority, whether the authority in question
be primarily that of a living teacher, or of past tradition.

It belongs, further, to the essential character of Christianity
that (in common with all the great prophetic and historical
religions) it claims to be a religion of revelation, and as such to
proclaim to mankind an authoritative Gospel in the name of the
living God.   " The idea of authority," writes Friedrich Heiler,
" is rooted in the revelational character of the prophetic type of
religion." [1]   This certainly has been the characteristic of Christianity from the beginning.   It appears to have been characteristic of the historical attitude of Jesus Christ, as may be seen from
the story of the scene in the synagogue at Capernaum in St. Mark
(Mark i. 21 sqq.).   It has been pointed out by the German scholar
Reitzenstein that the Greek word ἐξουσία, which we render
" authority," was employed in Hellenistic Greek to denote, in a
religious context, the idea of a combination of supernatural power
with supernatural knowledge of divine things. [2]   So in St. Mark's
narrative the word is used to suggest the combination in Jesus of
supernatural power with supernatural authority to teach.   " What
is this ?   A new teaching !   With authority, moreover, he com-
mandeth the unclean spirits, and they obey him ! " (Mark i. 27).
" He taught them as one having authority, and not as the scribes "
(Mark i. 22).   The Lord, as a matter of actual historical fact,
astonished people by teaching independently of scribal tradition,
with the unhesitating " authority " of immediate inspiration.   In
this respect His manner and method of teaching resembled that
of the great Old Testament prophets, but with the significant
difference that whereas the Old Testament claim to prophetic
authority was expressed through the formula " Thus saith
Jehovah," our Lord said simply " I say unto you."   The
authority claimed by the Lord Jesus in matters of religion may
thus be described as prophetic and super-prophetic : that is to
say, He claims for Himself, without any hesitation, the plenitude
of spiritual authority inherent in God's Messiah, *i.e.* in the Person
in whom God's spiritual purpose of redemption, in every legitimate sense of the word, is summed up and destined to be realised,

[1] F. Heiler, *Das Gebet*, p. 266.
[2] R. Reitzenstein, *Die hellenistischen Mysterienreligionen* (2nd edn.), pp. 14,
101, 125.

in the first instance for Israel, but ultimately also, through Israel, for mankind.

And this attitude of spiritual authority, characteristic of Jesus, is characteristic also, according to the New Testament, of the Church. To the Church as the redeemed Israel of God is entrusted the word of the Christian salvation as an authoritative Gospel, a message of good news, to be proclaimed as the truth of God " in manifestation of the Spirit and of power." " He that heareth you heareth me : and he that rejecteth you rejecteth me : and he that rejecteth me rejecteth him that sent me " (Luke x. 16). " As the Father hath sent me, even so send I you " (John xx. 21). Fundamental in Christianity is this claim of the Church to have been divinely commissioned, divinely " sent." The Church is not primarily a society for spiritual or intellectual research, but a society of which it belongs to the very essence to put forward the emphatic claim to be the bearer of revelation, to have been put in trust with the Gospel as God's revealed message to mankind, and to have been divinely commissioned with pro- phetic authority to proclaim it as God's truth to all the world, irrespective of whether men prove willing to hear and give heed to the proclamation, or whether they forbear. In this respect the tone of the Church must always be " Thus saith the Lord " : she must proclaim her message in such a fashion that men may receive it (like the Church of the Thessalonians in the New Testament) " not as the word of men, but as it is in truth, the word of God."

It is, moreover, in this sense—that is to say, as an authoritative Gospel—that the message of Christianity comes home, whenso- ever and wheresoever it does come home with effect, to the hearts and consciences of men. " Faith cometh by hearing, and hearing by the word of Christ " ; and the Gospel, thus authoritatively proclaimed, proves itself still to be " the power of God unto salvation unto every one that believeth." The apologetic work of reasoned argument and philosophical discussion, the dissipation of prejudices, the antecedent clearing away of difficulties, the removal of intellectual barriers, may in particular cases be the necessary preliminaries to conversion. But conversion to Chris- tianity, in any sense that matters, is not primarily the result of an intellectual demonstration. It is the work of the Spirit. " No man can say ' Jesus is Lord,' but by the Holy Ghost." Nevertheless, when a man *is* thus enabled by the power of the Spirit to say "Jesus is Lord," he does so for the reason that he has been made aware, in the very depths of his soul, that he has been brought face to face with a truth which he did not discover, but which has been spiritually revealed to him, even the truth of God, "as truth is in Jesus"; and he knows henceforward that he is no longer his own master : he has given in his allegiance, in free and deliberate self-committal, to the supreme authority of Him who is the truth : he is from henceforth "a man under authority," being "under law to Christ."

## 2. *The Relation of the Gospel to the Church*

With what has been thus far written, it is probable that the representatives of almost all types and schools of thought in Christianity would find themselves to be, upon the whole, in substantial agreement. It is common ground that "grace and truth came by Jesus Christ," and that the Gospel is God's authoritative message to mankind. The main difference between the Catholic and the Protestant traditions in Christianity lies in the kind and degree of recognition which is given, side by side with the authority of the Gospel, to that of the Church. How is the relation of the Church to the Gospel properly to be conceived ? Is the Church the creation of the Gospel ? Or is the Church, in a more direct sense than such a view would suggest, the supernatural creation of God—a divine institution—the Spirit-filled Body of Christ ?

Now, it can be recognised freely that the Spirit operates to-day, in varying measure, outside the borders of any institutional Church, that "the wind bloweth where it listeth," and that "Jordan overfloweth his banks all the time of harvest." Nevertheless it must be affirmed that according to the New Testament the Church (the idea of which is rooted in that of Israel, the holy people of God) is the covenanted home of the Spirit, and the Church is historically the society which is put in trust with the Gospel for the benefit of the world. The Gospel does not descend from heaven immediately, as by a special revelation. It reaches men through the instrumentality and mediation of the Church. This is true obviously in the case of all those who are born and brought up within the fold of the Church, and who acknowledge themselves to be her spiritual children. It is true equally, though less obviously, in the case of those Christians who would be disposed to deny the idea of any ecclesiastical mediation, and who would conceive themselves to derive their faith directly from the New Testament ; since it is a plain fact of history that the very existence of the New Testament presupposes the prior existence and activity of the Church, of whose authoritative tradition it forms a part.

The Church, therefore, is not the creation of the Gospel. The Gospel is rather the divine message of redemption which is entrusted to the Church. There is ideally no opposition or antithesis between " Catholic " and " Evangelical." If Catholicism has ever in any degree failed to be Evangelical, it has to that extent and in that degree failed signally to be true to its vocation. Catholicism stands, according to its true idea, both for the presentation of the Gospel of Jesus Christ in its fulness, and also for a certain wholeness, a certain completeness, in the development, maintenance and building up of Christianity as a system and spiritual " way," or manner of life. The Catholic Church in idea is not simply the redeemed Israel of God : it is also the missionary of Christ to the world, the society which is put in trust with the Gospel. It is bound therefore of necessity to regard itself as an authoritative society, in so far as it is entrusted with an authoritative message, and empowered with divine authority to proclaim it. Beyond this, as the Beloved Community of the saints, the familiar home and sphere of the operations of divine grace, the ideal Fellowship of the Spirit, the Church possesses a legitimate claim upon the allegiance of its members, and exercises over them a teaching and pastoral authority, an authority not of constraint, but of love, in respect of which those who are called to the office of pastorate are enjoined in the New Testament so to fulfil their ministry as to seek to commend themselves to every man's conscience in the sight of God.

There are accordingly different types and kinds of authority in the Church, all of which are important and real, even though admittedly all (because of the frailty of men, and of the earthen vessels to which the divine treasure is committed) are liable to abuse. There is the fundamental and primary authority of the Gospel, the divine message of revelation. There are the subordinate and totally different questions of disciplinary authority in the Church, of the administrative authority of Church officers, of the prescriptive authority of custom, of the obligation or otherwise, in varying degree, of different types of Church ordinances and rules. There is further the moral and religious authority of the saints, and of the devotional and ascetic tradition of Christendom, in relation to the proper development of the spiritual life in its most characteristically Christian forms. Any one who is wise will, if he desires to develop such spiritual life, go to school to the saints and pay heed to the devotional traditions of Christendom. The sciences corresponding to this type of authority are those of moral, ascetic and mystical theology. They are essentially practical. They presuppose the desire to make progress in the life of the spirit in its Christian form, and the readiness to learn from the experience of the saints and of former generations of Christians. But the proper concern of this essay is not with any of these forms of authority : it is with authority as a ground of belief—belief, not in the sense of what S. Paul means by *faith* (*i.e.* the response of the " heart," or of the whole personality, to the primary appeal of the Gospel) but in the sense of the acceptance of beliefs, the acknowledgment of particular doctrines or historical assertions as true.

### 3. *Authority as a Ground of Belief*

For it is, in point of fact, obvious that the preaching of the Gospel, considered simply as the proclamation of a divine message which is primarily prophetic in type, presupposes as the intellectual ground of its validity a number of truths—philosophical, historical, and theological—which it is the business of Christian apologetics and theology to substantiate, to interpret, and to defend. It is possible to point, even in apostolic times, to the inevitable tendency to draw up short statements of Christian truth, dogmatic summaries of the intellectual content of the faith. The work of the teacher in apostolic times went on side by side with that of the evangelist or preacher. The proclamation of the Gospel as a divine message of Good News presupposed, and required as its supplement, the teaching of doctrine. Unless certain dogmatic assertions are true, the whole Gospel of Christianity falls to the ground. The truths, therefore, which to the Christian mind have appeared to be implicit in the truth of the Gospel, or to be presupposed by the assumption of the validity of Christian Church life and devotional practices, were eventually formulated, more and more explicitly, in the shape of dogmatic propositions; with the result that a body of *credenda* arose, which in the traditionally Catholic presentation of Christianity are proposed for the acceptance of the faithful on the ground of the teaching authority of the Church.

From the point of view of the effectual handing on of the Christian tradition such a method of teaching was in practice inevitable, and has analogies in all branches of education. The acceptance of alleged truths on the authority of a teacher who is trusted is commonly, in the initial stages of the study of any subject whatever, the dictate of wisdom. Authority, for those who are under instruction, is always, at least psychologically, a ground of belief; nor is there anything irrational in the acceptance of beliefs on authority, provided always that there is reasonable ground for believing the authority on the strength of whose assurance the beliefs in question are accepted to be trustworthy, and that the degree of "interior assent" is proportioned to what is believed to be the trustworthiness of the particular authority concerned. There is nothing therefore *prima facie* irrational in the attitude of a man who in religious matters elects, even to the end, to submit his judgment to authority, and to accept the guidance of the Church, since it may be argued that in respect of such matters it is *a priori* probable that the wisdom of the community will be superior to that of the individual, and the question may be asked : If the Christian Church does not understand the real meaning of Christianity, who does ? The Church in each successive generation has always included within its membership a considerable proportion of such unspeculative souls, who have been content to accept such teaching as has been given to them " on authority," and to live spiritually on the basis of a faith the intellectual content of which they have not personally thought out, and the purely rational grounds of which they have not personally attempted to verify.

Even in the case, however, of those who could thus give no other intellectual account of their beliefs except to say simply that they had accepted them on authority, it is probable that the real grounds on which the beliefs in question are held are not exhausted by such a statement. A doctrine may have been accepted, in the first instance, on authority, but it remains inoperative (save as a purely abstract and theoretical opinion) unless it is at least to some extent verified in the experience of life. It is doubtful whether those who have accepted their beliefs on authority could continue to hold them, if the experience of life appeared flatly to contradict them ; and conversely the extreme tenacity with which Christian beliefs (seriously challenged, very often, by contemporary critical thought) are not uncommonly maintained by those who in the first instance accepted them " merely on authority," is to be explained by the fact that the beliefs in question have mediated to those who entertain them a spiritual experience—valuable and precious beyond everything else which life affords—of the genuineness of which they are quite certain, and with the validity of which they believe the truth of the beliefs in question to be bound up.

It was on an argument of this general kind, based on the pragmatic value of the " faith of the millions " (*i.e.* on the capacity of traditional Catholic doctrine and practice, as shown by experience, to mediate spiritual life), that the late Father George Tyrrell was at one time disposed to attempt to build up a " modernist " apologetic for Catholicism. And the argument is of value as far as it goes. It suggests that in such religious beliefs or religious practices as are discovered in experience both to exhibit " survival value," and also to be manifestly fruitful in the mediation of spiritual life of an intrinsically valuable kind, there is enshrined, at the least, some element of truth or of spiritual reality, of which any adequate theology or philosophy of religion must take account. It is the function of theology in this sense to interpret religion, to explain it, without explaining it away. The argument of Tyrrell at least constitutes a salutary warning against any such premature rationalism as, if accepted, would have the latter effect rather than the former.

But the argument of Tyrrell, while suggesting that in every spiritually vital religious tradition there is *some element* of truth, of which account must be taken, does not obviously justify the intellectual acceptance at face value of the *prima facie* claims of any and every tradition, as such. The plain man may be provisionally justified in accepting religious beliefs and practices upon the authority of the Church—or more immediately, in actual practice, upon the authority of some particular religious teacher whom he trusts—and may discover in his own subsequent experience of the life of the spirit, as lived upon the basis of such acceptance, a rough working test of the substantial validity and truth of the doctrine in question. But what the plain man is thus enabled directly by experience to attest is rather the spiritual validity of Christianity as a way of life, and the fundamental truth of the spiritual reality behind it, than the strictly intellectual adequacy or truth of the intellectual forms under which he has received it as a dogmatic and institutional tradition. Meanwhile, in the world of our time, all Christian teaching whatever is very definitely under challenge, and the issues are further complicated by the existence of variant forms of the Christian tradition, and of a number of more or less conflicting religious authorities. The plain man may indeed simply choose to abide by the tradition in which he has been personally brought up and which he has to a certain extent " proved " in experience, and to ignore the whole issue which the existence of current contradiction and conflict is otherwise calculated to raise. But a large number of plain men are not able to be thus permanently content with the practice of a religion which they have in no sense thought out, and with the acceptance of doctrines the properly intellectual basis of which they have never considered. They ask for a reason of the hope and of the faith that is in them. In some cases they become conscious of a vocation to serve God with their minds. The mere existence in the world of conflicting religious authorities raises problems enough. It is clear that religious authority has been claimed in different quarters for a large number of statements which, because of their manifest conflict, cannot all of them be equally true, and in some cases are definitely false. No claim has ever been made with more emphasis by religious authority than the modern Roman claim that the Bishop of Rome, under certain narrowly defined conditions, is possessed *ex officio* of a supernatural infallibility. The writers of this volume are united in the conviction that the claims made in this respect for the Papacy are in point of fact untrue. The question inevitably arises, What is the ultimate relation between authority and truth ? What of the intellectually conflicting claims put forward by different self-styled authorities in the sphere of religion ? Or again, What is the strictly rational authority of the main intellectual tradition of Christian theology ?

It is obvious that these questions, when once they are raised, can only be solved, in the case of any given individual mind, on the basis of an act, or a succession of acts, of private judgment. This is true even in the case of an individual whose solution of the problem assumes the form of submission to Rome. There is a recurrent type of mind, fundamentally sceptical and distrustful of reason, and yet craving religious certitude and peace, which will gravitate always towards Rome ; and for minds of this type it is probable that only the Roman Communion is in the long run in a position to cater. The demand of such souls is not for any form of strictly rational or verifiable authority. It is for authority in the form of a purely external and oracular guarantee of intellectual truth, an authority of which the effect, when once its claims have by an initial act of private judgment been definitely acknowledged, shall be to exempt them from any further responsibility of a personal kind for the intellectual truth of the religious beliefs which they entertain. There are indeed good reasons for believing that such a solution is an illegitimate simplification of the intellectual problems involved in religious belief, but it is clearly a solution the attractiveness of which to some minds is exceedingly strong. In the earliest days of Christianity the Church does not appear to have made claims of a kind strictly analogous to those of the Papacy. The modern Roman conception of authority is the result of a development in the direction of rigidity and absoluteness of claim, which appears to have been at least partly the result of reaction from, and opposition to, the religious confusions of Protestantism.

Reaction and antithesis are not commonly the pathways to absolute truth. In any case it would appear to be clear that for the allegiance of those who, in despair of existing confusions, demand simply the kind of authority which, in virtue of the sheer absoluteness of its claim, shall appear to be its own guarantee, independently of any further appeal either to reason or to history, no other Christian communion will ever be in a position effectively to compete with the great and venerable communion of Rome.

The rejection of the claim of the Roman Church to be possessed of authority in the form of what I have ventured to describe as an external and oracular guarantee of the intellectual truth of its doctrines carries with it, in the long run, the rejection of the purely oracular conception of religious authority altogether. Neither the oracular conception of the authority of the Bible, nor that of the authority of the ecumenical Councils and Creeds, is in a position to survive the rejection of the oracular conception of the authority of the Pope. This does not of course mean that the authority either of the Bible, or of the Church, or of the ecumenical Documents and Councils, has ceased to be real. It means only that such authority is no longer to be taken in an oracular sense, and that the final authority is not anything which is either mechanical or merely external, but is rather the intrinsic and self-evidencing authority of truth. It means that authority as such can never be ultimately its own guarantee, that the claims of legitimate authority must always be in the last resort verifiable claims. The final appeal is to the spiritual, intellectual and historical content of divine revelation, *as verifiable at the three-fold bar of history, reason and spiritual experience.*

This of course does not mean that the individual is capable in all cases, or in any complete degree, of effecting all these forms of verification for himself. It is the wisdom of the individual to pay reasonable deference to the wider wisdom of the community, and to regard as tentative the conclusions of his individual reason, save in so far as they are confirmed and supported by the corporate mind, as well as by the spiritual experience, not only of himself, but of his fellows. It does mean, however, that there exists a very real recognition and conception of religious authority which is capable of being reconciled with inner freedom, a conception of authority which is capable of forming the basis of such an essentially liberal and evangelical version of Catholicism as that for which the Anglican Communion, at its best, appears ideally to stand. It is not at all true to say that the Church, on such a theory of authority, would be precluded from teaching clearly and dogmatically those foundation truths on which Christianity may be reasonably held to rest. On the contrary, the Church will be enabled to teach doctrine with all the greater confidence in so far as she is content to make an essentially rational appeal—in so far, that is, as her authority is conceived to rest, not simply upon unsupported assertions, but upon the broad basis of continuous verification in reason and experience. The true authority is that which is able to flourish and to maintain itself, not simply under a *régime* of intellectual repression, but in an atmosphere of intellectual and religious freedom. I submit that it should be the aim of the Church so to teach her doctrines as by her very manner of teaching to bear witness to her conviction that they are true, and that they will stand ultimately the test of free enquiry and discussion : to teach them, in other words, not simply as the bare assertions of an essentially unverifiable authority, but as the expression of truths which are capable of being verified—spiritually verified, in some sense, in the experience of all her members ; verified intellectually, as well as spiritually, in the reason and experience of her theologians and thinkers and men of learning.

It is involved in such a conception of Church authority that the tradition of Christian orthodoxy will not be in its essence a merely uncritical handing on of the beliefs and conclusions of the past : it will rather assume the form of the stubborn persistence of a continuously criticised, tested and verified tradition. I have argued elsewhere [1] that the amount of strictly intellectual and rational authority which attaches to the broad theological consensus of orthodox Christianity is in direct proportion to the extent to which it can be said to represent the conclusions of a genuinely free consensus of competent and adequately Christian minds, and in inverse proportion to the extent to which unanimity is secured only by methods of discipline. There have been periods and countries in which the expression of unorthodox opinions has been attended by danger, not merely of ecclesiastical penalties, but of physical violence and suffering to those who professed them. To that extent what would otherwise be the overwhelming intellectual and rational authority attaching to the virtually unanimous orthodoxy of such countries and periods requires to be discounted. Nevertheless, intellectual sincerity is a virtue which cannot be wholly eliminated by any system of discipline from the minds of Christian men. It may fairly be argued that the broad doctrinal tradition of orthodox Christianity has both maintained itself through long periods under considerable intellectual challenge, and has also exhibited very considerable powers of recovery after apparent defeat—a good example being the revival of Nicene and Trinitarian orthodoxy within the Church of England, after the widespread prevalence in intellectual circles, during the eighteenth century, of Deism. The weight of rational authority attaching to the proposition that Trinitarian orthodoxy represents an intellectually true interpretation of the doctrinal implications of

---

[1] In the Bishop Paddock Lectures for 1923, published by Messrs. Longmans, Green & Co., under the title of *Authority and Freedom*, pp. 14 sqq.

Christianity in respect of the being and nature of God is, on any view, very far from being negligible.

To sum up the argument : The fundamental authority which lies behind the teaching of the Church is the authority of revelation, in the form of the (primarily prophetic) message of the Gospel, which the Church is divinely commissioned to proclaim. The purely dogmatic teaching of the Church represents the statement in intellectual terms of such truths as the Church holds to be either implicit in the truth of the Gospel, or else presupposed by the assumption of the validity of her spiritual life. The weight of intellectual authority which, in the purely rational sense, attaches to such statements is in proportion to the extent to which they represent a genuine consensus of competent and adequately Christian minds.

It will be obvious that, from the point of view of an argument which thus regards rational authority as attaching to statements of doctrine in proportion to the extent of their real acceptance, and to the impressiveness of the consensus which they may be said to represent, the weight of actual authority attaching to particular statements of doctrine will be a matter of degree. The weight of rational authority will be at its maximum in the case of such statements of doctrine as are commonly ranked as " ecumenical," and that on the ground both of the extremely wide consensus of genuinely Christian conviction which lies behind them, and also of the large number of Christian thinkers and theologians by whom they have been sincerely and freely endorsed. It will be at its minimum in the case of doctrines or practices which have either failed to gain wide-spread acceptance, or else are apparently only of temporary, local or insular provenance. Nevertheless, it needs to be recognised that *some* degree of rational authority attaches to every doctrine or practice which at any time or in any place has commanded the serious allegiance of Christians, and in the power of which men have been enabled to have life unto God, and to bring forth the fruits of the Spirit. What is merely sectarian or local need not necessarily be taken into account, indeed, at its own valuation. But it needs to be taken into account, and to have such truth and reality as it in fact represents fairly treated and adequately represented, in whatever may eventually prove to be the ultimate and finally satisfying statement of Christian theology.

## II

### THE AUTHORITY OF THE CHURCH
### BY WILFRED L. KNOX

#### 1. *The Divine Commission of the Church*

ALL Christians of whatever shade of belief would agree that the Church, in whatever sense the term is to be interpreted, is a body possessing a divine commission to preach the Gospel to the world. This claim proceeds inevitably from the belief that the one God, who revealed Himself partially to the prophets, law-givers and wise men of the old covenant, revealed Himself fully and finally in the person of Jesus, and continues to speak to mankind through the Holy Spirit, who dwells in the whole Church which is the Body of Christ. In this sense all Christians would agree that the Church has a divine authority, in virtue of which it can claim the absolute assent of the reason and conscience of all mankind. Unfortunately this agreement does not carry us very far towards solving the many controversies which have arisen with regard to the authority of the Church. These controversies concern the interpretation of the divine revelation committed to the Church by our Lord, the nature of the body to which He committed that revelation, and the means by which that body is able to formulate the true interpretation of His teaching. It is with these contro-versial matters that this essay is chiefly concerned.

#### 2. *The " Infallibility " of Scripture*

It will be convenient if we begin by clearing up a controversy which time and the progress of knowledge have solved for all but the blindest partisans. This is the old controversy as to the position of the Bible in Christian teaching. The Church from the outset accepted the old Jewish Scriptures and regarded them, just as the Jewish Church had done, as the verbally inspired teaching of God. It avoided the obvious difficulties of harmonising the letter of the Old Testament with the teaching of Jesus by the use of allegorical interpretations often of a rather desperate character ; in the conditions of human knowledge in the early Christian centuries it had no other means of solving the problem, unless it was prepared to abandon the whole claim that Christianity was the true development of the old Jewish faith. This the Gnostic heretics did ; but their attempt to reject the Old Testament, and where necessary parts of the New, was obviously fatal to the whole belief that Christianity is the one true revelation of God.

To the Old Testament the Church added its own Scriptures, the New Testament. With the origin and formation of the New Testament canon we are not here concerned ; it is sufficient to notice that for centuries before the Reformation the Church had possessed a body of sacred literature, which was universally accepted as divinely inspired and absolutely true, though the most important truth of certain portions might lie in an allegorical rather than in the literal meaning. In order to harmonise the Scriptures with the practice of the Church, as it had developed in the course of history, Catholics claimed that the Bible must be interpreted in the light of ecclesiastical tradition. Although the claim may often have been abused, and although the prevalent conception of the nature of ecclesiastical tradition may have been untenable (a point which will be considered later), there can be no doubt that the Catholic claim, that the Bible without some standard of interpretation cannot be applied to the daily life of the Christian individual or community, was in itself true. The Reformers claimed as against this that the Bible as it stands is the only source of authority for the teaching and practice of the Church. The Reformers were in many cases justified in appealing to the New Testament against the errors of much popular teaching and the abuses of their age ; but the claim that the Bible alone is the final and sufficient guide for Christian belief and morality was entirely untenable. In actual fact it involved not the appeal to the Bible, but the appeal to the Bible as interpreted by the system of some particular Reformer, who claimed that his particular system was the only true interpretation of the Scriptures ; the result was to produce a multitude of warring bodies, each holding to a different system of belief and anathematising all others ; the only ground of agreement being their denunciation of the errors of Rome.

The scientific development of the last century has rendered untenable the whole conception of the Bible as a verbally inspired book, to which we can appeal with absolute certainty for infallible guidance in all matters of faith and conduct. On the one hand the exact meaning of its various parts and the authority which they can claim are matters to be discussed by competent scholars ; it is hardly to be supposed that they will ever reach absolute unanimity as to the various problems which the Scriptures present ; and even such unanimity could only be provisional, for it is essential to scientific thought that it should always contemplate the possibility of further progress. On the other hand the Christian body as a whole needs a standard of faith and life which it can accept as being, if not absolutely true in every sense, yet absolutely adequate as a means of salvation. Obviously this distinction is one which will need careful examination later ; for our present purpose it is sufficient to point out that the Church as a whole, and the individual—at least the individual who is not a highly trained theologian—need some means of deciding precisely what the Christian message is. If the Church is to bring men to God through the person of Jesus, or if the individual is to come to God through Jesus, there must be some means of ascertaining Who Jesus is, and how we are to find Him. It is perfectly possible that many people have found Him by merely reading the Bible ; but it is obvious that we cannot merely hand the Bible to the inquirer, with no further guidance, and be certain that he will find Jesus there aright. In practice the Reformed bodies have attempted to solve the difficulty by drawing up their own confessions of faith ; but the drawing up of such confessions was really an admission of the inadequacy of the Bible, since these confessions, while claiming to be the only true interpretation of Scripture, are found to differ widely in important matters of doctrine. Clearly the claim that the Scriptures alone are a sufficient guide in matters of faith could only be maintained if all impartial inquirers arrived at the same conclusions. It may be added that the measure of agreement to be found in these documents is largely due to the fact that on many points of fundamental importance they adhered to the doctrines of the Catholic Church, which Catholics and Protestants alike believed to be clearly stated in the Scriptures ; in reality, however, these doctrines were only made clear by the earlier developments of Catholic theology. At the time they were not disputed by any party, and were therefore accepted by all as the clear teaching of the Scriptures ; it is now clear that they can only be regarded as the clear teaching of Scripture if it is admitted that the orthodox Catholic interpretation of the Scriptures on these matters in the first four centuries was in fact the correct one.

### 3. *Nature of the Authority of Scripture*

At the same time all Christians would agree that in some sense the Bible possesses a paramount authority in matters of belief and conduct. Although it can no longer be regarded as a collection of infallible oracles from which it is possible at any moment to draw with certainty a complete answer to any question that may arise, it would be generally admitted that any development of Christian teaching must very largely be judged by its compatibility with the teaching of the Scriptures as a whole. Opinions may differ as to what this teaching is, and how it is to be ascertained; in particular, Christian scholars and teachers, and organised Christian bodies may differ as to which elements both of the Old and New Testaments are to be regarded as of final and permanent importance, and which possess only a local and temporary value ; but it is universally recognised that the Scriptures contain a divine revelation, which in its essential elements lays down the lines which all subsequent developments of Christianity must follow. This authority proceeds from the nature of Scripture itself. The Old Testament shows us the process by which the religion of the Jewish nation was developed from a system of mythology and folk-lore similar to that of the other Semitic nations into a severe monotheism, based on the identification of the nature of God with ethical perfection, and safeguarded by an elaborate religious code from contamination with the lower religious systems of the ancient world. The New Testament contains the history of the full and final revelation of God to man in the person of Jesus, as recorded by the men who had lived under the influence of His earthly life, together with their interpretations of His life and teaching in its bearing on the relations of God to man.

It is impossible to believe that the literature which records and interprets this historical process was compiled by the human authors without a special measure of divine assistance. It is of course possible to deny the account of the origin of the Scriptures given above : but obviously to do so is to reject Christianity as in any sense a divine revelation. If it be accepted, it follows for the Christian that God must have chosen the men who were to carry out the task, and given them special gifts of the Holy Spirit for doing so. This need not imply in any way that they wrote with explicit consciousness of anything but ordinary human motives, or that they were divinely delivered from the possibility of human error. It does imply that these writings possess an inspiration different from that which is to be found in the greatest monuments of human literature and that they contain in substance the record of a divine dispensation to which all subsequent developments of Christianity must conform.

## 4. *The Method of Christian Development*

Anyone who is acquainted with the methods of modern investigation of the Old Testament recognises that the historical development of Israel was very different from that which the narrative describes. Instead of a series of catastrophic divine revelations to the patriarchs and Moses resulting in the permanent codification of the Jewish system of law and worship, we find a very slow evolution which only reached its final form some three centuries before the Incarnation. Although this evolution was largely due to the work of individuals whose writings we possess, it is obvious that their labours would never have led to any result, if they had not been able to appeal with success to the religious and moral ideas of their contemporaries. Any prophet or reformer in any branch of life depends for his success on his power to commend his message to his hearers. Their response may not be immediate ; but he must in some way gain the assent of those whom he addresses, if his work is not to be an absolute failure. Thus although we may truly say that the development of the Jewish religion was the work of the prophets and law-givers of the nation, yet it is equally true to say that it was the work of the hearers, who accepted the progressive stages of that process of modification which transformed the national faith from the worship of the original tribal deity and such other local deities as attached themselves to the nation in the course of its history into the worship of the one God, who is the Creator and Ruler of the universe.

We see the same process in the history of the earthly teaching of Jesus. Although He taught as one having authority, yet He does not appear as a teacher of a dogmatic system. Even in His ethical teaching He continually appeals to the conscience of His hearers to make it clear that the teaching He gives is the logical conclusion to be drawn from the Mosaic Law as accepted by them.

The first incident in His public ministry which has a really dogmatic importance is the question put to the disciples at Caesarea Philippi. "Who do men say that I am?" and the subsequent question, "But who say ye that I am?" The disciples are challenged to say whether in the light of their more intimate experience of His work and teaching they can regard the views of the general public as being in any way adequate; St. Peter's answer is an admission of their inadequacy, and a confession of the supernatural character of the origin and mission of Jesus, which is the germ of Catholic Christology. Its importance for our present purpose lies in the fact that it is only elicited by our Lord in reply to a question which presupposes some months of experience of His life and teaching; incidentally it may be noticed that it comes from one of the three disciples who had a more intimate experience of that life and ministry than the rest. A similar phenomenon may be observed with regard to the death of our Lord. It is only after the incident at Caesarea that He prepares His disciples for the shock of His crucifixion; and although at the moment the blow was too much for their faith, yet it did not completely destroy it. For the disciples were still an united body, apparently looking for some further development when our Lord appeared to them after His resurrection. In other words their experience of Him made it impossible for them to suppose that His death was really, as it seemed, a complete and final catastrophe.

If we examine the later history of the apostolic period we find a similar process of development. The first serious issue of controversy which the Church had to face was that which arose over the admission of uncircumcised Gentiles. Even the autocratic personality of St. Paul could only solve the question when the natural leaders of the Jewish party, St. Peter and St. James, had come to realise that the essential elements of Christianity lay in the new powers bestowed by Jesus on His followers, which rendered it unnecessary to insist on the old methods by which Judaism had preserved itself from heathen contamination. In the later books of the New Testament we see a steady process of development. The Fourth Gospel and the later Pauline Epistles show a marked tendency to appreciate more fully the implications of the belief in the supernatural character of the person of Jesus, and to concentrate the attention of the Church on this aspect of Christianity rather than on the supposed imminence of His return. In other words we see the mind of the Church, as reflected by the writers of these works, developing under the influence of Christian experience.

### 5. *The Meaning of Christian Experience*

Since the terms "religious experience" or "Christian experience" will play a considerable part in the remainder of this essay, it will perhaps be well to explain at this point the exact sense in which they will be used. By Christian experience is meant that apprehension of God through the person of Christ which is vouchsafed to all Christians who in any way attempt to live up to the standard of their profession. It may be no more than an experience of power to overcome temptation and to advance in the direction of Christian holiness in however rudimentary a degree. It includes any sense of communion with God in prayer and worship, whether that sense of union is of the elementary type described by theologians as "sensible devotion" or rises to the higher forms of prayer to which the great mystics have attained. It covers also such indirect forms of communion with God as the sense of deliverance from the burden of sin. To a greater or less extent, according to the religious development of the believer and his power to adjust his religious beliefs to his daily life, it covers the whole of his outlook upon the world in general. It is not in any way confined to any kind of mystical experience of God, nor yet to that "sensible devotion" which a certain type of modern theology seems to regard as the main element of religion. The person who finds no particular consolation in his prayers, but only knows that by using the means of grace he is able to attain to a higher standard of life than he would otherwise achieve, has a Christian experience as genuine as the greatest mystic, though of a much lower degree of intensity. On the other hand the higher forms of experience of God through our Lord are an important part of the whole sum of Christian experience, though not the whole of it.

Clearly from the Christian point of view religious experience cannot be treated as a purely natural phenomenon. It is the knowledge of God vouchsafed to man by the power of divine grace and the illumination of the Holy Spirit. Its method of operation has already been indicated in the foregoing section. The reforms of the religion of Israel by prophets and lawgivers were the result of their own personal experience of God, achieved by prayer and reflection on the nature of the divine Being. In the case of many of them it is obvious that the experience of God was of a peculiarly intense character. In the same way their ability to commend their message to their hearers depended on the fact that the latter had, in however elementary a form, some sort of consciousness of the nature of God, in virtue of which they were able to recognise the truth of the prophetic message. Naturally this recognition was only slowly effected, since the hearers as a rule possessed a far more limited consciousness of God than the prophet ; often no doubt it took several generations to enable the mass of the nation to assimilate even the general outlines of his teaching. But without some religious experience of however elementary a kind in their hearers the prophets would have had nothing to appeal to.

The same phenomenon appears in the New Testament. Our Lord appeals, as has been noticed above, to the religious consciousness of those brought up in the atmosphere of prophetic teaching and ardent Messianic expectation which prevailed in Galilee in His days. On the basis of this religious experience He builds up His own exposition of the true nature of the Kingdom of God, primarily in His disciples, but to a lesser extent in the general body of His hearers. In appealing to the Gentiles, St. Paul appeals to a religious experience already moulded either by familiarity with the Judaism of the synagogues of the Dispersion, or in a few cases by the highest religious teachings of Gentile philosophy. In both cases his main appeal is to a sense of sin as a barrier between man and God, and the impotence of Judaism or of human wisdom to provide a means of escape from it. His teaching is to a peculiar degree modelled on his own religious experience, especially on his conversion ; but it necessarily appeals to the religious experience of his hearers, however slight that experience may have been at the moment when he first addressed them.

### 6. *Religious Experience and the Development of Christian Doctrine*

In modern controversies on the subject of the nature of Christian authority and the proper organisation for its exercise, the part played by Christian experience has often been overlooked.

It may be doubted whether the sterility of these controversies has not in part at least been due to the omission.   In the actual history of the process by which the historical system of Catholic Christianity has been built up the part of the general religious experience of the whole body of Christians has necessarily been of primary importance.   The actual formation of the canon of the New Testament was almost entirely due to the general sense of the Christian communities of the first two centuries.   Books were indeed often admitted because they were believed to be the work of Apostles, but others were rejected although they bore no less venerable names.   But although the reason for their rejection was the belief that they were spurious, yet in an age which had little knowledge of critical methods the main test of authenticity was whether the doctrines laid down in such books were a correct interpretation of the implications of the religious experience of the Christian body as a whole.   In certain cases, indeed, we find appeals to a supposed body of unwritten teaching left by the Apostles ;   but although much teaching given by the Apostles must have been left unrecorded, there is no evidence whatsoever that there was any coherent body of traditional teaching which has not survived.   The appeal is fairly frequently met with in the first three Christian centuries, especially in the controversies of the Church with Docetism and Gnosticism.   But while it cannot be justified in this form, yet it represents a quite legitimate appeal to that interpretation of the original deposit of Christian doctrine to be found in the canonical books of the New Testament, as interpreted by the Christian experience of the Church in all places and in all generations since the Incarnation.   The importance attached in these centuries to certain sees which claimed apostolic founders was not justified, in so far as it was claimed that they possessed over and above the written records of the New Testament a further body of apostolic doctrine ;   it was justified in so far as the circumstances of their foundation and early history guaranteed that the Christian consciousness of those Churches had from the first rested on a basis of orthodox Christian teaching.

It may indeed be said that in these centuries it was mainly due to the general religious sense of the Christian community that these entirely destructive heresies were eliminated from the Church.   Although we possess the names and writings of some of the orthodox theologians of the time, it may well be doubted whether their labours would, from a purely intellectual point of view, have won the victory. On the other hand, their attitude was felt to represent the true development of the original deposit of the Christian faith, while the doctrines of the various heresiarchs were rightly rejected as alien additions or false interpretations which were fatal to that religious experience which the faithful felt themselves to have enjoyed in the Church. This reason for the rejection of these doctrines was perfectly legitimate. The claim of a religion to acceptance lies in its power to awaken religious experience in the believer — naturally the Christian claims that Christianity is unique in respect both of the nature of the experience it conveys and of the manner in which it conveys it. A doctrine which is fatal to the enjoyment of that experience must be rejected, unless we are to admit that the experience was an illusion, and to abandon the religion which appeared to convey it. This, of course, does not mean that the individual's judgment as to a particular doctrine is necessarily correct. On the other hand, the rejection of a false doctrine or the establishment of a true one can never be the work of an individual. Even when it is largely due to the labours of an individual theologian the reason for the success of his labours must in all cases be the fact that he has succeeded in commending his teaching to the general Christian consciousness. Just as the success of the Jewish prophet depended on his ability to commend his view of God to the nation, so the Christian teacher must commend his doctrine to the Christian consciousness as a whole, if his labours are not to perish. For our present purpose the point of primary interest is that in the first three centuries the Church overcame the gravest perils that ever faced her without any organised method of formulating the true developments of doctrine or rejecting the false ones by the instinctive action of the corporate consciousness of the Christian body as a whole. The orthodox Church proved the truth of its teaching by its survival : the falsehood of rival forms of teaching was proved by their disappearance.

### 7. *The Formulation of Christian Doctrine*

It is clear, however, that the general Christian consciousness is by itself a vague and fluctuating mass of individual opinions, approximating in each case to the truth, yet perhaps in no case fully grasping the whole truth with no admixture of error. Even in the most rigidly orthodox body of Christians different individuals will base their religious life more definitely on some elements of the whole Christian system than on others. A Christian who could grasp not only in theory but in the practice of his life the whole system of Christian teaching in all its fulness and with no admixture of error would obviously be a perfect saint and a perfect theologian ; he would indeed see the truth as it is present to the mind of God and correspond with it perfectly: for moral failure inevitably carries with it failure to apprehend the truth. The whole sum of the Christian experience of the Church at any given moment must be an inarticulate mass of opinion comprehending in general the whole body of divine truth as revealed in Jesus ; its only way of articulating itself will be its power to express approval of some particular statement of the faith as put forward by an individual theologian, unless the Church is to have some means for expressing its corporate voice. Hence it was natural that with the ending of the ages of persecution the Church should find some means of articulating her teaching and putting into a coherent form the sense in which she interpreted in the light of Christian experience the original deposit of faith which she had received from her Lord.

We are not here concerned with the history of the Councils which decided the great Christological controversies, nor yet with the process by which the decisive influence in all matters of doctrine passed, at the cost of the Great Schism between the East and West, into the hands of the Papacy. The important matter for our present purpose is to consider the claims which are made on behalf of the various definitions of Christian doctrine by bodies claiming to voice the authority of the Holy Ghost speaking through the Church, and the sense in which those claims can be regarded as justified.

It has in many if not in all cases been claimed that the various doctrinal pronouncements of Councils and Popes are simply the affirmation of what the Church has always believed. In the strict sense the claim cannot be maintained ; for it is easy to find cases in which theologians of the most unquestioned orthodoxy put forward doctrines which were subsequently condemned, or rejected doctrines which were subsequently affirmed as parts of the Catholic faith. Hence it is now generally admitted that such pronouncements are to be regarded as affirmations in an explicit form of some truth which was from the outset implied in the original deposit of the Christian revelation, though hitherto not explicitly realised.   This claim is in itself a perfectly reasonable one.   For the Christian revelation begins with the life of Jesus, presenting itself as a challenge first to the Jewish nation and then through His Apostles to the whole world, not with the formulation of a dogmatic system.   It was only when Christian thought began to speculate on the whole subject of the relations of God to man and man to God implied in that revelation that the need was felt for some body of authoritative teaching which would serve both to delimit the Christian faith from other religions and to rule out lines of speculation which were seen, or instinctively felt, to be fatal to the presuppositions on which the religious experience of the Christian body rested.   It should be borne in mind that the great majority of authoritative statements of doctrine have been of the latter kind, and that they usually aimed rather at excluding some particular doctrinal tendency, which was seen to be fatal to the Christian life, than at promulgating a truth not hitherto generally held.

In this sense it seems impossible to deny that the Church ought to possess some means for formulating her teaching, which will enable her to adjust that teaching to the developments of human thought, while eliminating doctrines which would, if generally accepted, prove fatal to the preservation and propagation of the life of union with God through the person of our Lord, which it is her duty to convey to mankind.   It might indeed be argued that even without such means for formulating her teaching the Church did in the first three centuries eliminate several strains of false teaching, which would appear on the surface to be more fatal to the specifically Christian religious experience than any which have threatened her in later ages.   It must however be remembered that unless the Church has some means of defining her teaching in the face of error there is always a grave danger that the simple may make shipwreck concerning the faith.   This might not be a very serious matter, if we were merely concerned with intellectual error as to some abstruse point of theology ; the danger is that large numbers of the faithful may fall into conceptions of the nature of God which are fatal to the attainment by them of the specifically Christian character and the specifically Christian religious experience. Even though in the long run the truth should, by the action of the Holy Ghost on the whole Christian body, succeed in overcoming error, the Church is bound to exercise the authority given to her by our Lord in order to preserve her children from this danger. If this account of the reasons which underlie the formulation of the teaching of the Church be accepted, certain conclusions will follow. The organ through which the Church pronounces must be in a position to judge correctly what the Christian religious experience really is. This involves not merely intellectual capacity to understand the meaning of any doctrine and its relation to the rest of the Christian system, but also that insight into the Christian character which is only derived from a genuine attempt to live the Christian life. The same applies to all theological thought : Christian theology no less than other sciences has suffered profoundly from the disputes of theologians and authorities who, often unconsciously, confused the attainment of truth with the gratification of the natural human desire to achieve victory in controversy or the natural human reluctance to admit an error.

It is however more important for our present purpose to observe that if the authority of the Church is to decide whether a particular doctrine is compatible with the religious experience of the whole Christian body, it must be able to ascertain what the religious experience of the whole body really is. In other words it must be able to appeal not merely to the religious consciousness of a few individuals, however eminent they may be in respect of sanctity or learning. So far as is possible, it must be able to appeal to the whole body of the faithful in all places and in all generations. It must inquire whether any particular form of teaching is compatible with that experience of union with God through our Lord which all generations and nations of Christians believe themselves to have enjoyed ; whether it is implied in it or whether it definitely destroys it. The extent to which any pronouncement can claim to be authoritative will depend on the extent to which it can really appeal to a wide consensus of Christian experience representing the infinite variety of the types of man who have found salvation in Christ. Naturally it will not be content merely with counting numbers ; it is also necessary to consider how far the consensus of the faithful on any given matter represents the free assent of men who were able to judge, or on the other hand merely represents the enforced consent of those who either through ignorance or even through political pressure were more or less compelled to accept the faith as it was given to them.

## 8. *The Claims of Catholic Authority*

It is from this point of view that the claims of the Catholic tradition are most impressive. For it cannot be denied that the Catholic tradition of faith and devotion manifests continuous development reaching back to the origins of Christianity. In spite of wide divergences in its external presentation of religion, it can show a fundamental unity of religious experience throughout all ages and all nations of the world, reaching back to the times when the Church had to propagate her teaching in the face of the bitter persecution of the State. Although in later times the Catholic Church has lost her visible unity, yet the general system of Catholic life and worship has shown its power to survive and even to revive from apparent death. The exercise of the authority of the Church has indeed been impaired by the divisions of the Church ; but the general unity of the trend of Catholic development in spite of these divisions is an impressive testimony to the foundations laid in the period of her unity.

None the less it is necessary to inquire exactly what measure of assent may be claimed for those definitions of doctrine which have the authority of the undivided Church, and how we may recognise those pronouncements which really have the highest kind of authority. It is usually held that any definition of doctrine promulgated by a Council which can really claim to speak in the name of the whole Church, as a doctrine to be accepted by all Christians, is to be regarded as the voice of the Holy Ghost speaking through the Church, and is therefore infallible. The same claim is made by those who accept the modern Roman position for pronouncements made by the Pope, in his character of supreme Pastor of the whole Church, on matters of faith and morals. The exact extent to which any pronouncement, whatever the weight of authority behind it, can be regarded as infallible will be considered in the following section. It is however convenient to consider first the whole conception of authority as residing in the nature of the organ which claims to speak with final authority. From this point of view it is in the first instance only possible to defend the claim that any organ can claim infallibility by means of the distinction generally drawn between doctrinal definitions which all Christians are bound to believe and disciplinary regulations intended to govern the details of ecclesiastical procedure and the popular exposition of the Christian faith.    In itself the distinction is a sound one ; for it is reasonable that the Church should have the right to exercise some control over such matters as the conduct of Christian worship and also the teaching of the Christian faith.    For instance, it may be desirable to control the extent to which new teaching, which at first sight seems difficult to reconcile with existing beliefs, should be expounded to entirely ignorant audiences.    A further complication arises from the fact that it is by no means always clear whether a particular organ has the right to speak, or is at any given moment speaking in the name of the whole Church.    For instance, there are numerous cases in which bodies professing themselves to be general Councils have promulgated decisions which have since been seen to be untenable.    It is usually said that these bodies were not in fact general Councils at all.    The same difficulty applies under modern Roman theories to papal pronouncements, for it is difficult to say with precision which pronouncements on the part of the Papacy are promulgated with the supreme authority of the Holy See and which are only uttered with the lesser authority of disciplinary pronouncements.    Hence it has happened in the past that the decisions of Councils which claimed to be general Councils have been reversed by Popes or later Councils, and that papal decisions have been tacitly abandoned.    Thus in fact the mere nature of the authority which utters a decision, whether Pope or Council, is by itself of no value as a test of infallibility.

If in fact we inquire what decisions made by authorities claiming to speak for the whole Church are generally regarded as infallible, we shall find that they are those which have won the general assent of the whole Christian body, or, as in the case of more modern Roman pronouncements, of a part of that body which claims to be the whole.    It has been urged above that the function of authority in the Church is to formulate and render explicit, where need arises, truths implied in the spiritual experience of the Christian consciousness, and it is therefore not unnatural to suspect that the measure of truth, which any such pronouncement can claim, is to be tested by the extent to which after its promulgation it commends itself to the authority which it claims to represent. In point of fact it is manifest that this is what has actually taken place. Pronouncements which have in fact commended themselves to the general Christian consciousness have gained universal acceptance and have come to be regarded as expressing the voice of the whole Church. Those which have been found in practice to be inadequate, or have been shown to be untenable by the advance of human knowledge, have been relegated to the rank of temporary and disciplinary pronouncements, or else the body which promulgated them has been held not to have spoken in the name of the whole Church, sometimes at the cost of a considerable straining of the facts of history.

It seems however more reasonable to recognise the facts rather than to strain them in order to suit a preconceived idea of what the authority of the Church should be. From this point of view it would appear that just as the inherent authority of a particular pronouncement depends on the extent to which it really represents a wide consensus of Christian experience, so the proof of that authority will lie in the extent to which it commends itself by its power to survive as a living element in the consciousness of the whole Christian body. Its claim to validity will depend very largely on the extent to which that body is free to accept it or not, and also on the extent to which it is competent to judge of the matter. It will be observed that this does not imply that the truth of a pronouncement is derived from its subsequent acceptance by the faithful. Obviously truth is an inherent quality, due to the fact that the Holy Ghost has enabled the authority which speaks in the name of the Church to interpret aright the truth revealed by our Lord and realised in the devotional experience of the Church, and to formulate that truth correctly. But the test of any individual pronouncement, by which it can be judged whether it possesses the inherent quality of truth or not, will be its power to survive and exercise a living influence on the general consciousness of Christendom over a wide area of space and time.

## 9. *The Certainty of the Catholic Tradition*

At this point the obvious objection will be raised that on the theory outlined above the Christian will at any given moment be unable to know precisely what he is bound to believe. He will never know whether a particular doctrine, which has for centuries enjoyed a wide veneration, but has in later days come to be assailed, is really as true as it seems to be. This objection is often raised in controversy from the Roman Catholic side and has a specious sound. In reality its apparent force is due to the fact that it rests on a confusion of thought. For it confuses the act of faith by which the individual submits his mind and conscience to the authority of Jesus in the Catholic Church with the quite different act of acceptance of the whole system of truth as the Church teaches it at any given moment. The first of these two acts is necessarily an act of private judgment pure and simple. The individual can only accept the faith on the ground of his own purely personal conviction that it is true, although that conviction may be very largely determined by the fact that the faith is accepted by others, and by the impressive spectacle of the faith of the Catholic Church. The second act is a surrender of the private judgment by which the individual, having decided that the Catholic faith as a whole is true, proceeds to accept from the Church the detailed filling-in of the main outlines which he has already accepted.

Now on the theory put forward in this essay the position of the individual is no worse than it is on the most ultramontane theory of ecclesiastical authority. For the determining factor in his acceptance of the Catholic system will be, as it must always be, the belief that it is the truest, and ultimately the only true, account of the relations of God to man. This act of faith, rendered possible by a gift of divine grace, can never rest on anything but the personal judgment that the Catholic system as a whole is true. As regards the structure of Christian doctrine he will find, precisely as he does at present, a large body of doctrine and ethical teaching which is set before him with very varying degrees of authority. Some elements in the system will present themselves to him with a vast amount of testimony to their proved efficacy as means for enabling the believer to attain to the genuine religious experience of Christianity, in other words to realise communion with God through the Person of Jesus, dating back to the most venerable ages of the history of the Church. Some, on the other hand, will present themselves as no more than minor local regulations, judged desirable by the Church as aids to his private devotion. Between these two extremes there will lie a certain amount of teaching which presents itself to him with varying degrees of authority. This he will accept as true on the authority of the Church ; and unless he be a competent theologian he has no need to trouble himself about it. He will know that it has behind it the guarantee that it has proved fruitful as an aid to the development of the Christian life ; and even if he is unable to find in some parts of it any assistance for his personal devotion, he will be content to recognise their value for others. If, on the other hand, he be a theologian, he will still respect the various elements in the Catholic system as a whole merely on the strength of the fact that they form a part of so venerable a structure. Further, he will recognise that every part, in so far as it has in practice served to foster the spiritual life of the Church, contains an element of truth which all theological inquiry must account for. The greater the extent to which it has served that purpose, the greater will be the respect he will accord it. At the same time he will regard the Catholic faith as an organic whole, the truth of which is guaranteed more by its intrinsic value as proved by past experience than by the oracular infallibility of certain isolated definitions. He will indeed reverence such definitions, and he will reverence them the more in proportion to the extent and the quality of the assent they can claim. But he will recognise that their claim to be regarded as absolutely and finally true is not a matter of absolute certainty or of primary importance. It may be that the progress of human knowledge will lead to a better formulation of the most venerable articles of the faith ; but it will always preserve those elements in them which are the true cause of their power to preserve and promote the devotional life of the Catholic Church. It will be observed that in acting thus he will be acting precisely as the investigator does in any branch of science, who recognises that any new advance he may make must include all the elements of permanent truth discovered by his predecessors in the same field, even though it may show that their discoveries had not the absolute truth originally supposed.

It should further be observed that the theologian will recognise that any formulation of doctrine by the Church has the highest claim on his respect. Even if he cannot hold its absolute truth, he will realise that it contains an element of truth which any new definition must preserve, and he will also respect the right of the Church to restrain him from putting forward his own views, where they differ from the authoritative statements of the Church in such a manner as to disturb the faith of the simple or to lead to unedifying controversy. He will admit that the mere fact that a particular statement has been solemnly put forward by the whole Christian body creates a strong presumption in favour of its embodying a very high degree of truth, and will be careful to avoid the danger of denying the truth which a formula contains, even if the formula seems to him to be defective.

It will certainly be objected that this view leaves the door open to " Modernism." The answer is that Modernism as hitherto expounded has obviously undermined the foundations on which Christian experience rests. If a new type of Modernism were advanced, it would either have the same effect or it would not. If it did not (we need not concern ourselves with the question of the possibility of such an hypothesis), there seems no reason to deny that it would be a valid restatement of the essential truth of the Catholic system, and it would stand simply as a more accurate statement of those truths which it is the function of the Church to teach to her children in order to attain to salvation through Jesus.

It may be added that the fear of " Modernism " seems to suggest a lack of trust in the power of the Church to eliminate false teaching from her system. It may be desirable to restrain the dissemination of teaching of an unsettling kind ; but the Christian should have sufficient confidence in the inherent strength of the Catholic system to view with equanimity the exploration of every possible avenue of inquiry. If a particular line of thought is really, as it seems to him at the moment, fatal to the whole content of Christian devotion, it will certainly come to nought. If his fears are unfounded, it can only lead to a fresh apprehension of the truth and the enrichment of Christian devotion.


## NOTES

### 1. The Holy Roman Church

Anglicans have tended in the past to a rather facile depreciation of the claims of the See of Peter. It must be admitted that the aggrandising policy of certain Popes was largely responsible for the division of Christendom ; but it must also be admitted that the

See of Constantinople was by no means free of blame in the matter. In the same way the papal court was largely responsible for the rejection of the demands of the more moderate Reformers ; but the excesses of the Protestant leaders rendered the preservation of Christian unity impossible. If the general position put forward in this essay be accepted, it will follow that there is some error in the claims usually made on behalf of the Papacy, in view of their proved tendency to destroy the unity of Christendom, but also an element of truth in that devotion to the Holy See which has done so much to preserve the Catholic faith in Western Europe.

As regards scriptural authority the Petrine claims cannot claim to be more than a development of the commission given by our Lord to St. Peter and the position held by him in the primitive Church ; it is only by the results that we can judge whether they are a legitimate development or not. Hence controversies as to their exact meaning are bound to prove futile. In general it may be said that the question at issue is whether the Papacy is to be regarded as the organ through which the Holy Ghost speaks directly to the whole Church, or whether it is the organ for articulating the experience of the Christian body as a whole, that experience being produced by the influence of the Holy Ghost on the corporate consciousness of the Church. It may seem that this is a somewhat subtle distinction ; but it is one of supreme practical importance. From the former conception is derived the tendency to regard the Pope as an autocratic ruler of the Church, responsible to God alone ; he has only to speak and the faithful are bound to obey. From the latter point of view the Pope is the representative of the whole Church, whose function is not to promulgate truth but to regulate the general line of Christian thought in so far as it may be necessary to save the simple from the disturbing effects of false teaching and to preserve that measure of uniformity in matters of faith and conduct which is necessary to the welfare of the Church. In this case he is to be regarded as holding a pastoral office as first among his brothers the Bishops of the Catholic Church. At the present time it is impossible to say which of these conceptions is the true one from the Roman point of view. Either can be made consistent with the definitions of the Vatican Council, and both are held in different quarters within the Roman Communion. It is clear that the former view is entirely incompatible with the position advanced in this essay ; but that does not justify

Anglicans in refusing to recognise the element of truth which may be claimed for the Papacy if it be regarded in the latter light. There can be no doubt that the Holy See has on many occasions preserved Catholicism from the gravest dangers ; but it has always done so by acting as the voice of the Christian community in general as against fashionable errors. It is when the Papacy has claimed to speak with the direct authority of the Holy Ghost and without reference to Christendom as a whole that it has aroused that hostility which has led to or kept alive the disruption of Christendom. In any question of reunion the vital issue is whether the Church can be safeguarded against that natural tendency to self-aggrandisement which is the besetting vice of all human institutions, and which has caused the Papacy to claim prerogatives which large bodies of Christians have felt bound to reject. But such a rejection of autocratic claims need not involve the rejection of the view that the Papacy has a special function to fulfil in the life of the Church. Further, just as the authority of the episcopate is held to be *de jure divino* on the ground that by a process of legitimate development the episcopate has become the repository of the authority given to the Apostles, so it might be held that the Papacy possesses authority *de jure divino* as having become by a similar process the repository of a primacy held by St. Peter. Anglican theologians can and should be prepared to discuss this possibility with an open mind. But while doing so they cannot concede the actual claims made or presupposed by the majority of Roman theologians in regard to the position and authority of the Papacy.

## 2. The Religious Experience of Protestantism

In this essay for the most part only the religious experience of Catholicism has been considered. Obviously, however, the various schools of Protestantism have in history proved for many a means of access to God through the person of our Lord of a very genuine kind. On the other hand, it is to be observed that the dogmatic systems of historical Protestantism are showing a tendency to disappear, if they have not already been tacitly abandoned. This fact shows that the element of permanent value in them was not the dogmatic systems which the original Reformers regarded as essential. This, however, is not intended to deny or to belittle the importance of the religious experience of historical Protestantism. It must, however, be observed that much of it has been drawn from its insistence on the power of the believer to enter into immediate personal communion with God through Christ, and its strong personal devotion to the humanity of our Lord. But these or similar features of historical Protestantism are simply aspects of the Catholic faith, which the Reformers regarded as having been obscured by the Catholicism of the time. It must be admitted that to a very large extent they were right in thinking so. Yet, in so far as it is these elements of Protestantism which have in the past given it value as a means of providing the Protestant with the experience of Christian devotion, and are still in fact a living force in the Protestant bodies, the strength of Protestantism lies in the fact that it emphasises certain elements of Catholicism. Further, Protestantism, although in its positive dogmatic systems it failed to establish any final truth, may claim to have rendered a genuine service to Christianity by showing the untenable character of much of the old tradition of Catholicism, and by its insistence on the necessity of justifying Christian doctrine by the appeal to the Scriptures and to human reason. In the sweeping away of false conceptions, and establishing a truer conception of the nature of the means by which truth is to be apprehended, Protestantism has played a vital part in the life of the Church and the progress of mankind.

# THE CHRISTIAN CONCEPTION
## OF GOD
### BY LIONEL SPENCER THORNTON

# CONTENTS

"THE God of Abraham and the God of Isaac and the God of Jacob. . . . He is not the God of the dead, but of the living ; for all live unto him." These words of our Lord take us to the heart of the Bible and the revelation which it records. The Christian's God is One who has to do with living men because He is Himself the living God. He is the Covenant-God who enters into the course of history and communicates the knowledge of Himself in a special way to a particular people, at first partially and in various stages, then finally and completely in the Person of Jesus Christ. All this is without prejudice to the truth that there is a wider and more general revelation of God given to all men, to which all religions bear witness, whose evidences are written in the book of nature and upon every human heart. If we claim that in the religious history of our race a special revelation occupies the foreground of the picture, nothing is to be gained by overlooking this far-stretching background. Yet from the point of view of historic Christianity the Gospel provides the clue which alone can interpret the riddle of God's world-wide Self-revelation.

The argument of this essay starts from the conclusions reached in a preceding essay on " The Vindication of Religion." Assuming the truth of theism, we are concerned with the content of that conception of God which the Christian Church has received. The subject falls naturally into two main parts : (i) The attributes of God ; (ii) The Holy Trinity. In discussing these subjects certain pressing questions of current thought will be kept in view, such as the idea of revelation, the possibility of reconciling different aspects in the traditional doctrine of God, and the meaning of personality in God.

## I

### THE ATTRIBUTES OF GOD

#### 1. *The Contrasted Aspects of Deity*

When religion is traced back to its beginnings in the history of man, nothing is more striking than the dominating position which it appears to occupy. Religion is the thread upon which

are strung whole systems of cultus, custom and taboo, tribal morality
and mythological explanation.   Thus from its first appearance
religion is concerned with the whole man and with the whole of
human life.   But again the first stirrings of the religious impulse
appear to take the form of definite emotional moods in which man
reacts to the mystery in his environment and to the mystery in his
own life.   Doubtless there were even in man's primitive experience
a variety of emotional moods and attitudes of this general character.   But all varieties ultimately resolve themselves into two
main types of attitude.   The object of man's worship is terrible
and awe-inspiring and yet in other moods is felt to be protective
and friendly.   Religion means abasement before divine majesty
and yet fascination which draws men to seek communion with the
divine.   The religious revelation given to Israel emerges out of
this dim background and continues in its progress to exhibit these
general characteristics.   There is the religious fear awakened by
local theophanies or manifestations of deity, or again by the infringement of some taboo ; and on the other hand there are homely
and joyful festivals at the local shrines.   Yahweh is revealed in
fire, thunder, and storm-cloud.   He marches with the tribes to
the destruction of his enemies ; He is a jealous God.   But there
is also another picture : the God who enters into friendly covenant
with patriarchs and kings, who promises protection and blessing
to the race.   When Hebrew religion rises to the level of theism
we still find these contrasted aspects of majesty on the one hand
and homely intimacy on the other.   But the combination attains
a new significance.   For in the development of prophetic monotheism the majesty of God is seen ever more and more clearly to
transcend the crude imaginations and limited horizons of primitive
religious thought until He is known in prophetic faith to be the
perfectly holy and righteous God who rules all the nations, the
Creator of heaven and earth.   Yet this revelation of divine transcendence does not crush out the more homely aspects of religion.
Rather those aspects are purified of their grosser elements and
reappear in deeper and more penetrating forms.

Meanwhile the religion of Israel, like other religions, concerned
itself with a people and all its national and local interests.   But,
unlike most other religions, it overleapt the boundaries of these
restricted interests and preoccupations and provided an interpretation of Israel's history and destiny which gave to that people an

unparalleled consciousness of divine mission and religious vocation. All the changing events of national experience are woven into the texture of this historical interpretation by a long succession of prophets and prophetic writers. Like other Semitic peoples they explained all events in terms of direct causation by the will of the deity. But the action of the divine will is related to a moral purpose which has nothing capricious or arbitrary about it. It is this purpose which gives unity and significance to history and to Israel's part in history. Thus through a prophetic interpretation of history in terms of divine purpose there is a steady enlargement of horizon and an enrichment in the content of religion and of religious ideas. The horizon is enlarged to include all events, international as well as national, within the scope of divine government. National interests are thus transcended and moral interests are made supreme. Once this point is reached, it involves a great deal more. The Lord of history is the moral Governor of the world, the Creator of the universe, the only true object of worship. Thus religion is enriched by entering into partnership with morality and reason, and a conception of God is reached which can satisfy all the awakening faculties of man. For in the last resort the higher needs of man cannot be separated. We cannot rest permanently in a moral revelation however sublime, unless it expresses the character of One who is the ground of our lives and of the universe in which we live. Nor could we yield the fullest worship of heart and reason to a Being who did not manifest His will in the form of a moral purpose controlling and overruling the course of events by which our destinies are shaped.

Now without going further at this stage into the biblical conception of God, we can see that the broad facts of Hebrew monotheism have already decided some of the conditions of our knowledge of God and the limitations which the subject imposes upon human language. For the God who is disclosed to us in Old Testament prophecy is already in effect the God of Christian theism. He is the supreme Reality behind all the phenomena of sense and the source of all intuitions of the human spirit. The external world-process and the interior world of human experience must both alike be traced to Him. The religious impulse can find adequate satisfaction only in such a God—One who is the ground of all forms of our experience, emotional, moral and rational. Consequently, when we try to state the content of our conception of God, such a statement must be in terms which cover all the various fields of our experience.    Now since there is a great diversity in the forms of human experience, our approach to the idea of God must be made along a number of different lines, each of which is an attempt to give rational form to some definite part of experience.    These different lines of approach give us what are called the attributes of God.    We can never attain to a completely synthetic view of what God has revealed Himself to be.    For that would involve a level of unified knowledge which can belong to none but to God Himself.    Such a simple and simultaneous knowledge of what God is must exist in God Himself.    But we on our part must be content to approach the sanctuary from the outside and from a number of different points of view.    But if this is our necessary starting-point it is also true that as we seek to penetrate from the circumference to the centre we find the lines of approach to be convergent.    Contrasted attributes are really interdependent and are mutually necessary to one another.    But here the proportion of truth often suffers from the inadequacy of our minds to grasp the whole.    All words that we can use are inadequate and more or less anthropomorphic in character, relating God either by affirmation or negation to human experience.    We cannot avoid this difficulty.    But it calls for a severe discipline of the mind and not least by criticism of such conventions of thought as happen to be familiar or congenial to ourselves or to the age in which we live.    For example, it has often been too readily assumed that, in dealing with moral qualities or categories which enter deeply into human experience, transference of such ideas from a human to a divine context can be effected with security in proportion to the familiarity of the ideas.    It has sometimes escaped men's observation that they have been defective in their grasp upon those very ideas from which they have argued.    Failure to realise this has been in part due to that very familiarity which has been the ground of confidence.    It is easy to detect this danger in the thought of the past.    It is not so easy to remember that it is still operative. When we look back over Christian thought about God we see, in different ages of history, special prominence given to this or that particular idea.    Thus we have the impassible divine substance or nature of Greek theology, the conceptions of legal justice which have characterised Latin theology through many centuries of its history, or again ideas of the omnipotent sovereign will of God dominating men's minds in the age of the Renaissance and the Reformation. The currents of thought in our own age are running strongly in other directions and largely in reaction from these ideas. In the necessary reconstruction we must needs be on our guard against being content with a mere swing of the theological pendulum, replacing the ideas of Augustine, Anselm, and Calvin by some modern version of Marcion's gospel.

## 2. *The Development of these Contrasts*

If we return now to our starting-point, the characteristics of Hebrew monotheism as it emerged from its origins in more primitive religion, there is another characteristic which needs further consideration. Reference has been made to two contrasted aspects of deity which are clearly developed in Hebrew prophecy, but which can be traced back to two different kinds of emotional mood everywhere present and operative in the religious experience of mankind. The contrast in question—between the majesty of God on the one hand and His willingness to enter into intimate relations with His creatures on the other—is one which can be traced through the whole course of revelation in the Scriptures. God is holy and righteous, yet also loving and gracious. He is Judge and King, yet also Father and Saviour. He is Creator of the world and Sovereign over the nations, yet He dwells with the humble and lowly in heart and the contrite in spirit. But once more, these ideas are not simply held in contrast. Again and again they are blended in one experience. In the experience portrayed in Psalm cxxxix. the writer's conviction of God's nearness to and knowledge of his own soul is blended with a parallel conviction of God's omnipresence and omniscience with regard to the world as a whole ; and the two ideas appear to reinforce one another in his mind. In the book of Job, which perhaps more than any other part of Scripture emphasises the inscrutable majesty and power of the Creator, it is precisely by a revelation of this aspect of the Godhead that an answer is given to all Job's searching questions about the divine handling of his individual life. Moreover, this experience of Job's is in line with the experiences through which some of the great prophets received their call. Isaiah and Ezekiel witness a theophany of the divine holiness and glory and then a Voice speaks to them and they are given a personal mission.

As the revelation of God to Israel moved forward it became more universal in form and at the same time more effectively concerned with individual worth and destiny, more penetrative of the spirit of man and on the other hand more transcendent of this world-order.    When we pass to the New Testament and the teaching of our Lord, we find that the heavenly Father of whom He spoke stands in a universal relationship to all men without respect of persons.    Yet this relationship reaches to the heart of man more completely than was possible under the Old Covenant.    The souls of sinful men and women are now set in concentrated rays of light and seen to be mysterious treasure, over which the Heart of God yearns and travails.    Moreover, these things are not simply set forth in idea.    They are already in operation.    They are part of the hidden reality of a Kingdom, which is here and now present as the action of God upon the world.    Christ Himself is the truth of the Kingdom which He preaches.    This Kingdom is proclaimed in the language of apocalyptic as something which altogether transcends the course of history and which finally breaks the bonds of mere nationalism.    Its claim is absolute against every earthly counter-claim.    Yet this Kingdom has come down to earth in the human form of Jesus Christ and it is actualised in the fellowship of His little flock.    Thus the Incarnation was the final ratification of the principle that God is revealed to us under contrasted aspects.    In the very inadequate language of theology we say that God is both transcendent and immanent.    But these two ideas are not sheer opposites in an insoluble contradiction. They exemplify that " double polarity " of Christianity with which Baron von Hügel has made us familiar.    The Incarnation not only ratified this principle of a union of opposites.    It embodied the principle in a new form.    Christianity is the universal religion, and at the same time it is the religion which raises individual personality to its highest power.    In the New Testament we see the creation of a wholly new experience of fellowship between God and man reaching down to the roots of the human spirit.    Yet the individual is thus recreated within the compass of a religious movement which breaks through all the old particularist limitations and claims for itself universal scope as the bearer of an absolute and final revelation of God.

The immediate effect, therefore, of God's love " shed abroad in our hearts " was an immense enlargement and enrichment of the whole idea of God. The idea now called for a new language in which it could be expressed. The search for such language already appears in some of the great doctrinal passages in the writings of St. Paul and St. John. As the development of Christian thought proceeded, it was impelled to borrow from philosophy's vocabulary of abstract words and impersonal categories of thought. Only by the use of such language, it was found, could justice be done to a revelation which was, as given to experience, intensely personal and concrete in form. Thus in the traditional list of the divine attributes there is a large proportion of such abstract and impersonal terms side by side with others which are drawn more directly from the vivid, personal language of religious experience. Again, although we are not as yet primarily concerned with the doctrine of the Holy Trinity, the formulation of that doctrine provides a further illustration of what has been said. To sum up, the limitations of the human mind and the facts of revelation alike require that the content of the idea of God should be formulated under a variety of aspects. No true simplification is effected by attempts to reduce the diversity of our religious experience, or to submerge under the dominance of any one idea the diversity of divine attributes which reflect that experience. Moreover, Christian theism, as the trustee of all religious revelation, bears witness to a fundamental duality running through all our experience of God ; and the contrasts which this experience implies are ultimately irreducible facts, of which theology is bound to take account. These considerations impress themselves upon the mind in a great variety of ways. God guides the stars and He also touches the heart. He embraces all the worlds and He is also the Voice that speaks in Jesus Christ. He is to be known in His cosmic relations through the severe impersonal studies of science and philosophy. Yet He can be vividly known to each one of us in the penetrating sway of conscience and in the hidden depths of prayer. We know Him through very varied schools of discipline and through many channels of revelation. None of these can be left out of account. For all contribute to the enrichment of each and every particular field of experience with which as individuals we may be most concerned.

### 3. *Revelation and the Attributes*

Much light is thrown upon these questions by two principles of great importance in the speculative thought of to-day. These are (*a*) the principle that there are different grades in the structure of reality ; and (*b*) the principle that all knowledge is trans-subjective. Both of these principles illuminate the religious concept of revelation and have an important bearing upon the whole subject of the divine attributes.[1]

(*a*) It is the glory of Christianity that God has been revealed to us in terms of a human life ; because humanity is what stands nearest to us. But if we consider man's place in the world-process this must mean a great deal more. For man is a microcosm of nature, and human life is the meeting-point of an inner world of spirit with the external world through all its levels. Further, the revelation of God in Christ is an historical revelation and, on any Christian interpretation, must be regarded as occupying the centre of history. Its universality is exhibited upon the background of the ages, through which its eternal principles are refracted both forwards and backwards for our clearer understanding. Here, then, we have a series—Nature, Man, History, the Incarnation— a series which forms a graded sequence with interconnections. The four factors in the sequence taken together provide all the data we possess for our knowledge of God. Revelation in its widest sense must be spread over the whole of this field and through all its stages and levels. Now it is precisely this fact which is represented in what are called the attributes of God. Moreover, as the different stages and levels of revelation are interconnected, so must it be with the attributes. There is here a real parallelism which is worthy of notice.

If we consider the attributes from this point of view we find, in the first place, that for Christian thought God is above the whole order of nature and the historical process of events which is unfolded upon nature's system. He is infinitely more than can ever be apprehended by man, the microcosm of nature and the subject

---

[1] For the first point cp. the recent Gifford lectures, *Space, Time and Deity* by Prof. Alexander and *Emergent Evolution* by C. Lloyd Morgan ; also W. Temple, *Christus Veritas*, ch. i., and F. W. Butler, *Christianity and History*, cc. i. and ii. For the second point cp. Von Hügel, *Essays and Addresses*, pp. 51–57, and L. A. Reid, *Knowledge and Truth* (a recent criticism of the " new realist," " critical realist " and other modern theories of knowledge).

of history, either through the medium of the external world and its temporal processes or through man's own inner life. God must for ever be contrasted with all the positive content of these things. This is the principle of negation. We do not know what God is in His ultimate Being. Such knowledge of Him as we possess is as a flicker of light upon a background of cloud and mystery. He is infinite, eternal, ineffable, absolute, inscrutable, wholly beyond this world of our experience and not subject to its changes and chances. In form these attributes are negative ; but their meaning for us is not simply negative. They are symbols of God's greatness and of our smallness, through which the attention of the mind is strained towards the Object of all desire. But, secondly, there is another knowledge of God which is mediated to us through the same series of our temporal experience. We may know the Creator through His creation, however in-adequately, yet with sufficient clearness and certainty to satisfy the cravings of the human spirit. God is revealed through all levels of creation in the measure which is possible to each level. What He possesses as an undivided treasure is refracted through nature and man in an ascending scale. God possesses in a more eminent sense all the true goods which exist in this world, all ful-ness of energy, life, mind and personality. He is rational, free, self-determining Spirit. In Him are realised all the values which these words connote. Thirdly, God is in active relations with His creation through all its stages as its ground, cause, and sustainer. All processes and events of the temporal order are within the com-pass of His knowledge and the control of His will. So, too, with the spiritual life of man and the expression of that life in society and in history. In this sphere also man can recognise what God is, both by contrast with himself and through the best in himself. God stands to man in a series of relations as Creator to creature, Deity to worshipper, Lawgiver to conscience, Sinless to sinful. These relations of contrast are asserted when we speak of God's majesty and glory, of His holiness, righteousness and goodness, of His perfect beatitude. Finally, through the Incarnation in its whole context and issues God is revealed as Love and Mercy, as Father, Saviour and Friend.

In this survey of the attributes we see a sequence which corresponds broadly to the factors or stages through which revela-tion is mediated. We move from the negative to the positive, from the abstract to the concrete, from transcendence to immanence, from the limitations of our knowledge to the light of positive revelation ; from nature to man as set in the order of nature and then to man on the field of history, from man in the social order of history to man the individual recognising his God through religious and moral intuitions ; finally from man and his aspirations to their fulfilment in the Incarnation.

(*b*) A prevailing characteristic of thought in the nineteenth century was its tendency to seek for an explanation of the world in terms of some one comparatively simple idea either of causation or of development.    Such a principle the mechanistic theory seemed at one time to provide, or, again, the idea of evolution conceived as the continuous and inevitable unfolding of what existed in germ or in essence from the first.    In all this the spell of Descartes' " clear and distinct idea " was still potent.    But as the sciences steadily won their way to autonomy, this method became less and less adequate.    Now we are faced with a new conception of reality in the graded series of matter, life, mind and spirit which the hierarchy of sciences discloses.    This change of outlook is driving out the old monistic theories of knowledge.    Descartes left the awkward legacy of an unresolved dualism between subject and object.    Upon this fierce onslaughts have been made ever since and are still being made.[1]    Yet even Professor Alexander, who surely sings the swan-song of evolutionary monism, is unable to eliminate this dualism of subject and object.[2]    Each grade of reality has its own " system of reference " and lays upon the knower its own categories of thought.    The real yields up its secrets only to those who accept it as something given, to which the mind must be receptive.    Now here we gain a flood of light upon the whole idea of revelation, which comes forth from its place in theology to claim a wider field.    This given-ness of the objects of knowledge persisting over every stage of so vastly varied a range throws a new meaning into the question as to what sort of knowledge we may possess in a revelation of God.    At every step in the scale the given reveals itself to mind as something of which we may have real knowledge ; and yet in such a way that our knowledge is never complete.    Knowledge is trustworthy as far as it goes ; yet the object always escapes from the knower's net.

[1] *E.g.* by the American " New Realists " and in the philosophy of Croce.
[2] *Space, Time and Deity*, vol. ii. bk. iii. ch. iv. B., pp. 109–115.

There is always attainable a degree of certainty sufficient for a further advance. But there is always an unsolved mystery left over. The higher we go in the scale of revelation the more significance this double principle attaches to itself. Moreover, throughout the whole series, consciousness of mystery remaining in no way conflicts with an assured confidence of knowledge already attained. We may even suggest that of these two characteristics the one is an ingredient in the other. The things which we feel are most worth knowing are known not as solved problems but as fresh vantage-grounds, providing new horizons and fascinating fields for further exploration. The more we are at home in the world which we know, the more strange and mysterious it is to us. How much more, then, is this likely to be true in the knowledge of that Being, who is the ground of all that is and all that knows, the source of all revelation and the all-inclusive object of knowledge. It is this truth which is reflected in the contrast of transcendent mystery and condescending love, which we have found to be a permanent factor in religious experience and in that intellectual formulation of the attributes, which endeavours to do justice to such experience. But this is not the whole truth. It has its complement in the fact that, unlike all finite objects of knowledge, God is Himself the ground of the knower. As the ground of all our experience He is less strange to us than any finite creature can be. He comes as the infinite Creator to the rescue of our finite powers and embraces our aspirations with immense condescension. The paradox of revelation has its reverse side. He who is wholly beyond us is infinitely near. The Creator's love is more native to our spirits than any affinity of His creatures can be.

The conception of revelation outlined above cuts across certain currents of theological thought which have been running strongly since Ritschl's day. These were congenial to that whole type of thought which we have seen to be characteristic of the last century. A variety of causes, into which we need not here inquire, led men to seek, in the break-up of traditional foundations, for some one clear and simple foundation upon which to build anew. They found this in the human figure of our Lord and in the moral revelation of divine love disclosed in His life and teaching. They rightly saw that here if anywhere the light of revelation shone most clearly. But they did not sufficiently consider the fact that what is in itself most luminous will not remain luminous if it is taken out

of its context.   The context of Jesus Christ is all that we can know
of nature, man and history.   The context of divine love is all
that we can know of God at all levels of reality and through all
channels of knowledge.   The Gospel is too tremendous to be
apprehended on any narrower stage, and that just because the
revelation of God's love in Christ transcends all other stages of
revelation and is the culminating point of the whole series.   Again,
underlying all these considerations is the fact that religion makes
its ultimate appeal to the whole of human nature.   Religion,
indeed, has its roots in emotional types of experience.   But it was,
as we have seen, the special province of Hebrew prophecy to bring
religion and morality into permanent alliance in such a way that
religion itself might ultimately claim the whole of human nature
and so be able to justify itself in satisfying the claims of both
morality and reason.   In the Old Testament revelation the
emphasis remains upon the moral response to God, that is to say
upon religion moralized in the form of obedience to the Law.
In the Gospel revelation of divine love religion becomes completely transcendent of morality, whilst taking morality up into
itself and transfiguring its character.   Thus the eternal fascination
of religion, which consists in man's deepest levels of desire being
met and satisfied by the self-communication of the divine—this is
now charged with moral quality and meaning ; and morality itself
in turn is fused with mystical and emotional power.   This is the
peculiar ethos of the New Testament.   It is summed up in the
word ἀγάπη, the most pregnant word of apostolic Christianity.
We therefore feel rightly that love is the most significant of all
the aspects under which God is revealed to us.   But it is so, not
as an idea which excludes other ideas, but as a ray of light which
illuminates everything which it touches.

## II

### THE HOLY TRINITY

The Catholic doctrine of the Holy Trinity is believed by the
individual Christian in the first instance on authority.   It is the
tradition to which he has been delivered at his baptism.   He has
accepted it in accepting the general trustworthiness of the Church's
mental outlook and the body of experience which that outlook
represents.   He continues in this faith because his own religious
experience corroborates the value of what he has received.   But in

the third place, in so far as he reflects upon the contents of his religious beliefs, he must necessarily seek to understand the Church's doctrine with the help of such light as can be obtained from human knowledge as a whole.    It is with this third stage that we are here mainly concerned.[1]

### 1. *The Word and the Spirit*

It is a familiar thought that revelation and inspiration are complementary ideas ; that the Word of God *aptat Deum homini* and that the Spirit of God *aptat hominem Deo*.[2]    In other words, all revelation may be regarded from the side of the object revealed and also from the side of the recipient of the revelation.    Thus we think of God's self-revelation as an objective manifestation mediated through nature, history, and the life of man.    But this idea requires for its counterpart an interior unfolding of man's powers of spiritual apprehension.    These two conceptions provide a background for the Christian belief that Jesus Christ is the revealing Word of God and that the revelation thus given has been committed to a community of persons whose inner life is quickened and illuminated by the Holy Spirit.

(*a*) In theology the doctrine that Christ is the Logos or Word of God has from the first had two contexts, both of which are to be found in the Prologue of St. John's Gospel.    There the Word is the author of creation and the light which enlightens mankind through a revelation given in the order of nature.    But the Word is also, in the same passage, said to have been manifested in history to His own people, in a process whose climax was the Incarnation. Following part of St. John's thought we may therefore regard the revelation in Jesus Christ as the goal towards which all earlier and lower stages of revelation were tending.    The conception of Christ as the goal of the world-process conceived as a single divine plan unfolding through the ages is also one of the leading ideas in the Epistle to the Ephesians.[3]    The word there used indicates, not that our Lord is the last term in a series, but that He is the summation of the whole series.    He includes in Himself all the

---

[1] The writer is not here concerned to raise, still less to prejudge, questions concerning the respective functions of authority, faith and reason in religion. The remarks in the text are confined to a general statement of facts.

[2] The phrases are taken from Du Bose, *The Gospel in the Gospels*, Part I, c. iii.

[3] Eph. i. 10 ; cp. also *ib*. iv. 13.

content of revelation as exhibited through all its stages. He is the final expression of the purpose of God as disclosed in nature, man and history. He is the "perfect Man." But we cannot rest satisfied with such an idea. There is a correlative truth stated emphatically by St. Paul and St. John. Creation is not only "unto Him"; it is also "through Him" and "in Him." He is not only the substance of all revelation given to man and its ultimate meaning. He is also the ground of the whole created order through which revelation comes.[1] The Christ of the New Testament is not evolutionary precisely because He is the Word, the absolute revelation. This antithesis becomes clear if we follow up the conception of revelation already outlined in this essay. In all revelation there is a disclosure to man of some aspect of reality which yet transcends our power of knowing. As we ascend the scale that which is given to knowledge increasingly transcends and escapes from the dissecting analysis of intellect; and yet at the same time comes ever closer to what lies within and at the root of man's most significant experiences. Thus at the top of the scale truth, beauty and goodness have infinitely larger meanings than we can ever find in them. Yet they correspond to our deepest intuitions, and are not only the ends which we seek but the grounds of our seeking. They are always beyond us and yet always with us. They are wholly native to our minds and yet altogether transcend every sequence in our mental and moral life. But they are only rays of that "light which lighteth every man," who is the Way, the Truth and the Life.

It follows that if Christ is the summation of that series in which such values appear and the goal towards which they point us, then the double principle of revelation must reach in Him its final and absolute expression. He sums the series of revelation because He transcends it entirely. He spans all avenues of revelation because He is the supreme Revealer, the personal Word, who is the source of all partial utterances of revelation and of all particular parts and sequences of that temporal order through which they are mediated to us. The Christ of history stands in an historical succession; yet He cannot be explained from within it. He enters it *ab extra*; and, to say the least, such an idea appears both rational and intelligible on the view that all revelation exhibits characteristics of transcendence. A previous essay has urged that

[1] Col. i. 15–17; John i. 1–4.

Nature and man are not self-explanatory, that both point to a supernatural world which is the ground of this world, and again that man himself belongs to both of these worlds.[1]  It is in virtue of such considerations that man appears pre-eminently fitted to be the recipient of a revelation from that supernatural order.  Now the Johannine doctrine that Christ is the Word made flesh declares that the whole revelation of God to man, the final summation of all that man can know of God, was projected into human life at a point in the historical sequence in the Person of Christ.[2]  The possibility of such an event St. John finds in the fact that He who enters thus into human nature is Himself the author and sustainer of the cosmic process, of that humanity which He took and of that historical succession into which He entered.  " In the beginning was the word and the word was with God and the word was God."  From this cycle of Johannine ideas springs that theological tradition which connects together Creation and Incarnation as two stages in one divine action, and which finds the ground of both in the deity of the Word or Son of God.  St. Paul reached the same result, but along a different line of approach. Here the experience of redemption from sin was the principle governing the process of interpretation.  Christ not only reveals God to man ; He also redeems man to God.  He brings down the supernatural to man and also raises man to that supernatural order. Where these two lines of thought meet, as they did conspicuously in St. Athanasius, there theology most truly reflects the balance of the New Testament.  But both lead to the same conclusion. For it is through the experience of Christ's redeeming action that God's character is revealed to us ;  and the substance of the revelation is that God is redeeming Love.  The conclusion in both cases is that God is revealed to man and man is redeemed to God by One who is Himself within the life and being of God.

(*b*) The idea of revelation requires for its counterpart the corresponding idea of inspiration.  Man is indeed fitted to be the recipient of a revelation by the fact that he is made in the image of the Word ;  since the Word is alike the author of man's being and the ground and substance of that revelation which is made to him.

---

[1] Essay II.

[2] This in no way precludes us from recognising the limitations of Christ's earthly life ; cp. what was said above on the " context" of the revelation in Christ, pp. 133, 134.

Nevertheless, since what is given in revelation is from a supernatural source, man stands in need of divine assistance or grace from the same supernatural source, that he may be able to apprehend what is revealed. This process of inspiration entering into the spirit and life of man goes forward *pari passu* with all stages of revelation. It is as wide in scope and as diverse in form as we have found revelation to be. But in particular, as the Old Testament revelation developed, Jewish thought distinguished the Spirit from the Word and looked forward to a full outpouring of the Spirit as a special mark of the Messianic Kingdom. This hope was fulfilled in the Pentecostal experience of the apostolic Church. The recipients of this experience traced the gift of the Spirit to their incarnate Lord, and found in the fellowship of the Spirit a new life whereby they were enabled to appropriate the meaning of that revelation which had been given in Christ. In the place of that objective historical manifestation of divine love in terms of human life which they had seen in Christ they now possessed an interior presence of indwelling love in the fellowship of the Christian community   This presence was personal in its action, creating a new social fellowship and renewing the life of individuals within that fellowship. The Spirit experienced as the source of such rich personal values was understood to be Himself personal [1] and yet distinguished from the incarnate Lord, whose revealing life He illuminated and whose historical redeeming action He transmuted into the form of an abiding interior principle of sanctification. There were, therefore, in this new cycle of experience two distinct features. God has revealed Himself through the redeeming action of Christ ; and God so revealed is present in the Christian community and in its individual members through the gift of the Spirit. The love of the Father is revealed in the grace of the Son ; and the grace of the Son is possessed and enjoyed in the communion of the Spirit. [2]

It does not fall within the scope of this essay to trace in full the development of the doctrine of the Trinity in the early Church until it reached its final expression in the fourth century. In the New Testament we find no formulated doctrine ; but rather the materials for such a doctrine taking shape in the form of a developing

---

[1] *E.g.* such phrases as ἐνεργεῖ . . . καθὼς βούλεται in 1 Cor. xii. 11 suggest an active subject rather than an impersonal influence. Still more definite is the use of the pronoun ἐκεῖνος in John xiv.–xvi.

[2] 2 Cor. xiii. 14.

experience which is already feeling its way vigorously towards adequate intellectual expression. This stage is already manifest in the Pauline epistles. It reaches its maturest expression in St. John's Gospel. Here Father, Son and Holy Spirit are Three "Subjects" or "Persons"; and on the other hand the distinctions drawn between the Three are balanced by emphatic statements of divine unity and mutual relationship. The development of patristic thought consisted in a series of attempts to do justice to such language and still more to the apostolic experience which lay behind it. Not all of such attempts were successful; each advance was made at the price of many abortive experiments. But the controlling principles of the process are sufficiently clear. The twofold experience of redemption through Christ and of new life in the fellowship of the Spirit is the continuous link between the apostolic Church and the Church of Tertullian and Origen, and again of Athanasius, Basil and Augustine.

## 2. *Personality in God*

It has often been pointed out that to the influence of Christianity must be assigned a large part in the development of modern conceptions of personality. The case is somewhat parallel to that of another comparatively modern conception, that of history. In both cases the development of the Christian idea of God in the Bible and in theology has had much to do with the emergence of these conceptions. Of history something has already been said in this essay. The question of personality confronts us in any discussion of the doctrine of the Trinity. In its modern connotation personality probably includes two main aspects. On the one hand there is the idea of mental life organised in relation to a conscious centre. What is distinctive of man as an individual, on this view, is self-consciousness. But on the other hand consciousness of self as a centre of mental life already involves the further idea of other such centres of consciousness. Personality has a sociological as well as a psychological significance. It involves the idea of relationship with other-than-self. It has a social as well as an individual aspect. It is awareness of self and of not-self. It means self-regarding reflection and activity on the one hand, and capacity for passing out of self into social relationships on the other.

There can be no reasonable doubt that religion has played an important part in the long process of thought which lies behind these developed ideas.    But the connection between the two ideas of God and of personality in human life becomes strikingly manifest if we concentrate attention upon the New Testament and the early Church.    Here we see blossoming forth new conceptions of God, of society and of individual life.    These are three aspects of one creative experience, three strands intertwined.    We see the Christian community emerge as a new sociological factor, a new experience of fellowship.    We see also the Christian individual with a new consciousness of his individual worth and ends and of their possibility of attainment.    A deeper meaning for personality in both its individual and social aspects has begun.    Thirdly, within the same movement there emerges a new conception of God, in which the living, personal God of earlier revelation becomes known as a fellowship of Persons.    We must now follow up this clue of a connection between personality in God and in man.

Any attempt to translate the formula of Three Persons in One Substance into modern language is beset with acute difficulties. For example, Descartes has given to the idea of " consciousness " a new meaning and emphasis for us which differentiates our habits of thought from those of the Nicene Fathers.    Such a phrase as " Three Centres of One Consciousness " represents a bold attempt to grapple with this difficulty.[1]    But do we know enough of consciousness to be quite sure of our ground ?    No formula can be adequate.    But, in view of the fluid state of modern psychology, it would perhaps be better to avoid the word " consciousness " altogether and to speak of *Three Centres of One Activity*.[2]    In the case of human personality relationship can exist only between separate individuals.    The Nicene formula, and any modern equivalent, must mean that such relationship exists in God, but *not* as between three individuals.    The three centres of relationship are here comprehended within the unity of One Absolute Activity.    Such a statement presupposes that personality exists in God after a manner to which human personality offers some analogy, but in a more eminent sense as is the case with all positive statements about God.[3]    The main difference would seem to be

[1] Bishop Temple in *Christus Veritas*.

[2] The word " Activity " was suggested to me by Professor A. E. Taylor, to whose kind criticism this essay owes much.

[3] As Professor C. C. J. Webb well says, we speak of " Personality in God " rather than " the Personality of God."    See his *God and Personality*.

that characteristics and functions, which at the human level of personality appear in tension and conflict as antithetical tendencies, exist in God within a unity and harmony which transcend all analogies from human experience. In man the individual and social aspects of personality are in tension and conflict. In God the self-regarding and other-regarding aspects of personality are integrated within the unity of one mental life. Within this unity there may indeed be tension, deeper tension than we can know But if so it is tension within harmony. We can dimly perceive that this means a higher kind of personality than ours. Moreover, although the mystery of the Blessed Trinity far transcends our powers of understanding, yet there are features of human experience which point directly towards the truth of the mystery.

We turn naturally to the special forms of experience within which the Christian conception of God as a Trinity first appears and to which reference has already been made.[1] Christianity came into the world as a way of life with a specific doctrine of life.[2] Man attains his true self through the principle of sacrifice or dying to self. By this means he may transcend the purely self-regarding aspect of personality and find a larger life of fellowship. The New Testament shows this transcendence of the self-regarding ego as the Way of the Cross which our Lord inculcated and which He Himself followed out, fulfilling that Way to the uttermost in His death. The same principle of self-transcendence is also set forth as something actually and vividly realised in experience by the early Christian community. It was realised in the fellowship of the Spirit and was recognised to be an operation of the Spirit. But what the Spirit wrought in the Christian life was a mystical union with Christ, whereby the self-transcending power of Christ's life passed into the soul and, bursting through its natural bonds of selfishness, carried it up to a supernatural level of love, where the dualism of self and other was in principle already solved. It was not, however, solved by the annihilation of self, nor by the merging of the individual's personality in the community, nor again by the absorption of that personality into the life of God in any pantheistic sense. What is characteristic, for example, of St. Paul's doctrine of mystical union is exactly the reverse of such absorption. The transcendence of self which is

---

[1] See above, pp. 139 f.
[2] Cp. Royce, *The Problem of Christianity*, vol. i.

there described leads to the transfiguration of self. " I live, yet no longer I but Christ liveth in me ; and that life which I now live in the flesh I live by faith which is in the Son of God. . . ." " I can do all things in Him that strengtheneth me." Where life is all grace, all Christ, all death to self, there also it means enlargement and enrichment of self. Now this supernatural experience, as we must call it, carries us both in promise and in fulfilment to a level beyond the range of natural human capacity. The development of culture and civilisation in itself shews no tendency to overcome the tensions existing between the individual and society and again between society as a whole and smaller groups within it. On the contrary the development of human society leads of itself to increasing stress and complexity.[1] The evolutionary process as a whole appears to be characterised on the one hand by increase of complexity and on the other hand by the emergence, at various stages, of new factors which take control of this growing complexity.[2] On this view the Christian experience of grace, union with Christ and the fellowship of the Spirit, might be regarded as the emergence in, or rather entrance into, the series of a yet higher factor, which takes control of the complexities of self-conscious human personality.

This Christian doctrine of life sets the movement of human life in train towards a goal already achieved in Christ, who in this way, as Pauline Christology declares, sums up in Himself the cosmic process. As has already been said, however, Christ is not only the goal but also the ground of this process in the developed teaching of St. Paul and St. John.[3] The truth of this now appears from another point of view. What Christian experience and the New Testament alike declare to be the true direction of human life, the higher possibility of self-conscious personality under the action of divine grace, *this* Christian theology from St. Paul onwards declares to be, not simply achieved within the historical order in the life of Christ and in process of attainment in the fellowship of the Spirit, but already existing in the life of God and in the eternal activities which belong to that life. The harmony of reciprocal personal relationships, which when carried to its highest

---

[1] This point has been worked out at length by Royce. See *op. cit.*
[2] On this point cp. J. Y. Simpson, *Man and the Attainment of Immortality*, cc. ix.–xi.
[3] Cp. pp. 135–137 above.

level is called ἀγάπη in the New Testament, this is the true end of man because it is the eternal mode of God's life. The inner reality of this mystery of Triune Love is something utterly beyond us. All thought and speech are helpless and impotent before it. Yet this same mystery is utterly near to us. For all avenues of Christian experience lead up to it and lead back to it. Because the truth of this doctrine is rooted in experience, its formulation was inevitable. No formulation indeed can be adequate. But we can at least endeavour to see what sort of difficulties must, from the very nature of the case, accompany all thought upon the subject.

### 3. *Two Primary Difficulties*

There are really two primary difficulties which beset human thought upon this matter. One is the difficulty of conceiving rightly the unity in the Godhead. The other is the difficulty of conceiving rightly the distinction of Persons. It does not matter which of these questions we consider first. For each leads eventually into the other. Our mental life is of such a kind that it is always bringing unity into the manifold of sense impressions through the medium of abstract concepts and ideas. Abstraction is the unifying principle of all intellectual activity. Consequently, the mind inevitably tends to think of unity itself as having the characteristics of an abstract principle or idea. It is a fact well-known in the history of thought that the philosophic and scientific mind finds personality difficult and intractable to system. From this point of view, if the idea of God is introduced, it is valued chiefly as providing a rational ground for the unity and order of the world-process. Modalism is the interpretation of the Trinity which is most congenial to this type of thought. The Persons become aspects, modes or phases of a single principle rather than centres of consciousness in relationship. This conception of unity is however very inadequate to reality as we know it to-day. The unities which the sciences reveal to us consist in the correlation of different kinds of energy and in the harmony and balance set up by the reciprocal interactions of these energies. As we move up the scale of reality the characteristics of unity necessarily change as the higher factors of life and mind emerge and take control. But the changes which occur move steadily in the direction of self-conscious personality and personal relationships. This series, as we know it, is unfinished. Personality, as known to the psychologist, is an imperfectly realised unity, in which conflicting tendencies have not yet attained to such a harmony as it is necessary to presuppose as the goal of personality. Moreover, this incompleteness in the unity of the individual is reflected in his corresponding inadequacy as the unit in a system of social relationships. Yet this unfinished series is a clue as to the direction in which we ought to look for our ideas about unity and personality in God.

A different line of approach is that of religious experience which starts, not from the idea of unity, but from the experience of personal relations. For that is in essence what religion means, even in the earliest stage of religious history, when the object of worship is not clearly recognised in terms of such relationship. The peculiar difficulty with which religion is beset is not abstraction but anthropomorphism. Consequently, religious thought, in attributing personality to God, finds it difficult to strip off from the idea of personality the associations of human imperfection and limitation which cling to it. Now the essential Christian experience of God is, in its completeness, what the New Testament records, namely personal communion with Father, Son and Holy Spirit, a threefold experience of personal relationship. This involves the idea of a fellowship of Persons in God ; and this fellowship is partially and imperfectly but truly reflected in the fellowship of the Christian community. On the whole, therefore, it seems true to say that, as reason is primarily interested in the unity of God, so religious experience is primarily concerned with the distinction of Persons. Owing to the difficulty referred to above, this distinction may easily be conceived in a form which approaches to Tri-theism. The human mind tends to think of the essence of personality as consisting in what sets one individual apart from another. The whole *nisus* of human personality towards self-realisation seems to confirm this idea ; because in our natural experience there is a deep fissure between the individual and social aspects of personality which it is hard to bridge over. But the Christian reading of this natural experience is that it is in large part to be explained in terms of sinful pride and selfishness. It points away from the true meaning of personality, not towards it. Philosophy also teaches a very different lesson. The higher values or goods of life are of such a kind that they can and must be shared For they can be fully realised or enjoyed by each only in community with others. If then we strip off our present limitations from the idea of personality, that idea in its most perfect form would mean something not less but more truly social than anything of which we have experience. It would mean precisely what is indicated in the mysterious doctrine that there is a complete mutual indwelling and interpenetration of the Three Persons in the Godhead.

## III
### CREATION, MIRACLE AND PROVIDENCE

In conclusion, something must be said as to the view of God's relation to the world and to human life which follows upon this conception of God. For Christians, creation has always meant that God made the universe " out of nothing." No other view is compatible with the absolute and transcendent character of the Deity as understood by Christian theism. It follows that God is the necessary ground of creation. Can we in any sense speak of creation being necessary to God ? Here there is need of careful distinction. Some philosophers seem to think that a perpetual process of creation is a necessary counterpart to the idea of a living personal God. Whether there is such perpetuity of creation is surely an irrelevant question, which we have no means of answering. The vital point is that God does not create under any necessity *external to Himself*, but by the perfectly free action of benevolent will. Since, however, there is nothing arbitrary in the divine will, this is the same thing as to say that He creates in accordance with the laws of His own nature. He does not create because He stands in need of creatures, but through the overflowing fullness of His love which must manifest itself in condescension. It is unfortunate that the English language possesses no convenient way of distinguishing between these two kinds of necessity. But whatever language we use the distinction must be maintained. Upon this difficult subject the doctrine of the Trinity throws a flood of light. In a Unitarian conception of God, where there is no subject-object relation within the Godhead, the idea of creation inevitably comes to mean that the world is the necessary object of divine activity. The world thus takes the place of the eternal Son, and God is subjected to external necessity. If, however, there are hypostatic distinctions within the Godhead, we can find in God an eternal ground and

L

possibility of creative action without introducing such necessity. The creative capacity which we know in human personality attains its ends through growth and succession ; and such attainment is but a mode of self-realisation within the created order of which we are parts.    But a transcendent Creator cannot be thought of as finding His adequate object in a created order, which is and must always remain less than Himself.    Such an adequate object the Father possesses in the Son, who is the eternal reproduction of Himself.    The doctrine of the Trinity indicates in God eternal activities of personal relationship such as provide a rational ground for creative activity.    Eternity is no mere negation of succession. For the most significant forms of human experience transcend successiveness and yet they are immanent in a succession.    We may therefore believe that in the eternal activities within the Godhead there exists in a more eminent way all that is abidingly significant in the temporal process.[1]

Closely connected with the subject of creation are important questions concerning miracles and providence.    Upon these matters nothing more can be attempted here than the indication of a point of view.    We have seen that the graded series of reality known to us through the sciences is actually an unfinished series.[2] Moreover, as new factors emerge in the series, horizons proper to the lower stages are transcended.    Again, the whole series is transcended by God its Creator.    It follows then that God's action upon the world as a whole must transcend our experience of what falls within the series.    The series itself contains the principle of transcendence and points beyond itself to horizons outside our experience of the system which we call Nature.    In other words, it points to a supernatural order.    It is, to say the least, hazardous, therefore, from our partial standpoint to prejudge the question as to what kinds of special action might or might not be appropriate to the fulfilment of God's redeeming purpose for His creatures.    The Christian conception of God and of His relation to the world involves at least the possibility of miracles.    Miracles may be defined as unusual events in which we catch a glimpse of a divine purpose which is actually embodied in all events.    Further, they are unusual to such a degree that in that respect they fall outside the horizon of our normal experience altogether.    The

[1] This is what I understand Dr. Temple to mean in *Christus Veritas*, ch. xv.
[2] See pp. 130, 132 f.

term "miracle," as thus defined, has a more restricted meaning than the term "supernatural," which covers operations of grace as well as abnormal events. The distinction seems to be mainly relative to our experience (we have continuous experience of grace, but not of miracle). If, however, miracles are *contra quam est nota natura*, the same is really true of the whole action of grace upon the soul. For the power of grace overcomes the sway of natural propensities and enables freewill to assert itself. Thus psychological laws are transcended by grace as physical laws are transcended by miracle. The idea of miracle belongs to a group of ideas which includes freewill, providence, prayer and grace. These in turn run back to creative will and a revelation of personality in God. We cannot properly dissociate any of these ideas from one another. There are as substantial arguments available against human freewill and against the validity of prayer as against any physical miracle. If it is appropriate for human freewill to break through psychological laws by the aid of divine grace, then we cannot rule out the possibility that it is appropriate for the Creator Himself, for sufficient reasons, to supersede the normal sequences of the physical universe. The universe exists, not primarily for the purpose of exhibiting unvarying sequences of law but, that it may be sacramental of God's glory and goodness and may be the medium through which God fulfils His providential purposes for man. The providence of God is directed towards personal ends and is concerned with the priceless treasure of human souls. In the last resort the universe is best understood as the unfolding expression of God's love. Its deepest secrets are disclosed in such sayings of our Lord as " Come unto me and I will give you rest " and " There is joy in heaven over one sinner that repenteth " ; or again in the words of St. Paul, " All things work together for good to them that love God." [1]

----

[1] In these brief remarks the writer has intentionally confined himself to one point only in the modern controversy about miracles, namely its metaphysical aspect, this being the only point which seemed relevant to the subject of this essay. The writer is well aware that other aspects are raised by the bearing of modern anthropological and psychological inquiries upon the evidence for particular miracles. An admirable discussion of the metaphysical aspect will be found in Dr. F. R. Tennant's recent work, *Miracle and its philosophical presuppositions*.

## ADDITIONAL NOTE
### By E. J. BICKNELL
#### THE TRINITARIAN DOCTRINE OF AUGUSTINE AND AQUINAS

THE aim of this note is to examine the statement that in Augustine and Aquinas the personal distinctions of Father, Son and Holy Spirit are reduced to mere functions or activities within one single divine mind or consciousness.

The terms " Una Substantia," " Tres Personae," are first found in *Tertullian*. While the precise meaning of " substantia " is disputed, there is a general agreement that " personae " is in origin a grammatical term, taken from texts used to prove the distinctions of the Persons, as where the Father addresses the Son, or the Spirit speaks of the Father and the Son, *i.e.* the Three are regarded as holding intercourse with one another. Hence, as in ordinary speech, " persona " means a party to a social relationship.

Augustine, unlike earlier Latin writers, approaches the Trinity from the side of the divine unity. " The Trinity is the one and true God " (*De Trinitate*, i. 4). " The Father and the Son and the Holy Spirit intimate a divine unity of one and the same substance in an indivisible equality" (i. 7). Whatever is spoken of God according to substance or, as he prefers to call it, essence (vii. 10), is spoken of each Person severally and together of the Trinity (v. 8). All that God is He is essentially. In Him are no accidents. For what is accidental can be lost or changed. His substance is at once both simple and manifold (v. 5, vi. 8). Each Person is as great as the other two or as the entire Trinity. It is hard to say either " the Father alone " or " the Son alone," since they are inseparable and are always in relation to one another (vi. 9). The divine substance is in no way a fourth term. We do not say three Persons out of the same essence in the same way as three statues out of the same gold, for it is one thing to be gold, another to be statues. Nor, are they like three men of the same nature, since out of the same nature can also be other three men. " In that essence of the Trinity in no way can any other person exist out of the same essence " (vii. 11). The truth that each is equal to the three is difficult because the imagination uses spatial images. In all their operations *ad extra* the Three have one will and activity (ii. 9). Their unity is by nature and not by consent. Hence the Son takes an active part in His own sending (ii. 9), and the Angel of the Lord in the Old Testament is the appearance not of the Son, but of God, that is the Trinity (ii. end).

Yet, though inseparable, they are a Trinity. As their names cannot be pronounced simultaneously, so in Scripture they are presented to us through certain created things in distinction from, and mutual relation to, one another, *e.g.* at the Baptism (iv. 30, cp. Ep. 169). The reality of essential distinctions within the Trinity is maintained by the theory of relations. The Persons cannot be accidents. But " every thing that is said about God is not said according to substance. For it is said in relation to something, as the Father in relation to the Son and the Son in relation to the Father, which is not accident." The terms are used reciprocally. " Though to be the Father and to be the Son is different, yet their substance is not different ; because they are so called not according to substance, but according to relation, which relation however is not accident, because it is not changeable " (v. 6).

Such teaching is only a development of the doctrine of coinherence as found in the Cappadocian Fathers. It is unfortunate that in vii. 7-12, through his ignorance of Greek, Augustine's treatment of their terminology is so confused that it is not worth discussion. They indisputably did not reduce the Persons to three aspects of a single self. Augustine goes further in this direction. The analogies of ix.-xiv. are all taken from the activities of a single mind. He begins by asserting that it is through love that we can best attain to the knowledge of the Trinity, and finds in the threefold nature of love a trace of the Trinity. " Love is of someone that loves, and with love something (or in one place someone) is loved. Behold then there are three things : he that loves and that which is loved and love " (viii. 14). Elsewhere he identifies the Spirit with the love of the Father for the Son (vii. 3-8), or with the will of God which is a will of love.

On the other hand, he did not wish to be a modalist. Though he disliked the word " Personae " as unscriptural, yet he recognized that something had to be said to deny the teaching of Sabellius (v. 10, cp. vii. 9). In his " Retractations " (I. iv. 3), composed at the end of his life, he corrects " He who begets and He who is begotten, is one," by changing " is " into " are," in conformity with John x. 30. Further, in a famous passage of the *De Trinitate* he expressly affirms that each Person has a knowledge and memory and love of His own. There emerges at length a view inconsistent with the idea of God as a single self (xv. 12). It cannot be set on one side as a mere slip. It is anticipated in xv. 7, and occurs independently in Ep. clxix. 6. It is so elaborately worked out that it represents an essential element in his theology. Lastly, though his psychological illustrations are borrowed from the functioning of a single self, he ends a prolonged apology for their inadequacy. " But three things belonging to one person cannot suit those three persons, as man's purpose demands, and this we have demonstrated in this fifteenth book " (xv. 45).

Two other considerations deserve notice. First, he gets more modalistic, the further that he gets away from Scripture into the region of logic. Secondly, the influence of Neoplatonism has at times led him to force the Christian idea of God into moulds of thought borrowed from pagan philosophy, so as to endanger its Christianity.

In Aquinas, the dominant analogy is that of distinct functions within a single human mind. The relation of Father to Son is that of a thinker or speaker to his thought. The Spirit is love. The Son proceeds by way of intellect as the Word, the Spirit by way of will as love. Is then the Son only the divine thought, and the Spirit the love which God has for the object of His thought? This simple explanation is hard to reconcile with other passages. " Persona " is defined, in the words of Boethius, as " rationalis naturae individua substantia " or " subsistentia " or " hypostasis." " Persona " is not used in the case of God in the same sense as in the case of creatures, but " excellentiori modo." It denotes a relation existing in the divine nature " per modum substantiae seu hypostasis," not as a mere accident. " Cum nomen ' alius ' masculine acceptum non nisi distinctionem in natura significet, Filius alius a Patre convenienter dicitur." We say " unicum Filium," but not " unicum Deum," because deity is common to more than one. A neuter signifies a common essence, but a masculine a subject (suppositum). " Quia in divinis distinctio est secundum personas non autem secundum essentiam, dicimus quod Pater est alius a Filio sed non aliud : et e converso quod sunt unum non unus " (*Summa Theol.* I. xxxi. 2). Again, " Apud nos relatio non est subsistens persona. Non autem est ita in divinis. . . . Nam relatio est subsistens persona " (xxxiii. 2). In xxxvii. the name love is only applied to the Spirit as " personaliter acceptus." In his discussion of the Incarnation he decides that though it was fitting that the Son should become incarnate, it was equally possible for either of the other Persons to have been incarnate (III. iii. 5 and 8). Further words predicated of God and creatures, are predicated not univocally, but either analogically or equivocally (I. xiii. 5). In xxxix. 4, he shows that persona is not used equivocally. Therefore it must be used analogically. This analogous use implies some likeness between the divine and human persons.

In short, even in Augustine and Aquinas there is evidence of the inadequacy of the single human mind with its functions to furnish a complete illustration of the threefold process of the divine life. It suggests that it needs to be supplemented by something like the analogy from a perfectly unified society.

# THE CHRIST OF THE SYNOPTIC GOSPELS
BY SIR EDWYN CLEMENT HOSKYNS, Bt.

# CONTENTS

"There is an absence of all reason in electing humanity to Divinity."
TERTULLIAN, *Apology*.

"Beloved, outward things apparel God, and since God was content to take a body, let us not leave Him naked and ragged."—JOHN DONNE.

"Doe this, O Lord, for His sake who was not less the *King of Heaven* for Thy suffering Him to be *crowned with thornes* in this world."—JOHN DONNE.

> "Wherein lies happiness ? In that which becks
> Our ready minds to fellowship divine,
> A fellowship with essence ; till we shine
> Full alchemiz'd, and free of space. Behold
> The clear religion of heaven."
>
> KEATS, *Endymion*.

> "'What think you of Christ,' friend ? when all's done and said,
> Like you this Christianity, or not ? "
>
> ROBERT BROWNING, *Bishop Blougram's Apology*.

# I

## THE PROBLEM

FOR the Catholic Christian "*Quid vobis videtur de Ecclesia, What think ye of the Church ?* " is not merely as pertinent a question as "*Quid vobis videtur de Christo, What think ye of the Christ ?* " : it is but the same question differently formulated. This unity between Christ and the Church, vital though it is for Catholic religion, raises a historical problem as delicate as it is important : delicate, because of its extreme complexity ; important, because the study of the history and development of primitive Christianity has a subtle though direct bearing upon Christian belief and practice.

The problem is this : What is the relation between the life and teaching of Jesus of Nazareth and the Christ of St. Paul, of St. John, and of Catholic piety ? And further, what is the relation between the little group of disciples called by Jesus from among the Galilean fishermen and the *Corpus Christi* of St. Paul or the *Civitas Dei* of St. Augustine ? This problem was first clearly recognised, when, in the latter half of the eighteenth century, the exegesis of the books of the New Testament was taken out of the hands of the dogmatic theologians and entrusted to the historians. Since that time many theories have been advanced in order to explain the development of Christianity in the apostolic age, and many attempts have been made to analyse and describe its essential character. These, however, show such radical disagreement, and are so mutually exclusive, that it can occasion little surprise if the intelligent observer grows sceptical of the ability of the historian to reach conclusions in any way satisfactory ; " facts being set forth in a different light, every reader believes as he pleases ; and indeed the more judicious and suspicious very justly esteem the whole as no other than a romance, in which the writer hath indulged a happy and subtle invention." [1]

The chaos is not, however, so great as would at first sight appear. There is at the present time a fairly widespread agreement among a large number of scholars as to the main outline of the development within primitive Christianity. The conclusions arrived at accord so well with modern demands that they have strayed into quite popular literature, and are found to be exercising considerable influence outside strictly academic circles.

## II

### The Liberal Protestant Solution

The reconstruction is roughly as follows [2] :

Jesus was a Jewish prophet, inspired by the Spirit of God at his baptism by John, and called to reform the religion of

[1] Henry Fielding, *Joseph Andrews*, Book III, chapter i.

[2] The more popular exposition of this view may be found in the following books : E. F. Scott, *The New Testament To-day* ; J. Estlin Carpenter, *The First Three Gospels* ; W. Wrede, *Paul*, English translation by E. Lummis, preface by J. Estlin Carpenter ; C. Piepenbring, *La Christologie Biblique* ; B. W. Bacon, *The Beginnings of the Gospel Story*, esp. pp. 38–40 ; A. Harnack, *What is Christianity?* ; T. R. Glover, *The Jesus of History, Jesus in the Experience of Men*, esp. chap. ix ; G. Frenssen, *Dorfpredigten*.

Such expositions are largely based upon elaborate literary and historical critical studies, and upon the more important critical commentaries on the books of the New Testament. The following have been of especial importance : H. J. Holtzmann, *Hand-commentar zum Neuen Testament, Lehrbuch der Neu-Testamentlichen Theologie* ; A. Harnack, *Beiträge zur Einleitung in das Neue Testament, Lehrbuch der Dogmengeschichte* ; E. Klostermann, Commentary on the Synoptic Gospels in the *Handbuch zum Neuen Testament*, edited by H. Lietzmann ; J. Wellhausen, *Das Evangelium Marci, Das Evangelium Lucae, Das Evangelium Matthaei* ; R. Jülicher, *Die Gleichnisreden Jesu* ; A. Loisy, *Les Évangiles Synoptiques* ; W. Bousset, *Kyrios Christos* ; R. Reitzenstein, *Die Hellenistischen Mysterienreligionen* ; Claude Montefiore, *The Synoptic Gospels* ; F. J. Foakes-Jackson and Kirsopp Lake, *The Beginnings of Christianity*, (esp. I. pp. 265–418).

the Jews, which in the hands of the scribes and Pharisees had
been overlaid with burdens which the common people were
unable to bear, and in the hands of the Sadducees had been
bereft of all spiritual content. After the death of John, he
continued the Baptist's work, discarding, however, his crude
and inhuman asceticism. Jesus came to interpret the Mosaic
Law and to awaken in men the love of God and the love of
one another. A true Jew, he felt himself one of the great
line of prophets and proclaimed that union with God and the
brotherhood of men depend upon righteousness and purity of
heart. In the Sermon on the Mount, with unerring insight,
he emphasised the essential characteristics of that righteousness
which is pleasing to God, and his teaching was embodied in
his life. The authority of his teaching and the power of his
life rested upon his own intense faith that God was his Father ;
a belief which, owing to his regular practice of silent and lonely
prayer, led to an actual experience of union with God. In
the parables his simple teaching was presented to the crowds
in language which they could understand, and his miracles of
healing were the natural expression of the power of the spiritual
over the material. It is true that at times he chose the
exaggerated and poetic language of Jewish eschatology as a
vehicle for his teaching, but such language was natural at
the period in which he lived, and causes little surprise. His
essential Gospel is not to be found in the eschatological
speeches, but in the Sermon on the Mount, and in the parables
of the Sower, the Prodigal Son and the Good Samaritan.[1]
Whether or no he claimed to be the Messiah, and in what
sense he used the title, if he did use it of himself, we cannot
now know. Nor can the modern historian recapture the
exact significance of the phrase the ' Son of man ' ; perhaps
it was but the expression of his consciousness of the dignity
of his essential humanity. These are problems which need
further consideration, and which may perhaps be insoluble.

[1] Recently, however, since the publication of Johannes Weiss' monograph,
*Die Predigt Jesu vom Reiche Gottes,* and of the works of Albert Schweitzer,
*Skizze des Leben Jesu, Das Abendmahls Problem,* and *von Reimarus zu
Wrede,* most New Testament scholars have been compelled to treat the eschatological element in the teaching of Jesus far more seriously. The consequent
readjustment in the reconstruction of the development of primitive Christianity
is best studied in Kirsopp Lake's *Landmarks of Early Christianity.*

But one negative conclusion may be regarded as certain.    He did not claim to possess a divine nature.    The possibility, however, must always be allowed that his sense of union with his Father in heaven may have led him at times to claim to be the Messiah and even the Son of God ; if so, these titles were the expression of his sense of divine vocation and of the complete surrender of his human will to that of his Father.

The crucifixion was the greatest of all human tragedies. True to their traditions the Jews killed the greatest of their prophets.    But history has reversed the judgment of Caiaphas. He is only remembered as the man who chose to hand over Jesus to Pilate as a leader of insurrection against the emperor, rather than to accept his teaching and himself undertake the reform of the Jewish religion.

The divinely inspired ethical humanitarianism of Jesus, originally evolved within the narrow sphere of an attempt to reform Judaism, could not be thus permanently confined. At times Jesus seemed to feel that his religion was capable of infinite expansion, for if every human soul were of infinite worth in the eyes of the Father of all, there could be no peculiar people and Jewish particularism was therefore undermined at its foundations.    But he foresaw no formal mission ; he founded no Church to propagate his ideals ; he left them to grow and expand in the hearts of those who had heard him, conversed with him, and lived under the influence of his personality.

The influence of Jesus over his disciples was immensely increased by their belief that he was still alive after the crucifixion.    The importance of the resurrection experiences for the later development of primitive Christian faith cannot be exaggerated.    The disciples were convinced that Jesus was the Messiah, and that he would shortly return in glory to destroy the power of evil and inaugurate the final rule of God. By a process of enthusiastic reflection upon the death and resurrection of Jesus, and upon vague memories of certain obscure sayings of his, they advanced the first step toward Catholicism.    Whereas Jesus had preached a Gospel, his disciples preached him.    And yet they still remained Jews, loyal to the traditions of their fathers, and distinguished from other Jews only by their claim to know the Messiah, and by the intensity of their expectation of his coming. They waited for Jesus, the Christ.

This Messianic enthusiasm spread, as such beliefs are known to spread in the East ; but its progress can with difficulty be traced, for it moved underground, just as the piety of the Balymous (Plymouth) brothers spread up the Nile valley during the nineteenth century. Groups of disciples appeared at Damascus and at Antioch and even some Greeks were converted to the new faith. With the mission of St. Paul the number of believers grew, and, since his converts were drawn chiefly from the Greeks and not from the Jews, popular Greek ideas penetrated Christianity, and his epistles were largely influenced by this new element. Paulinism both in form and content is popular Greek paganism Christianised. Jesus Christ became the Lord and Saviour, the centre of a sacramental cult based upon the interpretation of His death as a sacrifice, and Christian phraseology was so turned as to suggest that the Oriental-Greek cult deities had been superseded by Jesus, the Son of God. What was historically the gradual apotheosis of a Jewish prophet under the influence of Greek-Christian belief and worship was then thrown back upon the Jesus of history and the story of his life and death was related as the Epiphany of the divine Son of God. This stage of Christian development was completed when the author of the Fourth Gospel completely re-wrote the narrative of the life of Jesus, and borrowed the language of Greek philosophy in order to interpret his significance for the world. He was the Logos incarnate.

Thus Christianity became a mystery religion which tended increasingly to express its doctrines in terms of Greek philosophy. In other words, by the beginning of the second century the main features of Catholic Christianity had been evolved. In one respect, however, Christianity was infinitely superior to all other mystery religions. Christian immortality was morally conditioned to an extent which is not found elsewhere. Initiation involved moral conversion, and the Eucharist involved a moral conformity to the footprints of the Son of God, the *vestigia Christi*. In this way the teaching of the Jesus of history was preserved within the growing Catholic Church ; it was not altogether submerged under the mythical interpretation of his person. This moral sincerity ultimately saved Christianity from the fate of other mystery religions. They perished, but it endured. The gradual disappearance of the Jesus of history, however, constituted a grave danger to the persistence within Catholicism even of this moral earnestness.

The rediscovery of the Jesus of history in our own days by the application of the historical method to the study of the earliest Christian documents, and the consequent reconstruction of the development which issued in the Catholic Church of the second century, is far more than a monument to the skill and honesty of the historian. A basis is now provided for a new reformation of the Christian religion, capable of ensuring its survival in the modern world. In the Gospel of Jesus is to be found the pure religion of civilised and united humanity. Thus the assured results of liberal historical criticism form as necessary a prelude to the Christianity of the future as the preaching of John the Baptist did to the original proclamation of the Gospel.

## III

### Its Reflection in Catholic Modernism

This reconstruction of the origin and development of primitive Christianity is undeniably attractive, not so much on account of the sanction which it gives to modern idealistic humanitarianism, but because for the first time Christian historians have presented a rational account of the relation between the Gospel of Jesus and the Catholic Religion, on the basis of a critical analysis of the documents contained in the New Testament. The method is historical and the conclusions are supported by evidence drawn from the documents themselves. These conclusions have not left even Catholic scholars unmoved, and Catholic Modernism is, in one of its aspects, an attempt to explain and defend Catholicism on the basis of this historical reconstruction. It is maintained that Catholicism is the result of a development in which the Gospel of Jesus formed but one element. The dogmas of the Church and its sacrificial sacramentalism are pagan in origin, and for this reason can be shown to correspond to demands essentially human. Catholicism is a synthesis between the Gospel of Jesus and popular pagan religion ; and, because it is a synthesis, Catholicism can claim to be the universal religion.[1] Thus, while Liberal Protestantism tends to find the religion of the future safeguarded by the discovery of the Jesus of history, and by the consequent liberation from the accretions of Catholicism, so foreign to the modern mind,[2] Catholic Modernism welcomes the broadening of the basis of Christianity, due to the recognition of its having preserved and purified the mythology and worship of countless ages of men, and feels no regret that a way of escape from the tyranny of a Jewish prophet has been so solidly secured by the historical and critical approach to the study of the New Testament.

The conclusions, which give this newly discovered liberty the sanction of unprejudiced and scientific historical research, have, however, been shown to be open to very severe criticism, which is by no means confined to those who may be suspected of a desire to defend orthodoxy. These critics do not only question the details of the reconstruction ; they judge the whole to have sprung less from a nice historical sense, than from an impatient anxiety to interpret primitive Christianity " in terms of modern thought." [3]

Those who regard the writing of history as a gentlemanly accomplishment which requires little more than sufficient leisure to ascertain the relevant facts, and a certain facility for embodying them in adequate literary form, not unnaturally discover in the

---

[1] Loisy ably defended Catholicism along these lines in his *L'Évangile et l'Église* (esp. chap. iv). The book was a criticism of Harnack's *What is Christianity?* and of A. Sabatier's *Esquisse d'une Philosophie de la Religion.* Loisy's point of view was developed by G. Tyrrell in *Through Scylla and Charybdis* and in *Christianity at the Cross-Roads* ; it appears in more modern form in Friedrich Heiler's recent book, *Der Katholizismus* (esp. pp. 17–78, 595–660).

[2] "Above all, the figure of Jesus stands out all the more grandly as the mists of theological speculation are blown away from him, and we come to discern him as he really sojourned on earth. It is not too much to say that by recovering for us the historical life of Jesus criticism has brought Christianity back to the true source of its power. The creeds, whatever may have been their value formerly, have broken down, but Jesus as we know him in his life, and all the more as his life is freed from accretions of legend, still commands the world's reverence and devotion. The theology of the future, it is not rash to prophesy, will start from the interpretation of Jesus as a man in history."—E. F. Scott, *The New Testament To-day*, pp. 89 ff.

[3] G. A. van der Bergh van Eysinga, *Radical Views about the New Testament* ; Arthur Drews, *The Christ Myth* ; P. L. Couchoud, *The Enigma of Jesus*, preface by Sir J. G. Frazer ; V. H. Stanton, *The Gospels as Historical Documents* ; Pierre Batiffol, *The Credibility of the Gospels.* To these must be added the learned and voluminous writings of Theodor Zahn. These authors agree in recognising that the Gospels stand within the sphere of Christian orthodoxy ; they disagree, however, completely as to their historical value.

disagreements of the critics nothing more than a fresh instance of that persistent and irrational hatred which theologians are commonly supposed to feel for one another.  Those who assume that the Gospel of Jesus was a simple gospel are equally irritated by the inability of the critics to reach agreed conclusions, and attribute this disagreement to the innate tendency of the academic mind first to complicate what is obvious, and then to perform mental gymnastics as prodigious as they are unnecessary.  Books written under the influence of such prejudices are, however, calculated rather to inflame the imagination than to sharpen the intellect, and fail to lead to an accurate appreciation of the canons of historical criticism or of the peculiar problems which confront the historian of the beginnings of Christianity.

English theologians, trained in the study of the Classics, and accustomed to an exacting standard of scholarly accuracy, have looked with suspicion on such popular accounts of Christian origins, and have shown far less confidence in the "assured results of modern criticism" than their colleagues in Germany, Holland,[1] and France.  The effect of this tradition of learned conservatism has been that, whilst English theologians have made important contributions to the study of the history of the text of the New Testament, to the literary analysis of the first three Gospels, technically known as the Synoptic Problem, and to the exegesis of the various books of the New Testament, they have generally refrained from attempting any comprehensive reconstruction of the development of primitive Christianity on the basis of these exhaustive preliminary studies, and have been content mainly with a criticism of the critics.

## IV

### NEED OF A SYNTHETIC SOLUTION

It can hardly be denied that English theology stands at the cross-roads.  The preliminary studies with which it has been chiefly concerned are now on the whole so well-worn that the results have passed into the textbooks ; and the attempt to force the energy of all the younger men into these channels threatens to involve them in work which must be largely unproductive.  On

---

[1] Eldred C. Vanderlaan, *Protestant Modernism in Holland*, provides a useful survey of recent Dutch literature ; cf. K. H. Roessingh, *De moderne Theologie in Nederland*, and *Het Modernisme in Nederland*.

the other hand, the analysis of the religious experience within primitive Christianity, and of the beliefs by which it was stimulated, offers a new line of approach to the history of Christian origins, and provides a field of investigation almost untouched, except by those who have little or no first-hand knowledge of the necessary prolegomena. If this be a correct statement of the present situation, there can be little doubt that the time has come for English theology to make its contribution to the study of Christian beginnings, a contribution which may be all the more valuable for this long preparatory discipline. An examination of the reconstruction outlined above provides a convenient point of departure. Should it survive the examination, it only remains to perfect the whole by a greater attention to detail ; if it be found unsatisfactory, an alternative reconstruction must be attempted and submitted to the judgment of scholars. The main purpose of this essay is to state the problem afresh, and to indicate the lines along which a solution may perhaps be found.

## 1. *Literary Structure of the Gospels*

The literary analysis of the four Gospels has shown that the first three Gospels are closely related documents. Both St. Luke and the editor of St. Matthew's Gospel made use of St. Mark's Gospel in approximately its present form, and also of an early Christian collection of the sayings of Jesus. Since both writers, apparently independently, made constant use of the same documents, it may not unreasonably be deduced that they regarded them as of especial importance. In addition to the material common to the First and Third Gospels each editor has incorporated into his narrative special material not found elsewhere. Therefore, if St. Mark's Gospel be called $M$, St. Matthew's Gospel $T$, St. Luke's Gospel $L$, the collection of sayings $Q$, the special material in St. Matthew's Gospel $S_1$, and the special material in St. Luke's Gospel $S_2$, $T$ is composed from $M + Q + S_1$ and $L$ from $M + Q + S_2$. But it must not be assumed that the editors incorporated their sources unchanged. They show considerable freedom in the use of their sources, a freedom which is however considerably curtailed when they record actual sayings of Jesus. The literary construction of the First and Third Gospels may therefore be expressed by the formulae $T (M + Q + S_1)$ and

M

$L (M + Q + S2)$.   The first three Gospels depend ultimately upon tradition, which was preserved not in the interest of accurate history, but for the guidance and encouragement of the Christians.   It is therefore always possible that the tradition may have been transformed before it was committed to writing.   It must be borne in mind, however, that the belief that the same Jesus who had been taken from them into heaven would return in like manner may well have been more powerful in preserving an accurate tradition of His words than any theory of unprejudiced historical investigation.

The Fourth Gospel occupies a peculiar position in the New Testament.   In form it is a narrative of the actions and sayings of Jesus ; that is, it is a Gospel.   In substance it is primarily an interpretation of Christianity in the light of Christian experience. The author has no doubt made use of oral tradition, or of a part or the whole of the Synoptic Gospels, or of apostolic reminiscences, or of all of these, but they have been transformed in such a way that it is almost impossible to disengage the tradition from the interpretation.   Therefore, whereas the historian is free to make full use of the Fourth Gospel in describing the Christian religion at the close of the first century, it is dangerous for him to use it as an authority for the earliest form of the Christian tradition.

Since none of the Gospels can have been written down in their present form before the second half of the first century, the Pauline Epistles are the earliest written Christian documents which survive.   The Epistles, therefore, offer important evidence of the primitive Christian tradition in those passages where St. Paul refers to the teaching he had " received," and where, when writing to those who had not been converted through his preaching, he assumes certain beliefs to be held by all Christians alike.

If this literary analysis be accepted as sound, it follows that though the documents do not provide sufficient material for a detailed " life of Jesus," they ought not to be dismissed as entirely untrustworthy.   There is no reason to assume that the characteristic features of His teaching could not have been accurately preserved, or even that incidents recorded as giving rise to sayings of especial importance were entirely due to the creative imagination of the Christians.   This, however, needs careful testing.

The investigation of the origins of Christianity must begin with the exegesis of St. Mark's Gospel $(M)$ and of the sayings common to Matthew and Luke (*Q*), and then proceed to an examination of the Matthean-Lucan corrections of *M* and of the variant forms in which the *Q* source has been preserved. The treatment of the special material (*S*1, *S*2) is best reserved until this has been completed, since the valuable check afforded by a comparison of Matthew and Luke is no longer available.

Assuming the exegesis of *M*, *Q*, *S*1, *S*2 and of the Matthean-Lucan corrections of *M* and *Q* to have been completed, two important questions arise. Do these surviving extracts from primitive Christian tradition agree or disagree in their description of the Gospel proclaimed by Jesus ? and Do they agree or disagree with the tradition received by St. Paul ?

The Synoptic Tradition consists of sayings, miracles, parables, and a careful record of the events which immediately preceded the crucifixion. A Gospel as a literary form emerges when, not merely the events immediately preceding the crucifixion, but the whole tradition is arranged and narrated as the Way of the Cross crowned by the resurrection. This arrangement gives unity to the whole, and the reader is hardly conscious of the fragmentary nature of the parts. Whence came this order ? Was it a literary device of the Evangelists ? Was it the result of the faith of the Christians ?[1] or did it go back to the Lord Himself ? No reconstruction of the Gospel of Jesus is possible unless it is possible to answer these questions.

The unity which is achieved by ordering the material so as to secure movement towards a fixed point is also achieved by the central position given to the Kingdom of God, or of Heaven, as a concrete reality ; the whole tradition, including the narrative of the crucifixion, being brought into the closest relationship with it. The recognition of this unity of direction and standpoint leads, however, to a simplification more apparent than real. The Kingdom eludes definition. It is both present and future. The full significance of the phrase " the Kingdom of God " is presumed to be intelligible only to those who believe in Jesus as the Christ, and yet when Peter declares his belief, the obscure title Son of Man is

[1] The literary structure of the Gospels has been minutely examined by three German scholars since the war. The conclusion arrived at is that the Gospel framework is a literary creation, which emerged from the Hellenistic Christian community ; *cf.* K. L. Schmidt, *Der Rahmen der Geschichte Jesu,* 1919 ; M. Dibelius, *Formgeschichte des Evangeliums,* 1919 ; R. Bultmann, *Die Geschichte der synoptischen Tradition,* 1921.

substituted for that of the Christ (Mark iv. 11, viii. 29–32). Thus the Christology underlies the idea of the Kingdom, and the title Son of Man underlies the Christology, and the eschatology underlies the whole. The problem which has to be solved can be clearly formulated. Is this complexity due to the existence within the Synoptic Tradition of various strata of Christian piety with which the original tradition has been successively overlaid, or is the origin of this obscurity to be sought in the life and teaching of Jesus ? If it be maintained that the latter is demanded by the evidence of the documents, then a synthesis of the apparently divergent elements in His teaching must be found.

## 2. *Canons of Historical Criticism*

No solution of these intricate problems is possible without strict adherence to carefully defined canons of historical criticism. Some of these need stating by way of illustration. (1) Passages which do not occur in the earliest documentary sources, but which are found in later sources, should not be dismissed as necessarily originating at the date of the document in which they are found. Therefore $S1$ and $S2$ may be as valuable as $M$ and $Q$. They may be even more primitive. (2) Editorial corrections of an older document need not necessarily be bad corrections. If a document be open to misinterpretation, an editorial correction, however clumsy, may nevertheless correctly elucidate its meaning. Therefore the Matthean-Lucan alterations of $M$ and $Q$ require careful and sympathetic attention. For example, " Blessed are the poor *in spirit* " (Matt. v. 3) may well be an admirable gloss on the saying recorded by St. Luke, " Blessed are ye poor " (Luke vi. 20). (3) If a word occurs only in a comparatively late document, it does not follow that what is expressed by the word is secondary. Therefore, for example, from the fact that the word " Church " is not found in the Synoptic Gospels except in $S1$, and then only twice (Matt. xvi. 18, xviii. 17), it cannot be assumed that the existence of a corporate body of believers, into which men and women could enter and from which they could be excluded, did not form an integral part of primitive Christian tradition.[1] (4) If the analysis of a document disentangles distinct strata of subject-matter, it must not

[1] Commenting on Matt. xvi. 18, Montefiore writes : " This passage could only have been written after the death of Jesus, for the Christian community was hardly founded by Jesus, but only after his death on the basis of his supposed

be presumed that the dates of their origin can be arranged in definite chronological order.[1] Therefore, if the analysis of the Gospels reveals Jesus as a prophet, as the Messiah, and as the Saviour of the world, and His teaching as consisting of moral exhortations, of eschatological predictions, and of the promise of supernatural regeneration and immortality, it does not follow that this represents merely successive stages in the development of Christian faith and experience. And as a rider to this it also follows that, in dealing with religious texts which chiefly record supernatural events, and yet contain much that is normal and human, it must not be assumed that what can easily be paralleled from human experience is historical, and that what is supernatural has been superimposed by the irrational credulity of later enthusiastic believers. It must, nevertheless, be allowed that an experience felt to be supernatural tends to be expressed symbolically, and the symbolical language or actions are capable of misinterpretation as literal fact, without, however, the symbolism being thereby necessarily obscured. Alterations in religious texts, which appear at first sight to be caused merely by a " love of heightening the miraculous," are more often due to an instinctive desire to perfect the symbolism in such a way that the reality may thereby be given more vivid and adequate expression. Therefore, for example, when it is found that $S2$ contains a parable, the subject of which is the destruction

resurrection." With this may be compared the interpretation of Matt. xviii. 15–18 given by Estlin Carpenter: " The church whose authority may be invoked is very different from the Master's ' Kingdom of God ' ; and the rejection of the evil doer on to the level of the heathen or the publican hardly savours of the tireless love which came to seek and to save the lost. Here, likewise, may we not say, the practice of the later community seeks shelter under the Founder's sanction" (*The First Three Gospels*, chap. i. 4). Compare the conclusion most solemnly stated by H. Holtzmann : " Therefore it is generally recognised that Mt. (in xviii. 17) has substituted the Church for the Kingdom of God just as he has done in xvi. 18, 19. To-day, the impossibility of finding in Jesus a founder of a church is accepted by all theologians who can be taken seriously " (*N. T. Theologie*, 2nd Ed., vol. ii, p. 268, n. 3).

[1] Upon this assumption Bousset built the theory which he elaborately developed in *Kyrios Christos :* " There will emerge from the presentation (i.e. of the history of the Christology) a clear distinction between the original community in Palestine and in Jerusalem, and between Jerusalem and Antioch. At the same time it will, I hope, become clear how far Paul belongs pre-eminently to the Hellenistic primitive communities, thus making a contribution to the solution of the great problem of the relation between Paul and Jesus. The first two chapters of my book, which treat of the primitive community in Jerusalem, form also no more than the introduction, the starting-point, for the presentation which follows " (*Kyrios Christos*, p. vi).

of a fig-tree (Luke xiii. 6–9), and that *M* includes an incident in which a fig-tree is cursed and destroyed (Mark xi. 12–21) it is possible that the latter is a later form of the former. But in both cases the fig-tree symbolises Judaism, which failed to produce the fruit (righteousness) demanded by the Messiah, and the transformation of the parable into a miracle emphasises rather than obscures the symbolism. Considerable portions of the Synoptic Tradition may perhaps have been influenced by similar transformations.

Finally, (5) In cases where a word or a phrase in an ancient document can be translated or paraphrased by a word or phrase in common use at a later period, it does not follow that the meaning of the original is best reproduced by such a translation or paraphrase : it may be even completely obscured. For instance, " Thou art my beloved Son " seems an obvious rendering of the original Greek in the narrative of the Baptism (Mark i. 11, Luke iii. 22), but the suggestion of uniqueness, which belongs to the Greek word ἀγαπητός [1] is in no way reproduced by the English word " beloved." Hence the use of such phrases as " the call of Jesus," or " the supreme intuition of his divine mission," [2] tends to obscure the meaning of the passage, by employing easily understood language to paraphrase language which is strange and allusive.

### 3. *Fallacies in the Liberal Protestant Reconstruction*

Tested by such canons as these, the popular reconstruction of the various stages in the development of primitive Christianity is found to rest upon a series of brilliant and attractive intuitive judgments rather than upon a critical and historical examination of the data supplied by the documents. *S*1 and *S*2 are used just in so far as they are convenient. The parable of the Prodigal Son (Luke xv. 11–32, *S*2) is held to be original because forgiveness of sin is not complicated by any reference to the atoning death of the Christ, whilst the speech at Nazareth (Luke iv. 16–30, *S*2), which concludes with the prophecy of the rejection of Jesus by the Jews and of His acceptance by the Gentiles, is treated as a Lucan

---

[1] Cf. *The Journal of Theological Studies*, July 1919, pp. 339 ff., Jan. 1926, pp. 113 ff., and the detached note on " The Beloved " as a Messianic title in Armitage Robinson, *St. Paul's Epistle to the Ephesians*, pp. 229 f.

[2] Loisy, *Évangiles Synoptiques*, i. 408, quoted by Montefiore, *The Synoptic Gospels*, i. 47.

composition [1]; and the important sayings, " But I have a baptism to be baptised with ; and how am I straitened till it be accomplished ! " (Luke xii. 50, *S*2), and " Fear not, little flock ; for it is your Father's good pleasure to give you the kingdom " (Luke xii 32, *S*2) are hardly mentioned. The subject-matter of the Sermon on the Mount is accepted as authentic throughout (Matt. v.–vii., *Q* + *S*1), but no reference is made to the parable of the Drag-net (Matt. xiii. 47–50, *S*1), or to the saying addressed to St. Peter, embedded in the episode of the Stater in the Fish's Mouth, " Therefore the sons are free " (Matt. xvii 26, *S*1).

St. Mark's Gospel is regarded as a primary source, but the narratives of the Stilling of the Storm, the Walking on the Sea, and the Transfiguration are dismissed as altogether untrustworthy, even though they record the awe experienced by the disciples in the presence of Jesus and their halting, stammering questions, " They feared exceedingly, and said one to another, Who then is this ? " (Mark iv. 41), " They were sore amazed in themselves " (Mark vi. 51), " They became sore afraid . . . questioning among themselves what the rising again from the dead should mean " (Mark ix. 6, 10). Nor is any serious attempt made to explain the significant fact that this attitude is accepted and even encouraged by Jesus, which suggests that He regarded a true interpretation of His Person as only possible on the basis of some such experience. Sayings firmly rooted in the tradition, such as

---

[1] Montefiore comments on Luke iv. 14–30 : " Luke now makes a great change from the order of Mark. B. Weiss supposes that in doing this he followed his extra special authority (L) ; it is more probable that the transportation of the rejection in Nazareth to this place, and the variants in, and additions to, the story are entirely the work of the Evangelist. His aim is to symbolise the rejection of the Gospel and the Christ by the Jews, and their acceptance by the Gentiles. The miracles which Jesus is said to work outside Nazareth represent the diffusion of the Gospel beyond Israel. The widow of Sarepta and Naaman are types of Christians who were once heathen" (*Syn. Gosp.*, ii. 872). Commenting, however, on Luke xv. 11–32, he describes the parable of the Prodigal Son as " the purest Judaism," and quotes with approval the remarks of J. Weiss: " The gospel of the grace of God is announced without any reference to the cross or the redemptive work of Christ. There is no hint that the love of God must first be set free, so to speak, or that a redeemer is needed. Jesus trusts in His heavenly Father that without more ado He will give His love to every sinner who comes to God in penitence and humble confidence. Thus our parable is in fact a ' gospel ' in miniature, but not a gospel of Christ or of the cross, but the glad tidings of the love of the heavenly Father for His children " (*Syn. Gosp.* ii. 991 ; cf. Jülicher, *Die Gleichnisreden Jesu*, ii. 365).

" The Son of man is delivered up into the hands of men, and they shall kill him ; and when he is killed, after three days he shall rise again" (Mark ix. 31), or "The Son of man came not to be ministered unto, but to minister, and to give his life a ransom for many " (Mark x. 45), are held to be secondary and to owe their present form either to the influence of Paulinism or to the first efforts of the Christians to create formulas which were developed later into creeds entirely foreign to the teaching of Jesus.

The use in the New Testament of language which can be paralleled from the surviving records of popular Greek and Eastern religious cults is presumed to imply an assimilation of primitive Christian piety to Greek-Oriental models.   The possibility that such language may have expressed and effectually reproduced a relationship to Jesus which existed from the beginning, and which it had been the main purpose of His life and death to evoke, is hardly ever seriously discussed.

The assumption that the original preaching of the Gospel was simple and at once intelligible to ordinary people, and was only misunderstood by the Jewish authorities, whose sympathy had been perverted by hard and unbending ecclesiasticism, underlies the reconstruction outlined above, and conditions the manipulation of the analysis of the subject-matter of the Synoptic Gospels.   What is supernatural is transferred to the period of growth, what is human and merely moral and philanthropic and anti-ecclesiastical is assumed to be primitive and original.   The miracles and the Christological passages are, therefore, treated primarily as presenting literary and historical rather than religious problems. Consequently their value as evidence for the existence of a unique experience dependent upon a unique faith is entirely overlooked. The possibility has, however, to be reckoned with that the experience of salvation through Christ, or as St. Paul calls it, Justification by Faith, rather than an ethical humanitarianism was from the beginning the essence of the Christian religion, and that the conviction of salvation was from the beginning the peculiar possession of the body of the disciples who surrounded Jesus, and that the peculiarly Christian love of God and of men followed, but did not precede, the experience of salvation by faith in Christ, and the incorporation into the body of His disciples.   In other words, not only may the supernatural element have been primitive and original, but also that exclusiveness, which is so obviously a characteristic of Catholic Christianity, may have its origin in the teaching of Jesus rather than in the theology of St. Paul.

These criticisms are not, however, wholly to the point unless the exegesis of the Marcan narrative of the Baptism, upon which the whole reconstruction ultimately rests, can be shown to be unsatisfactory and misleading. It is claimed that the natural meaning of the narrative is that Jesus, conscious of the need of repentance, and therefore possessing a sense of sin, came to be baptised by John. At the moment of His baptism He passed through a religious experience, of which He alone was conscious, and that He then felt Himself called to associate Himself with the work of the Baptist. Thus, in spite of all the later Christological accretions, there is preserved in St. Mark's Gospel a genuine reminiscence of the consecration of Jesus to the work of a prophet, in the light of which the claim to the Messiahship, if He did make the claim, must be interpreted. The Matthean version of the Baptism shows the early church in the process of obliterating all traces of this human experience by the insertion of the preliminary conversation between Jesus and John, and by the substitution of " This is my beloved Son " for " Thou art my beloved Son," which has the effect of transforming an intimate personal experience into a public proclamation of Jesus as the Messiah (Mt. iii. 13–17, $M + S1$).

But is the Marcan narrative really capable of such psychological treatment ? And is it necessary to convict Matthew of such wilful and unprincipled editing ? The Second Gospel opens with the description of John the Baptist as the forerunner of the Christ, preparing " the way of the Lord," and proclaiming the advent of the Messiah to baptise with the Holy Spirit. Jesus is then immediately introduced, coming unknown and unrecognised among the crowd, and His baptism is narrated as the fulfilment of the great Messianic passages in Isaiah xi. 1–9, xlii. 1–4, lxi. 1–3, and in Psalm ii. 7. Most significantly the latter half of the citation from the Psalm (ii. 7), " This day have I begotten thee," is omitted, and an echo of Isaiah xlii. 1, " In whom I am well pleased," substituted for it.[1] No less significant is the inser-

---

[1] The citation from Ps. ii. 7 is completed in some manuscripts of the Lucan version of the Baptism (D a b c ff²). Canon Streeter considers this to be the original reading of Luke iii. 22 (*The Four Gospels*, pp. 143, 276). It is more easily explained as an assimilation to the Psalm. Even if it were original in Luke, its Christological significance cannot be unduly pressed, since in Acts xiii. 33 the citation is applied to the resurrection.

tion of the word " beloved," which at least suggests uniqueness, and may be a synonym for "only begotten." [1]   Thus the intelligent reader, who is expected to feel the allusions, is from the outset initiated into the secret of the Messiahship of Jesus.   The question as to whether there was or was not a moment when He became the Son of God is neither raised nor answered by the Evangelist. Having made it perfectly plain that Jesus is the Christ, the Son of God, he proceeds to record the steps by which the disciples were led to accept Him as the Messiah.   The introduction to the Gospel which consists of the preaching of John the Baptist, and the account of the Baptism of Jesus, must therefore be interpreted by the whole narrative which follows, and especially by the Transfiguration, the Crucifixion, and the Resurrection.

If the Marcan narrative be open to this interpretation, the Matthean corrections admit of a comparatively simple explanation. They do not involve the transformation of a human prophet into a supernatural Messiah, since the Marcan source itself implies a supernatural Christology.   They do, however, gloss over the reiterated emphasis laid by St. Mark on the fact that the Messiahship of Jesus was recognised by none except by the evil spirits until the confession of Peter, and that it was not proclaimed in public until the trial before Caiaphas.   The use of the baptismal narratives for an analysis of the religious experience of Jesus is at best a very hazardous procedure, and almost inevitably results in confining His experience within a framework supplied by an incomplete knowledge of the psychology of vocation.

The conclusion to which these arguments have been leading is that, so far as the subject-matter of the Gospel is concerned, no one of the Synoptic Gospels can be contrasted with the others, nor can portions of the Gospels be set over against the remainder, nor is there any evidence of the existence of older lost Christian documents which contradict those which survive.   The main problem of the origin of Christianity can, therefore, be stated with considerable precision.   Was this unity of subject-matter achieved in the period between the crucifixion and the date when the Christian tradition was first committed to writing ?   Or did

---

[1] In the LXX the Hebrew word יָחִיד is translated indiscriminately by μονογενής or ἀγαπητός (Judg. xi. 34; Tob. iii. 15, vi. 14, Ps. xxxv. 17; Gen. xxii. 2, 12, 16, Am. viii. 10, Jer. vi. 26 ; cf. Mk. xii. 6, Lk. xx. 13, vii. 12, viii. 42, ix. 38).   See references, p. 166, note 1.

it originate with the teaching of Jesus ? In solving this problem the personal judgment of the historian can never be wholly eliminated. For example, even if it be granted that the Marcan narrative of the Baptism implies a supernatural Christology, it is still possible for the critic to claim that Mark was himself influenced by a developing Christology, and that he has allowed his narrative to be controlled by it. This must, however, remain no more than a supposition so long as it is supported by no documentary evidence ; and the necessity for some such supposition is considerably reduced if it can be shown that the elements which together form the subject-matter of the Gospels are capable of a synthesis.

## V

### GOVERNING IDEAS OF THE GOSPELS

#### 1. *The Kingdom of God*

The petitions of the Lord's Prayer, " Thy Kingdom come. Thy will be done, in earth as it is in heaven," indicate that the phrase " the Kingdom of God," or " of Heaven," is more than a poetical representation of an ideal. It presumes that the Kingdom of God exists in heaven. In the immediate presence of God His sovereignty is complete and absolute, and heaven is the sphere in which that sovereignty operates perfectly and eternally. The genitives which qualify the word " Kingdom " are primarily genitives of origin. If the Kingdom is to be established on earth, it must come from God or from Heaven. Thus the salvation of men, that is their incorporation into the sphere in which the sovereignty of God operates, is only possible either by their ascension into the heavens, or by the descent and extension of the supernatural order from heaven to earth. Salvation is therefore conceived of as necessarily dependent upon an act of God. The conception that the human order can be transformed into the Kingdom of Heaven by a process of gradual evolution is completely foreign to the New Testament.

The Synoptic Gospels assume throughout that the supernatural order has descended to earth. The Kingdom has come. The Beelzebul speech (Mark iii. 20–30, Matt. xii. 22–30, Luke xi. 14–23), in which our Lord's interpretation of His miracles, of the call of the disciples, and of their acceptance of His call is recorded, gives this classical expression.   Beelzebul, the Prince of the evil spirits, has usurped authority over men, and has become, as his name indicates, the master of the house (*cf.* Matt. x. 25).[1]   The miracles of Jesus are effectual signs that a stronger than Beelzebul has come.   The Mighty One is robbing the Prince of evil of his authority, and spoiling his goods.   When the twelve accepted the call of Jesus, they passed from the sovereignty of Beelzebul under the authority of the Christ ; and the family of Jesus who do the will of God is thus sharply distinguished from the house of Beelzebul (Mark iii. 33-35, *cf.* Matt. xii. 30, Luke xi. 23).   But the underlying distinction is between the Kingdom of God and of His Christ, and the Kingdom of Satan.   The Matthean-Lucan addition to the Marcan narrative, " Then the kingdom of God is come upon you " (Matt. xii. 28, Luke xi. 20), is admirably appropriate.   The authority of Satan is undermined by the advent of the Christ, and by the descent of the Kingdom of God (*cf.* Luke x. 18).   The new supernatural order has descended upon earth, and is realised in Jesus and His disciples.   Because He is the Christ from heaven, they have become the sons of the Kingdom and the Messianic people of God, to whom the mystery of the Kingdom has been given.   The true love of God and of men is thus embodied in a living organism.

Judaism is, therefore, superseded and fulfilled.   The authority exercised by the chief priests and scribes and Pharisees passes to the disciples of the Christ, and especially to the twelve apostles, who as the twelve patriarchs of the new people of God are to lead the Messianic mission to the world, to cast out devils and fish for men.   Finally, they will sit on twelve thrones judging the twelve tribes of Israel : " Fear not, little flock ; for it is your Father's good pleasure to give you the kingdom " (Luke xii. 32, xxii. 28-30, Matt. xix. 28, *cf.* Mark i. 17, xii. 9).   This radical attitude to Judaism, which gives point to the parable of the Wicked Husbandmen and to the Cursing of the Fig-Tree, underlies the whole of our Lord's teaching.   Judaism is superseded, not because a new

---

[1] The name *Beelzebul* may mean either *Lord of dung* or *Lord of the habitation*.   Mt. x. 25, and the whole sense of the Beelzebul speech, seem to demand a play upon words.   Jesus is the true, Beelzebul the false, *Lord of the house*. The variant reading *Beelezebub*, which occurs in no Greek manuscript, is best explained by assimilation to 2 Kings, i. 2, 6, when the significance of the name *Beelzebul* was not understood (*cf.* Swete, *St. Mark* ad Mk. iii. 22).

prophet has arisen, but because the Messiah has come and effected the purification of the heart and brought into being the new People of God.    The Messianic Kingdom has arrived and Judaism is fulfilled by the advent of the Messiah and by the actual righteousness which belief in Jesus carried with it.    Of this Messianic purification and illumination the miracles are signs and symbols.    The blind who see, the dumb who speak, the lepers who are cleansed, the hungry who are fed, and the dead who are raised have their more important counterparts in the apostolic vision of the Christ at the Transfiguration, in St. Peter's convinced declaration after a long period of inarticulate stammering that Jesus is the Christ, in the cleansing of Mary Magdalene, Levi, and Zacchaeus, in the Eucharistic bread and wine, and in the eternal life which is promised to those who leave all and follow Jesus.    The apostles, having heard the call of the Christ and having been incorporated into the supernatural order of the Kingdom, are the true believers in God and the true lovers of men, and as such are given especial authority. They are the salt of the earth, and to them is entrusted the Messianic purification of the world.


## 2. *The Humiliation of the Christ*

During the earthly ministry of the Christ all this is veiled in obscurity, not because the Kingdom will only come with the end of the world, but because He must first complete His work.    The humiliation of the Christ of divine necessity (Mark viii. 31) precedes the apostolic mission to the world, because this mission, to be effective, depends upon His death and glorification.    Until this is accomplished His disciples are ignorant both of the meaning of His life and teaching and of their own significance for the world. The humiliation of the Christ underlies the Synoptic Tradition throughout, and is carefully emphasised, as a comparison with the Apocalypse clearly shows.    He was subject to temptation, His power was dependent upon faith and prayer, the sphere of His work was limited to Jews resident in Palestine, He was compelled to face the united opposition of the Jewish authorities.    He spoke in parables and His actions were symbolic, because the Gospel could not be nakedly expressed.    Of this humiliation the crucifixion was both the climax and the completion, for by it the Christ was both freed and glorified.

" I have a baptism to be baptised with ; and how am I straitened till it be accomplished ! " (Luke xii. 50).

" The Son of man must suffer many things, and be rejected by the elders, and the chief priests, and the scribes, and be killed, and after three days rise again " (Mark viii. 31).

The death of the Christ was, however, far more than a necessary stage in His personal glorification; it inaugurated a new order, as the sacrifice on Mount Sinai inaugurated the Old Covenant. Our Lord's words at the Last Supper must be taken primarily as assigning to His death redemptive significance.

### 3. *The Via Crucis*

It is not, however, suggested that this liberty of the Christ, accomplished through His death and glorification, will carry with it at once the liberty of His disciples. They must remain in the world and succeed to His former position. If He was the humiliated Son of God, they are to be the humiliated sons of God. The persecuted and humiliated Christ is to be succeeded by the persecuted and humiliated disciples ; but whereas His work was limited to Jews, the sphere of their work will not be thus bounded (Mark xiii. 9–13, 27). In other respects they must follow in His footsteps. Possessing supernatural power, they will be tempted from within and from without to misuse it ; their power will be dependent, as His was, upon faith and prayer ; they must take up their cross, for they also will be brought before governors and kings for His sake [1] ; they must be willing to die. For some, as for Judas, these demands will prove too severe and they will return whence they had been rescued—that is, they will pass from the Kingdom of God to the Kingdom of Beelzebul. Into this life of Christian humiliation the disciples were initiated by the words spoken at the Last Supper. The Last Supper, therefore, both

---

[1] Professor Burkitt (*Christian Beginnings*, p. 147) holds that " governors and kings " (Mark xiii. 9) are Roman officials and Herods in Palestine, and that " the mental horizon is still Palestine, not a formal worldwide evangelization." In the context, however, in which the saying stands, the horizon is not Palestine merely (xiii. 8, 13, 27). The eschatological mission of salvation before the End can, it is true, hardly be described as a *formal* evangelization. Mark xiii. contains no suggestion of *formality*. If it be granted that the chapter refers to an eschatological mission which, after the death of the Lord, the disciples are to lead beyond the boundaries of Palestine, there seems every reason to regard Mark xiii. as, at least, reminiscent of words spoken by Jesus.

gave formally to the death of the Christ its redemptive value and also formally initiated the disciples into the mystical and actual participation in His sacrifice and of its benefits. The disciples must share in His *broken* Body and His *outpoured* Blood. Only thus could they be enabled to continue His work, to share in His victory over sin and death, to take up their cross confidently and follow Him, and to endure the hostility of the world until the End.

### 4. *The New Righteousness and Eternal Life*

The Synoptic Tradition presumes eternal life to be dependent on moral conversion effected by belief in the Christ and by incorporation into the body of the disciples of Jesus. The apostolic Gospel, therefore, is both a gospel of supernatural moral purification and a gospel of immortality. Possessing the supernatural righteousness of the heart, the disciples possess also eternal life, and those who have received and maintained this righteousness need not fear the Judgment which is to come. The Christian gospel of immortality has its roots in Jewish eschatology as transformed by our Lord, rather than in the cycle of ideas and experiences characteristic of Greek-Oriental mystery cults.

The character of the new Messianic righteousness, upon which the Christian hope of ultimate immortality is based, is illustrated in our Lord's teaching on marriage and divorce. Moses, He allowed, wisely permitted divorce, because of the hardness of men's hearts, and Judaism rightly followed his teaching. But with the coming of the Christ and the consequent entrance of those who believe on Him into the sovereignty of God, this hardness of heart has been removed, and His disciples can not only, therefore, fulfil the law of God promulgated in the second chapter of Genesis, " Therefore shall a man leave his father and his mother, and shall cleave unto his wife : and they shall be one flesh " (Gen. ii. 24, quoted Mark x. 7, 8, Matt. xix. 5), but they can even, for the sake of the Kingdom, remain celibate without falling into sin (Matt. xix. 12). Hence adultery and fornication among Christians are not to be regarded as lapses from a moral law, but as apostasy from the Kingdom. Similarly, the purpose of the Sermon on the Mount is to describe the new Messianic righteousness by which the old is authoritatively superseded and fulfilled, rather than to construct a new moral law on the basis of the old. Still less is the Sermon on the Mount a loosely constructed list of ideal moral virtues. The advent of the Christ and the existence of the Messianic community which He has brought into being are presumed throughout. The most serious humiliation of the Christians is that this righteousness which they have received has to be maintained in the face of manifold temptations, and may be lost. It is possible for the salt to lose its savour, and of this Judas becomes the terrible symbol.

The emphasis on the humiliation of the Christ and on the subsequent humiliation of His disciples is crossed by the eschatology which alone renders the whole position tolerable and intelligible. Though the humiliation of the Christ ends with His death and resurrection, the humiliation of His Ecclesia must last until He returns, not this time unknown and unrecognised, but in glory, on the clouds, and visible to all. Then the righteous will be separated from the unrighteous, and the Kingdom will be established in glory and for ever. The final reunion of the Christ and His disciples is also foreshadowed in the words spoken at the Last Supper. The Eucharist looks forward beyond the humiliation of the Christ, beyond the humiliation of His disciples, to the time when it will be no longer possible for them to share in the sacrifice of His body and blood, for He will drink the wine new with them in the Kingdom of God (Mark xiv. 25). The Eucharist is, therefore, as St. Paul says, the commemoration of the Lord's death " *till he come* " (1 Cor. xi. 26). But when the Kingdom will come in glory, or when the Christ will return, no one can know ; of this even the Christ Himself was ignorant. Only this is certain : the Gospel must first be preached to all nations, and, what is a far more difficult task, it must be preached in all the cities of Israel. But the impression given by the Synoptic Gospels is that the End will not be long delayed.

## VI

### CONCLUSION

From this reconstruction it will be seen at once that a whole series of contrasts underlies the Synoptic Tradition. These contrasts, however, do not break the unity of the whole, since they are capable of synthesis. The failure of most modern scholars to formulate the contrasts correctly has led to their failure to recognise the possibility of a synthesis. The contrast is not between the

Jesus of history and the Christ of faith, but between the Christ humiliated, and the Christ returning in glory ; the two being held together by the title Son of Man which suggests both (Ezek. ii. 1, Psalm viii. 4–6, Dan. vii. 13, 14, interpreted by Enoch xlvi. 2, 2 Esdras xiii.) : " The Son of man must suffer " (Mark viii. 31) ; " The Son of man hath not where to lay his head " (Luke ix. 58) ; " Ye shall see the Son of man sitting at the right hand of power, and coming with the clouds of heaven " (Mark xiv. 62) ; " And he said unto his disciples, The days will come when ye shall desire to see one of the days of the Son of man, and ye shall not see it. And they shall say to you, Lo, there ! Lo, here ! go not away, nor follow after them : for as the lightning, when it lighteneth out of the one part under the heaven, shineth unto the other part under heaven ; so shall the Son of man be in his day. But first must he suffer many things and be rejected of this generation " (Luke xvii. 22–25). The double significance of the title Son of Man may have caused our Lord to use it for the interpretation of His Person, in preference to the easily misunderstood title " the Christ." The contrast is not between a reformed and an unreformed Judaism, but between Judaism and the new supernatural order by which it is at once destroyed and fulfilled : not between the disciples of a Jewish prophet and the members of an ecclesiastically ordered sacramental cultus, but between the disciples of Jesus, who, though translated into the sovereignty of God, are as yet ignorant both of His claims and of the significance of their own conversion, and the same disciples, initiated into the mystery of His Person and of His life and death, leading the mission to the world, the patriarchs of the new Israel of God. The contrast is not between an ethical teaching and a dreamy eschatology, or between a generous humanitarianism and an emotional religious experience stimulated by mythological beliefs, but between a supernatural order characterised by a radical moral purification involving persistent moral conflict and the endurance of persecution, and a supernatural order in which there is no place either for moral conflict or for persecution. Thus stated the contrasts are capable of synthesis by a fairly simple view of history. Judaism is fulfilled by the advent of the Christ, who inaugurates the new order, which is the Kingdom of God on earth. The existence, however, of the Kingdom of God and of the kingdoms of the world together involves conflict and opposition, which is to last till the return of the Christ and the final destruction

N

of evil, when the Kingdom will come in earth as it is in heaven, or, to use St. Paul's phrase, when God shall be all in all.

A synthesis of the contradictory elements within the Synoptic Tradition having been thus achieved, the last step in the historical reconstruction of the origin of the Christian religion is almost inevitable. This was the Gospel proclaimed by Jesus, and these were the claims made by the Jesus of history for Himself and for His disciples. Ultimately this conclusion is, and must be, a subjective judgment, but it is a conclusion from which it is exceedingly difficult to escape.

It remains only to point out what is gained by this alternative reconstruction. The historian is freed from the necessity of being compelled to assume that a foreign influence was exerted upon primitive Christianity between the crucifixion and the appearance of the earliest Pauline Epistles, and he is therefore enabled to treat the development represented by the Pauline Epistles, the Johannine writings, and the literature of the Catholic Church of the second century primarily as a spontaneous Christian development. The commentator will find that the New Testament is one book, not merely because certain documents have been collected together by ecclesiastical authority or by common Christian usage, but because it presumes an underlying unity of faith and experience.

In conclusion it may be suggested that the results of a purely historical investigation of the origins of Christianity have a more than purely historical importance. There seems no reason to doubt that the characteristic features of Catholic piety have their origin in our Lord's interpretation of His own Person and of the significance of His disciples for the world. The religion of the New Testament provides, therefore, a standard by which the Catholicism of succeeding generations must be tested, and which it must endeavour to maintain.

# THE INCARNATION
BY JOHN KENNETH MOZLEY

# CONTENTS

THE doctrine of the Person of Christ, in its historic form, gives the fullest illumination to the doctrine of God and the fullest expression of the doctrine of grace. That is because the *theologia Christi* is essentially, as Kaftan, the theologian of the Ritschlian right wing, says, the doctrine of Christ's Godhead. "Christ is spoken of as God" : so, in opposition to assailants of the Lord's real divinity, writes an anonymous author quoted by Eusebius, with an appeal to the Fathers of the second century. If Christ is perfect in His Godhead, then in Him God's self-revelation reaches its highest point, nor is there any peak beyond this peak which man will, under the conditions of his earthly life, ever need to ascend in order to gain the light of a fuller knowledge of God. The Catholic doctrine of the Incarnation rules out every thought of a repetition of that supreme act in which God became man. It is concerned with one who is truly God incarnate, not a temporary *avatar* of deity. And the wealth of God's favour to man is pledged and given in the gift of the Son. "How shall He not with Him freely give us all things?" The great problems of theism, as they affect both speculative inquiry and practical religion, come to the fullest rest which man can enjoy, in that faith which has been the foundation of the victories of Christianity in the world and the power in which those victories have been won. Browning only puts in an absolute form the confidence which the doctrine of Christ's Godhead inspires :

> I say, the acknowledgment of God in Christ
> Accepted by thy reason solves for thee
> All questions in the earth and out of it.

It is natural enough that round this doctrine the most dramatic controversy in the history of the Christian Church was fought out ; it is equally natural that in the religious world of to-day, with all its cross-currents and hesitations, it is in relation to this same doctrine that the most real divisions, productive of the most far-reaching consequences, appear. The religious discussions and confessions of faith, to which so large a space has recently been given in popular journalism, all come to their critical turning-point, whether the writers have perceived the fact or not, when the choice has to be made between a Jesus as divine as the Father and a Jesus whose divinity, if the term is used, is the immanental divinity of the race at the highest point which it has yet reached. And it is the crisis within all that calls itself Christian as well as between Christianity and the world that lies without.

## I

### THE DOCTRINE AND THE GOSPELS

In the previous essay the question has been approached from the side of the study of the Gospels and of the picture which they give of Jesus Christ. Such a treatment is indispensable. In the Christian religion historical facts and theological doctrine cannot be detached from one another and put into separate compartments. That issue was effectively settled in principle when the Gospels came to be written. But the relation between the Gospels as documents which certainly intend (let us for the moment put it no higher than that) to record facts of history and the doctrine of the Incarnation calls for much accurate discrimination. In the first place, the Gospels are products of the doctrine in the form which that doctrine possessed about the middle of the first century or a few years later, and witnesses to it ; they were not written to establish it ; that is no more true of St. John's Gospel than of St. Mark's. And, secondly, it is not necessary to hold that one, and only one, evaluation of the historical matter in the Gospels is essential to the doctrine. Among the various attempted reconstructions of the Gospel history and delineations of the central Figure, some, of course, make the interpretation which the Church regards as the one true interpretation at least difficult. But even radical criticism may compel the recognition of a mystery *sui generis* about the Person of Jesus, and not compel but allow of the belief that nothing less than the Catholic doctrine is an adequate explanation of the facts. That the " reduced Christology," to use Dr. Sanday's phrase, of the liberal theologians of Germany did cohere more or less closely with views as to the unreliability of the Gospel narratives, especially of the Fourth Gospel, in the report of sayings and doings of Jesus in which the element of transcendence comes notably to the front, is undeniable. But it makes a great difference whether this element is judged to have been intruded into the history, because an examination and comparison of strata and traditions can be brought to show or suggest the unauthentic character of the Gospels at the points in question, or whether the Gospels are pronounced to be unreliable in the relevant passages because of the intrusion of this element. It is not necessary, nor would it be right, to present these alternatives as though, in practice, they could be quite clearly and sharply differentiated from one another. But in so far as a place has to be found for the second alternative, we are thrown back on to distinctively theological issues. For the determining of those issues other considerations must be present than the data of the Gospels can by themselves, if taken in isolation, supply.

## II

### THE REACTION AGAINST THE DOCTRINE

We turn then to the doctrine itself, to the belief that in the Person of Jesus Christ we have the incarnation of the eternal, divine Son of God; and, first of all, to the reaction against that doctrine, or, at least, the deflection from it, characteristic of the many Christologies which can be studied from rather different angles in Schweitzer's " Quest of the Historical Jesus," and in Sanday's " Christologies Ancient and Modern." It is noteworthy that the very idea of a Christology, of a doctrine of Christ's Person, implies that in that Person there is present something, some overplus, as compared with what is true of other persons. It is possible to adopt what may be called a wholly humanitarian view of Jesus. Some world-views necessitate such a conclusion. In such cases the break with the Christian tradition is absolute. But whenever, against a theistic background, it is recognised that there is something in respect of the relation of Jesus to God which can be associated with none other than Him, a step has been taken within the borders of Christology. Though they may not be aware of the fact, modern writers often raise just the same problem as underlies the doctrine of the Church. But in their thought there is less thoroughness and less care than is manifested in the theologians of the Church. It is a curious fact that the accuracy with which the theologian feels that it is necessary for him to try to approach the expression of a coherent world-view seems, at times, almost to be imputed to him as a fault, whereas the metaphysician is not subject to this charge.

What are the objections to a Christology which, while admitting an overplus in the Person of Jesus, surrenders the Catholic doctrine of Christ's Godhead, thus opposing itself to the Creed of Nicaea not less than to the Definition of Chalcedon? In the first place the break, at this point, is made with tradition precisely where tradition is strongest. For the strength of tradition consists not merely in consistency of belief but in the sense of what is indispensable to life and health. If the Christian conception of the meaning of existence is untrue, then the doctrine of the Incarnation falls; but if that conception is maintained and defended as giving the true religious interpretation of the world; if that interpretation is found to be consistent only with a doctrine of a personal God whose relations with the world are expressed by such terms as creation, providence and redemption; if, further, Jesus is regarded as, in a special way, illuminating and even mediating some of those relations, as possessing (a point on which Ritschl laid great stress) a unique historical vocation; and if, finally, a distinct place is kept for the truth and importance of the resurrection of Jesus, with whatever dissent from the form of the Gospel narratives—then, in such case, the rejection of the doctrine which has, in the history of Christian thought, been associated not formally and externally, but by the most intimate of internal connections, with the affirmations of Christian faith and the struggles, heroisms and achievements of Christian practice, needs to be justified by weightier arguments than are usually forthcoming. The pages of criticism in Loofs' small book "What is the Truth about Jesus Christ?" may be referred to as a careful and temperate, while definite, attempt to show that the Catholic doctrine is untenable. But apart from the fact that the Incarnation, as a possibility for God, cannot be disproved by the exhibition of resulting paradoxes which are then pleaded in support of the view that the doctrine is irrational, it is, I think, fair to say that the weakness of Lutheranism, and of German liberal theology in general, in its grasp of the idea and importance of the Church, makes it difficult for Loofs to appreciate the force of a question which might be written across his book taken as a whole—If, in such large respects as this work reveals, what the Church has believed about Christ is true, is not the Church likely to be right in that further belief about Him which makes of the Church's faith a coherent unity? Obviously it is impossible to reach more than a measure of probability along the lines of such a question, and the argument involved possesses in this context the characteristics and the limitations of an *argumentum ad rem* : nevertheless, it ought to be faced by those who agree that the Church is right in ascribing to Christ a unique place in relation both to God and to man and in striving to bring the world to an acknowledgment of this His position, but is wrong in the interpretation it offers—an interpretation which, in the fourth century crisis, was essential to the survival of Christianity as vital religion. Anyone who reads the fascinating account of the beginnings of the Arian controversy, and especially of the contrasted doctrines of Arius and Athanasius in Harnack's " History of Dogma," may well feel that he is preparing for himself a position of unstable equilibrium if he tries to make his own what is, in effect, Harnack's conclusion, that Athanasius was religiously at the centre, dogmatically absurd.[1]

Then, secondly, Christian experience decidedly favours the Nicene doctrine of Christ's true Deity.   Warily though it is necessary to walk in the attempt to apprehend the character and to determine the tests of the argument from experience, it is possible for any careful observer to arrive at certain results after a broad survey of the course of Christian history.   And whether attention be directed to the Church as a whole or to the great Christian souls who have revealed themselves to us, or, so far as that can be known, to the piety of the individual Christian who has achieved no supereminent degree of saintliness and progressed not far along the mystic way, the strength and the inspiration of life has been that devotion and self-committal to Him, that trust in Him as Saviour and loyalty to Him as Lord, which finds its completion in the adoration of Him as God.   But that is not all : not only are Christian piety and the Christian life historically bound up with the confession of the Godhead of Christ, so that each is intellectually coherent with the other, but the highest ascents and the most far-going adventures of Christian saints who have made of life a continual means of sacramental or mystical communion with God have been, at the same time, the attempt to win a fuller

[1] I have adapted a phrase quoted by Mr. H. G. Wood as used of W. Herrmann, " religiously at the centre, dogmatically worthless." Like all such epigrams it is too sweeping.   But Herrmann's view of the relation of Christian religion and faith to dogma makes it intelligible in his case, whereas in the case of Athanasius the disjunction is far less tolerable.

knowledge of Christ, and to discover more of the meaning of what has been already confessed. If Christians had not believed in the Godhead of Christ, both the most distinctive and the most wonderful things in Christian experience would never have come into existence. That to which they witness is that from which they have sprung. It is not simply a case of the creed being an intellectual explication of the experience. If that were all, there would be comparatively little difficulty in allowing that a change in the creed would, after the necessary readjustments in thought, make no difference to the future history of the experience. But what has happened, when belief in Christ's Godhead has been given up and some other form of doctrine has taken its place, gives no ground for any such idea. If the richest and the most penetrating kind of Christian experience is to continue, its conditions will remain what they have always been.

And, thirdly, whereas the Catholic doctrine gives a rational interpretation of the Person of Jesus in relation to God, and, in connection with Him, of God in relation to the world, the Christologies which stand on the other side find it hard to rise above description to explanation. After accounts with historical criticism have been settled the individual scholar or theologian must, if he wishes to go as far as possible into the depths of his subject-matter, put to himself such questions as " How is it that Jesus was the kind of person that the sources, after cross-examination, show Him to have been ? " and " Why did the primitive communities think of Him after the fashion revealed throughout the New Testament ? " It is not easy to answer the first question along the lines of a non-Catholic Christology, while keeping a firm hold on the uniqueness of Christ. Arianism, in its historic, dogmatic form, is as dead as an opinion can be, but the root-difficulty of Arianism remains in Christologies which are quite differently expressed and seem free enough from everything of a mythological character. Historic Arianism made of Christ an intermediate being whose physical characteristics isolated Him both from God and from man. The Christologies of modern times do not isolate Christ so far as His nature is concerned ; as to that He is man, simply and exclusively, with whatever affinities to God man possesses in virtue of his Creator's will, or, if the background of thought is pantheistic rather than theistic, of the terms of the cosmic and evolutionary process. But the grand solitariness of Christ, His moral and spiritual difference, has been constantly emphasised, and much made of those features in His life and teaching which belong to Him as they do not belong to others, and which we do not associate with mankind in general. As to how and why this should be so, a Christology which rejects the doctrine of the Incarnation cannot readily explain. As the medium of the conceptions of the world and of God's dealings with men which appear in the teaching of Jesus, Messianic and apocalyptic notions may rightly be exhibited. But these do not account for Him, and that is the heart of the problem. The belief that in Jesus the Spirit of God was present in the highest degree is the nearest approach which liberal Christologies make to the Catholic doctrine : but this doctrine does not so much solve one problem as raise another, namely how we may understand the action of God in the choice of a particular person at a particular time for this superlative endowment ; or, if the stress is laid rather on the achievement of Jesus than on the work of God, how we may understand the supremacy of Jesus in the moral and spiritual sphere. Christologies of an immanental or inspirational character involve in this case an ethical development *per saltum* to which no parallel can be offered. This perplexity, at least, does not confront the believer in the Incarnation, since in that case what we have is not a sudden break in the normal moral history of the race, but a new beginning. St. Paul's contrast drawn between the first Adam and the second is one way of expressing the difference which Christ makes for mankind. But to find the material for such a difference in the history of one individual member of the race involves an assertion of spiritual relevance in this one person such as challenges us to go further into the meaning of a truth of which the phenomenon of His life affords the one and only example.

But the belief that the historic doctrine of the Church has advantages of a purely rational character over its rivals ought not to prevent those who hold it from feeling a very real sympathy with others who have been able neither to make the Church's doctrine their own nor to evacuate the Gospels of personal mystery. A logic which may seem insuperable to others should not lead to the attempt to force hard and fast alternatives on those who can more easily be impaled upon a dilemma than saved by one. The Liberal reconstructions in Christology were not built to be immortal; yet amid all the confusion of an era which inevitably set its sons searching for guiding-posts to take the place of their fathers' landmarks, which were for the time at least, and some thought for ever, being submerged beneath the incoming flood of discovery and criticism, they did service to their own generation and even beyond. They aimed at showing the religious view of the world to be concentrated in and mediated through the Person of Jesus; they refused to admit that Christianity was merely a department of religion, and religion of philosophy. When all the reservations on which they insisted had been made, it was still clearly the case that the history of Jesus Christ and of Christianity was much more than one chapter in the comparative history of the religious experiences of mankind.

### III

### Liberalism and Eschatology

A word may be said on the greatest difference in scientific outlook between the Liberals on the one hand and their critics from the side of eschatology on the other. For the former it was natural to try to present the Person of Jesus as rationally intelligible and interpretable in terms of the standards and ideas of an age far later than His own. That age, their own, was being immensely affected in its world-view by the science and criticism which were so striking a feature in the development of its intellectual life. It would almost seem as though the unconscious notion prevailed that He could be of use to the nineteenth century only by being shown to lack the characteristics of a Jew of the first. So rationalisation entered not only into explanations of narratives in the Gospels but also into the delineations of the figure of Jesus. Against this the eschatologists set their faces, and with much right. They had strong arguments to bring forward both in criticism and in theology. And when those who have stood on this side have been penetrating enough, as was the case with von Hügel, they have deepened the impression of mystery, to which the Liberals were not insensitive, in connection with Jesus. They have called attention to the strain and tension which the Gospels reveal, by what they report of some of His words and of His actions, to have beset Him. And so, especially in connection with the life of the Church and its dependence upon Him, they have heightened the sense of something extraordinary attaching to His Person by the very fact that they have viewed it in its historical context. The eschatological side of the Gospels, even if we admit the truth contained in von Dobschütz' valuable phrase " transmuted eschatology," involves perplexities which neither the critic nor the theologian can hope wholly to straighten out. But perplexity is not the only word. The eschatological sayings of the Lord give us, as perhaps no other part of the Gospels does, the power of appreciating something of the results in consciousness that might be expected to follow upon that bringing together of God and man which the doctrine of the Incarnation presupposes. Von Hügel speaks of the "junction between Simultaneity and Successiveness"; and unless the human were to be simply lost in the divine, it would seem inevitable that conflict, or at least strain, should follow upon junction. The narrative of the Temptation suggests its presence in one way, the eschatological sayings in another. In both cases it is in connection with Christ's Kingdom that the signs of tension appear, and, even more fundamentally, in connection with Jesus as King. In comparison with this side of the Gospels the language of Nicaea and still more of Chalcedon seems to present us with a static impassive union of two elements human and divine. But the comparison is not apposite, and ought not to be raised to the level of a contrast. In a formulary the content of a historical situation does not need to be mentioned, except in the briefest way and with reference to some fact that has a special dogmatic significance, as when in the Nicene Creed, it is said that Christ " was crucified also for us under Pontius Pilate." The abstractions of a formulary are not to be taken and applied as they stand to the concrete experiences of which historical narratives tell. The four words of the Chalcedonian Definition which we translate " without change, without confusion, without division, without separation," do no more than say that in Christ what is divine remains divine and what is human remains human, while they are not isolated from one another as they would be if there were one Person who was divine and another Person who was human. How the divine and the human acted in relation to and upon each other in Christ they do not try to declare. Such statements were, indeed, not lacking; but, whatever be thought of them, they are not essential deductions from the language of approved dogmatic decisions.

## IV

### THE DOCTRINE OF THE TWO NATURES

If criticism has at times its conventions which are obstacles to a clear understanding of the way in which progress may best be made, that is also true of theology.   In the doctrine of Christ's Person the disparagement of the formula of the Two Natures has become in some circles almost a convention.   It is one from which we have gained very little.   Chalcedon can be criticised as offering to us a psychological puzzle which we can never hope to solve by any help which it gives us ; but if the doctrine of the Incarnation is true, we cannot escape from a psychological puzzle. If either the divine or the human element could be abandoned or explained away we could avoid such puzzles.   But if the elements are allowed to be there, in the life, then, whether we do or do not use the phrase Two Natures, we recognise what the formula recognises and puts on record.

But, it is said, the doctrine of the Two Natures is incompatible with the unity of Christ's Person.   Dr. Mackintosh, in his well-known and highly (and rightly) valued book, " The Person of Jesus Christ," lays great stress on this :—" The doctrine of the two natures, in its traditional form, imports into the life of Christ an incredible and thoroughgoing dualism.   In place of that perfect unity which is felt in every impression of Him, the whole is bisected sharply by the fissure of distinction.   No longer one, He is divided against Himself. . . . The simplicity and coherence of all that Christ was and did vanishes, for God is not after all living a human life.   On the contrary, He is still holding Himself at a distance from its experiences and conditions.   There has been no saving descent.   Christ executed this as God, it is said, and suffered that as man." [1]

Now it is quite true that inferences can be drawn from the traditional statement of the doctrine which are very prejudicial to real unity, and that a mode of expression, " He did this as God, that as man," became habitual, which seems to suggest that the danger was not avoided.   But that is not to say that the Chalcedonian phraseology is no longer possible for us, still less that we cannot make the meaning of Chalcedon our own.   Certainly Christ was, and is revealed in the Gospels as, really one.   His personal unity is as unquestionable as Dr. Mackintosh affirms,

[1] P. 294.

and as the theologians, who spoke in ways which suggest the bisection of which he complains, would most sincerely have confessed. And following out the line of thought of which Dr. Moberly made so much we shall say that all the experiences of Christ were the experiences of God in manhood. But unless we are prepared to say that the divine is human and the human is divine, we must admit a distinction between the two in the Person of Christ and discover a relationship between them which is dependent upon the fact that each of the terms " divinity," " humanity," expresses a real truth about the one, whole Person. Let us take three descriptive phrases from documents of the fifth century and see how the truth expressed by the Two Natures' formula can be expressed in language which lacks the disputed phrase, while at the same time exactly the same distinction is made as that which is inherent in the theology and terminology of the Two Natures. In *Quicunque vult* the writer points out, as against views which were supposed to follow from the principles of Apollinarius, that in the oneness of Christ we are to see not a conversion of the Godhead into flesh, but a taking of the manhood into God. That does not mean a change of the substance of manhood, but a new relationship of manhood to Deity under the new conditions which have come into existence with the Incarnation. Again, Leo in his " Tome " speaks of Christ as " complete in that which is His, complete in that which is ours " ; the distinction is clear enough, but so also is the intimacy of the relationship, since everything falls within the circle of the unity of the one Person. Lastly, the Chalcedonian Definition itself says that the one Lord Jesus Christ is " complete in Godhead, complete also the selfsame in manhood."

If what the Church means by the word " incarnation " is a true belief, it is impossible not to speak in such ways as the above references illustrate. If the words φύσις and *natura* had been scrupulously avoided, the problem, except for a greater exactness in definition, would have remained just the same.

The famous passage in Ignatius concerning the one physician who is " spiritual and fleshly, of Mary and of God," [1] contains the whole theological meaning and truth of the doctrine of the Two Natures. And when we say, as believers in the Incarnation are bound to say, that Christ is truly God and truly man, while

[1] *Ad Ephes.* vii, 2.

at the same time we do not and cannot allow that He is the one in virtue of being the other, we affirm what the traditional statement affirms and mean the same thing.

In the passage which I have quoted, Dr. Mackintosh exaggerates the dualistic impression which methods of employing the doctrine of the Two Natures can convey, through not allowing for the orthodox emphasis on the unity of the Person which is the correlative of the emphasis on the duality of the natures. And further, when he charges the doctrine with leaving no place for a human life as lived by God, one may ask what the truth is which this phrase implies and which Chalcedon omits and by implication denies. For it is the one orthodox doctrine—and all orthodox theologians, whatever differences appear among them, agree in this—that all the experiences that fall within the circle of the incarnate life are experiences of the one divine Person. If the objection is that in the traditional theology a number of experiences are selected as essentially human, and Christ is said to have had them in respect of the flesh or of His humanity, one may agree that, in so far as this suggests an alternation or action by turns on the part of Christ, now as God, now as man, an artificial oscillation as between the human and the divine is introduced into the picture of a life which is at unity with itself. And further, it may be allowed that we can get very little way along the lines of such distinctions within the sphere of the Incarnation. But unless we are to be greatly embarrassed by a drift in the direction of pantheism we must bring in the idea of human nature as intermediate between God and human experience. The Alexandrine Christology, with all its stress upon the divine aspect of the Incarnation, was compelled to do this when, in its best representations, it stopped short of monophysitism. So Cyril of Alexandria in his " Epistola dogmatica " explains the ascription to the Logos of birth and death.

The doctrine of the Two Natures does not endanger the unity of the Person when it is associated with that other doctrine to which so much exception has been taken, that Christ's human nature is impersonal. This difficulty arises from the failure to distinguish between the abstract and the concrete. Catholic theology never meant that, in the concrete, the human nature of Christ lacked its *persona*. Leontius of Byzantium brought in no new idea by his employment of the term *enhypostasia*. All that went on within the incarnate life, all that was static and all that was dynamic, was covered, if the word is permissible, by the Person of the Son. But regarded in abstraction the human nature of Christ is rightly spoken of as impersonal, since in this case and this alone discrimination can be made between human experiences and a human subject of the experiences.

The Chalcedonian Christology holds its ground as the only one which has a right to be regarded as fully Catholic. But, for the very reason that its implications undoubtedly present difficulties, and that the attempt to follow out the meaning of the doctrine to its further conclusions in respect of the incarnate Christ can be made only with the utmost care—while yet, if it is to be made at all, it must be made with the boldness that comes from a grasp upon first principles—honourable reference is due at this point to the chapter entitled "Towards Solution" in the late Bishop Weston's "The One Christ."[1]  No one but a real theologian could have written it.  Its peculiar strength lies in the consistency with which Bishop Weston conceives of the manhood of the self-limited Logos as the one medium of all that took place within the state of the Incarnation.  When the Logos "took human flesh which, with its own proper and complete soul, He constituted in Himself so that He became truly man, living as the subject or ego of real manhood,"[2] He imposed upon Himself such a "law of self-restraint" that "He has, as Incarnate, no existence and no activity outside the conditions that manhood imposes upon Him."[3]  This law, as we may call it, determined the character of all the relationships involved in the state of incarnation.  With this Bishop Weston combined the thought of "the essential inseparableness of the universal relations of the Logos from His relations as Incarnate, seeing that all are based in one and the selfsame Person."[4]  The same idea appears in "Christus Veritas," where the Bishop of Manchester speaks of the value of thinking of God the Son as most truly living the life recorded in the Gospels, but adding this to the other work of God.[5]  And to such a conclusion the logic of the Christian doctrine of God may point, but even the best of analogies (and Bishop Weston's were more than ordinarily good) can do very little to enable us to form a conception of the reality involved.

[1] Second edition, 1914.    [2] Pp. 150 ff.    [3] P. 153.
[4] P. 181.    [5] P. 143.

## V

### FURTHER CONSIDERATIONS IN RESPECT OF THE CHALCEDONIAN CHRISTOLOGY

On the strictly theological side the objections to the Chalcedonian Christology as a statement of the doctrine of the Incarnation are less formidable than the propounders of them suppose. And the failure to replace the old terminology by something equivalent in value and equally effective as a bulwark against restatements which involve an alteration not only in the form but also in the substance of the doctrine is important ; for it is an argument against the view that it is no serious loss if we regard the Definition put out by the Council as possessing only the interest which attaches to an historical landmark, and of no inherent validity for the guidance and regulation of our conceptions. On the philosophical side the difficulties are greater. A doctrine of Christ's Person that approached adequacy and completeness would go along with a satisfactory doctrine of personality. Such a doctrine did not exist in the fourth and fifth centuries, and though the problem of personality has come to the front in philosophy as one that demands serious attention, the stage of an agreed solution has not yet been reached. If what Dr. Cave, the writer of the latest monograph in English on the subject of Christology, calls " the beginnings of a philosophy of personality " [1] in the works of modern philosophers is further developed, theologians may find avenues of insight into the Christological problem opening out before them from the side of metaphysics. Du Bose, had he been able to handle the question simply as a philosopher, and been gifted with greater lucidity of expression, might have contributed much in this connection.

As it is, while the Chalcedonian doctrine neither answers nor professes to answer all the inquiries which naturally arise out of the faith in Christ as one who is both God and man, it remains the bulwark of that faith, and does not, as is the danger with some modern restatements and speculations, render the faith itself precarious. It has not barred the way to the study of the conditions of our Lord's life on earth, and it has left ample room for different types of devotion, resting on the clearer apprehension of His Godhead or of His manhood. And it decisively prevents the conversion of a doctrine of incarnation into the highest form

[1] *The Doctrine of the Person of Christ*, p. 240.

of a doctrine of divine immanence.    This latter mode of thought gives us a Christ who is as we are, except that He has in richest measure what we have in small portions.    Grace is poured into Christ, as into us, but in His case without stint.[1]    But, that being so, there is no place for the thought of an absolute dependence upon Christ as Redeemer.    He does not have for us the value of God.    Something in Him does, since the value of that which indwells Christ is divine.    But so it is with ourselves.    And if Christ is, by virtue of God's indwelling within Him, the most highly privileged member of the human race, then the faith, the mysticism and the ideas of sacramental union which we find in the New Testament, directed towards Him and placing Him in a position where He Himself and not something in Him becomes everything to man, cannot be justified.    It is not as though immanence and incarnation were two theological ways of expressing the same thing.    They are the beginnings of different religions, though along the divergent lines there may be points of resemblance. We do not know all that it means to say that God is immanent in a man ; and we do not know all that it means to say that God is incarnate ; but we know enough, and the religious history of mankind helps us, to see that a real difference is involved.

The faith of the Church and its doctrinal expression set before us Christ as one who is man, but also God.    That is its account of the facts, but what kind of a thing, viewed apart from the facts, the incarnation of God would be it does not try to say.    But if we take the idea of the Two Natures as one which asserts the diverse realities of divinity and humanity, and then try to conceive of the consequences of those two realities being united, neither fused nor lost, in a Person who does not result from the union but is precedent to it and enters into new conditions because of it, we shall come under the unescapable difficulties which attach to the attempt to determine in the abstract the character of what is, *ex hypothesi*, a new kind of fact and the single instance of it.

[1] Cf. S. J. Davenport, *Immanence and Incarnation*, p. 229 : " Does the immanental theory imply that . . . given a perfect man *ipso facto* we are presented with an Incarnate God ?    If such is a necessary implication of immanentism, then, as we have argued above, this is not the Christian conception of Christ.    He is Absolute.    Even a perfect man a priori would derive his perfection through the Logos, from whom he derives his constitution, his existence.    Perfection is by no means synonymous with hypostatic union, for the former is possible, abstractly, for all men, but the latter belongs to the Second Person of the Trinity alone, that is, to Jesus Christ.''

If the word " incarnation " is rightly used, then the fact of the Incarnation is the one instance of the particular being its own universal. We should have to say the same thing in another way if we possessed no heritage from Aristotle and the Scholastics. But as to speculations in Christology, the data afford us little opportunity for supposing that we can lay down rules for the testing of the validity of our conclusions. There have been such speculations, but they fall right outside the faith and the dogma of the Church, which is concerned to make decisions only with reference to the concrete historical fact. So it is with regard to kenotic theories, and, in partial opposition to them, to specu- lation as to the work of the Logos outside the circle, but during the period, of the incarnate life. Such a tentative idea as Dr. Temple has put forward in " Christus Veritas," [1] that supposing from the life of Christ the presence of God incarnate were with- drawn we should not be left with nothing, but with the life of a man, belongs to the same order of untestable suggestions. All that the Church asserts as positive truth is what must be asserted if we are to think of a real incarnation. For that, Christ must be both God and man, not successively and by division but wholly and simultaneously.

## VI

### FINAL DIFFICULTIES AS TO THE DOCTRINE OF THE INCARNATION EXAMINED

When all necessary explanations have been given, two obstacles to faith may still remain. The first is that the notion of incar- nation involves an incredible relationship between God and the finite order ; that God, the Eternal, cannot be thought of as entering into time after the manner expressed in this doctrine. In popular form the objection takes exception to the discovery of a final

---

[1] Dr. Temple writes (p. 150) : " If we imagine the divine Word withdrawn from Jesus of Nazareth, as the Gnostics believed to have occurred before the Passion, I think that there would be left, not nothing at all, but a man." If the Bishop had stopped there, one might feel that an incursion had been made into the region of the most unverifiable speculation, and that behind it lay a really inadequate view of the meaning of the Incarnation. But he continues, in words which (especially with the note calling attention to the avoidance of the phrase " human person ") make all the difference in substance, whatever be thought of their form, " yet this human personality is actually the self- expression of the Eternal Son, so that as we watch the human life we become aware that it is the vehicle of a divine life, and that the human personality of Jesus Christ is subsumed in the Divine Person of the Creative Word."

revelation in something which happened a long time ago in an obscure corner of the world. A full consideration of this objection and of the answer to it would necessitate an examination of the significance of the pre-Christian history to which the title *preparatio evangelica* is given, and a discussion of the doctrine of God as the background against which the idea of incarnation becomes intelligible. Here it must suffice to point out that while Christian theology has repudiated all explanations of the Incarnation which imply that God immerses Himself in such a manner in the finite order that He becomes for a time no more than part of it, it has presented the doctrine as the one in which alone the gap between God and the world is effectively overcome. The world-order is raised potentially to the level of the divine life which has been manifested within it. That is the truth of the idea of deification. But this idea is not construed as though the Incarnation worked like leaven to the production, by a quality of permeation, of a human super-nature. The Christian tradition, if account is taken of its chief emphases and of its total character, has viewed the Incarnation in relation to God's redemptive and ethical purposes, which man must receive and make his own if he is to know the joy of communion with God. The ethical confusion to-day is the result of uncertainty as to the existence of an ethical interpretation of life, which is the real meaning of life and not superimposed upon life, while a grasp of the ethical character of life becomes less firm in the absence of knowledge of where to look for the true ideals, standards and laws of moral well-being. The Incarnation brings light at the point where lack of light must work out in lack of power. It gives the assurance of the reality of moral values in God and in the world-order. It reveals God as making Himself one with man, and entering into the world's moral life and undergoing the passion which is born of the travail of good in its struggle with evil. It is only as we view the Christian Church and the Christian life, both of which derive from the Incarnation, that its moral fruitfulness begins to be manifested both extensively and intensively. But immediately following upon conviction of the truth of the Incarnation comes the realisation of a new unity accomplished, which gives the best of all answers to those most poignant of all doubts, in which the drama of the world and of the soul seems to have nothing moral at its heart and to move towards no moral end.

The other principal difficulty arises out of the study of the Gospels. The picture which they bring before us is held to be incompatible with the faith in Jesus as God incarnate. Something that bears on this has been said earlier. The extent of the difficulty will depend upon the judgment formed as to the miraculous sections of the Gospel.[1] But it is largely the consequence of *a priori* assumptions, which may be held with no full consciousness of their nature, as to the form which an incarnation of God will take. The sense of injurious speculation concerning the Person of Christ which kenotic doctrines often produce must be ascribed to preliminary judgments of what is both possible and fitting in the case of one who is God incarnate. But the doctrine of the Incarnation, as the one that best satisfies all the facts which are bound up with the beginnings and history of Christianity as religion and way of life, is not to be rejected on the ground that the life of Jesus contains features of a surprising and unexpected character. Like the Apostles we have to learn that apparent stumbling-blocks may be the way in which God effects His will. If the Cross has not prevented the confession of the Godhead of Jesus, but has revealed the full glory of the self-impoverishment of the Eternal Son, the recognition of limitations in His knowledge and His power while on earth need not do so.

The question of the finality of Christianity as the "absolute religion" has come into some prominence of late. It is a question which depends altogether for any valid answer upon the view taken of Christ. Christianity is not primarily the most satisfactory philosophy of religion, embodying in the most perfect form certain universally valid religious principles, but faith in a Person, to believe in whom is to believe in God. If that is not true, then all that is most distinctive in Christianity falls, and even though a sentiment about Him and an attachment to Him remain, Jesus Christ will no longer be the Way, the Truth and the Life. The Church at least knows what is at stake. Her life is not centred in herself but in Him. Her tradition, derived in the first instance from the faith of the apostolic age, is the rational account which she has given of her experience. And believing herself to be the trustee, not only of the Christianity which deserves the name, but of vital religion and of its continuance within human life, she sees no future for her office and no security for

[1] See the appendix to this essay.

her efforts except in the acknowledgment and adoration of Jesus
Christ as Lord and God.

## APPENDIX ON MIRACLE

The stage which the question of the miraculous element in the Gospels
has reached seems to be describable as follows : The opposition to miracle
from the side of those sciences which reveal the orderly flow of sequences
in nature, and are thereby responsible for the phrase " natural law," is
no longer formidable.   It is clear that no decision can be reached without taking into account the prior questions which arise around the problem
of theism.   With regard to literary criticism of the Gospels, no discovery has been made which suggests the existence of any primitive non-
miraculous documentary deposit which has been overlaid by later strata.

On the other hand, there is no sign of a return to the old kind of
argument which built upon miracle (and upon prophecy) for evidential
and theological purposes.   The miracles are not taken just as they stand,
as though no problem were raised by their appearance.   Though they
may be regarded as " in place " in the life of Christ, they are
so regarded in consequence of an interpretation of His Person ;
they are not usually appealed to directly for establishing the truth of
that interpretation.   It is inevitably impossible to reach a settlement
which could be put forward as representing objective truth, since the
approach to a decision can be reached only along the lines of this or
that *praejudicium*.   The non-Christian, and more definitely the non-
theist, may admit that the historical evidence has its strong points, that
the narratives are not far removed in time from the facts, that they are
not worked up into a form which suggests mere legend-mongering, and
that they are embedded in a context which there is no reason to distrust.
But even so he will reject them because it is impossible for him to find a
place for them in a non-theistic world-view.   His non-theistic successor
ages hence may be able to accept them on the basis of knowledge which
is at present hidden.   But that is mere hypothesis ; at the present time
a non-theist will not and cannot accept the truth of the Gospel miracles.
He may or may not be able to explain the accounts in a way satisfactory
to himself and to others.   But even if he cannot do that, even if his con-
jectures seem as absurd as some of the methods taken to find a way round
the Gospel-narratives of the morning of Easter Day and of the resurrection,
he will be guilty of no irrational behaviour when he denies that these
wonderful things happened.   His fault lies further back.   Where he
is wrong is in not believing in God, and in Christ as the Son of God.
In other words it is, broadly speaking, only from within the Christian

tradition that he is capable of a true verdict upon the miracles of the Gospel.[1]

But because the Christian is free from a *praejudicium* which is anti-miraculous because it is anti-theistic, he will not necessarily go on to the assertions which the other has denied. He still may feel difficulties. Unless he believes in the verbal inerrancy of Scripture he is not able to affirm that a miracle which appears in one of the Gospels must have happened as a miracle. He knows that stories of miraculous events appear all over the world in connection with different religions, and he is probably not prepared to accept those which have their place in religions which are rivals to Christianity. What is it, he may ask, which gives the New Testament miracle-narratives a special claim to be accepted as true statements of wonderful occurrences in the natural order?

I can do no more than suggest the lines along which an answer may be found. In the first place I would say that the problem of miracle concerns not God's will to produce certain results through acts attributable immediately to Him without the appearance of any mediate agencies, but God's will to produce those results under certain conditions which involve a particular relationship between Him and the human soul. There is a mediate agency, namely man in fellowship with God. In a theistic world-view, which finds the greatest of all powers under God to be those of spiritual beings in fellowship with God, and cannot regard the material side of existence to be at any point simply intractable and unmalleable, it is impossible to set limits to the results which might be produced, given favourable conditions in respect of communion with God.

Then, secondly, whatever be the case with other conditions under which miracles have been said to have occurred, the context of the Gospel miracles raises no difficulty. That Jesus Christ lived in the most intimate communion with the Father, that His power was the natural fruit of that communion, and was manifested in a moral holiness which, apart from questions of " Christology," gives evidence of His pre-eminence among men, is the picture of His life which we can derive from the Gospels. That in His case, in response to the faith in which He drew upon God for help, certain things happened in God's world of nature, which revealed in a way that we call miraculous the supremacy of spirit over matter, is not surprising. And the miracle-narratives do not appear in their context oddly and awkwardly as might be expected if they were really

---

[1] That seems to me true with this reservation. The evidence for the resurrection possesses a specially impressive character, and makes a more general appeal than any other miraculous section in the Gospels. Why this should be so is not difficult to understand. The truth of Christianity and the truth that Christ is risen are inseparable, and part of the evidence for the resurrection is the account of the tomb that was found empty.

out of place. If the element of miracle in them is untrue, they are, if not conscious inventions—a most improbable supposition—, the product of pious imagination misinterpreting certain natural phenomena. Such a view does not, at least as a rule, arise spontaneously out of the study of the Gospels without the presupposition of a theory adverse to miracle.

And, thirdly, if Christianity is the true religion because Jesus Christ is the Son of God incarnate, the record of the Gospel-miracles possesses this essential difference from the record of other miracles, that the personal Subject differs from all other persons. His divine-human sovereignty in the sphere of the spirit, in virtue of which He is Lord, Judge, Saviour and King, has as its other side a divine-human sovereignty in the sphere of nature. The Son of Man has power in both. Incarnation and miracle do not, perhaps, cohere so closely together as to enable us to say that where the one is the other must be found; but, on the other hand, if the Incarnation is in any real way apprehended as the greatest event in human history, miracle cannot be ruled out as possessing no fitting occasion for the manifestation of such a mode of divine operation.

These considerations may be particularised in reference to the miracle which, through its relationship to the beginnings of our Lord's earthly life, Christian theology has viewed in specially close connection with the doctrine of the Incarnation. Here, I think, we may legitimately contrast with great clearness and sharpness two propositions. On the one hand, if we did not believe that Christ was truly the Son of God, we should not believe that He was born of a Virgin. Some of the Ebionites could do so, but that does not matter : no lengthy argument is needed to convince us that their position is untenable. On the other hand, if we do believe that Christ is truly the Son of God, the Virgin-Birth appears as a truth in respect of His advent into this world congruous with the truth of His eternal being and essential Deity. Chary as we may be of pressing arguments which cannot be conclusive because they contain an element of unverifiable speculation, the difficulty, to which defenders of the orthodox tradition, most recently the learned American Baptist scholar Dr. A. T. Robertson,[1] have called attention, of combining the notion of incarnation with the belief that Jesus was the Son of Joseph and Mary, is not an unreal one. And the fact that disbelief in the Virgin-Birth, and belief in other doctrines of the Person of Christ than that He was the Son of God incarnate, do very largely go together suggests that the Incarnation and the mode thereof are neither easily nor truly dissociated from one another. The possibility of theoretical abstraction of the one from the other does not prove that they are not, in fact, a living unity.

There is one point to which attention may be drawn. May we not lay stress on the part actively taken by the Blessed Virgin in co-operation with God, coming along the avenues of mystical experience? The

[1] In his book, *The Mother of Jesus*, p. 28 f.

importance of this idea, which is not inconsonant with the story of the Annunciation in St. Luke's Gospel, lies in the fact that it recognises in connection with the physical miracle the relevance of the human, spiritual, mediate agency. Mary did all that she could do, by making her will one with the will of God, to make it, from her side, possible for the Son of God to be born of her. It is, therefore, quite wrong to treat the Virgin-Birth as though no spiritual significance were to be discovered in connection with it. A narrative in which the woman's part was of no essential worth, and nothing emerged except a divine decision that a particular birth should be brought about in a miraculous way, might fairly be regarded as of no spiritual consequence, except for the exhibition of the power of God. But that is not St. Luke's narrative. In his account the faith and willingness of Mary show that, even in such an event as this, all the factors are not exhausted in the one idea of divine omnipotence. There is spiritual response and spiritual preparation from the human side. We cannot define the exact character of the Annunciation. We may quite properly hold to its objective reality without thinking of the angel coming to the Blessed Virgin in any way parallel to a person coming into a room through its door. The word "vision" may help, and so may the word "experience." In any case St. Luke has given us what he did not make up, a most appropriate spiritual context for the physical wonder of the Virgin-Birth. And both the context and the wonder are appropriate to Him who came, in the fulness of time, true God made man.

# ASPECTS OF MAN'S CONDITION

## BY EDWARD JOHN BICKNELL

### AND

## JOHN KENNETH MOZLEY

# CONTENTS

# I

## SIN AND THE FALL.

### BY E. J. BICKNELL.

### 1. *Basis in Experience of the Theological Doctrines of the Fall and Original Sin*

(*a*) THE doctrines of " original sin " and " the Fall " are pieces of theology. Theology is the science of religion. It springs from the effort of man to understand his own life. Always religion comes first, and theology second. Experience precedes reflection on experience, and the two must not be confused. Man lives first and thinks afterwards. Accordingly we shall not be surprised to find that these two doctrines, so closely connected, were not revealed ready made, but have behind them a long history of development in time. Our first duty therefore will be to consider what are the facts of experience which they attempt to express and to correlate. What is their relation to practical religion ?

Let us start from common ground on which all Christians are agreed. We all have no difficulty in understanding what is meant by " actual " sin. It is a concept that can be denied by no one who believes in a personal and righteous God and in some measure of free-will in man. Actual sin denotes an act of disobedience to God or the state of mind and heart that results from such acts of disobedience. Christ depicts sin as the alienation of the will and heart of a child from an all-righteous and all-loving Father. It is important to remember for our present discussion that sin is always against God. The term belongs to the vocabulary of religion, not to that of moral or political philosophy. To an atheist sin can only appear to be an illusion. " Against thee and thee only have I sinned " is always the cry of the awakened sinner. No doubt historically the content of the term sin has varied enormously in accordance with the conception of the character of God attained by the community. Even within the Bible we find a development in the idea of sin *pari passu* with a development in the understanding of the character of God. In primitive times

sin is simply that which displeases God.    Exclusive attention is
paid to external acts, not to motives.    Individual responsibility is
hardly recognised.    Ritual irregularities are not distinguished
from moral offences.    Unintentional breaches of custom are put
on a level with wilful disobedience.    But gradually personality
comes to its own and distinctions are made.    The root of sin is
seen to lie in the will.    Merely ceremonial defilement is felt to be
of small account beside moral evil.    The development reaches its
culmination in the teaching of Christ that nothing from outside a
man can defile him but only that which comes from within.    Still
always and everywhere sin is that which offends God.    We do not
wish to discuss here the difficult question of the relative degrees
of guilt or accountability which sin involves.    We only assert
summarily that in the last resort only God who knows the heart
can estimate the exact measure of guilt in any case.    Nor can we
discuss the relation between sin and the sense of sin.    We deliberately
put these problems on one side.[1]    All that we are concerned to
maintain is that the one constant element in the concept of sin is
that which puts man out of fellowship with God.

(*b*) So far our path is clear.    When, however, we look into
ourselves we discover the fact, so mysterious to all who believe in a
good God, that we find there evil tendencies and desires, similar to
those which result from indulgence in actual sin, but which are prior
in time to, and independent of, any such actual sin.    For these bad
tendencies and impulses we do not recognise any personal responsibility.    They are not the consequences of our own acts of choice.
They seem to come to us ready made.    Yet, quite as fully as those
bad habits which are the result of actual sin, they incapacitate us
from full fellowship with God.    They hamper and thwart our
better purposes.    They are not simply imperfections : they are
positively evil.    They are loyalties that conflict with and weaken
our loyalty to God.    Nor do we show any signs of outgrowing
them.    They do not disappear as we get older.    In other words
our nature, as we receive it, appears to be not merely undeveloped
but to possess a bias towards evil, a disunion within itself, an inability
to rise to higher levels.    We find ourselves out of sympathy with
God from the start.

This analysis of human nature is confirmed when we look

[1] For a discussion of them see Bicknell, *The Christian Idea of Sin and
Original Sin*, pp. 43-49.

*[Margin handwritten note:]* Of course in see sin thought and desire are prior to action. and it is scarcely true to say that we feel no sense of moral responsibility for such predisposing thought and desire.

*[Bottom handwritten note:]* Such inherited tendencies of which we early become conscious would seem to partake of the nature of original sin.

outwards and study human life as disclosed in history and politics. The history of the race is that of the individual writ large. There is no doubt marvellous progress in many directions. It is the recognition of this that prompts the objection that man has not fallen, he has risen. But the rise is only in certain limited directions. He has gained an increased mastery over the material world. He has accumulated a vast amount of experience and turned it to good account in ministering to the needs and comforts of the body. He has also advanced in intellectual knowledge. He has before him more material from which to draw conclusions and better methods of sifting and arranging that material. He has also developed more complex and refined moral ideals. There is among civilised men *Is there in 1943?* less open brutality and cruelty, less violence and unabashed lawlessness. But there is no evidence that his moral and spiritual powers have proportionately developed. The wonderful inventions of science are in themselves morally neutral. They may be used in the interests of the common good or for selfish ends. Science provides impartially a hospital or the latest poison bomb. It may well prove that man's moral powers are so inadequate to stand the strain of all this increasing mastery of the material world that he will use it to destroy himself. So, too, though the outward forms of human selfishness have changed, there is no ground for believing that men are at the bottom less selfish than they were. The highwayman has been superseded by the profiteer, but the only gain is a loss of picturesqueness. Nor do improved conditions of life necessarily go hand in hand with an improved condition of soul. Men can be as selfish and godless in a palace as in a slum. Vice does not cease to be vice because it is gilded. The polite and polished self-indulgence of the smart set hides the glory of God even more effectually than the brutality and coarseness of the savage. Nor does mere learning carry with it an increase in holiness and righteousness. A professor can be further from the kingdom of God than a coal-heaver. Nor is it enough to have higher and more elaborate ideals. The real question is how far we live up to them.

In short when we study the causes that underlie the decay of nations and the degradation of public life, or the misuse of new powers and knowledge, we always come back to man himself. There is nothing outside him that hinders a triumphant upward movement turning all fresh discoveries into means for promoting the highest welfare of each and all. The hindrance lies in man himself, in his inability to love the highest when he sees it and to subdue his antisocial impulses. History lends no support to the idea that these are being outgrown. At bottom the problem is one of moral and spiritual weakness.

(c) This impression is deepened when we turn to the human life and example of Jesus Christ. There we see man as he was intended in the divine purpose to become. We realise anew his imperfection and degradation by placing ourselves beside the concrete picture of the ideal. Christ shows up not only the weakness but the fallenness of human nature. His life throughout is based on unbroken communion with God. He exhibits a perfect harmony between all the faculties and impulses of His human nature. His growth is uniform and unbroken. He is in full sympathy with the mind and purpose of God. Taken by itself, the life of Christ might well only provoke us to despair. We see in it what we acknowledge that we ought to be, but what we are wholly unable in our own strength to attain. It makes us all the more conscious of the evil impulses within us. It shows up our " fallen " condition. Thus introspection, a study of human history, and the example and teaching of Christ all unite in witnessing to our present state as unnatural. By what name are we to designate it ?

(d) Since it is indistinguishable in all except the consciousness of personal responsibility from that condition of heart and will which results from actual sin, in theology it has long received the name of " original sin." Indeed the two are so closely intertwined in actual experience that it is often hard to distinguish them. The alienation from God that they produce is almost identical. We cannot wonder at the choice of the term. To-day, however, the term " original sin " is widely criticised, and with good reason. Many writers argue that the word sin should be restricted to actual sin—that is, to states of character or conduct for which the individual is personally responsible by acts of moral choice. The wider use of the term, they say, only leads to confusion of thought and endangers morality. It is a relic of the days when the concept of sin had not yet been moralised. Its retention to-day only tends to blur the sense of the heinousness of sin or to lead to morbid scruples. If we were starting theological terminology, there would be much to be said for a clearer distinction. But the use of the term sin to include other states of character than those for which the individual is personally responsible, not only has a long history behind it, but witnesses to certain truths of great importance. What are we to substitute for the phrase " original sin " ? Various suggestions have been made, but none of them are entirely satisfactory. " Inherited infirmity " expresses the important truth that our unhappy condition does not carry with it guilt in the sense of accountability or expose us personally to the wrath of God, but is hardly adequate to the seriousness of the situation. " Moral disease " has the advantage that it brings out the positive danger to spiritual health. But neither phrase sufficiently emphasises the important truth that by this state of heart and will we are disqualified for that full communion with God which is the indispensable condition of all sound human life. Religion is not mere morality, but is a walking with God ; and " two cannot walk together unless they be agreed." Further, the old term has this additional advantage that it leaves room for the idea of corporate sin. In his moral and spiritual life the individual is interpenetrated by the community. The will of the community is not simply the sum-total of the wills of the individual members who compose it, though indeed it has no actual existence outside of or apart from them. There is such a thing as a group mind, though probably not a group consciousness. And though an act of moral choice can only be made by an individual, he makes it not as an individual, but as shaped and moulded by the community. Thus we find corporate action which can only be described as sinful since it is objectively opposed to the will of God, though it is certain that not every member of the body is personally responsible for it. Our Lord judged not only individuals, but cities, as Capernaum or Jerusalem. If we attempt to limit sin to states of character or acts for which the individual is personally in the sight of God responsible, we shall find ourselves in difficulties about those corporate sins which are both recognised in the teaching of Christ and implied by modern psychology

## 2. *Various Forms of these Doctrines in History*

If, then, we decide to retain the term in spite of its manifest disadvantages, that does not mean that we accept all doctrines of original sin. It is most important to study the various forms which this doctrine has assumed.

P

(a) If we begin with the Old Testament, we find there a full recognition of the badness of human nature, but hardly any theory of original sin or any attempt to account for it. In the third chapter of Genesis there is a vivid picture of temptation and of actual sin by an act of disobedience to a command of God recognised as binding, but though the act of disobedience is followed by punishment, it is not suggested that this included a bias towards evil in Adam's descendants. Further, when the conspicuous wickedness of a later generation is recorded, the explanation of it is found not in Adam's transgression, but in the strange tale about the " sons of God " and the " daughters of men." Nor is there any certain reference to the story of Adam to be found in the whole of the canonical books. When we pass on to the post-canonical literature, we find more than one apparent attempt to account for the empirically universal wickedness of man. There is the Rabbinic doctrine, based on Genesis viii. 21, of the evil impulse already existing potentially in the heart of man and only waiting for the right stimulus to emerge in a sinful act. There are the more popular theories which connect man's present condition with the disobedience of Adam or with the unions of evil angels and women. Thus it may be said that a doctrine of original sin in some form was held by many in the Jewish Church in the time of Christ, but hardly as an official doctrine of the Church. Nor was there any agreed doctrine of the fall of man. The word " fall " does not occur in this connection in the canonical writings. It is first found in a quite untechnical sense in Wisdom x. 3.

(b) In the teaching of Christ Himself as recorded in the Gospels there is no formal theology of original sin. Indeed we should not expect such. What we do find is the full recognition of the facts of human nature and history which the theological doctrine was formulated to express. It is not too much to say that in His teaching and ministry He assumes that all men are in a condition of " fallenness." They are sick and need a physician. They cannot cure themselves. They need not only enlightenment, but redemption. They are in bondage to a strong and cruel tyrant. They are no longer free and cannot deliver themselves. They are not only undeveloped, but misdeveloped, and therefore must undergo not simply growth and education, but new birth. The existing world order is largely under the domination of evil powers. It resembles a field in which an enemy has sown tares

It would seem that original sin in the sense that this article discusses it is implied in all our Lord's teaching. Of course the guilt of original sin is another matter. Though Jesus clearly spoke of His death as a ransom.

among the wheat. The wheat and tares are hopelessly inter-
mixed both in the hearts of man and in all human life. Nothing
is more startling than the way in which He assumes the presence
of evil in all human hearts. " If ye then, being evil, know how
to . . . ," He says. The Lord's Prayer includes a petition for forgiveness. The only class of people of whom He seems to despair
are those who are unaware of any need for repentance or change of
mind. We cannot develop this subject at length, but it is plain
that in all His teaching He implied that mankind as a whole had
strayed from the right path and swerved away from God's purpose.
This judgment on all men is in the sharpest contrast to His own
claims to an unbroken communion with the Father and undimmed
insight into and sympathy with His purposes. While He sum-
moned all men without exception to repent He displayed no need
of repentance Himself. No prayer for pardon or amendment for
His own life passed His lips. His own sinlessness, if we use
what is too negative a term to express the positive and harmonious
energy of His life towards the Father, shows up the failure and
disharmony of all other human lives.

(c) In St. Paul we find the beginnings of a Christian doctrine
of original sin, starting from the Jewish speculation which connected
man's present condition with the disobedience of Adam. In the
famous sentence " as through one man sin entered into the world,
and death through sin ; and so death passed unto all men, for that
all sinned : for until the law sin was in the world : but sin is not
imputed where there is no law," we find a foundation on which
many large and imposing structures have been built. Unfortunately St. Paul's meaning is most obscure. His primary interest
in the whole chapter is in the universality and completeness of the
redemption brought by Christ. Man's sinful condition is only
brought in as a foil to this. Indeed the actual sentence which
speaks of all men sinning is never finished. It may simply make
the statement that as a matter of fact all men after Adam did for
some reason or other commit sin, without connecting this with
Adam's sin. That is exegetically possible, and it may be argued
that if " in Adam " was to be added, the addition is so important
that it must have been expressed. But the context is against this
interpretation. The whole passage is based on the parallelism
between Adam and Christ, and there is little doubt that the words
" in Adam " are to be supplied in thought, though the fact that

St. Paul did not actually insert them proves that the dominant purpose in his writing here was not to give a theory of the origin of sin.   Further, what is the connection between the sin of Adam and the universal sinfulness of his descendants ?   Is the tendency to sin transmitted by heredity ?   The passage gives no answer to such questions.   They clearly were not in St. Paul's mind at this moment.   Perhaps all that we can say with certainty is that Jewish tradition connected man's present sinfulness with Adam's transgression, and St. Paul assumes a general familiarity with this idea.   If we press for a closer examination of St. Paul's meaning, we may perhaps find a clue in the parallelism between " in Adam " and " in Christ " which pervades the whole context.   Christians are " in Christ," and a study of his general line of thought shows that this means more than that they individually adhere to Christ by personal faith, though it includes this.   It also conveys the idea of membership in His Body the Church.   For St. Paul the Christian life was always mediated by fellowship in the divine society, the people of God.   So "in Adam" may well convey the idea of membership in an unregenerate humanity.   This would suggest that Adam's sin affected his descendants not merely by way of bad example, but by the subtle influences of social tradition in all its forms.

It is also important to remember, though the point is often overlooked, that when at the opening of the Epistle, St. Paul develops the picture of mankind as wholly given over to sin and needing a new power for righteousness, he never mentions Adam. He never suggests that Jew and Gentile have fallen away from God because they inherited a weakened or depraved nature.   He blames them for wilfully turning away from the light given to them.   His language is consistent with a recognition of the social nature of sin but hardly with a strict theory of heredity.

(d) When we turn to the early Church, it is long before we meet any formulated doctrine of original sin.   Before the time of St. Augustine there is neither in East nor West a single and consistent theory of original sin.   The early Christian writers were more concerned with deliverance from demons from without than with deliverance from an inherited bias towards evil within.   In the main, the Greek Fathers represent a " once-born " type of religion.   Under the influence of St. Paul's language, they often allow that Adam's sin has affected his descendants, but it is very difficult to be certain of the way in which they regard this effect. The general tendency is to lay stress on the inheriting, through the solidarity of the race and its unity with its first parent, of the punishment of Adam's sin rather than of the moral corruption of the sin itself. Where emphasis is laid on the effects of the Fall on human nature, they are regarded rather as a *privatio* than as a *depravatio*, a loss of supernatural light and gifts. There is always a strong insistence on the reality of free will and responsibility. Even though in Origen and in Gregory of Nyssa we find the germs of a doctrine of original sin similar to that of St. Augustine, there is no doctrine of original guilt and the consequences of such a doctrine are not thought out.

In the West, Tertullian's traducianism led him to formulate a theory of a hereditary sinful taint—" vitium originis." Adam's qualities were transmitted to his descendants. Yet, as his arguments for the delay of baptism show, he was far from regarding human nature as wholly corrupt. Nor did he deny free will. But he established a tradition in the West which was continued by Cyprian and Hilary and developed by Ambrose until it attained a systematic form at the hands of St. Augustine.

(*e*) In St. Augustine we reach for the first time a systematic theology of original sin. In considering it we must take into account all the factors that have gone to its construction. We place first among these the profound spiritual experience which he had undergone in his sudden and violent conversion, similar to that of St. Paul. His religion was essentially that of the twice-born type and gave him an insight into the meaning of St. Paul's Epistles possessed by few of that age. As he reflected on his experience, it seemed to him that his former life had been one of entire badness from which he had been rescued by an act of divine love. God had done all ; he had done nothing, except to offer a vain opposition to God's irresistible grace. Secondly, in the face of this conviction, the teaching of Pelagius that every man at any time, whatever his past conduct, was able to choose equally and freely either right or wrong, seemed unmitigated folly. No less inadequate was the Pelagian view of grace as primarily the nature bestowed on man in virtue of which he enjoyed this free will, or a merely external assistance such as the example of Christ, or at most an inward inspiration useful indeed as seconding man's efforts but in no way indispensable for salvation. Accordingly in revolt against Pelagius, who taught that all men at birth receive a sound and uncorrupted human nature, he emphasised to the utmost the corruption of human nature. Mankind was a " massa perditionis." [1] We do indeed possess free will by nature in the sense that the sins which we commit are our own choice, but we do not possess a truly free will in the sense that we have the power to choose right. Apart from the grace of God we can only choose sin. In support of this teaching he appealed to the authority of St. Paul. The Pelagians argued that practically universal sin was due to the following of Adam's bad example and to the influence of bad surroundings, regarded in a purely external way. Against this, relying on the mistranslation of Romans v. 12, " In whom (*in quo*) all sinned," he taught that Adam's sin involved the sin of all his descendants and that they in some sense sinned when he did. Thus, going beyond the teaching of St. Paul, he insisted not only on original sin, but on original guilt, a conception which it is impossible to reconcile with either reason or morality. When driven to offer a defence for this indefensible position, his replies were by no means either clear or consistent. At times he put forward the theory of our seminal existence in Adam, as Levi existed in the loins of Abraham. At other times he fell back on a mystical realism in which he held that not only Adam's nature, but his personality were shared by his descendants. Elsewhere he appealed to the mystery of divine justice. In close connection with this view of inherited guilt involving the further assertion that unbaptised infants were condemned to hell, was the theory familiar to Gnostics and Manicheans, but strange in the writings of a Christian teacher, that inherited sinfulness consisted mainly in that concupiscence through which the race was propagated, since under the present conditions of a fallen world marriage, in itself right and sinless, was inevitably accompanied by passions which are sinful. Few theories have had more disastrous results in later Christian thought. Such teaching as this would seem logically to carry with it some form of traducianism, but, though he inclined towards it, he never actually adopted it.

In this short summary of St. Augustine's teaching it is clear that he has gone very far beyond the teaching of St. Paul. Not only does he omit the other side of St. Paul's teaching where he insists on the need of human effort, but the novel conception of

---

[1] e.g. *De correptione et gratia,* 12.

original guilt gives a new colour to the concept of original sin. To St. Paul, original sin is of the nature of a deadly spiritual disease disabling man from full fellowship with God, objectively contrary to the will of God and in that sense sinful, but not blameworthy. Men stricken with it are unable to help themselves, but their plight appeals to God's pity rather than to God's wrath. This teaching does full justice to man's need of redemption, and is in full accord with the facts of life. St. Augustine on the other hand ignores a large field of facts, and though his interpretation of religion goes far deeper than that of Pelagius, his theology is one-sided. His doctrine of man as inheriting a totally corrupt nature by physical transmission from a historical Adam and involving guilt in the sense of accountability is often taken to be the Catholic doctrine of original sin, but this is by no means the case. We must not confuse the doctrines of the Fall and of original sin with the Augustinian presentation of them.

A short survey of Church history is sufficient to show that the complete Augustinian system has no claim to be considered Catholic in the true sense of the term. As we saw, the teaching of the Fathers before him, even in the West, gives no certain voice on the subject. The Church agreed with him in his rejection of Pelagianism, but was by no means ready to accept the system that he offered in its stead. The Eastern Church has never received Augustinianism as a whole. Its teaching on original sin does not at most go beyond that of Gregory of Nyssa. In the West his views aroused at once considerable opposition, especially in South Gaul. The so-called Semi-Pelagian School protested with effect against his doctrine of grace and election as a novelty, and maintained that even man as fallen had some power of free choice, though weakened, so as to be able to co-operate with grace. The celebrated " Commonitorium " of Vincent of Lerins, in which " semper, ubique, ab omnibus," is laid down as the test of Catholicism, was probably aimed at the teaching of Augustine. The Synod of Orange in 529 maintained a considerably modified Augustinianism. While emphasising the need of grace, including prevenient grace, it expressly condemned the idea of predestination to evil which was implied in the doctrine of irresistible grace. As regards the Fall it asserted that Adam's sin affected not only himself but his descendants, and that it has impaired not only the body but the soul. Nothing however is said about entire corruption.

In the Middle Ages the general movement was away from the stricter teaching of St. Augustine, in spite of the veneration for his name.    Aquinas taught that on the positive side original sin was a wounding of nature, a disordered condition, the result of a loss of superadded graces which Adam had enjoyed in his state of original righteousness.    In contradiction to Augustine he denied that natural goodness was forfeited by the Fall or free will destroyed, and held that concupiscence is not properly sin.    Duns Scotus represented an even greater departure from the standpoint of Augustine.    He insisted more strongly on man's freedom and taught that the first sin, whose gravity he tended to minimise, had affected not man's nature, but only his supernatural gifts.    The Council of Trent with an ingenuity worthy of our own Thirty-Nine Articles contrived, while using the language of St. Augustine, to produce a formula which could be interpreted in accordance with the much milder Scholastic teaching.    The Fall is said to have involved the loss of original righteousness, the tainting of body and soul, slavery to the devil, and liability to the wrath of God. Original sin is propagated by generation.

It is to the Reformers that we must principally look for a revival of Augustinianism.    Calvin and Luther agree in describing the depravity of human nature in the strongest terms, in insisting on the guilt of original sin, and in maintaining the doctrine of irresistible grace.    They both did what Augustine shrank from doing, namely, taught explicitly that some men are predestined to evil.    Here again, if we study the history of Protestantism, we find an increasing reaction against such teaching.    It is hardly too much to say that modern Protestantism, so far as it has any doctrine of the Fall and original sin, has repudiated the stern but logical teaching of Calvin and Luther.

### 3. *The Need for Restatement*

Within the last century new knowledge has accumulated which compels a reconsideration and restatement of the whole question. New data unknown to the theologians of the early Church and of the Middle Ages may well cause us to revise their teaching in the interest of truth.    All that reverence for Catholic tradition demands is that the new theology of original sin should be no less adequate to the facts of the Christian life and should possess the old spiritual values.

We may especially consider three sources from which fresh light has been thrown on the subject.

First, literary and historical criticism have shown beyond any reasonable doubt that the opening chapters of Genesis do not give us literal record of fact. They are, to use a phrase of Bishop Gore, "inspired mythology." This does not diminish their value for religion, however. The picture of the temptation to disobedience followed by the act of sin is of abiding value as an analysis of the spiritual drama that is constantly being re-enacted in our own souls. No words could bring out more clearly the subtlety of temptation, the nature of actual sin, and the alienation from God that it brings. On the other hand the value of these chapters as literal history has been for ever shattered. There is a strange reluctance in many quarters to face the consequences of this discovery. Historical facts can only be proved by historical evidence. We have therefore no right to draw from the stories in Genesis deductions about the condition of Adam before his disobedience and make them a basis for theories about the condition of unfallen man. How much theology has centred round the purely hypothetical supernatural graces of an Adam for whose existence we have no historical evidence ! The chapters of Genesis do indeed bear witness to man's conviction that his present condition is unnatural and not in accordance with God's will. They attest a sense of fallenness, but give us no information whatever about a historical Fall.

Secondly, we have come to realise that man has been evolved from a non-human ancestry, and that he has inherited impulses and instincts which he shares with the lower animals. Recent psychology has emphasised the fact that not only the human body, but the human mind has been thus evolved.

Thirdly, psychology has given us the concepts of the " unconscious mind and purpose." Whatever be the ultimate verdict about the theories connected with the names of Freud and Jung, there can be very little doubt that they have thrown light on the structure and mechanism of the human mind, and that this will have to be taken into account in all attempts to understand and deal with our spiritual life.

How, then, can we apply these considerations to the doctrine of original sin ?

*A point worth mentioning too is that the instincts of animals do not lead to the depths [variety and intensity of evil as do man's uncontrolled impulses.*

(a) We owe to Dr. Tennant the first attempt, at least in England, to reinterpret the doctrine in the light of biology. It is quite unfair to regard his treatment as merely naturalistic. He limits the term sin to actual sin, claiming that this limitation brings out all the more clearly the seriousness of sin. So-called original sin he regards as the survival in man of animal tendencies, useful and necessary at an earlier stage, but now felt to be an anachronism. Our consciousness of divided self is due to the fact that these animal impulses are only in process of being moralised. As man has evolved he has exchanged a life of merely animal contentment and harmony for one of moral struggle and effort. He has become dissatisfied with his brute life and contrasts his animal passions and habits with what he would fain become. So his sense of dissatisfaction is really a sign of moral advance and is the inevitable outcome of man's development.

Though we are unable to accept this as an adequate explanation of all the facts, we owe much to Dr. Tennant for his treatment of the problem. But we feel that he has underestimated the gravity of the situation. He has explained admirably the origin of the raw material of our evil impulses and tendencies, but the real problem is not the possession of these animal tendencies but the universal failure to control them. We believe that the human life and character of Christ were based upon just such elements of instinct, but in Him they were directed and harmonised into a perfect whole. There is in this material of instinct and impulse nothing that is intrinsically evil. It is all capable of right direction. The problem is that men universally fail to control and direct it. The mere possession of these impulses could not be called sinful in any sense of the term. It is in full accord with the will of God. But it certainly results in very much that cannot be in accordance with the will of a good God. We may also criticise Dr. Tennant on the ground that he regards sin as a purely moral problem. He passes over lightly the religious aspect. He has replied indeed that there was no need to emphasise the fact that sin is against God, because no one had ever disputed it.[1] But there is always a danger of allowing too little weight to considerations which are taken for granted. Sin is a religious term and religion is more than mere morality. The seriousness of original sin is that it cuts man off from God and from that fellowship with Him for which man was made.

[1] *Journal of Theological Studies*, Jan. 1923, p. 196.

(*b*) Let us then look at the facts again. Science and psychology unite in teaching us that we must regard human nature not statically but dynamically. It does not come to us ready made. It is a process. When we are born, we are so to speak candidates for humanity. We inherit a number of quite general instincts out of which we build up our life through experience. We also inherit certain mental dispositions and capacities, though there is a wide difference of opinion as to their number and nature. Our powers are undeveloped. What if this mental structure has been already misformed before the conscious life begins? May we not find on these lines an explanation of those phenomena which are comprised in the term "original sin"? Older theology regarded men as inheriting a tendency to evil by generation much in the same way as physical peculiarities. This is still the official doctrine of the Roman Church, following St. Augustine. It comes very near to reducing moral evil to a physical taint. Further the transmission of any such bias to evil would be a case of what is called the transmission of an acquired characteristic. The possibility of this is strongly denied by the dominant school of biologists. They hold that modifications acquired during the lifetime of an organism cannot be passed on to its descendants by heredity. It is true that many scientists are of an opposite opinion, but until science has made up its mind on the question—and it is for science to decide—it is rash to explain original sin by heredity. Further, it is hard to see in what way any element in our nature can have become intrinsically bad, since God created nothing evil in itself. Rather it is the balance of our nature that is upset, and desires and impulses good in themselves and necessary for the completeness of our human life have become attached to wrong objects or got out of control.

We suggest therefore that more weight should be attached to what is often called, not quite accurately, "social heredity." We have already called attention to the fact that there is no such thing as a mere individual. The individual only comes to himself as a member of a community. This truth long familiar has received a new application through modern psychology. We have come to see that from his earliest moments, even perhaps in the period before birth, the infant is having his tastes and tendencies moulded by the influence of those around him. And all through life we are being shaped by social tradition in all its many and subtle forms.

In all his moral and spiritual life the individual is being inter-penetrated by the moral and spiritual life of others. There is a real solidarity of mankind. Herd instinct prompts our conduct far more than we like to assume and, let us remember, herd instinct is in itself at best morally neutral. When we have attained a certain stage of development, mere herd instinct tends to lower the moral level of the individual. We must distinguish between mere herd or mass suggestion and the group mind or mind of an organised society, which is able to raise the minds of the members of a group to higher levels of moral and intellectual life. This innate capacity for social life is then itself morally neutral. As it may be the condition of progress, so it may be equally the condition of movement away from the purpose of God. We may see in original sin the result of misdirected social influence. Some such concept is an intellectual necessity. Social sin is as much a fact as social righteousness. All societies possess in a real sense a corporate mind, the product not only of its present members but of its past members also, and all who belong to and share its mind come consciously or unconsciously under its sway. We suggest that original sin is to be found not simply in the possession of animal impulses and passions imperfectly disciplined and in the failure to discipline them by the individual, but rather in the positive mis-directing of such instinctive tendencies by bad social influences at every stage. Psychologists have invented a new term "moral disease" to describe a mental condition in which instinctive tendencies which conflict with moral standards have been repressed into the unconscious and from there exercise a pernicious influence on the conscious life. Without committing ourselves to the position that original sin consists merely in repressed complexes, we may see here one way in which the moral life may be disordered through no fault of the individual but simply through social environment.

In a review of Dr. Tennant's book in the " Journal of Theological Studies " [1] Mr. C. S. Gayford wrote : " Granted that the propensities which constitute the *fomes peccati* come to us from our animal ancestry, and are in themselves non-moral, the last step in the evidence should tell us what attitude the will itself at its first appearance is seen to adopt towards these propensities. Is it neutral ? Does it incline towards that higher law which is just

[1] April 1903, p. 472.

beginning to dawn upon the consciousness? Or is it found from the first in sympathy and alliance with the impulses which it ought to curb?" Modern psychologists would complain that this language treats the will as a separate faculty, whereas they regard it rather as the whole man moving in response to some stimulus. But if we modify this view of the will, the quotation corresponds to our suggestion. When man becomes responsible for his actions, his power of choice is limited and perverted by "sentiments" and "complexes" formed under the influence of his social environment during the time when his power of moral choice was still undeveloped. While these do not destroy his power of free choice, they curtail the range within which such choice is now possible.

(c) Dr. Tennant's view has also been attacked from another direction. It has been argued in several quarters lately that we cannot isolate the evil tendencies in man from the evil in nature : that the process of evolution was vitiated long before man ever appeared on the scene. It is impossible to suppose that a perfectly good and wise God would have created, say, the cobra or the cholera germ. It is not enough to say that the world is imperfect. The existence of "dysteleology" in nature, the ruthless competition and cruelty all go to show that it does not perfectly express the will of God. So the nature which man inherited from his animal ancestry was fallen before ever he inherited it. He appeared on the scene burdened by an inherently self-centred nature dominated by instinctive structures of animalism whose overpowering bias towards evil he could not be expected to control. Those who maintain such views as these make out a strong case. They argue for a "Fall," but a Fall which is "pre-organic"—that is, prior in time to the whole evolutionary process. Certainly this idea clearly emphasises the reality and seriousness of original sin.[1]

## 4. *The State of Fallenness*

The doctrine of a Fall of some kind is an inevitable deduction from the recognition of original sin. If we hold that our present condition is not in accordance with the will of God we must believe that the race as a whole has fallen away from the divine purpose. As we have seen, we can no longer use the story in Genesis as historical evidence. Nor have we any other source of

[1] See e.g. Formby, *The Unveiling of the Fall*.

*It must be remembered that Science does not tell the whole of man's story nor even the higher part of it. History has a big word to say. Civilisations do rise and fall. Progress is neither inevitable nor continuous and there is much to be said for the*

light on the moral and spiritual condition of primitive man. We do
not even know for certain whether all mankind are descended from
a single pair or not. Nor does the study of the scanty remains of
primitive races throw light on our problem. It seems as if man
had made one or two false starts, and that races who had attained to
a certain degree of development died out. It can also be inferred
from the possessions buried with the dead that they believed in some
kind of future life, and therefore had some kind of religion. More
than this we cannot say, nor does it seem as if we shall ever get any
clear evidence on this point. It is quite conceivable that there once
was a time when the human race was developing on right lines,
a period of what we might call, to use the old term, " original
righteousness." Science is more ready than it was to admit of
leaps forward in evolution. We can picture one such when man
became aware, however dimly, of a spiritual environment and of
his capacity to correspond to it. It may have been that for a
time long or short he did respond and began to develop on right
lines and then failed to respond. He refused to make the moral
effort to live up to his calling and so forfeited that full fellowship
with God which could alone give him the power to control his
animal impulses. Science cannot say anything against such a
hypothesis. Indeed, Sir Oliver Lodge in his last book puts forth
a similar view. Man experienced " a rise in the scale of existence,"
but fell " below the standard at which he had now consciously
arrived. The upward step was unmistakable ; mankind tripped
over it and fell, but not irremediably." [1]

Another possible view is that there never existed in actual
history any period when man fulfilled God's purpose for him,
but that before ever he emerged, the evolutionary process was
marred by some rebellious spiritual influence. Some have
attempted to revive Origen's teaching of a Fall of individual souls
in a pre-existent state. This is open to all the arguments against
pre-existence and is hard to reconcile with the justice of God.
If our present lot is the rightful consequence of disobedience in
some previous existence, then it is morally useless to punish us
for it unless we are able to remember it. Others again have put
forward a theory of a world-soul which by some pre-cosmic act
was shattered and defiled so that the life-force is in itself tainted.
This is a piece of pure mythology, and corresponds to nothing in

[1] *The Making of Man*, pp. 84, 151.

human experience. It is difficult to criticise it because it eludes both the understanding and the imagination. It is more reasonable to conjecture that the world-process has been distorted by rebellious wills other than human. There is nothing irrational in supposing that there are other conscious beings than man in the universe. We know in our own experience the possibility of disobedience to the will of God. If sin can arise in our own lives in this way, it is not unreasonable to hold that it arose in like manner in other beings who, however unlike ourselves, resemble us in this, that they enjoy some measure of free will. This certainly can claim the support of Scripture, which assumes the activity of rebellious spirits other than human behind the world-order. St. Paul includes in the redemption won by Christ not only mankind, but angels above man and nature below man.

To sum up : Christian tradition and experience unite in bearing witness to a belief that mankind as a whole and not merely individual man has fallen away from the purpose of God. What is important is to recognise the fact of fallenness. The practical value of this belief is great. To believe in original sin is to face the facts, but not to take a depressing view of human life. It is to make an act of faith that we ourselves and human society are not what God intended us to be, and that our present condition is a libel on human nature as He purposed it. The human race as a whole and every member of it needs not only education and development, but redemption. It cannot save itself, but must be as it were remade or born again. And we believe that in Christ God has provided exactly what we need. In Him the human race made a new start.

Further, just as we saw that original sin was propagated by membership in a fallen humanity, so in the Church, the Body of Christ, we see the new people of God, the new humanity. The Church is in literal truth the home of grace. By baptism[1] the

[1] The question may be asked whether the rejection of much of the traditional theology connected with the Fall of man does not necessitate a revision of our doctrine of baptism. We must first insist that much of the language employed in connection with baptism, which is taken from Scripture, was used in its original context to refer to adult baptism. It dates from a time when, as in the Mission field to-day, infant baptism was the exception and not the rule. Accordingly when it is transferred to apply to infant baptism we cannot wonder that its meaning needs to be modified. Thus an adult coming to be baptised needs forgiveness of his past actual sins. He needs not only to be cleansed but to be pardoned. But an infant is not in the least responsible for

Christian is born again, because he is brought within the sphere of the new life achieved by Christ and imparted normally by membership in His Body. "For as in Adam all die, so also in Christ shall all be made alive." Over against original sin we set the redemptive power realised through fellowship with God and with one another in Christ.

## II

### GRACE AND FREEDOM

### BY J. K. MOZLEY

#### 1. *The Idea of Grace*

THE differences which inhere in any two individual lives are, in part, the result of the differences of the two persons concerned. But they are also, in part, the result of the differences of the two particular environments. For no two persons, at any stage, is environment precisely the same, and the secret of a life, which may be revealed though very incompletely at some moment in its course, and is more fully disclosed when that course has reached its earthly end, is the secret of the interaction between the self and its environment. Yet this is not the whole truth. The Christian sees the deeper truth of the self and its earthly environment in the

his share in a fallen humanity. He needs indeed the grace of God to counteract the perverting influences which have already begun to work upon his life, but God cannot be said in any sense to blame him for his present condition. Nor can we believe that infants are personally exposed to the wrath of God. All that we can assert is that God hates and condemns that condition of humanity which shuts men out from fellowship with Himself. Only in this quite abstract sense can sin that is only "original" be said to deserve God's wrath. The unhappy use of St. Paul's phrase "children of wrath" in the baptismal service has been responsible for many misunderstandings. In its context, as all New Testament scholars agree, it only means "objects of wrath." There is no reference whatever to infancy. St. Paul insists that men by "nature," that is apart from the assistance of God's grace, cannot overcome their evil tendencies and be pleasing to Him. Even so God's wrath is directed, as we have seen, against their condition, not against themselves. God cannot condemn men for a state for which they are not accountable. Rather, as suffering from a disease of the soul which disqualifies them for the highest life, they are the objects of His pity and redeeming purpose. So, again, when infants are said to be born "in sin," the term is being used in its widest sense, to include all tendencies of life that are contrary to the divine purpose. The phrase means "born into an environment that will mis-shape them."

light of the relation of each to a higher order of reality which supplies the only adequate account both of what is and of what is intended to be. There is a unity underlying variation. A two-fold relationship, constituting a twofold environment, forms the permanent setting of the life of every individual. We are one through our membership of a fallen and sinful humanity ; we are one through our membership of a redeemed humanity which offers us the hope of such a final liberation from all sin and every form of evil as will mean the fulfilment of a glorious destiny.[1]

Both these are real environments. They give the spiritual conditions of our lives. There are certain moral facts connected with humanity, out of which no individual can contract. This is clear enough of the evil. It has penetrated too deeply for any sort of Pelagianism to hold its ground, when the appeal goes to the facts. It is on the moral side that pessimism has its strength. There is a real facing of a mass of evidence in the belief that though humanity is conscious of a call to moral idealism and achievement it neither has nor ever will have the power to attain. The other condition is not equally clear. Indeed, to some it may seem too great a paradox to speak of humanity both as though in it a kingdom of evil held sway, and also as in fact redeemed. Some who reject pessimistic conclusions, while seeking to face bravely and honestly the widespread signs of evil strongly entrenched, would probably prefer to describe humanity and the world as to be redeemed rather than redeemed. But the Christian Church will never allow its songs of triumph to be set in the minor key. The work of Christ means something more than a specially powerful movement in the long warfare between good and evil. The two great epistles *Colossians* and *Ephesians* bear testimony to that. We have but dim conceptions and inadequate words for expressing what is known as the cosmic work of Christ. A veil hides from us the mysteries both of creation and of redemption. But the Church with all the richness of its life is not to be understood as the means to the attainment only of moral ends, nor is the Kingdom to be reckoned as no more than that " far-off divine event " which will some day close the book of world-history. The Church is here, and the Kingdom comes because of the eternal present value of Christ's work of salvation. We have our place in a new world-order as truly as in that which binds us with the chains of its ancient evil.

[1] *Cf.* Romans viii. 18–25.

But though the belief in a new order is characteristic of Christianity, the relationship of the individual to this order in which the old things have become new is not " given " in the same sense as his relationship to that sinful humanity which represents the continuance of the old order.  For the efficacy of his membership in it depends upon his personal response to it and use of it. He himself, for this to be possible, must become a new creation. No utterance of the New Testament better expresses the nature of the environment in which the believer has his dwelling and of the change which the reaction between it and himself involves than 2 Corinthians v. 17 : " In Christ . . . a new creation " ;  that description briefly comprehends the reality of the new life as possessing and possessed by the individual.  And the word which gives the best and fullest description of this new life, expressing both its nature and also the individual's proper reaction to it, is the word Grace.

This word is one of the classic words of Christian theology, as an exposition of its frequency and importance as χάρις in the New Testament, and of its standing in the great dogmatic *schemata* of Catholicism and of Protestantism, would show.  Yet the framing of a wholly satisfactory conception of it has not been unattended by special difficulties, and both in popular religious thought and in theological interpretations, it has occasioned misunderstandings and perplexities which have not been chiefly on the surface or at the circumference of Christian faith.  We must allow first of all for impressions, which can hardly be called intellectual conceptions, of grace as an impersonal force, a " thing " which can be brought into touch with persons by some process of permeation. That is the danger of the phrase " infused grace."  We cannot abandon it.  It has both too honourable a history and too essentially religious a meaning.  But we must not let it convey to our minds the idea that grace is a kind of invisible fluid which passes into persons and produces effects through contact.  The materialism of attenuated and etherialised substances is still materialism ; and though matter and spirit are not contrary the one to the other, seeing that each is dependent upon God and serves God's purposes ; though, further, matter can be used in the highest interests of spirit, else the Incarnation would be impossible and the sacraments possess no inward part ; it is always true that spirit remains spirit, and matter matter.  Grace stands for the personal dealings of God with man in various ways and through various media. He does not start a process which ends in the pouring of grace into man ; but grace means God in action, regenerating, blessing, forgiving, strengthening. It is the suggestion of impersonal operation which has found an entrance into the terminology of grace that needs to be eradicated. Then, secondly, difficulties arise in connection with the place given to grace and with the effects ascribed to its activity. It is both intellectually justifiable, and also of great spiritual value, to believe that man is not the victim of illusion when he claims to possess a measure of freedom, and that that freedom is never overwhelmed or destroyed. Man's free self-expression is variously limited, and in no two persons is it of exactly the same quality, but the moral aim of life is towards an expansion not a contraction of it, and in all moral attainment free action of personality is involved. Now the workings of grace have been so expounded as to leave no place for freedom. The Augustinian tradition so emphasised the necessity of acts of will being in accordance with the state of human nature which lay behind the will, that grace was in danger of being regarded as an invasive and irresistible force which so changed man's nature that man was then "free" to do what had formerly been impossible for him. For Augustine the true freedom was the *beata necessitas boni*,[1] and the goal of the spiritual life. To this description of the ideal no exception is to be taken : but there is grave objection to the idea that the human will, or, better, the willing person, never makes any contribution in connection with salvation except that of willing what he has to will because his whole being is in the control of a force which turns it like a ship's rudder.

There is no hope of escape from this annulment of freedom by the delimitation of the moral and the religious life as two different spheres, with freedom the characteristic description of the one, and grace of the other. This is an unsatisfactory and unreal compromise. Even if grace could ever be regarded as operating in man in such a way as to leave his freedom alone and not to invade that region of his life in which moral decisions have to be made and moral values achieved, that could be applied only to quite low levels of experience. Only on such levels is any divorcement between ethic and religion conceivable. Ethic is not religion, and religion is not ethic, but

[1] Cf. *De Civ. Dei*, xxii. 30. The phrase itself I take from Harnack's *History of Dogma*, v. p. 113.

only as they meet and interpenetrate in experience are the highest levels of either attainable.[1]    If grace is to be allowed for at all, that is progressively the case as the moral life grows to higher stature and becomes richer and more comprehensive.    And the consciousness of dependence upon grace is the best way to moral attractiveness.    It is the lack of this consciousness which is the most serious and suggestive defect in the pagan moral ideal.    How little Aristotle conceives of a way out of the moral struggle whereby the individual may reach a higher state of goodness and abide therein is clear from his comparison in the seventh book of the "Ethics" of the ignorance of the incontinent man, and its cessation, with the phenomena of sleep and awakening.    There is simply an alternation of contrary experiences.    As for the Stoic sage, we may admire him, without impulse or desire to imitate him.    Whatever theory be held of the matter, it is the union of religious dependence with moral independence in the Christian saint which gives him his pre-eminence religiously and morally.    It appeals as a unity, not as two admirable but isolated facts lying side by side within one personality.

## 2. *The Idea of Grace in the Bible and Christian Theology*

Before we go further into the question of the presence and scope of grace in the Christian life, and of the character of its relation to freedom, a sketch of the idea of grace as we find it in the Bible, and of the place it occupies in the historical development of Christian thought, will be useful, and may point us in the right direction for a solution of the difficulties which have gathered round the subject.

We may note at the start that the general notion involved in the word "grace" is, when viewed in relation to God or the gods, that of divine favour flowing outwards to man, and, when viewed from the side of man as the recipient of that favour, enhanced powers which may reveal themselves in physical or spiritual growth and capacity.    According to the character and development of religion, so will be the conception of grace.    If we take two definitions of grace when it is conceived in accordance with the whole Christian outlook—that of Dr. Gore that it is "God's love

[1] Otto's insistence on this point has been strangely overlooked by many of his critics.

to us in actual operation," [1] and that of Dr. W. N. Clarke who describes it as " the suitable expression, in such a world as this, of the fact that God's gracious purpose is to bless sinners " [2]—we see how far such phraseology goes beyond the primitive ideas of grace which we find in ethnic religions.[3]   But wherever there is the conception of a mysterious power or virtue attaching to particular things, or, more personally, of beauty and strength bestowed on men by a divine being, there we may recognise the rudiments of what was to become the Christian belief in grace.   A passage in the " Odyssey " shows how χάρις can be construed as a physical gift from the gods.   Before his meeting with Nausicaa Odysseus is beautified by Athene ;  she makes him " greater and more mighty to behold, and from his head caused deep curling thick locks to flow like the hyacinth flowers . . . and shed grace about his head and shoulders.   Then to the shore of the sea went Odysseus apart, and sat down, glowing in beauty and grace." [4] Yet, though materialistic or quasi-physical conceptions of the gods involve similar conceptions of grace, we must not exclude a primitive moral interpretation.   The favour of the gods possesses this moral connotation, in that the opposite of the divine favour, namely the divine anger issuing in punishment, is the result of offences which draw down upon individual or tribe supernatural wrath.   And though, at early stages of religion, no sharp division between the ceremonial and the ethical is possible, allowance must be made for the presence of an element truly, though in quite primitive fashion, ethical.[5]

The Old Testament is permeated with the conviction of God's gracious dealings with man.   But we must recognise different levels of insight into the character of these dealings.   There is the primitive conception of grace as it comes before us in the story of Noah's sacrifice [6] ;  there is the highly developed teaching of the Prophets whose doctrine, on its side of hope and promise, is one of grace specially directed towards the Community.[7]   There is

[1] *The Epistle to the Romans,* i. p. 49.
[2] *The Christian Doctrine of God,* p. 89.
[3] For primitive notions of grace and the concept of " mana " see R. R. Marett, *The Threshold of Religion,* pp. 101 ff.
[4] *Odyssey,* vi. 229–237 (tr. Butcher and Lang).
[5] See the chapter entitled " Morality " in Dr. F. B. Jevons' *Introduction to the Study of Comparative Religion.*
[6] Genesis viii. 21.
[7] *Cf.* Amos v. 15 ;  Hosea xiv. 2 ;  Is. xxx. 18.

nothing akin to pagan conceptions of grace as won from supernatural powers through magical processes.　In the sacrifices of
the Law, it is God who through the cultus gives man the means of
approaching Him and being accepted by Him.[1]　Where the Old
Testament, as a whole, is incomplete is in placing so predominant
an emphasis on the national covenant-relationship with God that
the individual is in danger of being overlooked, and in the confine-
ment of God's gracious purposes and blessings to Israel.　But the
manifestation of grace as the antithesis of sin and the source of
mercy and forgiveness is constantly found in the Old Testament,
beginning with the Protevangelium.　It would take us too far
away from the subject to pursue this thought further, but it may
be said that modern misconceptions of the religion of the Old
Testament and its doctrine of God are largely due to a failure to
pay attention to the place and importance given in the Old Testament to God's manifestation of His grace.

In the New Testament, though the word " grace " is unevenly
distributed through the various portions of its literature, the reality
for which the word stands is of the essence of the revelation of
God's attitude towards man.　The Gospel is always one of grace.
It is so in our Lord's preaching of the fatherhood and the love
of God, nowhere more prominently than in the parables which
St. Luke has preserved for us.[2]　And when we pass to St. Paul's
epistles, grace appears as " that regnant word of the Pauline theology " [3] in which is contained the answer to the fact and problem
of sin, bound up with the Incarnation and cross of the Son of God,
and linked on, as the Dean of Wells shows, with the extension of
the Gospel to the Gentiles.[4]　Any adequate discussion of St. Paul's
understanding of grace would have to take account of problems
which can only be mentioned.　These concern the universality of

---

[1] *Cf.* Lev. xvii. 11.

[2] *Cf.* Dr. Townsend's *The Doctrine of Grace in the Synoptic Gospels.*　On
p. 106, writing of the first two parables in St. Luke xv. he says : " In the Christian
religion the emphasis is on the divine quest of God for man.　God is the seeker,
and these parables affirm the restlessness of His grace in Christ, until that which
was lost is found."　*Cf.* what St. Paul says of " being known of God " in 1 Cor.
viii. 3 and Gal. iv. 9.

[3] Miss E. Underhill's expression in *The Mystic Way*, p. 178.

[4] See, in his edition of *Ephesians*, the exposition on ii. 10, pp. 52–3 : " It
was the glory of grace to bring the Two once more together as One in Christ.
A new start was thus made in the world's history.　St. Paul called it a New
Creation."

grace, the relationship in which it stands to the divine righteousness, its doctrinal connections with the Apostle's theology of the indwelling Christ and of the Holy Spirit, and its bearing upon his conception of the sacraments.   It is sufficient for our purposes to point out that the problems or even dilemmas of which he was conscious, at least in part—and we still more when we try to systematise the controlling features in St. Paul's religion—must not be solved or evaded by any compromising formula which is always in danger of missing the point of the Apostle's meaning.   For him the true interpretation of religion depends on the recognition of the priority of grace to all human endeavours.   This grace he found at its richest and most illuminating in Jesus Christ, the Son of God, crucified and risen, and when he thought of the working out of God's purposes in the ages to come, he saw it as an increasing manifestation of " the exceeding riches of his grace in kindness towards us in Christ Jesus." [1]

As in the New Testament, so in Christian theology, grace is one of the dominant words.   Yet in the first centuries it gained no special attention.   The sacramental associations of grace are, as early as Ignatius, deriving from the Incarnation and pointing forward to a climax in " deification." [2]   No one was concerned to go deeply into the question of the effect of grace upon human freedom.   Origen has something to say on the matter, and ends his discussion with the declaration that both the divine and the human element must be maintained. [3]   But for the full significance of grace to be expounded, both a man of quite uncommon religious history and genius and the occasion of a great controversy were necessary. The need was supplied by Augustine and the issues which rose round the sharp reactions from one another of himself and Pelagius. We must leave on one side the story of that first great clash of rival efforts to state a Christian anthropology.   Suffice it to say that Augustine's whole doctrine of grace rests on two pillars which rise from the ground of one of the profoundest of religious experiences.   One of them stands for the absolute necessity of grace, as the source of all real goodness, the other for the character of grace as real power infused into the human heart.   A determinist   in   the   modern   philosophical   sense   Augustine   was

---

[1] Eph. ii. 7.
[2] *Ad Ephes.* xx.   *Cf.* also Irenaeus, *Haer.* v. 2, 3.
[3] *De Principiis,* iii. 1, 22.

not.[1] But the only freedom which interested him was freedom to do right, and that freedom was obtainable through grace alone. His opponents, on the other hand, conceived of grace as no more than a help, interpreted it, partly at least, as a description of such external assistance to well-doing as law and doctrine,[2] and displayed great zeal for the emphasising of man's natural freedom to choose the good, and of the obligation resting upon him precisely in virtue of that freedom. Augustine triumphed, but within the Catholic Church Augustinianism as a fully articulated system has, practically from the first, been subject to reservations. When in A.D. 529 the Council of Arausio or Orange, while maintaining against Pelagianism or Pelagianising tendencies that grace was necessary and prevenient and not based on antecedent merits, declared that sufficient grace was given to all the baptised,[3] a place was left for the action of the will which involved by implication a kind of differentiation between grace and freedom that Augustine could not have admitted.[4] For Augustine identified salvation with the gift of final perseverance, which was not bestowed on all the baptised ; and as that gift was both in itself indispensable for salvation, and the culmination of the economy of grace, sufficient grace, in the sense of being sufficient for salvation, was not, in Augustine's view, a gift of which every member of the visible Church had the advantage.

Large contributions to the theology of grace were made by the Schoolmen, and the conception of actual grace as the motive

---

[1] " The *libertas arbitrii* in the psychological sense he never denied ; within the region of his ability man possesses a *liberum arbitrium* (that is freedom of choice) : Augustine was no determinist." Loofs' *Leitfaden zum Studium der Dogmengeschichte* [4], p. 411.

[2] In the *De gestis Pelagii*, 30, Augustine refers to Pelagius' repudiation of an opinion ascribed to Coelestius that " the grace and help of God is not given for individual acts, but exists in free-will or in law and teaching." Thus interpreted, grace becomes the revelation of what we ought to do, and the formal possibility of doing it, not a re-enforcement of man's will by divine power. Harnack, while allowing that just at this point it is hardest to reproduce Pelagian views, concludes that the Pelagian doctrine " in its deepest roots . . . is godless " (*Hist. of Dogma*, v. p. 203).

[3] Towards the end of *Capit. XXV* it is said : " This also we believe according to the Catholic faith, that through the grace received in baptism all the baptised, Christ helping them and working with them, can and ought, if they are willing to strive faithfully, to accomplish those things which concern the soul's salvation."

[4] For Augustine the way in which freedom and grace are related to one another is all-important. He says (*De corrept. et grat.* 17) " the human will does not attain grace by freedom, but rather attains freedom by grace."

power whereby habitual grace, consisting in the natural or theo- ∧
logical virtues, is exercised, is in line with the Augustinian tradition,[1] though the scheme is much more elaborate. When at
the Council of Trent neither the Dominicans, carrying on the
Augustinian doctrine, as it had come down through St. Thomas
Aquinas, nor the Jesuits, with their much more definite semi-
Pelagianism and affinities with Scotist thought, were able to secure
full dogmatic expression for their views, the result was an Augustinian assertion of the necessity of grace, which, at the same time,
refused to treat the will as other than a real co-operant, with its
own part to play by assent and by preparing itself for the grace of
justification.[2] It is a synergistic doctrine, and, in view of it,
Jansen's later attempt to revert to the severest conclusions of the
logic of the great African Father was sure to fail. With regard
to the sacraments, the Council in its seventh Session taught that
these contained and conferred the grace which they signified.

The rigour of Augustine's doctrine reappeared in the Continental Reformers. Both Luther and Calvin by insisting on
the bondage of the will of the natural man under sin left no room
for any factor in salvation except that of grace, while Calvin's
emphasis upon a double Predestinarianism, in the absoluteness of
which he went beyond Augustine, closed the circle so completely
that man appeared as a wholly passive instrument controlled by
forces which he could do nothing to help or resist. The Continental Confessions of Faith give formal statements in accordance
with these estimates of grace and the will. An instance may be
given from the Canons of Dort. In them it is taught that as a
result of their corrupt nature, " all men are thus children of wrath,
incapable of any saving good ; without regenerating grace neither
able nor willing to return to God, to reform the depravity of their
nature, nor to dispose themselves to reformation." The knowledge of God which belongs to man through the faint light of

---

[1] " Besides the supernatural superadded ' organism ' (habitual grace, virtues,
and gifts), the human soul, in order to produce supernatural actions meri-
torious of life everlasting, requires, each time, the impulse from God, which
enables it to perform now a supernatural action " (" Grace, Doctrine of (Roman
Catholic)," in Hastings' *Encyc. Rel. Eth.*, vol. vi, p. 368).

[2] Session VI, chapter V, of the decree on Justification. The beginning
of justification springs from the prevenient grace of God, who calls sinners in
such a way that " through His awakening and assisting grace they may be
disposed to convert themselves with a view to their own justification, by freely
consenting to and co-operating with that same grace."

nature has no saving value. Salvation results from God's un-
feigned calling, and as to the unsaved " the fault lies in men themselves, who refuse to come and be converted. But that others
obey and are converted is not to be ascribed to the proper exercise
of free will whereby one distinguishes himself above others equally
furnished with grace sufficient for faith, but it must be wholly
ascribed to God who calls effectually in time the elect from eternity,
confers upon them faith and repentance . . . that they may glory
not in themselves but in the Lord." [1]  It is the paradox which goes
back to Augustine : the wicked are rightly condemned because
they will evil, yet apart from grace it is impossible for them to will
anything else.

Where the Reformation theologians broke with Augustine
was in substituting the doctrine of justification by faith only for that
of infused grace. Yet at this point there was not perfect consistency. Luther, who in connection with the baptism of infants had
invented the idea of infused faith, taught an Eucharistic doctrine
which involved the thought of the infusion of the power of Christ's
body and blood. The notion of the sacraments as *efficacia signa
gratiae* belongs to him as much as to the twenty-fifth article of the
Church of England. Earlier articles reveal, on the problem of
grace and freedom, an Augustinianism which avoids the full rigour
of that system by not pushing its positive statements beyond a
certain point and by the indeterminate character of its exposition
of predestination.

With a brief account of the bearing of certain aspects of modern
religious thought upon the subject with which we are concerned,
this section may close. It is a natural deduction from all the
evidence we possess that, to understand the place which grace holds
in Christianity, we must view it against the background of belief in
revealed religion as involving in a very definite way the incursion
of the supernatural. It was precisely that belief which the growth
of sceptical and deistic philosophies in the seventeenth and eighteenth centuries assaulted ; and that meant a depreciation of the
need for grace, for if Christianity was " as old as creation," the
whole notion of supernatural grace, however interpreted, directed
manwards through, and as a result of, the Incarnation, was
jeopardised. Stages in the progress of this tendency may be observed in Socinianism with its " school-Christianity " and its

[1] See W. A. Curtis, *History of Creeds and Confessions of Faith*, p. 245.

Pelagian outlook, in the pantheistic philosophy of Spinoza, in the Arianism and Deism which so suddenly threatened the dogmatic well-being of the Church of England and of English Dissent, in the anti-miraculous thought of Hume, in the philosophy of the "Enlightenment" on the Continent, and even in Kant. For Kant's profound moral reaction against the "Enlightenment" left no place for the idea of grace, inasmuch as he held it necessary to exclude something which seemed to him prejudicial to human freedom and so to a real morality. Kant here stands in almost formal opposition to Augustine, since for him " the only true means of grace is a morally good life." [1] At the same time Kant came nearer to the orthodox standpoint and refused to range himself with a merely facile liberalism in that he both left a place for original sin and did not deny man's reception of supernatural help as a supplement to his own endeavours. In the nineteenth century the " liberalising of theology," which was on the whole anti-sacramental as against Catholicism and anti-evangelical as against the Reformation *doctrine*, was inimical to any emphasis upon grace, though the greatest of nineteenth-century liberal theologians, Albrecht Ritschl, refused to interpret Christianity either as the climax of natural religion or as the supreme ethic. But one must allow that his exact position as to grace is not at all easy to grasp. In England, while liberalism in theology had its influence, that could hardly be described as a positive and reconstructive one in the fields either of dogmatics or of the Christian philosophy of religion. On the other hand, the Oxford Movement laid the fullest stress on the supernatural, and brought once more into prominence the sacramental system as a principal means for the bestowal of grace; while, in a very different quarter, the Keswick School, with its special devotion to the theme of the work of the Holy Spirit in sanctification, proclaimed the inspiration of grace in the Christian life.

### 3. *The Supernatural Order, Grace and Freedom*

The question, What is grace and wherein may we recognise it? is wrapt up in that larger and most crucial question, What is the supernatural and where may we look for its manifestation? Exception is sometimes taken to the word " supernatural," but it is on any adequately Christian view impossible to dispense with the

[1] C. C. J. Webb, *Problems in the Relations of God and Man*, p. 95.

idea for which it stands. And whether the word be favoured or not, this idea of the essentially transcendent which establishes itself by a special kind of immanence within the natural order, and gives to that order a new centre, control and destiny, could hardly be denied by any believer in the Incarnation. But the Christian understanding of the relation of the supernatural to the natural is not content to see it concentrated in one supreme manifestation. The new unity in Christ's Person overflows into the whole of life with the power of unifying all life on a new and higher level. There is no denial of natural goodness or the value of natural and this-worldly ends. But when that goodness and those ends are isolated from their true destiny—which is to be integrated into an excellence and to serve purposes which transcend their own nature—then the Apostle's vision of a redemption of the natural order is retarded not only by the positive evil which has found a place within it, but also by the short circuit of its own virtues. So, as a recent writer has pointed out,[1] the New Testament conception of a moral life is that of one " deriving from, and determined by, fellowship with God," a life to which, minting a phrase of more than common value, from a passage in the Epistle to the Hebrews, he has given the title the " worshipful life." And I believe that he is entirely right and gives intelligible application within the sphere of morals to the distinction between the natural and the supernatural, when he writes : "that there is a fundamental difference not merely between good and evil, but between good and good, in the spiritual condition of men ; that the second includes but transcends the first ; and that it is the second which is of primary significance for religion, because it is concerned with men's relationship to the eternal Good Himself—these are propositions which appear to have overwhelming testimony in the mind of the Christian Church." And the secret of the power of the higher good lies in the revelation of the supernatural in the light of that Eternal Light which came into the world in the Person of Jesus Christ full of grace and truth. With this belief in a supernatural order belief in grace will be found congruous, since grace stands for the outflow into the existing given natural order of the powers of the world to come, the world which *a parte temporis* is conceived of as subsequent to our world and yet in present relationship to it. But that

---

[1] E. G. Selwyn in *The Approach to Christianity*, pp. 138–145.

is not the only result. One of the problems which has followed
in the wake of modern science and has engaged the attention
of those who have sought to vindicate the reality of the mental
and spiritual side of human life and to refute that account of it
which involves the conception "that all mental states are *epi-
phenomena*, superfluous accessories, which arise in the course
of the connected series of bodily changes," [1] is the problem of
freedom. A one-ordered interpretation of reality makes it, at
least, exceedingly difficult to find any place for freedom. Stoicism
is prophetic in the consequences of its monism. Its teaching
was that the only freedom possible was freedom to follow
obediently the leading of the world-order, of Zeus or Destiny.
In any case "follow still I must," is the testimony of Cleanthes.[2]
Modern determinism has no other message. Entirely different
is the witness of the New Testament. Unconcerned as it is,
except by way of implication, with speculative problems that
belong to the territory where science, philosophy and theology
all try to make themselves at home and stake out their claims,
it leaves us in no doubt where it stands on this issue. Its Gospel
is a Gospel of freedom in the moral life from the bonds of a world-
order which, so far as it had organised itself apart from God,
meant slavery for all who were caught in its net.[3] With the
will as the subject of philosophical discussions neither the Old
Testament nor the New is at pains to deal. With man as the
servant either of God or of his own lusts and the powers of evil
the Bible is occupied from beginning to end. And had our
modern expressions been at the disposal of the Biblical writers,

---

[1] A. E. Taylor, *Elements of Metaphysics*, p. 318.

[2] The four lines run thus: "Lead me, O Zeus, and thou, O Destiny,
whithersoever I am appointed by you to go. I will follow without shrinking ;
but if I turn evil and refuse, none the less shall I follow."

[3] At this point I insert the following note by Professor A. E. Taylor:
"*Cf.* the allusions of St. Paul to bondage under the στοιχεῖα, which seem to mean
the planets. Is not this aimed directly against the current astrology which, as
is now known, was, in its Hellenic form, definitely Stoic ? The thought is that
true freedom consists in getting loose from the evil world-order which is subject
to the planetary revolutions. You get this thought equally in the Hermetic
writings, where the main point is that the divine part in the soul came from
God who is above the planetary system, or from the super-planetary "aether"
where God dwells. But *how* this direct contact with God is to be established
is just what the Hermetists cannot tell us and St. Paul does tell us. It is the
thought of the starting of the process *from God's side* which is lacking to Stoics,
Hermetists and Neo-Platonists alike."

they would not have said that the character of man's service was wholly determined by the circumstances of his human nature and its environment—that is, by the world-order expressing itself through him and controlling him through his physical and psychical constitution. We must not generalise too widely ; but it is a fact that the ruling out of the supernatural order and of grace does not tend to strengthen belief in human freedom. If we think of the Christian view of the world as one which holds to the reality of freedom as the condition for there being any life truly deserving the title of "moral" at all, we see the significance of the fact that a threat to one is often a threat to both. It suggests that grace and freedom alike are living forces only when we view reality as a whole as something richer and deeper than it is in the power of the natural sciences by themselves to reveal to us. And it also suggests that, as this enlarged world-view is able to provide satisfaction for those who wish to maintain the truth of human freedom, and also for those who assert that religious experience and its theological interpretation are not astray as to the actions upon and within human life of that divine energy which is called grace, it is a reasonable supposition that grace and freedom are not antitheses, and that the notion of discord between them errs by conceiving of them as though they were objects occupying space, and the one were excluded by the fact that the other was already in possession.

To consider the question more closely. When we think of the meaning of grace, not simply as the energy of the divine favour and good will, but as that energy operative within the conditions of human life, bringing man into such contact with God that life is progressively raised to a higher than the natural level of this-worldly experiences, we see that grace involves a dependence of man upon God, a set of relationships between man and God over and above the fact that man is God's creature. And because man's one true end is God, it is clear that the fuller his dependence upon God the truer will the direction of his life be and the richer will be its content, since it will neither consciously limit itself to the goods of the natural order nor fail to interpret and use those goods for purposes whose realisation lies beyond that order. So for St. Paul the body, while belonging to the natural order, is also a temple of God, to be redeemed and raised in glory.

Now when we seek to understand the meaning of freedom

we find it impossible to give any rational account of it which does not take into consideration the sphere or order within which it is or may be a real fact, and the ends for which it exists. Freedom, in isolation, means nothing, and when, being expounded as a "freedom of indetermination," it is held to imply that "our choice between motives is not determined by anything at all," [1] it has neither philosophical sense nor religious value. Freedom is not given once for all. Rather do we begin to give it its true place only when we remember that life is the opportunity for man's progressive growth in independent moral personality, so that his personality represents something truly individual and distinctive. Of course if the moral world—what Professor Ward has called the Realm of Ends—is itself an illusion, then, so far as freedom is concerned, *cadit quaestio*. But if it is reality, and a higher reality than the physical world, then each person can enter into that realm only by making moral ends his own. He cannot do so by being wound up like a clock to a state of exact correspondence with the objectively good. Nothing but a purely external relationship would thereby be brought about. The objectively good must become goodness in him, the very stuff of his life. And this goodness is of his own choice. He is good because he chooses to be good. If we deny this, we not only destroy freedom but endanger personality as well ; for how shall we preserve the distinction between person and thing, unless we say that a person recognises certain purposes as purposes for him, and makes active contribution towards the bringing of those purposes within the circle of his own life ? This is what no thing can do, and animals other than man can do, if at all, only to a very limited extent.

When we think of the religious relationship to God and the life of grace, the moral relationship to goodness and the life of freedom, dependence and independence, we seem to postulate two circles, never intersecting, yet each enclosing human life,

---

[1] The late Dr. McTaggart's view of freedom as understood by its defenders, on which he based his attack. In the article, "Libertarianism and Necessitarianism," in *Encyc. Rel. and Eth.*, vol. vii, Dr. Pringle-Pattison's quotation of and repudiation of Dr. McTaggart's interpretation is given. Professor Taylor finds the true place of freedom to lie in the comparative judgment of the goodness of two objects of pursuit, A and B. When the judgment is made the will is determined by the judgment, but the judgment is not decided in advance by character up to date plus circumstances. William James, it may be remembered, insisted on the freedom of attention.

each indispensable. But in point of fact these relationships, blessings and ideals are held together within the unity of the personal life, and the moment we begin to think of the matter concretely, on the basis of what we can experience or observe, the whole idea of the delimitation of spheres, of so much being given to freedom and so much to grace, fades away.[1] It is not that we can be satisfied simply with an interpretation of freedom as " ideal " freedom, freedom to do right, as contrasted with the faculty of self-determination ; but the unconstrained activity of personality directed towards the attainment of ends which will involve in the case of the personality itself a self-realisation or self-fulfilment lies within that system of relationships which represents God's continual re-creative energy upon and within the world-order with a view to its establishment in a true religious and moral attitude to Him. This is not a work of divine omnipotence. A kingdom of good cannot be established by force ; there would be no value in man being constrained from without to become what he was not becoming from within.[2] At the same time, to suppose that anything good which he becomes from within he becomes in detachment from divine grace, or, differently expressed, from the inspiration of the Holy Spirit, is an atheistic delusion, since it means a discrimination at some point between goodness and God. If we treat the problem as one that concerns the relations of two abstractions known as " grace " and " freedom " to one another, we pose it in a *milieu* which forbids the hope of the discovery of a way out. For it implies an isolation of man from God just at the point where religion, and especially Christianity, affirms that isolation is exactly the wrong

[1] *Cf.* the quotation in von Hügel, *The Mystical Element of Religion*, vol. i. pp. 69 f., from St. Bernard, *Tractatus de Gratia et Libero Arbitrio*, cap. xiv. § 47 : " That which was begun by Grace gets accomplished alike by both Grace and Free Will, so that they operate mixedly not separately, simultaneously not successively, in each and all of their processes. The acts are not in part Grace, in part Free Will ; but the whole of each act is effected by both in an undivided operation."

[2] Two sayings of early Christian writers may be quoted in this connection. The author of the *Epistle to Diognetus* argues that in the sending of His Son God was saving men by persuasion, not compulsion, " for compulsion (βία) is not an attribute of God " (vii. 4). And Irenaeus, in a very interesting passage (iv. 62, in Harvey's edition), suggests that the education of the human race towards perfection is due to the fact that, whereas " God was indeed able to give man perfection from the beginning, man was unable to receive it for he was a child."

word and conception. No religion has contributed as much as Christianity to faith in the value of man, to appreciation of his dignity, and to hope of his destiny. It has done so by viewing him as the redeemed child of God, enabled by grace to enter upon his inheritance.

When we speak of the grace of God we mean that the divine favour goes forth towards man and rests upon him to bless and strengthen him. Spirit communicates with spirit ; the personal God is active towards the sanctification of the persons He has created and redeemed. He has ways at His disposal beyond our power to search out or define. Yet the phrase " means of grace " certainly stands for a method of His activity on which we can count, for instruments or channels which He uses, through and in which we can be sure that what He wishes to give us is to be found. Like more than one other famous expression of Christian theology it is capable of being misconstrued. It could be taken to allow of the idea that grace was a quasi-physical substance poured into men, which would mean a passing out of the region of moral relationships into the region of impersonal forces. But avoidance of such an error will enable us to make free and natural use of such words as " means " and " channels," which stand for truths congruous with the character of Christianity as the religion which, above all others, asserts the harmony and not the discord of matter and spirit. And while grace is present and operative in the historical process, in the formation of institutions and in the material order, so that we shall not seek to exclude it from anything but sin, with which it has a different kind of relationship, there are points within the historical, the institutional and the material at which grace is revealed as of special potency and relevance. We do no injustice to the universal operation of grace when we point to the cross as the place where God has manifested the full measure of His graciousness, or to the Church as the body in which that gracious-ness is the consciously realised background and meaning of all its distinctive actions,[1] or to the sacraments as objects which God selects, that through them as *efficacia signa* He may bring Himself into contacts of particular kinds with men and enable them to realise what He does. In them the divine life, everywhere

---

[1] *Cf.* Dr. Bicknell's remark on p. 223 : " The Church is in literal truth the home of grace."

present, imparts itself in ways which answer to man's need, not only of a general environment of God's graciousness, but also of acts and ordinances which mediate to him the blessings which the gracious God gives in answer to his various necessities.    And the life of man, enriched by these blessings, and making a response which is itself possible only because man himself is never simply a natural phenomenon, becomes different.    It is in that difference as it is expressed in moral and spiritual progress that we recognise the grace which sanctifies.    There is nothing automatic, nothing magical, nothing unethical intruded at this point.    Sacramental grace does not involve any such incredible supposition as that God, in this province of His loving energy on our behalf, ceases to deal with us as persons and treats us as though we were things. It would indeed be an astonishing paradox if the richness of the sacramental life, rooted in and bearing its flowers in the ground of the conviction of the reality of sacramental grace, flourished alongside of so profound a misunderstanding of its own nature. It is possible, of course, to think of the sacraments sub-personally and sub-ethically, but so it is possible to do of God's grace and love, quite apart from the sacraments.    When we think truly, as the Gospel inspires us to think, of God's grace and love as realities which express the being of One in whom is the perfection of moral and personal life, we shall think of no other grace and love as given to us in the sacraments, that we may grow up into the ever fuller self-identification with the ideal of the καινὴ κτίσις.    Nor is there any obliteration of freedom.    The life strengthened by the sacraments is one in which man, by making his own the one true objective and personal ideal which exists for him, the ideal of the perfect humanity of Jesus Christ, is on the way towards that highest personal achievement which we understand by the word character.    And the more character is unified in its tendency and moves towards unity in expression, the freer, because the more completely himself, does man become in the correspondence that exists between himself and the spiritual order.    More and more is he raised above the natural order, to which he is indeed linked as an element within it, but which is neither the explanation of him nor his home.    It is only in his true home, and as he begins to be a native of it, that he learns the salvation which is God's purpose for him, for which God's grace is given.    And as he learns that, depending at all times upon the grace to which he owes the redemption won for him by Christ, he becomes what he already is, his Father's son, and gains his own self.

Christianity is the religion of redemption. And, not in addition to that, but in and through that, it is the way of the highest moral life and the completest personal attainment, a life of service wherein is perfect freedom. All this it is, and as a unity, and no one word so well explains this many-sidedness and this unity as the word Grace.

## ADDITIONAL NOTE

To those who are acquainted with that very remarkable book, " Grace and Personality," by Dr. John Oman, Principal of Westminster College, Cambridge, it may well seem strange that I have not hitherto referred to it. I desire neither to overlook the book, which, in fact, I reviewed in *The Journal of Theological Studies* (July 1920 : xxi. 84), nor to fail to acknowledge the debt which I owe to its author. But I should have overburdened my pages had I referred at the various relevant points to Dr. Oman's positions, or dwelt on controversial matters where I should feel it necessary to diverge from his conclusions. " Grace and Personality " is written round the conviction that the distinguishing characteristic of a moral person is autonomy, and that grace must be a personal relationship between God and man, involving fellowship between God and man, and not suppressing freedom. The problem as he sees it is that of combining the dependence upon God which is an essential quality of a religious person and the independence which is an essential quality of a moral person. And the way to unity is neither by a compromise between religion and morality nor by the isolation of one from the other, but by such a relationship that " our absolute religious dependence and our absolute moral independence are perfectly realised and made perfectly one " (p. 82). I am sure that he is right in holding that the problem of grace can be handled properly only when all vestiges of sub-personal relationships are excluded from our thought of what can be true as between God and man. And neither the Augustinian emphasis upon the irresistible might of the grace which saves those who are called according to God's purpose, nor the Pelagian appeal to the obligation of obedience to the moral law as indicating that man has the power to keep the commandments, necessarily involves that thorough personalising of relationships. On the other hand, Dr. Oman is pressing his point too far when he attributes a kinship to the "extremest Catholicism and the extremest Evangelicalism . . . just because both depend on the same conception of grace as arbitrary acts of omnipotence." Not only would most of the theologians implicated in this indictment have vehemently rejected the word "arbitrary" : they would also have been justified in doing so because they did not find the source of right in God's particular appointment, but in the unchangeable moral perfection of God's nature. Even as to Duns Scotus important reservations have to be made,[1] while it is certainly no part of St. Thomas's doctrine that "God's appointment makes things reasonable and right," though Dr. Oman associates the two doctors in this belief (pp. 163–4). Dr. Oman insists on the need to recognise that "in all things God is gracious," and that we should not treat "the rest of experience as mere scenery for operations of grace which are canalised in special channels" (p. 174). Certainly ; but Catholic theology knows quite well that it must seek to do justice to the world and experience as a whole, and that it must exclude the possibility of contact with God and of doing God's will from nothing whatsoever except the morally evil. At the same time, whatever language be used, the Incarnation is a special channel of God's graciousness, and the religion sprung from belief in it reflects that fact in ways which do not at all impair the truth that all experience is usable for the knowledge of God and for fellowship with Him. Dr. Oman seems to me to be too much outside the particular and characteristic field of sacramental praxis and theology which we

---

[1] See the article "Scholasticism" in *Encyc. Rel. and Eth.* vol. xi. "Assuming that the content of duty depends on the constitution of human nature, it follows that, if human beings were constituted differently in certain fundamental ways, then the content of morality would be fundamentally altered. There is, however, no evidence that Duns Scotus intended to teach that morality could be determined differently by the will of God, human nature being constituted as it is." Professor Taylor draws my attention to Bonaventura, *Breviloq.* vi. 1, 5 (ed. minor, Quaracchi, p. 205) : "Huiusmodi sacramenta dicantur gratiae *vasa* et *causae* nec quia gratia in eis substantialiter contineatur nec causaliter efficiatur, cum in sola anima habeat collocari et a solo Deo habeat infundi ; sed quia in illis et per illa gratiam curationis a summo medico Christo ex divino decreto oporteat hauriri, licet Deus non alligaverit suam potentiam sacramentis."

associate with Catholicism to be first a satisfactory interpreter and then an adequate critic. There is not enough sympathetic penetration, at least at this point; and mental, and even spiritual, power, richly as his book is endowed with both, do not make up for that lack. He sees negatives in the positions of others which they would deny, or of which they would give a different description. The positive in his own position which he knows at first-hand is of very high religious value.

# THE ATONEMENT
## BY KENNETH E. KIRK

# CONTENTS

## The Problem of the Death of Christ

*Ex ore infantium* . . . The Catholic theory of the Atonement, with all its affirmations, its reticences, its possibilities of diverse interpretation, its consequent or collateral problems, is stated more clearly perhaps in three verses of the children's hymn than in any other document. Taking them as a starting-point, we shall have an opportunity of gathering, first, the affirmations in which all Christians are agreed ; then those to which Catholic theology is more firmly wedded than other modes of Christian thought ; finally the problems which are raised by the contrast between Catholic affirmation and non-Catholic doubt or silence.

> He died that we might be forgiven,
>   He died to make us good,
> That we might go at length to heaven,
>   Saved by His precious blood.
>
> There was no other good enough
>   To pay the price of sin,
> He only could unlock the gate
>   Of heaven, and let us in.
>
> Oh dearly, dearly has He loved,
>   And we must love Him too,
> And trust in His redeeming blood,
>   And try His work to do.

"He died that . . . " Christ's death is *central* in Christian thought. Christ's submission to death was *purposive*. On these two points there is substantial agreement between all types of Christian thought. *Why* it is central, or with *what* purpose He submitted to it, is the question which it is the object of this essay to consider. It suffices at the moment to say that those who would hush reason to silence at this point, and let loving faith dwell on the mystery without seeking to pierce its truth or meaning, ignore the God-given desire to know and understand which is the inheritance of every thoughtful man. Thought must go on till it is checked by the failure of its own powers : it admits no other or more artificial barriers.

The problem, therefore, of the purpose of the Lord's acceptance of death, or (in other words) of the manner of the Atonement, cannot be evaded. We must notice, however, a tendency among Christians, particularly of the present day, to take " death " as a mere paraphase or metaphor for " life." To them it would be the same or almost the same if our hymn ran—

> He *lived* that we might be forgiven,
> He *lived* to make us good,
> That we might go at length to heaven,
> Saved by His precious *love*.

The death of Christ, appealing, arresting though it is, is in their view no more than the focus of His life—" it only added a crowning illustration of the ethical principle which ran through all His teaching." [1] There was no absolute need for the cross and passion, nor anything new contributed by them ; they have no " exclusive efficacy " [2] ; they are simply accessories introduced by the cruelty of circumstance. They point the moral, no doubt ; but in strict thought they do no more than adorn the tale. If (as some of Athanasius's opponents urged) Christ had lived the same life of purity, self-denial and love, but passed away in a quiet and honourable old age, the dramatic appeal would have been less (for " no other way of ending the earthly life could so fully embody or symbolize the fundamental thought of Christianity that God is love "),[3] but the atoning effect the same. To such a conception our hymn, as it stands, offers no obstacles ; yet the divergence from traditional Christianity and from the New Testament writers is really extreme. We must, at some stage of our argument, face the question : If the death or " blood " of Christ saves, does it do so merely as summarising in itself the message and purpose of His life which is the true medium of salvation ; or does it contribute some-

---

[1] H. Rashdall, *Idea of Atonement*, p. 46.
[2] Rashdall, *op. cit.* p. 149.
[3] Rashdall, *op. cit.* p. 361.

thing to our salvation which His earthly Incarnation, had it ended in any other way, would not have secured to us ? Is His death, and that the death on the cross, a *sine quâ non* of salvation ; or no more than an appropriate but not strictly necessary conclusion of His life ?

## II

### ITS NECESSITY FOR SALVATION

" There was no other good enough . . . " " He only could unlock . . . " Here there can be little explicit [1] disagreement. Even though some writers use language which suggests that (given Christ's *life* on earth) His *death* was a mercy strictly speaking superfluous, vouchsafed to men by the abundant love of God to point the moral of His life, few would go so far as openly to allege that the life itself was, in the same strict sense, superfluous. This would involve a belief that man can save himself (whatever is meant by salvation) if he only bestirs himself sufficiently ; and that the Incarnation was a divine gift which no doubt makes it easier for us to bestir ourselves, but with which the most saintly and noble souls can dispense. Such a theory we can unhesitatingly reject. No coherent body of Christian thought has ever consciously regarded the incarnate life of Christ as a mere luxury, easing the moral man's path to perfection indeed, but in no way making that path practicable for the first time. If man had not sinned, perhaps, it might have been so ; but since sin entered in, we have " no power of ourselves to help ourselves " ; our sufficiency—if ever we attain to sufficiency—is " of God," and of God " through Christ alone."

As to this necessity of an atonement, however, different minds will be impressed by different arguments. The point is one to which we must recur [2] ; at the moment we need do no more than establish its inherent probability. That probability depends upon a doctrine which clearly dominates St. Paul, that sin and circumstance are inextricably allied as forces from which man longs for

---

[1] The words "explicit," "openly," "consciously," are used in this paragraph because, in the writer's opinion, the theory he has ventured to call "exemplarist" involves an implicit though probably unconscious denial of the position here stated. See further, Note A, fin. p. 276.

[2] *Infra*, pp. 267–270.

deliverance. " Sin," to the apostle, is a force hostile to God and goodness permeating all life and nature, and manifesting its power at every point. To adopt the words of another New Testament writer, here is an enemy or a combination of enemies, in fear of which every man goes " all the days of his life." [1]   He may have little sense of moral sterility within himself—and it is in this respect, no doubt, that the " sense of sin " most fully manifests itself ; but he is conscious of an environment full of menaces, dangers, and hidden possibilities, all of them potent enough to destroy in a moment the work of his hands, and to reduce his efforts and aspirations to a cipher.   Against such an environment he sees himself to be in fact powerless ;  though it tolerate and even further his activities for the time, he cannot tell at what moment it may turn against him and overwhelm his work in disaster.   From all such dread of circumstance he needs—and indeed, if he be a man of any sensibilities at all, he desires—" salvation," and he feels himself to be incapable of finding it spontaneously.   He may not see in Christ his Saviour ;  but at least he says, " There is *none other* good enough."

This deep-rooted disorganisation of the universe, investing all man's efforts with pain and threatening them with annihilation, of which every serious-minded man is conscious and from which he must naturally seek deliverance, is presented in the early chapters of Genesis as the consequence or punishment of sin.   If the invariable imminence of death be taken as its most obvious symbol, then St. Paul is found to be in complete agreement ; death is the wages of sin.[2]   Such a representation of the dependence of physical upon moral disorganisation is not without its difficulties —death and disaster appear to have been laws of nature at epochs before conscious morality or immorality were possible.   Yet there is a connection between the physical and the moral in this matter so intimate and unbreakable that to apply the name " sin " to both, and to recognise both together as that from which man needs to be saved, is wholly warranted.   That connection shows itself in two respects at least.   (i) As we have said, sin and circumstance combine to frustrate, or threaten with frustration, all man's hopes and efforts ;  they form thus an unholy alliance, or conspiracy, against him, so intimate that one name fitly covers both. (ii) Without a change of moral attitude (a " salvation " from " sin "

---

[1] Heb. ii. 15.        [2] Rom. vi. 23.

in the narrower sense) no change in man's environment could make him happier, or better, or more confident of the future, *i.e.* could "save" him from "sin" in the wider sense. He might be assured that Nature would further his every effort and crown him with length of days, but reflection would still convince him that his own moral deficiencies might bring disasters more bitter than Nature's worst ; health, prosperity, rank, reputation avail nothing to lighten the burden of sin upon a guilty soul. Escape from circumstance would be valueless except to those who could also escape from sin. To equate the idea of "salvation" with anything less than "full personal righteousness" is not merely—as Dr. Moberly so fairly pointed out [1]—"a pagan rather than a Christian" thought ; it is also a thought in itself futile and doomed to disillusionment.

Scripture has good grounds, therefore, for regarding sin and circumstance together as an alliance of enemies from which man needs deliverance. And it is just this fact of the alliance between physical and spiritual menace which makes it so natural for us to assert that man cannot "save" himself. Were our enemies spiritual only, we might not be able to prove that man is so debased in moral capacity as to be unable, unaided, victoriously to meet them. But they are physical, or cosmical, as well. This, on the one hand, enhances the demand for moral effort, for a new moral outlook to make man master of his fate and captain of his soul ; on the other it threatens all such effort with futility. Of what avail will be self-sacrifice, devotion to the cause of others, patience, courage, endurance when all but hope is gone, if there is only one event to the good and the wicked, if man is no more than dust, and to dust must return ?  "Salvation"—at the very least—demands not merely that new moral outlook of which we have spoken, but also the assurance that Christian fortitude must in the end triumph over all the powers of cosmic evil ; that the gates of hell cannot prevail against it. And such an assurance the experience of human life does not seem to give. The grave is still the inevitable termination of all our hopes. There is a further aspect of this corporate or cosmical character of sin, to which we shall come. But even the aspect just suggested is enough for our present purpose. We are forced to the conclusion that man cannot save himself ;—that, apart from Christ, there can be "none

[1] R. C. Moberly, *Atonement and Personality*, p. 72.

other good enough " to overcome that combination of spiritual and physical enemies which St. Paul personifies as Sin.

## III

### Its Function as an Example

" Oh dearly, dearly has He loved, and we must love Him too." Here again all are, almost without exception, agreed. The life and death of Christ (whether the death stands by itself in purpose, or is simply the appropriate consummation of the life) constitute an example which calls for human imitation within the measure and limits of human capacity ; whose call, moreover, is of infinite power in inspiring men to a new and devoted service of God and their fellows. Whatever other benefits may have been secured for us by this mystery which we call the Atonement, one benefit was not secured, offered, or intended—that man should be saved without any contributory effort of his own will towards good. Phrases have been used by Christian thinkers which some- times can be distorted into this latter meaning, as of the sacraments, so of the death of Christ. But no responsible theologian would ever have accepted the implication. Some indeed might be so full of the thought of " grace " or " communion " as the means of holiness (whether mediated by the sacraments, or given apart from visible channels in response to the appeal of naked faith ; and whether, again, thought of primarily as a moralising force, or as a force lifting man into a realm far transcending all moral distinctions) as to suggest that man's efforts should primarily be directed, not to the imitation of Christ, but to the pursuit of " grace "—" grace " itself, on some theories, being thought of as attainable on conditions other than those of a constant striving after moral excellence.[1] But even so, it would be admitted by all except the most extreme, that *if* in the " state " or " life " of grace moral problems arose demanding a " yes or no " answer—problems of the form, " Must I do this ? " or, " May I do that ? "—the life and death of Christ must form a final test or standard by which to measure the rightness or wrongness of the action contemplated. As an example, that life and death can be neither surpassed nor

[1] For the exaggerated teaching of Luther in these directions see H. Rashdall, *Idea of Atonement*, pp. 401–409.

ignored. At the very least they mark out a path from which we deviate at our peril. At the most they constitute a challenge which, in the last event, no human will, unless far advanced on the road to perdition, can disregard. And to all the world they present, as realised in actual history, the picture of an ideal which few would not be glad to have constantly before their eyes, to keep their efforts from flagging and their hope from extinction.

## IV

### Criticism of Exemplarist Theories

So far all ways have lain together. Theologians of every shade of thought travel in company. The landmarks they have passed are these : (*a*) No man can save himself ; (*b*) the life of Christ Incarnate was therefore *essential* to man's salvation, though its significance hitherto has mainly been found to lie in the fact that it makes the one appeal without which humanity could never have raised itself far out of the slough of sin ; (*c*) the death of Christ, even though no more than the appropriate consummation of the life, was *so* appropriate that it may, symbolically at all events, be regarded as itself necessary also. But at this point many theologians halt. No more (according to them) is required by man, no more has been given by God ; the example of Christ's suffering and obedience is all-sufficient.

Theories which go so far and no further have been designated by two names, equally question-begging ; their upholders call them " ethical," their opponents " subjective." [1] " Ethical," of course, they are, and " subjective " also, in the best senses of those much-abused words—that is to say, they demand of the human subject an ethical or moral effort towards righteousness. But, in this respect, all genuinely Christian theories are ethical and subjective. Nor can it even be said that the type of theory we have under consideration is *necessarily* more ethical or subjective than any other ; that depends entirely upon the degree of effectiveness with which the interpreter endows the example of Christ, which (as we have seen) is the only lever of salvation recognised by the theory. If he says (as for the theory's sake alone he might be

---

[1] Though Dr. Rashdall constantly uses the word " subjective " of his own theory with approval.

induced to say) that the moral appeal of the death of Christ is so overwhelming that no reasonable man can resist it, his theory partakes to an almost unlimited extent of the " unethical " or " objective " character which he deprecates in, or which his opponents claim for, the fuller theories to which we are to come. He is saying in effect: " The lion hath roared, who will not tremble; the Lord God hath spoken, who will not prophesy ? "—" Christ's death makes such an appeal to all that is best in human nature that only the insensate can remain unmoved ; all others *must* rise up from sin in the desire to imitate." The analogies on which the theory rests [1] are just those instances in which the example of one human personality removes out of another's path stumbling-blocks which hitherto have remained insuperable. A single hero may, by the stimulus of example, turn a craven rabble into a band of heroes like-hearted with himself ; and under that stimulus they can and do perform—with ease and without reflection upon the cost—acts of valour which at an earlier stage appeared entirely impossible. Their efforts, no doubt, are still voluntary and conscious (and therefore " ethical " and " subjective "), but so inspired by the example and magnetism of a great personality that they have ceased to be " efforts " in any ordinary sense of the word. The leader has lent his followers his own strength and daring. They are themselves and yet other than themselves ; or—we may say—they are their real selves at last, and no longer the cowards they appeared to be.

Here is a theory of the Atonement at once comprehensible, admirable and inspiring—one, moreover, without doubt true to life ; but the more the influence of Christ's example is emphasised, the more He is thought of as lending His followers His strength, the less can it be called " subjective," or " ethical " either, in any sense in which emphasis is laid upon the efforts of the Christian to imitate. If we must have a name for theories of this type, let us choose a non-committal term and call them " exemplarist "— because their emphasis is upon the moral value of Christ's example. Terms such as " ethical " or " subjective " simply confuse the issue ; they suggest either that partisans of the theory claim too

---

[1] *E.g.* the " leader of men," Rashdall, *op. cit.* p. 43 ; *cf.* p. 51—our Lord thought of His death " as a kind of service which His disciples ought to imitate." As a matter of fact, and naturally enough, few exemplarist writers emphasise this " objective " aspect of their doctrine. *Cf.* p. 257, note.

much for it, or that opponents attack it at points where it is not necessarily assailable.

The " exemplarist " theory is not therefore, at first sight, either unworthy or unchristian. It is indeed a part, and a vital part, of every theory that can be called Christian. It might even be urged that it exhausts the data of Scripture, and is wholly adequate to the needs of man. But brief consideration will show that, whether it be the only truth derivable from reflection upon the death of Christ or no, its adequacy is a very different question. The example of Christ, we are told, appeals to love and will ; and so it does. But it does so, except in the case of His historical contemporaries, indirectly and at not one but many removes. It appeals to love and will only by way of imagination ; the mind which cannot visualise the life and death of Christ, as an example of self-sacrificing devotion, must go untouched. And imagination is a weak, fickle and erratic servant ; if we are to depend upon *this* for our salvation our chances are tenuous at best. In the long run, therefore, exemplarism holds out little hope to the ordinary man. The will, as we know, we can to some degree command, even in our state enfeebled by sin. But imagination and emotions are our servants only to a far slighter degree ; if the dedication of the will is to depend upon a prior captivity of emotion and imagination, our state is precarious indeed.

This criticism might perhaps be met by the addition to the theory of a doctrine of objective grace, to be won on such conditions that not even the most unimaginative soul would stand at a disadvantage as regards salvation [1]—and such indeed is the character assigned to grace in traditional Christian thought. But few exemplarist theologians seem disposed to make this addition. The cause of their reluctance does not concern us here ; it is connected with a shrinking from the objectively supernatural in general, characteristic of much modern thought. But the absence of any such doctrine of grace in exemplarism marks the theory out not only as inadequate to human needs, but also as profoundly inequitable. On the exemplarist theory, those will benefit most

[1] Such a theory, on strictly exemplarist lines, is involved in that " objective " aspect of exemplarism to which we alluded on the preceding page. But to adopt it would be to introduce an element of objectivity as aggressive as any contained in the traditional doctrines of grace. It is for this reason that exemplarists as a whole ignore the interpretations we have suggested.

by the example of Christ, *ceteris paribus*, who are most highly endowed with the capacity for emotional or imaginative quickening. Less moral effort will be required of them than of others of more stolid natures. In some cases, indeed, the force of example playing upon imagination and emotions will be so potent that a minimum of conscious moral effort will serve, when aided by this influence, to achieve results which in other natures, less richly endowed, even heroic struggles may fail to reach. The traditional theories, whatever form they take, all assume as a fundamental proposition something which common sense and Christian sentiment alike endorse—that (in the measure in which man is called upon to co-operate with God and grace in his salvation) the greater the moral effort the greater the certainty, if not the degree, of achievement. This plain and obvious piece of natural justice exemplarism sets aside ; it makes attainment depend primarily not upon moral efforts for which the man is consciously responsible, but upon accidents of heredity for which he can claim no merit. The theory is not merely *less* ethical than traditional Catholicism ; it is even more unethical and arbitrary than any but the most absolute Predestinarianism.[1]

Finally, the insufficiency of mere exemplarism is shown once more by the fact that it does not, in itself, provide any hope against that complete disorganisation of the universe which we have seen to be comprehended under the title of " sin." The moral appeal of the character of Christ is infinite and compelling ; but what guarantee does it give of a successful issue to the struggle ? The universe conspired to drive Him to the cross and to a forgotten grave ; was not this total failure ? There is still one event to the good as to the evil ; " vanity of vanities, all is vanity." The Christian is forced to proclaim the victory of his Master's earthly life by appealing to the truth of the resurrection ; and once that appeal is made, exemplarism, whilst never losing its elements of truth and final value, is forced into a secondary position. New factors come into view which wholly change the balance of doctrine : factors which traditional Christianity has always placed in the forefront of the scheme, though the exemplarist, by the very urgency with which he advocates the essentials of his own theory,

[1] For a possible reply to this argument, and further discussion, see Note A, " Exemplarist Theories of the Atonement," at end of this essay.

is compelled to give them little attention, if not wholly to ignore them.[1]    What these are we must briefly consider before passing to the central affirmation of Catholic doctrine.

V

### The Resurrection the Guarantee of the Atonement

"He only could unlock the gate of heaven, and let us in." We must add then to the inspiration of the example of Christ the guarantee of ultimate victory over all the powers of evil, of disorganisation, of the malignancy of circumstance, given by the resurrection of Christ.    Our primary emphasis will no longer be upon the heroism with which He struggled against the powers of evil, but upon the manifest victory with which the struggle was crowned.    St. Paul in various passages arrays the army of forces against which the Christian has to fight, or from which he desires deliverance ;    in other passages he is meticulously careful to show that each of these forces has been severally and individually conquered by Christ—robbed of its sting ; stripped of its power ; nailed to the cross ;    made a mockery.[2]    Similarly he never tires of speaking of the " redemption " won for us, as though we were prisoners emancipated from captivity or slaves bought back into freedom in the market-place.[3]    The meaning of all this is transcendently clear.    The resurrection and ascension of Christ, above all if taken in connection with the doctrine of the Holy Spirit as the agent through whom man accepts and makes his own the obedience which was in Christ, guarantee as a certainty what the world had always groped after as a pious aspiration.    The ills of this life, against which a moral revelation of character would indeed strengthen us to endure (though only transcendent faith would enable us to believe the endurance to be more than a noble but quixotic vanity), will come one day to an end for the moral man.

[1] This point is noticed in regard to Abailard by Canon Storr, *Problem of the Cross*, p. 132.

[2] So of " sin," Rom. viii. 3 ; " death," 1 Cor. xv. 54 ; the " law," Rom. x. 4, Gal. iii. 25, Eph. ii. 15 ; *cp*. Col. ii. 14 ; the " curse," Gal. iii. 13 ; the " present evil world," Gal. i. 4 ; the " powers of darkness," Col. ii. 15 ; etc.

[3] λυτροῦσθαι and compounds, Rom. iii. 24, viii. 23 ; 1 Cor. i. 30 ; Eph. i. 7, iv. 30 ; Col. i. 14 ; 1 Tim. ii. 6 ; Tit. ii. 14 ; ἀγοράζεσθαι and compounds, 1 Cor. vi. 20, vii. 23 ; Gal. iii. 13, iv. 5.

His struggles shall usher him into a glorious immortality of body as well as soul, where there shall be no more crying nor any pain, and God shall wipe away all tears from his eyes. Redemption, won by the cross, is guaranteed by the resurrection ; and for the righteous, at least, it shall be redemption not merely from temptation and the sinfulness of the flesh, but also from all the disorganisation and hostility of the universe. For him at least there shall be a new heaven and a new earth, for the old heaven and the old earth are passed away. St. Paul goes further, and in a mystic passage suggests that the whole universe, inanimate as well as animate, shall be relieved from a condition so terrible that it can be described only as a " universal moaning in pain." [1]

Is such a consummation guaranteed by the resurrection of Christ ? The question, properly, belongs to other chapters of this book, but two points may be noticed here. (i) The advantage of a doctrinal position which emphasises *not merely* the example of Christ's life and death *but also* the guarantee of His resurrection, over any theory which concentrates solely upon the example, is independent of any theory of grace, sacramental or otherwise, which may be taken into account. Its superiority stands assured even though no doctrine of the agency of the Holy Spirit be added to it. We are for the moment considering questions merely of example and guarantee—questions, that is, of purely " natural " influences, into which " supernatural " considerations do not enter at all. If " grace " and " the Spirit " be thought of as no more than summary terms to describe natural operations such as these—and in this manner, it may be conjectured, do most exemplarists conceive of them—we shall indeed have little enough comfort to offer to the sick soul ; but even so it remains true that a guarantee of victory as well as an example of heroism is a greater gift, or act of " grace," than the example taken solely by itself could be. Our contention that no doctrine of the atonement is complete apart from explicit emphasis upon the Lord's resurrection is independent therefore of any controversy as to, let us say, the personality of the Spirit, or the character or means of grace ; it can be considered (as the preceding paragraphs have considered it) on its own merits alone.

(ii) It gives to the death of Christ, and in particular to the special circumstance of tragedy with which it was surrounded,

[1] Rom. viii. 22.

exactly that unique significance which we have seen that Catholic theology has always attributed to it. A tiny example may inspire, in others, efforts altogether out of proportion to itself in magnitude ; but the adequacy of a guarantee always depends upon an *a fortiori* argument. The example of the spider inspired, no doubt, in Robert Bruce heroism far greater than that which the spider itself manifested ; but it could give him no guarantee of victory, because the obstacles which the insect overcame were not demonstrably more serious than those which confronted the patriot. He might reasonably have argued : " The example of this persevering animal is no doubt highly laudable, but what evidence does it give me that a renewal of *my* efforts will not be crowned with disasters even greater than the present one ? " The example was adequate ; the guarantee insufficient.

But the resurrection of Christ does give a guarantee ; and where it is combined with a doctrine of grace which puts the assistance of the Spirit of God within the reach even of the most unimaginative man, we may fairly urge that the guarantee is one of triumph over every conceivable obstacle. The guarantee is sufficient, precisely because the death of Christ was attended by every circumstance which could conceivably add completeness to the apparent defeat sustained in it. The treachery of a familiar friend ; the cowardice and flight of all who were most bound to stand their ground ; the *volte-face* of a multitude demanding to-day the crucifixion of Him whom yesterday they claimed as King ; the uprising of the leaders of religion against one whose only concern is with religious integrity and ideals ; the failure of a justice which, by its very indifference to purely national and sectarian interests, might reasonably be supposed impartial ; even the deliberate refusal of the Sufferer Himself to call upon the legions of angels who only waited His summons to intervene ;—these, far more than any physical pangs, constitute the real tragedy of the crucifixion. These too, to every sensitive mind, exhibit in their highest degree the cruel refinements of that adverse circumstance which it is the aspiration of Christian virtue to conquer and transcend. The death of Socrates is often quoted as a parallel to the crucifixion of our Lord ; in effect it provides, not a parallel, but a glaring contrast, which only enhances the offence of the cross. Beyond a combination of events such as those which culminated in Calvary, the mind can scarcely picture anything more terrible ; and therefore the resurrection of the Lord is a guarantee that the tyranny of circumstance is not eternal and unconquerable, just because it is a resurrection following upon *such* a death and not upon one less unnatural or cruel.    It is for this reason that He is able to help *to the uttermost* them that call upon Him.

We have reached a second halting-place.   Here again many theologians are content to rest in their exposition of what is called the doctrine of the Atonement.   The death and resurrection of Christ are not merely an example of righteousness, but a guarantee that the righteous man who sets himself in the way of salvation (at least if this be thought of as a life ennobled and strengthened by grace) may triumph over every temptation, hindrance, or power that sin and circumstance can array against him.    But our hymn carries us further still ; it proclaims that there is yet another factor in man's degradation and weakness of which we have taken no account ; but that the Lord took account of it, and provided by His death a remedy.

## VI

### Christ's Death the Price of Sin

" He died that we might be forgiven . . . to pay the price of sin."    It is of phrases such as these that Catholic thought finds itself most called upon to offer an explanation.   We may dismiss at once any explanation which leans to the suggestion that a ransom had to be paid to the devil to rescue man from his clutches ; or that God demanded a victim—*any* victim, but still a victim—on whom to wreak vengeance for man's sin—" as if God did, according to the manner of corrupt judges, take so much money" (it matters not from *whom*) " to abate so much in the punishment of malefactors." [1]    It need scarcely be pointed out that theories of this kind find no support in the New Testament.   They have at times no doubt been popular in Christian thought, and their popularity has left marks upon Catholic language which may sometimes prove misleading ; but we must distinguish between such mere phrase-survivals and the deeper and truer thought to which, by a not unnatural transition, they have become attached.

Put in its simplest form, that thought is something as follows. The benefits of the death of Christ to which we have so far alluded

[1] R. Hooker, *Eccles. Polity*, vi. 5.

are all directed towards enabling man, as we may say, to "turn over a new leaf," to adopt a new and nobler attitude for the future towards both temptation within and adverse circumstance without. Yet if a sinner were so to lay hold upon grace and turn from sin without any allusion to, or apparent recognition of, his past offences, we should all rejoice, no doubt, at the result ; but equally we should all feel that something demanded by the circumstances of the case remained unsatisfied. "An improved attitude on the part of men to the law, a moral re-identification with it, is not sufficient ; for the temporal future cannot meet the demands of the temporal past." [1] "Afterward he repented and went" is without doubt a better conclusion to the story of the elder brother in the parable than "he went not" to the story of the younger, and the word "repented" may cover a multitude of acts of reparation. But if we take the story at its face value we cannot resist the conviction that the elder brother was something of a boor. He had refused his father's request, and that abruptly and insolently ; and though his subsequent repentance cancelled, in a sense, the original refusal, the abruptness and insolence must have created an atmosphere of mutual tension which it would take more than the formal obedience of the mood of penitence to dispel. Some kind of apology, acknowledgment or recognition of the intentional and uncalled-for offence offered to the father would have gone far to restore the family relationship which the son's perversity had subjected to so severe a strain. "Afterward he went" is no doubt a technical expiation of "I go not" ; but a sullen "going," without apology, could hardly restore the original harmonious relationship to which the father appealed with his courteous "Son, go labour to-day in my vineyard." The offence was a slight one, and no more than a mere apology was needed ; yet, as the story stands, the elder brother's repentance seems less adequate to the circumstance than that of another son, of whom it was said, "He fell at his father's feet saying, Father, I have sinned against heaven and before thee . . . ."

Where offence has been offered, therefore, a mere cessation of the offence does not restore the original relationship which existed before the offence. Even a complete reversal of behaviour can scarcely be thought to suffice, though it comes

[1] J. K. Mozley, *Doctrine of the Atonement*, p. 210 ; *cf.* Augustine, *Serm.* 351 (ed. Ben.) ; Anselm, *Cur Deus Homo*, i. 11.

nearer to sufficiency. Something more is demanded—something in which the offender explicitly acknowledges his fault and asks for forgiveness and restoration, even though he knows that forgiveness and restoration are his without the asking. But when we come to say *what* it is which demands this reparation for the past, our limited knowledge of eternal truth makes it difficult to give an answer. Phrases have been multiplied to express the source of the demand. "God's offended majesty," "God's holiness," "natural justice," the "craving of the soul for expiation," "the constitution of the universe as a moral order," all suggest the truth, yet we hesitate to say that any one of them expresses it fully. Perhaps we can do no more than borrow a theological term popular in many other connections ; it is πρέπον, *conveniens*, "fit" that the past be explicitly acknowledged in this way, before we turn to the future with its hoped-for newness of life. Such reparation is a part of the "natural fitness" of things.

It may indeed be alleged that in employing the phrase "the demand of natural fitness" rather than, let us say, the "demand of God's holiness," we have availed ourselves of a facile euphemism to evade a real difficulty.[1] Such an objection would be true enough if the substitution involved any suggestion that the ideal demands of nature did not coincide with the demands of God ; to contrast God and nature in this way would reduce theology to confusion. In common fairness it must be admitted that "natural fitness" and "divine decree" do mean the same thing ; and that the necessity for what we have called explicit recognition of past sin is to our mind of divine institution. Nevertheless, something is gained, in this connection, by using the name of "nature" rather than that of "God." For to say that God "demands" such and such things involves, in much modern anthropomorphic and unphilosophical thought about God, the

---

[1] A similar criticism could with some plausibility be urged against Canon Storr's theory that while the "consequences of sin" (degeneration of character, etc.) may fitly be called "the divine reactions against our sinning, expressed in the laws of the universe" (*Problem of the Cross*, p. 86), they can *not* be described as "the direct, personal acts of God" (*ib*. p. 84). It is difficult to see what is gained by this delicate distinction—or indeed whether it is a real distinction at all. At best it marks a difference between two modes of divine action—on the one hand, antecedent legislation ; on the other, *ad hoc* intervention. But this difference does not affect in any way the real question, which is simply, "Are the 'consequences' of sin of divine ordinance or not ?"

attribution to Him of characteristics at once tyrannical and pedantic :—tyrannical, because it suggests that He selects, of his own unfettered choice, conditions which He then imposes upon man as necessary preliminaries to salvation ; pedantic, because it might be inferred that, once He had laid down the law, He suffered not the slightest deviation from it to go unpunished whatever extenuation could be pleaded. Until Christian thought has wholly emancipated itself from the possibility of interpreting God's " demands," " decrees," or " laws " in an unnatural and unethical sense, it is wiser perhaps, and certainly safer, if we wish to argue the essential morality of a principle such as that of acknowledgment of sin, to base the argument upon phrases whose appropriateness and cogency all will recognise, rather than upon others which, though just in themselves, are at the moment liable to misinterpretation. When Christendom regains its appreciation of exact theology it will be possible to say plainly : " God, in no arbitrary or vindictive spirit, calls for acknowledgment of past sin as a piece of natural justice " : and the conscience of man will recognise the essential truth of the statement without falling into the errors so common in modern thought.[1]

At all events it is easy to show that some such idea as that which has been indicated underlay the whole Jewish system of sacrifice, crowned as it was by the final aspirations of the Day of Atonement. Other ideas were present no doubt—ideas which have an integral place in the scheme and which, like this one, have their own counterpart in Christian doctrine—ideas of communion with God, of sharing in His nature. But the " covering " of sin by sacrifice, the offering of atonement, is a primary thought of the system. With a humility as deep as their sense of sin itself, the Jews believed that only unwitting offences could be atoned for in this way ; for the "sin with a high hand " there was no known form of atonement. And with a like humility the greatest of their prophets invariably reminded them that the whole system of sacrifice could never be

[1] M. Rivière puts the argument of the above paragraph with inimitable precision and effect : " Nous ne prêtons pas à Dieu, comme on nous en accuse, je ne sais quelle susceptibilité mesquine de grand seigneur piqué ; et la raison en est que l'honneur de Dieu n'est pas, à vrai dire, un droit personnel et comme une affirmation hautaine de sa supériorité : il se confond avec la loi de subordination nécessaire des êtres, avec ce qu'on appelle parfois—d'un mot vague, mais juste—l'ordre des choses."—J. Rivière, *Dogme de la Rédemption*, p. 4.

regarded as *adequate* atonement for the past. Sacrifices were a symbol of penitence no doubt—an explicit recognition of sin before God—but in no way a substitute for that newness of life which He desired to see. And this introduces a consideration of primary importance. The function of sacrifice is wholly different from the function of newness of life ; the latter is the end after which man, by God's grace, should strive ; the former a necessary preliminary as restoring, by the admission of wrong done, the condition of harmony making future sanctification possible. Sacrifice and conversion, therefore, are two separate acts in the restoration of man ; each has its distinct part to play. Only a debased mind will infer, from the necessity of sacrifice, that it can take the place of conversion ; only a shallow mind, that conversion is adequate without sacrificial reparation.

The fact that sacrifice to the prophetic mind appeared value-less unless accompanied by a genuine effort of contrition brings out a further truth of real importance—that the intrinsic cost of the sacrifice to the offerer is not in itself a condition of its reality or worth. It must not indeed be so valueless as to make it only another insult to the offended person ; but because it is the explicit symbol of an implicit sense of sin rather than an act of legal restitution, appropriateness to the occasion rather than cost to the offerer should be its dominant characteristic. If we revert to the Parable of the Two Sons, we see that all that was required to restore the ruptured relationship was the utterance of a single sentence of regret. " Restitution " such as the cir-cumstances demanded was made by the work in the vineyard, it was the apology that was lacking. Without the restitution, indeed, the apology would have been an added insult ; without the apology the restitution was at best ungracious and inconsiderate. But to one genuinely intent on the restitution the apology could scarcely, in the case in question, have involved a great additional effort ; it is not so much the actual as the symbolic value of the sacrifice that makes it acceptable. From this it may further be inferred—and the inference is one of crucial importance—that, if A has no appropriate sacrifice of his own that he can bring to the altar, he can avail himself of, associate himself with, B's offering ; if he is, for any reason, tongue-tied, another can speak the necessary words for him, provided only that he signifies his assent. Another's gift can still be offered validly, if the desire to offer sacrifice is there, and no other means avail.

The importance of this conclusion for Christian theology becomes at once apparent. To all who fail to find within themselves adequate means for that expression of real contrition of which we have spoken, the Church offers her doctrine that the death of Christ is the divinely appointed means of help in this respect, as in those other respects which have been considered above. " On the cross," she says, "we see One wholly akin to ourselves offering a sinless life to the Father as representative for man. There is no confession of sin on His lips, for He did no sin ; otherwise His sacrifice would have been, in its measure, imperfect as ours have always been. And if we attribute to the Father the intent to give His only-begotten Son for the world's salvation, we can scarcely be wrong in seeing in His death this purpose also, that man should be provided with an adequate sacrifice and symbol of penitence—a symbol sufficient to satisfy the demand of ' natural justice ' or the ' fitness of things.' "

That one who has no other means of adequate sacrifice at his disposal may associate himself with another's offering we have already seen. That the sacrifice of Christ is *appropriate* for this purpose need hardly be argued ; that it is *adequate* will scarcely be doubted by anyone who sees in Jesus the Son of God, of the essence of the Godhead, incarnate for the salvation of the world. The only question that arises is whether we can in all strictness call the death of Christ *necessary* in this respect, as in those others in which its necessity has already been argued ; or rather, whether this aspect of the matter *demonstrates* that necessity for the death which our earlier arguments only led us—though with a high degree of cogency—to assume.[1] Is man unable adequately to make an appropriate acknowledgment of his sin ? Some will have no doubt on this point. " Christianity," they will say, " gives us a doctrine of human depravity which renders it antecedently unlikely that any-one not far advanced in spiritual grace could appreciate the depths of sin into which he had fallen, and give his appreciation adequate expression. Experience, again, teaches us that no acknowledgment of sin before God of which we are capable is wholly free from selfish sentiments and motives. It is mingled with wounded self-respect

[1] *Supra*, pp. 251-253.

and remorse for folly unbefitting the sinner's fancied dignity ; it is not without unworthy hopes of a response of divine favour showing itself even in temporal benefits ; it is hypocritical, as promising in the moment of emotion a dedicated life which it knows it cannot guarantee." Confession of sin may be a higher thing than sacrifice ; but arguments such as these suggest that it can never on human lips be pure enough to satisfy that natural fitness of which we have spoken.

Those who are convinced by these and similar lines of argument will not hesitate to agree that " some better sacrifice " than the blood of sheep and goats—better even than contrition of the heart and confession with the lips—was universally necessary ; and they will the more unhesitatingly and willingly accept the claims made by the Church for the death of Christ in this regard. Others, not so convinced, may believe themselves—theoretically at least— *capable* of such contrition and confession as is needed by the circumstances of their sin. Yet, even so, it is unthinkable that they should actually be *content* with any contrition they had exhibited or confession they had voiced. Contentment of such a kind would be of the very essence of self-righteousness ; it would indicate not sorrow for sin, but complete analgesia towards the real character of sin in the soul. If, then, there should be a genuinely spiritual man who said "I see the need for confession, but not the need for sacrifice as well," he would never reject without examination any offer of help that *might* conceivably enable him to make his confession more adequate ; rather he would *only* reject such offered help if it proved either idle or immoral. He might indeed be less inclined to emphasise the necessity of Christ's death in this respect. But, on the arguments hitherto advanced, he would not hesitate to attribute to it sacrificial character in the fullest measure. He would recognise the unspeakable gift of God which enabled him to say : " Whether my own life, renewed as it is by the Spirit of God, is an adequate expression of sorrow for my past sins, I cannot say. But I know that some such expression was a necessary condition of my reconciliation with my Father in Heaven ; and my own attempts at expression, be they sufficient or otherwise, are infinitely enhanced when I contemplate the cross and say 'There, O Father, is the sacrifice I would have made if only I could. There is the sinless life of obedience unto death which—if I could offer it—

would be a fitting reparation for the past. Accept, I pray, this sacrifice on my behalf. It is not mine ; yet by every grace given to me I associate myself with it, promising to mould my life upon that pattern not only for righteous service in the future, but also, and equally, as my open acknowledgment of grievous sin in the past.' "

Yet even this consideration moves within too limited a circle of argument. "Sin," as we have seen, involves a deep-rooted disorganisation of the universe, mysteriously bound up with human sin, yet infinitely more terrible than even the complete sum of all the sins that ever have been or can be committed. "Sin" is a corporate matter involving both animate and inanimate creation, and to the reflective mind even an endless offering of individual reparations would not suffice to repair the breach thus made between the creation and the Creator. Natural fitness, we may say, demands that human nature—if not universal nature too—shall in one symbolic corporate act express the conviction, shared by God and man alike, that sin is foreign to its ideal constitution. If the boorish son of the parable had been not one but fifty in number, individually and collectively offending against the father's love, separate and private acts of reparation, however complete, would not have effected the necessary reconciliation. A conspiracy can only be expiated by the corporate submission of the conspirators ; ideal justice remains unsatisfied if they merely pass over, severally and one by one, to the side of the aggrieved. And whatever be the truth of the disorganisation of nature, it is clear that human sin partakes of this character of conspiracy. Men make an implicit compact not with Death and Hell alone, but with one another, to hold down the truth in unrighteousness, to connive at an outraged social order, to tolerate the inertia of selfishness, to prostitute the divine standard of purity to the debased usage of the world. Once we revert to the Pauline conception of the corporate character of sin, the absolute necessity for some such act as the death of Christ becomes transcendently clear. We are in a position to endorse the familiar statements that in Him humanity paid the price as a whole, and that He died as the Representative Man ; for it is only a soul preoccupied with the thought of " my sin " to the exclusion of that of " sin " as a whole which can hesitate any more to confess that, without such an offering, the sacrifice demanded by natural fitness is still unoffered, and salvation, which must at least involve full and final reconciliation with the loving Father of all mankind, remains not merely difficult or doubtful of attainment, but completely and finally impossible.[1]

## VII

### The Vocabulary of the Atonement

There is no " Catholic " doctrine of the Atonement in the sense in which, for example, there is a " Catholic " doctrine of the Incarnation. Conciliar definition has never asserted any one theory of the manner in which Christ's death avails for the salvation of men. But the main stream of Christian thought has carried along with it certain definite phrases as applicable to the Atonement, and it is by reference to these that we may test what has been written above. That, on the theory thus outlined, the death of Christ may with peculiar appropriateness be called a *sacrifice* is self-evident, and in this respect the test is wholly satisfied. That it provides *expiation*, or due acknowledgment, for the past sin of mankind, and so removes the obstacle on man's side which impedes the resumption of harmonious relationship between man and God, we have already argued ; that it *propitiates*, or *satisfies*[2]— not, indeed, an arbitrary, angry, or tyrannical deity, but that natural fitness which is none the less a divine ordinance for being also an admitted demand of human reason, has been our main contention. Similarly, there can be no doubt as to the description *vicarious* ; the death was offered by the divine Victim on man's behalf, and, as we have argued, is available for man to identify himself therewith. That it can fitly be called *substitutionary* is not, on the theory we have stated, very apparent ; but we have frankly to recognise that, whilst the New Testament constantly speaks of Christ suffering " on our behalf," it very rarely indeed uses language suggesting that he suffered " in our stead " [3]; and it may reasonably be supposed that such language crept into Christianity through an interpretation of Isaiah liii. which neither the author

---

[1] See further, *infra*, p. 276, Note B, " Dr. Moberly's Theory of the Atonement."

[2] See further, *infra*, p. 277, Note C, " The Term ' Satisfaction ' as applied to the Death of Christ."

[3] *Cf.* Rashdall, *op. cit.* p. 93.

nor, for example, his Septuagint translators would for a moment have endorsed, or from a similar vulgarisation of the ritual of the Day of Atonement.

We may pass on to a much more important problem, and that our last one : have we done sufficient justice to the undisputed fact that the death of Christ on the basis of New Testament evidence is constantly spoken of as winning for us *justification* and *forgiveness* of sins ?

This is scarcely the place for a detailed discussion of the meaning of St. Paul's *justification by faith*. Two facts, however, are sufficiently clear : (i) that he discards the gospel phrase of *forgiveness* whilst introducing and emphasising that of " justification " ; (ii) that no amount of argument can rob the latter word of its primary forensic sense ; it is redolent of the Law.[1] These facts are surprising and disturbing enough in all conscience. It would seem that the apostle of the Gentiles showed himself, at the central point of his gospel, more Jewish than the Jew, a Pharisee of the Pharisees in the worst sense ; that he abandoned the free air of the new law for the bonds of Rabbinic legalism just at the point where such a lapse would prove most disastrous. The motive may, indeed, have been mainly controversial—to prove to his opponents *not* that " forgiveness " must be taken in the sense of " justification," but rather that " justification " could have no religious meaning unless set in a context of " forgiveness." Yet even so it can hardly be denied that St. Paul perpetuated, in Christianity, a Jewish idea singularly difficult for the Gospel to assimilate with other elements as fully, or more fully, integral to itself—the idea of the " wrath of God " from which man has to find " justification " ; and that he added to it a conception which to many appears equally infelicitous—the conception, namely, that this wrath could be evaded, by the unrighteous, on the basis not so much of a conversion to righteousness as on that of the appropriation of justification—a righteousness not of obvious fact but of apparent legal fiction—from another source.

Yet we have to notice that he is not happy in his adoption of the phrase " the wrath of God "—he tends throughout to

---

[1] *I.e.* " to deem righteous." Modern commentators are practically agreed on this point : W. L. Knox, *St. Paul and the Church of Jerusalem*, p. 117, and A. C. McGiffert, *Christianity in the Apostolic Age*, pp. 143, 144, are the principal dissentients.

avoid it and substitute an impersonal "wrath." [1]   This tendency eliminates—partially, if not entirely—one of our difficulties.   We can interpret this "wrath" in the sense of that "fitness of things" or "natural justice" which demands of a sinner some overt recognition and abhorrence of his past sin.   Such a recognition, as we have seen, is independent of "newness of life," fulfilling as it does a different function ;   it can therefore avail itself, for its explicit self-expression, of the actions of another.   So, too, St. Paul's "justification" is independent of "newness of life." Ideally, sanctification follows it ;   but St. Paul is clear that Christians, already "justified," will still have to answer "in the body" for their life after justification, and that an unsanctified life will not be able to evade condemnation by any appeal to precedent "justification."   That being so, the element of "evasion by fiction" goes.   Justification is far from being salvation ;   it is just that acknowledgment of past offences without which salvation is impossible, but which does not in itself guarantee salvation.   The Jew, St. Paul suggests, had made his mistake in identifying justification with salvation, and the identification was a false one.   It is necessary to "justify" oneself for the past, or to associate oneself with another's act sufficient to secure "justification" ;   but this is only the beginning of the righteous life, not (as the Jew supposed) the beginning and the end as well.

We come, then, to the other question, In what sense does the death of Christ win "forgiveness of sin" ?   Forgiveness obviously means resumption, by the injured party, of the same *attitude* towards the offender (*e.g.* an attitude of friendliness) as was exhibited by him before the offence.   Forgiveness, therefore, is (in strict thought) different from the resumption between the two parties of the same *relations* as before the offence.   It is the act of one party—the injured—and not of both.   But the *goal* of forgiveness is obviously the resumption of the relations of which the resumption of the attitude (of friendliness or the like) is a part but no more than a part.   There is therefore a sense in which forgiveness may be called incomplete until these relations are resumed ;—it is not incomplete in character indeed, but it is incomplete in its effects.   No one has put this paradox more finely

---

[1] ὀργή with Θεός, Rom. i. 18, iii. 5, ix. 22 ; Eph. v. 6 ; Col. iii. 6 ; without Θεός, Rom. ii. 5, 8, iv. 15, v. 9, ix. 22, xii. 19, xiii. 5 ; Eph. ii. 3 ; 1 Thess. i. 10, ii. 16, v. 9.

than Dr. Moberly. " Love wears the form and carries the name of ' forgiveness,' " he writes,[1] " in its anticipatory and provisional relation to the penitent. We *call* love ' forgiveness ' just when and just because the penitent, whose very life it is, yet makes and can make no claim to deserving it. But the *full forgiveness* to which I aspire is the righteous love which, *seeing in me at last the very righteousness of Christ*, embraces in me the righteousness *which is really there.*" Although, therefore, the death of Christ does not alter God's attitude to man—that attitude of unswerving love could never and needed never to alter; indeed, it showed itself in its highest degree in the self-oblation of Christ—it *does* alter the relations subsisting between man and God, and in such a way that God's forgiveness of man, formerly incomplete, is put on the road to consummation. There may be other and deeper ways in which Christ made atonement for man ; but even the way suggested above makes it possible to say with a meaning in every respect conformable to the tests of Christian tradition and of unbiassed reason, and passing beyond everything contained in our previous affirmations, that " He died that we might be forgiven," that " He paid the price of sin," and that we are " saved by His precious blood."

That being so, we may with confidence revert for the last time to the New Testament and to Catholic thought, and draw from them one more universal phrase to express our meaning. It is true that St. Paul eschewed the words " forgiveness of sins " ; but it is profoundly untrue that he did so to substitute for them the idea of justification ; the new idea—his great contribution to Christian soteriology—was the word " *reconciliation*," " atone-ment." Furthermore, his consistent use of the word implies that the fulfilment of God's purposes depends even more upon man being reconciled to God than upon God being reconciled to man.[2] But it is in reconciliation that forgiveness first comes to rest and finds its goal ; without reconciliation forgiveness remains an offer to which no answer is vouchsafed. And reconciliation sums up in itself every aspect of that restoration of relations between the offender and the offended which we have seen to be the crucial need in man's salvation. Where sin is not thought of as an offence

---

[1] Moberly, *Atonement and Personality*, pp. 62–72, condensed ; the italics have been added.

[2] Sanday and Headlam, *Romans*, pp. 129, 130 ; Rashdall, *op. cit.* p. 100.

against the living God, it is true this need cannot be felt ; but where sin is not so thought of, the soul has far to go before it begins to realise the fulness of its needs.    Even so, Christ's death has a message and a promise for it—the message of example to inspire present effort, the promise of victory in the end.    Is it not true to say that meditation upon the goodness of God revealed in this promise and message must lead to a sense, by contrast, of human unworthiness of God—unworthiness whose most piercing sting lies just in the fact that it is the result of human sin ; and that this sense must sooner or later bring with it the knowledge that frank penitence and open confession are the first steps towards reconciliation ?    Once this knowledge is attained, the need for a sacrifice is felt ; and where the need is felt, in whatever degree, great or small, to recognise that in the death of Christ God has Himself provided a Lamb for the sacrifice is to lay aside remorse, despondency and despair, and to be reconciled to God.

NOTE A.—EXEMPLARIST THEORIES OF THE ATONEMENT (see p. 258)

It is perhaps in a subconscious effort to avoid the criticism here adduced that Exemplarist writers lay more stress upon *gratitude* than upon *respect for example* as the motive to which the death of Christ appeals (*cp.* Rashdall, *op. cit.* p. 101 *et pass.*) ; for " gratitude "—" the last spark of the divine image to disappear from the soul of man " (Rashdall, *op. cit.* p. 361)—may be thought of as a more widespread emotion than "respect for example," and so less dependent upon the intermediary offices of imagination. If this, however, is the real object of the insistence upon gratitude, it depends on a fallacy. A man can only be grateful in response to some objective service, and on the Exemplarist theory the *only* objective service contributed by the death of Christ to man's salvation is its appeal as an example of unswerving obedience to the will of God. That this is an objective service we need not deny, indeed (as we have attempted to show above, p. 256) it has more objectivity about it than Exemplarist writers would care to admit ; but the *realisation* of its objective value depends wholly upon its appeal to the imagination ; and therefore the question as to whether it will or will not in any given case elicit responsive gratitude depends in equal measure upon that appeal. The shifting of emphasis from the motive of *respect for example* to that of *gratitude* is a specious obscuring of the issue, which leaves the real gist of our criticism untouched.

It might however be held that *any* theory of the atonement depends for its efficacy in eliciting a response from the individual upon an appeal to the imagination, and that this is evidenced by the facts that all theories of justification alike are theories of justification *by faith* ;—for faith in the atoning work of Christ for us is only possible when imagination has been stirred to embrace its atoning value. On such grounds it would appear that the assertion in the text above, that in the traditional doctrines of grace the unimaginative man stood at no disadvantage as compared with his imaginative brother, was wholly illusory. This objection, however, depends upon a dangerous confusion between imagination and common sense. The older theories of atonement, however inadequate or misleading they may have been—the Ransom theory, the *Wergeld*-satisfaction theory, and the like—all depended upon an appeal to common sense which would be universally recognised. Man is Satan's prisoner,—*of course*, therefore, someone must ransom him ; man owes a debt to God which justice cannot remit,—*of course*, therefore, someone must pay it for him. As Canon Storr has pointed out (*Problem of the Cross*, pp. 10-13), these traditional theories were erected upon the universally accepted axioms of contemporary thought. Common sense would therefore at once see their relevance and necessity ; no effort of imagination was necessary ; faith—and consequently grace—was in reach of the most pedestrian and prosaic mind. But the Exemplarist theory is not so. Here common sense is satisfied with some such dictum as " Man must live the moral life ; conscience, Scripture, the Church tell him in what that moral life consists " ; it does not rise to the affirmation, " *of course* he must have an example." Whether a given example—even the highest—will help a sinner or not depends, therefore, wholly upon the exercise of his imagination.

No doubt the verdict of common sense changes with the ages ; and what to patristic or mediæval thought seemed obvious may appear to us fantastic or untrue. But modern " objective " theories are all of them attempts to find a basis in common sense—in some proposition whose cogency will be universally admitted—and not in imagination. Thus the theory outlined in the later paragraphs of this essay (pp. 262-270), however imperfect and inadequate it may be, must stand or fall entirely in accordance as the reader's common sense accepts or rejects the postulate on which it depends—namely, that where offence has been committed, " natural fitness " demands not merely reformation of character but also some form of overt acknowledgment as an appropriate and adequate means of restoring ruptured relations.

Dr. Denney (*Death of Christ*, p. 177) launched a somewhat confused criticism of the appeal to gratitude in Exemplarist theories, based on the fact that *some* Exemplarists had forgotten to emphasise the objective value of an example of loyalty to the service of God and man. By restoring the emphasis, Dr. Rashdall had little difficulty in rebutting this criticism at its face value (*op. cit.* pp. 440 ff. —note that the references to the pages in *The Death of Christ* appear to be incorrect). But the real point of Dr. Denney's criticism remains unaltered. The " rational connection " between the death of Christ and the " responsibilities which sin involves and from which that death delivers "—the " intelligible relation " between the two—is scarcely apparent to the ordinary mind, unless the " natural fitness" of the explicit acknowledgment of guilt be admitted. Without that admission a relationship may indeed be established, as we have admitted, between the example of Christ and the needs of man, even on the Exemplarist basis ; and in his implicit denial of this Dr. Denney would seem to have overstepped the limits of his argument. But it is certainly not a *rational* relationship ; for, as the argument in the text is designed to show, it makes grace proportionate not so much to the moral earnestness as to the imaginative capacity of the recipient.

One final criticism of exemplarism may be mentioned. The theory fails to show any grounds for belief in the *necessity* of the death of Christ. The ultimate arguments for that necessity must be drawn, as we have seen, even more from the *corporate* character of human sin (demanding as it does corporate or representative acknowledgment—see above, p. 269) than from its *cosmic* character (above, pp. 251-253). It is just this need for a corporate acknowledgment which the Exemplarist denies ; his theory loses all distinctiveness unless he insists that the example and teaching of Christ were the *only* benefits conferred on man by His life and death. Were he to allow that possible interpretation of his theory which emphasises (p. 256 above) a psychological compulsion to Christian heroism objectively resulting from the example of Christ, we might still be in a position to assert the necessity of that example with some appearance of plausibility ; the more the compelling character of the example were emphasised, the more it would appear unlikely that without it (and consequently without the death of Christ) man could work out his own salvation. But few Exemplarist writers care to emphasise this aspect of their theory, for the reason that they wish to avoid *any* suggestion (not merely that involved in so-called " transactional " theories) that a change in man's spiritual condition can be brought about by any agency external to his own conscious moral efforts. They are therefore compelled to postulate that the example of Christ can only be effective in the lives of those who *consciously meditate* upon His life and death. We should be the last to deny the supreme value and importance of such conscious meditation ; but if this be the *only way* in which the life and death of Christ can alter man's spiritual condition, it must be conceded that it can hardly be a *necessary* way. For it to be necessary it would have to be asserted that *no other possible subject* of meditation could be depended upon to rouse the Christian to a moral effort sufficient to win salvation ; and such an assertion would at once be too unsubstantiated, and too suggestive of a " magical formula," unfailingly efficacious in the case of all who had recourse to it, to commend itself to Exemplarist thought.

It follows, therefore, that on the strict logic of the Exemplarist theory, its supporters would be unable to subscribe to the belief that man cannot be saved apart from the death of Christ, without sacrificing all the distinctive positions for which they are really contending. Where writers of this school of thought commit themselves to language which appears to assert the universal necessity of Christ's death for men, the fact can only be attributed to a failure to grasp the full implications of their system ;—or better, and probably more truly, to the victory of a genuinely Christian sentiment over a faulty human logic.

It remains only to notice Canon Storr's version of exemplarism. To him the death of Christ is principally not an example of obedience to the will of God, but a revelation of God's sympathy with sinful man and His consequent suffering on account of man's sin (*Problem of the Cross*, pp. 133, 136, 152, etc.— with quotations from Canon Wilson and Dr. White). It is noteworthy that although this position (which of course contains in itself a profound and wholly Christian truth) might establish a better case for the necessity of Christ's death than other versions of exemplarism, Canon Storr himself evades the test (" The burden lies on the shoulders of those who criticise," p. 139), which elsewhere he regards as " very important " (p. 108) and applies rigorously to theories which he rejects (pp. 93, 108, 111). However this may be it remains true that the other criticisms we have urged against exemplarism hold with equal force in this case.

### Note B.—Dr. Moberly's Theory of the Atonement

The debt which this essay owes to Dr. Moberly's *Atonement and Personality*, and especially to the sixth chapter of that great book, is so obvious that any comment on its position might seen unnecessary. But those who, with the present writer, find themselves continually recurring to Dr. Moberly's pages for fresh light upon the mystery of the Atonement, will notice in this essay the omission of two of his most important phrases—" Christ the Perfect Penitent " and " Christ inclusively man." Canon Storr (*Problem of the Cross*, ch. ix.) has published a very fair and friendly appreciation of the merits and defects of these two phrases to which little need be added. The first (" Christ the Perfect Penitent ") is a beautiful and arresting paradox, whose meaning cannot be obscure to any but the most pedantic and literal mind ; it has not been avoided here of strict purpose, and its meaning has as far as possible been expressed in analogous ways. The second (" Christ inclusively man ") is perhaps more open to question, as witness Dr. Rashdall's criticisms (*Idea of Atonement*, pp. 424, 425 ; *J.T.S.* iii. 178–211—Dr. Rashdall censures similar phrases used by Dr. Ottley and Mr. Mozley ; Canon Storr also quotes a kindred passage from Dr. Du Bose). The phrase covers three (if not four) distinct ideas which it is well to keep apart, as confusion between them may produce an erroneous impression that their implications have not been fully thought out, if not that the phrase itself is virtually meaningless : (*a*) that atonement by a Representative is the *natural* or even the *necessary* way in which corporate guilt can be acknowledged ; (*b*) that such representative acknowledgment, if fitly expressed, will be adequate in the case of each individual offender who chooses to associate himself therewith ; (*c*) that " incorporation in Christ," of which the sacraments are at once a symbol and a means, is for Catholic thought the most obvious way in which man can (i) associate himself with Christ's acknowledgment of sin on his behalf, and (ii) derive from God those other benefits of the death and resurrection of Christ (victory over sin and circumstance and the like) to which allusion has been made. It has been the purpose of this essay to keep these separate implications of the phrase as distinct from one another as possible (for (*a*) see p. 269 ; for (*b*), pp. 266 f.; (*c*) (i) has not been dealt with here, but is fully treated in the concluding essay of this book ; for (*c*) (ii) see p. 261) ; and to this end the phrase itself has not been used. But analysis is not necessarily the best way of expressing Christian truth ; and though the writer has thought himself bound, in the present case, to use the analytic method, he would take this opportunity of wholly and gladly associating himself with what he takes to be the rich complex of meanings underlying Dr. Moberly's synthetic phrase.

## Note C.—The Term " Satisfaction " as applied to the Death of Christ

A note on the traditional (but not Scriptural) term *satisfaction*, as applied to the death of Christ, will not be inapposite, especially as it is the term to which critics of the doctrine of Atonement most commonly take exception. The application is first made by Radulphus Ardens in the eleventh century (Rivière, p. 289), but it was really popularised by Anselm. It is often thought to be derived from the Teutonic concept of the *Wergeld*, or compensation paid by (*e.g.*) a homicide to his victim's clan (see reff. Rivière, pp. 308–309 ; *cp.* Rashdall, p. 352, note 1) ; and the necessary corollary that Christ (on the theory of satisfaction) paid a penalty due from man which exempted man from any further responsibility is rightly stigmatised as clearly immoral. But there seems to be no doubt that the phrase was in fact borrowed by soteriology from the penitential system of the Church, where it had been used since Tertullian's time to designate the penitential acts (or, as they are now called, *penances*) which should accompany contrition (Rivière, Rashdall, *ut sup.*). At first sight this does not appear to affect the inherent immorality of the theory, until the full implications of *satisfactio* are seen. In legal Latin the word meant not so much " compensation " as " surety," " guarantee "—not that which satisfies a creditor in full, but that which satisfies him of the good faith of the debtor. " Non idem sunt *satisfacere* et *solvere* ; nam *solvit* qui creditori pecuniam omnem numerat ; *satisfacit* qui quocumque modo creditorem placat—v.g. cautione, satisfactione, pignore, partis debiti solutione " (Forcellini, *Lexicon*, s.v.). Hence in classical

Latin, when applied to offences, it may mean no more than " making suitable apology"—"purgare se de injuria illata, verbis excusare, deprecari, veniam petere culpam fatendo " (*ib.*) ; cp. *Digest*, 46, 3, 52.

No doubt the idea of "payment in full" attached itself in popular thought to the term in its penitential usage (*e.g.* to avoid the *poena temporalis* of sin) ; but the other conception was never lost. Thus Ambrose, *de poenit.* ii. 9 (80), points out that penitential works could never *merit* forgiveness ; though called " satisfaction " the idea of " full compensation" was wholly absent. So too Hooker, commenting upon Tertullian, points out that " repentance and the works thereof are termed *satisfactory*, not for that so much is thereby done as the justice of God can exact, but because . . . they draw the pity of God towards us (*illices divinae misericordiae*—Tert. *de poenit.* 9)." " Satisfaction as a part [*i.e.* as distinct from contrition] comprehendeth only that which the Baptist meant by works worthy of repentance " [καρποὺς ἀξίους τῆς μετανοίας Lk. iii. 8] (Hooker, *Eccles. Pol.* vi. 5). Furthermore, " satisfaction" was not a *sine quâ non* of absolution ; the latter could be given before penance was performed (as in the present discipline—which Hooker (*ut sup.*) indeed calls a " strange preposterous course," though what he is really inveighing against is the distinction between eternal and temporal punishment on which many of its defenders based it) ; or could be waived by the Bishop (*Conc. Anc.* can. 5 ; *Conc. Nic.* can. 12)—though there was always some doubt as to the validity of this (Bingham, *Origines*, xviii. iv. § 6).

From this it would appear that we are not going beyond the strict limits of patristic thought if we say of satisfaction (in the sense of " penitential works ") that though (*a*) generally necessary, it is (*b*) quite different from repentance, (*c*) inoperative without repentance (this is universally agreed), (*d*) not an "adequate compensation " to God for the offence committed, but rather a " suitable acknowledgment" thereof, and a pledge of newness of life. This gives to " satisfaction" in Christian theology a meaning identical with that assigned in the text above to " reparation " (pp. 263 ff.), and allows us to use the term of the death of Christ (as in the case of the Anglican Prayer of Consecration) not with any implication of the idea of an "angry God " who has to be placated, but as suggesting that Christ, by His death, provided a suitable symbol of human guilt with which man, to make that due acknowledgment of his sin which otherwise could not be made, can associate himself.

Space forbids any discussion of the meaning of the word " propitiation." In the text above it has been used as the equivalent of " satisfaction " ; but note should be taken of Westcott's contention that " the scriptural conception of the verb is not of appeasing one who is angry . . . but of altering the character of that which, from without, occasions a necessary alienation and interposes an inevitable obstacle to fellowship." " The ἱλασμός, when it is applied to the sinner, so to speak, neutralizes the sin." (Additional note on 1 John ii. 2, *Epistles of St. John*, pp. 83 ff.) If Westcott's view be adopted, *propitiation* would correspond with the meaning we have given to *expiation* ; considerations suggesting caution in the acceptance of this view will be found in Sanday and Headlam, *Romans*, p. 130 ; and Moulton and Milligan, *Vocabulary of Greek Testament*, s.v. 2 ; Deissmann, *Bible Studies* (E.T.), pp. 124 ff ; Driver, Art. " Propitiation " in Hastings' *Dictionary of the Bible*, should also be consulted.

# THE RESURRECTION
## BY EDWARD GORDON SELWYN

# CONTENTS

# I

## INTRODUCTORY

THE resurrection and ascension of Jesus Christ have from the earliest days formed a cardinal element in the *credenda* of the Christian Church. They focus with peculiar intensity that faith in the Gospel as at once historical and supernatural, which enabled Christianity to conquer the pagan religions of the Græco-Roman world ; and by the same token they focus also those doubts and problems which are characteristic of modern criticism and enquiry. If it be true that the religion of Christ belongs at once to this world and to the other ; if it claims to provide a synthesis between the agelong antinomies of Time and Eternity, of Nature and Supernature, of Successiveness and Simultaneity, of Fact and Value ; and if it asserts that the secret of this synthesis lies in the mediation of a Person ;—then clearly supreme importance attaches to those happenings in history in which the Mediator is alleged to have decisively and finally vindicated His character. In an earlier essay it has been shown that the Christ of the Synoptic Gospels must remain " a stranger and an enigma " to us unless we recognise the reconciliation of the two principles of suffering and of glory in the unity of His single experience as giving the clue to His life and teaching ; and others have drawn out the dogmatic implicates of this fact, and its reactions upon human sin, freedom and forgiveness. It remains to be shown that the revelation thus made to the reason and the redemption thus offered to the will are not illusory, but were sealed as genuine by a divine action credibly attested in history and in character with the momentous issues at stake.

Various causes combine to make the task one of great complexity. The resurrection, and still more the ascension, in so far as they are facts, are facts on the borderland of history and symbol. In the case of the ascension the symbolical element greatly outweighs the historical ; one might almost say that the faith of the Church would not be other than it is, if by some mischance the few verses in the Acts which St. Luke devotes to the ascension had not survived. The primary evidence, that is to say, is the Church's experience of Christ's sovereign power from St. Stephen's day to our own. The resurrection presents a far closer balance between the two elements. Who would not feel, for example, if we were without the last chapter of each Synoptic Gospel or the last two of the Fourth, that the whole significance of the story had been changed ? The precise determination of the fact behind these records is perhaps impossible ; but that some historical fact of an unusual order occurred at that point is required not only by the existence of the documentary evidence, but by the evidence of Christianity ever since. Yet here two important cautions must be borne in mind. In the first place, while the Christian creed asserts an unequivocal belief in the fact of the Lord's resurrection, it lays down nothing as *de fide* in regard to the manner of it ; and on the latter point many different interpretations have been given by theologians of unquestioned orthodoxy at different times. This does not mean that any such teaching, particularly if it seems to endanger the faith-values of the fact, should be exempt from criticism. But it does mean that the Christian scholar may claim here a large latitude of enquiry and thought, and that such criticism as he either makes or receives should be frankly *in foro theologiae*. In the second place, it must be observed that the risen Lord appeared only to believers. The fact was not of a kind, that is to say, to convert men by its stark and palpable marvellousness against their will. We may assume, then, that much will depend for our understanding of the resurrection on the atmosphere or " spirit " of our minds. It belongs to that order of " spiritual things," of which St. Paul says that they must be " spiritually discerned." Apologetics must beware, therefore, of trying to do too much—of trying to demonstrate to the natural reason a fact which in its historical happening was witnessed only by those whose minds had been trained by Jesus. If we reach a point where we have to admit that the historical evidence can only give probabilities, we may well remember that *a priori* in a matter of this kind historical evidence cannot be expected to do more.

The method which I propose to adopt in this essay is the familiar one of arguing from the better known to the less known ; or, in other words, from the doctrine to the fact. We do know with singular precision what was authoritatively taught and believed in the Church within a generation of Pentecost ; and we can determine the significance, and observe the centrality, of Christ's resurrection in relation both to doctrine and ethics for those first writers and believers. The first section will therefore be devoted to considering the resurrection as part of the apostolic teaching. But we cannot stop there. The Apostles are convinced that what they preach as the resurrection was a fact of history for which unimpeachable testimony existed. Examination of this testimony will show that it is concerned partly with "appearances" of the Lord, and partly with circumstances of a different kind pointing to the fact that He had risen from the dead. In the second section of this essay, therefore, I propose to discuss the evidence for the "appearances" as evidence relating to the experience of the disciples, to appraise their meaning, and to consider how far they provide an adequate explanation for the Catholic dogma ; while the third section will be devoted to an estimate of the probabilities in regard to the remainder of the evidence.

## II

### THE RESURRECTION IN THE APOSTOLIC TEACHING

Christianity went out into the world as a gospel of emancipation. To the Jew it brought emancipation from the cramping fetters of the Law ; to the Gentile from the doubt and despair which haunted the pages of its greatest teachers ; and to both a new freedom from the power of sin. It did this by opening up afresh, on the strength of a new and authoritative revelation, the true nature of God. It proclaimed Him to be transcendent both above the Law, which had once been the embodiment of His will, and above those circumstances of sin and death which seemed to set such inexorable limits to the possible worth of human life. Moreover, this opening up of truths and riches as yet unguessed in men's conception of the Being of God carried with it the uncovering of new worlds for the spirit of man to move in. Access was now given to that heavenly and supernatural order of fellowship with God, whose doors had seemed fast closed hitherto : the citizenship of Christians was in heaven, and they were heirs of eternal life. This call involved new powers and new hopes— new powers of conquering sin in this life here, new hopes of

immortality hereafter.　　And the fact which more than any other
was asserted as the ground of this whole revelation, opportunity
and call was the resurrection of Jesus Christ.

In this first preaching of the Gospel the resurrection is set
forth as primarily a mighty act of God in relation to His only-
begotten Son.　　It is a revealing act which at once designates the
Son and declares the nature of the Father.　　It designates Jesus as
the head of the corner, the only Saviour of men,[1] the Fulfiller of
Messianic prophecy,[2] the Lord and Judge of men,[3] the Son of
God.[4]　　At the same time it declares the nature of the Father as
" a living and true God "[5] ; it was through His power that Jesus
was raised and now lives[6] ; Christ's resurrection and ascension
are demonstrative proofs of God intended to lead men to repose in
Him their faith and hope.[7]　　And this new understanding of God
through Christ and His resurrection bears the hall-mark of a true
revelation in spiritual experience.　　It is, that is to say, fundamentally vocational.　　This sense of call or mission, of a new and
divine direction given to life, is one of the means by which men
are made aware of that element in the transcendent Deity called by
Otto " energy " or " urgency."　　The resurrection of Jesus was
felt by the first Christians to be a signal example of this divine
urgency, laying upon them generally the duties of their vocation
and upon their leaders in particular their apostolic commission.
The power and purpose of God stand out now with a new definiteness and a richer content.　　In it St. Paul finds rooted his one title
to be an Apostle[8] ; by it the disciples are emboldened to claim to
obey God rather than men[9] ; through it believers are made certain
of the limitless spiritual resources now put at their disposal.[10]
Faith in the resurrection has thus mediated a new experience and
vision of God—a vision and an experience which are attested in
the positive fruits of new vocation.

This revelation of the purpose of God and of His power to

---

[1] Acts iv. 11, 12.　The identity of teaching as to the resurrection in the
speeches in Acts and in the Epistles is one of the important points of internal
evidence in favour of the genuineness of the former, as at least a reliable reflexion
of the Christian ideas of the time : though a modern historian such as Eduard
Meyer regards the external evidence as in itself sufficient.

[2] Acts ii. 25 ff.　　　　　　　　　　　[3] Rom. xiv. 9 ; Phil. ii. 9 ff.
[4] Rom. i. 4.　　　　　　　　　　　　　[5] 1 Thess. i. 9.
[6] 2 Cor. xiii. 4.　　　　　　　　　　　[7] 1 Pet. i. 21.
[8] Gal. i. 1 ; 1 Cor. i. 1 ; 2 Cor. i. 1 ; *cf.* 1 Cor. ix. 1.
[9] Acts v. 29.　　　　　　　　　　　　[10] Eph. i. 19.

achieve it has its counterpart in a great expansion of men's ideas as to the meaning and worth of human life. In the age which witnessed the dawn of Christianity no conviction was more widespread than that of the vanity and corruption of the world and all that pertained to it. What the Gospel did was not to deny this, but to change its significance by showing that the world was only a part of that whole structure of reality with which men had to do. It was true that the creation was " subjected to vanity " ; but it was of God's set purpose and for a time only. For the natural order—so St. Paul says in a famous passage—is but the vestibule of the supernatural ; its bondage is but the presage of liberty ; its corruption preparatory to a glorious redemption ; the world as we know it is no more than a kind of enclave, soon to be removed, within the reality of eternal life.[1] And the assurance of this reality derives from the resurrection of Jesus.[2] It is the risen Lord who has " abolished death and brought life and incorruption to light through the gospel." [3] Once before in history God's people had known what it was to enter upon a new inheritance. It was when Israel saw the fulfilment of long-cherished hopes at the entrance into Canaan. But there the analogy ends. For the new inheritance opened up to Christians is infinitely more satisfying than their storied land ever was to the Jews. Its wealth is incorruptible, its boundaries inviolable, its resources permanent, its nature not of earth but of heaven. And its possession is secured to believers by Christ's resurrection.[4] New ends are thus proposed to human life ; its destiny is given a fresh scope ; man's spirit breathes in a new air.

One effect of this changed outlook and proportion is a transvaluation of those very experiences in which man enters most sensitively into the sorrow and vanity of the world. In a passage of poignant intimacy [5] St. Paul tells how the Christian life, and particularly the life of an Apostle, is a perpetual reproduction of the Lord's death and resurrection. In his weariness, perplexity, persecution he feels himself to be " always bearing about in his body the dying of Jesus." But it is compensated for and balanced by a parallel manifestation of the life of Jesus, both in the Apostle himself and yet more signally in the life of the Church he serves.

[1] Rom. viii. 18 ff.  [2] Rom. viii. 11, which governs the context.
[3] 2 Tim. i. 10.  [4] 1 Pet. i. 3 ff.
[5] 2 Cor. iv. 7–15.

Here we have that principle of life through death and glory through humiliation, which is the clue to the synoptic portrait of the Christ, transferred from the Master to the disciple, from the field of history to that of spiritual experience. The gospel of the resurrection is a gospel of salvation, because it offers fellowship with God in a new quality of life, and this is the ground of rejoicing. But this rejoicing does not mean that the Christian is exempt from trials ; it means that he finds in them a new significance as a test and proof of his faith.[1]

But it is the moral element involved in the new relation to God which the Apostles press most urgently upon their converts. St. Peter at Cæsarea and St. Paul at Antioch in Pisidia alike insist that the message of the resurrection is a message of " the remission of sins." [2] He who was "delivered up for our trespasses" was likewise "raised for our justification." [3] The resurrection makes a new start in the moral life of men, which every believer is called to reproduce and manifest in his own case. New ethical motives, new powers of conquering sin, new standards of right living are now proclaimed and accepted. Christ risen from the dead now "lives unto God," and creates in the hearts of believers a life motived by a like fellowship with God [4] ; the purpose of His death and resurrection was that men might abandon their selfish interests and make Him the centre of their affections and the end of their activities.[5] And the moral resolutions so originated are capable of achievement. The power of God manifested in the raising of Christ from the dead is what has raised Christians from paganism to the moral freedom of the converted life [6] ; and it is for ever available to them as a potent instrument for the conquest of sin. The purpose of the resurrection was that believers should be joined with the living Christ,[7] and find grace through that union. And this privilege carried with it obligations of a most definite kind. It involved renunciation of sin and of the "lusts of the flesh." In writing to the Corinthians St. Paul lays particular emphasis on the incompatibility of any breach of the law of purity with the Christian profession.[8] But it would probably be an

---

[1] 1 Pet. i. 6–8 ; *cf.* 2 Tim. ii. 8–10.    [2] Acts x. 43, xiii. 38, 39.
[3] Rom. iv. 25.    [4] Rom. vi. 4.
[5] 2 Cor. v. 15.
[6] Eph. ii. 5 ; Col. ii. 13 ; Rom. viii. 2.    [7] Rom. vii. 4.
[8] 1 Cor. vi. 14, 15.

error to restrict his allusions to the mortification of the flesh to impurity alone.[1]  Rather we should interpret them as coterminous with the whole range of purely selfish impulses and desires which in St. Paul's philosophy are characteristic of the natural man.  In reference to all of them the faith of the resurrection meant for the Christian the deliberate pursuit of the " purgative way."  But it involved likewise new standards of positive conduct—a walking in " newness of life." [2]  A fresh worth-whileness has been given to the spiritual life as such.  " If then ye are raised together with Christ," says the Apostle, " seek the things that are above, where Christ is, seated on the right hand of God.  Set your mind on the things that are above, not on the things that are upon the earth." [3] Thus the claims of the unseen order upon men's thoughts and interests are laid upon them by virtue of their relation to the risen Lord.

So decisive is the ethical teaching of the resurrection that St. Paul can write definitely, " If Christ hath not been raised, your faith is vain ; ye are yet in your sins." [4]  It is part of one of the arguments he uses against sceptical opponents at Corinth who mocked at the notion of immortality.  He would not have done this, and the argument would not have served its purpose, had not Christian morality been regularly and closely linked with Christ's resurrection in his own and the Church's teaching.  He seems indeed to be prepared to admit the strength of the Epicurean—or rather the Cyrenaic—argument for pleasure as the highest good, if the resurrection is a myth.  For the resurrection is the one sure pledge and guarantee men have of the reality and claim of that other order of ends and values whose evidence proves the fallacy of hedonism.  Christ's resurrection, the Christian's experience of moral redemption, and his hope of immortality are three facts so closely locked together that none of them can be disowned without the repudiation of the others.  It is significant of the whole outlook of the first age of Christianity that this great chapter on the Christian hope should close with the note of practical exhortation.  " Wherefore, my beloved brethren, be ye steadfast, unmovable, always abounding in the work of the Lord, forasmuch as ye know that your labour is not in vain in the Lord." [5]

---

[1] Rom. vi. 12–19, viii. 12.           [2] Rom. vi. 4.
[3] Col. iii. 1 (The Epistle for Easter Day).
[4] 1 Cor. xv. 17 ; *cf.* 1 Cor. xv. 32.       [5] 1 Cor. xv. 58.

But we are already trenching upon that further issue which for large numbers of Christian believers throughout the ages has given to the resurrection of Jesus its most significant appeal.   It is true to say that thousands to whom the doctrinal or the moral bearing of the Easter message means little or nothing yet pin their faith to it as the main assurance we have of the life beyond the grave.   And in this the popular sentiment of Christendom undoubtedly reflects the mind of the New Testament.   It is by that act of raising Jesus from the dead, and by that in unique measure, that God has certified believers of their immortality.

A full discussion of the New Testament doctrine of immortality would fall outside the scope of this essay ; and we must confine ourselves to those aspects of it which have a direct and detailed bearing upon the problem of the resurrection of Christ.   The two passages of particular importance are both to be found in the letters which St. Paul addressed to the Church of Corinth.[1]   It is not an accident that that cosmopolitan city should have elicited a peculiarly full treatment of the subject.   The Church there contained both Jews and Greeks, and it was in close contact with a world where every phase of speculation passed rapidly from mouth to mouth.   Thus the Jewish element found little difficulty in believing in a resurrection ; but they were no less exercised than the Jewish Christians of Thessalonica as to what the belief portended for those who died before the " coming " of the Lord.   To the Greek element, on the other hand, the whole idea of resurrection was perplexing.   If they had avoided the current scepticism of the philosophical schools, it was usually through recourse to some Orphic or Platonic conception which asserted only the immortality of the soul and despaired altogether of the body.   St. Paul, who was at once Jew and Greek, was well equipped for handling such a situation ; and we can, in fact, see him in 1 Corinthians xv. addressing himself now to the Jewish and now to the Greek section among his readers.[2]

The Apostle's teaching in this chapter, so familiar to us from the Burial Service, may be summarised as follows.   Christian immortality is conceived after the analogy of a grain of corn, which is sown in the earth dead and renews itself in the grains of the ensuing harvest.   It involves, that is to say, a continuity of indivi-

---

[1] 1 Cor. xv. ; 2 Cor. v.
[2] *Cf.* Lake, *Earlier Epistles of St. Paul*, p. 218.

dual life, but a transformation of the form or " body " in which that life finds expression. There is a connection between the earthy body and the heavenly body, in that each in its time is appropriate to the individual life which it embodies ; though the point is emphasised that the heavenly embodiment is the gift or act of God. In the case of Christians already dead, or dying before the Lord's " coming," the transformation from the earthy to the heavenly body entails the dissolution of the former in death, followed by a period of waiting ; whereas for those who survive to that day the transformation is immediate and sudden. But in point of fact death is really irrelevant for Christians. For them the only thing in connection with death which matters is sin. They share the physical mortality of all the sons of Adam ; but, if they have laid sin aside, this mortality is overwhelmed in and swallowed up by that other life which Christians also now share, the immortal life of Christ.

The irrelevancy of death as a barrier to immortality, and the certainty of the spiritual body, are proved by Christ's resurrection. In one sense the Greeks are right ; " flesh and blood," the material particles of the body, cannot as such inherit eternal life. But they are wrong in not seeing that there must be a body in that life. At the same time there are differences between the resurrection of Christ and that of those who are His, corresponding to the difference of rank which belongs to Him in the hierarchy of spiritual beings.[1] So He experienced " on the third day " that completeness of trans-formation for which Christians who are dead have to wait until His " coming." He is distinguished from Christians already dead in that His body knew no decay ; from Christians now living in that the spiritual body is already His. His bodily transformation, though it involved death, did not involve corruption ; and, though it involved resurrection, did not involve an interval of waiting.[2]

---

[1] 1 Cor. xv. 23. Canon Streeter's whole treatment of the resurrection in *Foundations* is governed, as he admits, by the assumption that the parallelism between the resurrection of Christ and that of Christians is complete. But this is surely too facile. What is true, as Professor Lake points out, is that certain important features in St. Paul's view of the resurrection of Christians are based on his knowledge of the resurrection of Christ.

[2] The argument is not affected if we adopt Dr. McNeile's thesis (*The Problem of the Future Life*, p. 107) that " in some sense the formation of the spiritual body has already begun [*sc.* in this life here], and is being progressively formed with our spiritual progress." The idea is attractive, and, as he points out, is consistent with much N.T. teaching. But it would still remain true that for

That is the gist of St. Paul's teaching in the two great passages under review.    It is sometimes said that the later passage (2 Cor. v.) is inconsistent with the earlier.    But careful examination does not endorse this.    There is a change of phraseology through the use of the metaphors of a heavenly " house " and of heavenly " clothing " to describe the spiritual body.    There is a change in the practical point of the argument, which in the earlier passage turns on popular doubts and questionings, in the later on the contrast between the sufferings of the present and the glory of the future. And there is, further, the addition of a new idea—the idea that Christians already dead are if anything more privileged than those still living, because they are in closer proximity to their Lord. But so far as the main principles of the teaching are concerned, there is no alteration.    It still remains true that, for St. Paul, immortality means a body of different texture from that of earth ; that this body is an endowment given to each believer by God ; that Christians already dead pass by resurrection, after a period of waiting, to the manifestation of this transformed or spiritual body, while those who survive to the "coming" enter upon it suddenly and without delay ;  and that of both these hopes the resurrection of Christ is the great security and pledge.

It has been necessary to describe St. Paul's teaching in these chapters with some fulness, because it is sometimes stated that his doctrine would not be stated as it is, if he had accepted the traditional ideas connected with the empty tomb.    That, however, is to overstate the case.    Not only is there a very wide agreement among critical scholars, including even Schmiedel, that one who like St. Paul had been brought up in Pharisaical circles must be assumed to have accepted these traditional ideas, unless he definitely states the contrary ;  but it also ignores some important considerations.    It ignores, for example, the care with which St. Paul sets Christ in a " rank " of His own distinct from those of other Christians ;  and still more it fails to recognise that details of the manner of Christ's resurrection would be foreign to the argument which the Apostle is here developing.    On the other hand, it can fairly be urged that the very fact that St. Paul keeps these details in the background, even though he assumed them as part of the

St. Paul Christ's resurrection is differentiated from that of Christians in that the process of transformation was in His case completed without corruption and within a very brief period of time.

regular belief of the Corinthian Church, is not without its significance ; while the emphasis he lays upon the difference between the earthy and the spiritual body in the case of Christians does require us to suppose that he conceived of Christ's risen body as spiritual too, transcending the ordinary properties of matter, in conformity with that heavenly order into which at the resurrection He had passed. It will be important to bear this in mind, when we come to deal with that subject more closely.[1]

# II

## THE APPEARANCES OF THE RISEN LORD

### 1. *The Nature of the Evidence*

We have considered at some length the evidence for the reaction of the resurrection-faith on the first generation of Christians ; and we have seen that it postulates the occurrence in the historical order of some fact of transcendent significance touching Jesus Christ. It is now time to examine the more direct historical evidence. In part, we have already touched it ; for St. Paul's teaching in 1 Cor. xv. is prefaced by a brief historical summary, which is in fact the earliest documentary testimony we have as to the resurrection. Its date is somewhere in the middle fifties of the first century ; and it points back to still earlier dates—one the period of St. Paul's first preaching in Corinth, which may be placed in A.D. 49 or 50 ; the other that of his conversion, probably in 35 A.D., when he received authoritative instruction in the truths of the Gospel. The facts, that is to say, of which he reminds the Corinthians, are facts which he had received and believed for several years past ; and they were the common property of the Church in Jerusalem within at most six years of the crucifixion. The summary itself, moreover, falls into two parts. The first has all the marks of a primitive *credo*. It not only contains the death, burial, resurrection, and appearances of Jesus, but notes that

---

[1] It may be pointed out, further, that both the passages we have been considering may be dependent on the Book of Wisdom. *Cf.* W. L. Knox, *St. Paul and the Church in Jerusalem*, pp. 128 f.

the death was "for our sins," that the resurrection was "on the third day," and invests both events with the dignity of religious dogma by adding that they were fulfilments of Scripture. The second part contains further allusions to appearances of Jesus, closing with that which had been experienced by the Apostle himself ; the purpose of this second section being to reinforce the evidence for the resurrection, to expand its significance, and to account for St. Paul's own title to be an Apostle.[1]

The evidence of the Gospels is naturally of a different kind from that of St. Paul ; for here we are dealing with narratives definitely purporting to be historical. Nowhere does the criticism of the Gospels present more complicated literary and historical problems than in regard to the resurrection.

The earliest narrative, St. Mark's, unfortunately breaks off after recording the discovery of the empty tomb and before coming to speak of any appearances of Jesus ; and the concluding twelve verses are usually recognised as a précis, compiled by a much later hand, of other accounts then current in the Church, some of which are more fully given in our other Gospels. St. Luke appears to have material of his own for this part of his story no less than for that of the Passion, derived perhaps from some member of the Herodian household [2] ; and it is possible that his concluding chapter may have belonged to the first edition of his work,[3] if such were indeed prepared, and so have been written no later than St. Mark. The internal evidence of this Gospel cuts both ways : for while the naturalness of the narrative, especially of that of the walk to Emmaus, tends to bear out the high opinion of St. Luke's trustworthiness as a historian which his own preface and the study of his works as a whole have led scholars to form, yet there are features in it which many will regard as secondary and as presuppos-

---

[1] A division of this kind seems to me necessitated by the phrasing. To the end of verse 5 ("then to the twelve") each clause is introduced by the conjunction ὅτι, while from verse 6 onwards the direct statement is used (ἔπειτα ὤφθη). Moreover it is impossible that the record of the appearance to St. Paul himself (v. 8) could have been part of the primitive *credo* ; so that a division somewhere in the list of appearances is inevitable. This is also Meyer's view. At the same time it is quite possible that the whole list represents an agreed statement arranged between St. Paul and the other Apostles on one of his visits to Jerusalem, with a view to making clear his title to the Apostolate.

[2] *Cf.* Sanday, *Outlines*, p. 172.

[3] *Cf.* Canon Streeter's hypothesis of a Proto-Luke, which has secured influential support.

ing problems and questionings of a later day than the resurrection itself.[1]  Nevertheless it is important to remember that St. Luke was brought into close touch with St. Paul and the other Apostles, and no doubt had access to several streams of oral testimony.  St. Matthew's account is from the historian's point of view perhaps the most baffling.  It has commonly been supposed to incorporate part at least of the " lost ending " of St. Mark ; but this is impossible to prove, and internal evidence points to certain features of the record as having been amplified in transmission.  The verdict of the historian on the Synoptic evidence for the resurrection would recognise that in St. Mark and St. Luke we have two independent lines of testimony of whose general worth we can form a clear estimate ; while the first Gospel, if in some respects it follows St. Mark, also incorporates elements of floating tradition the value of which cannot to-day be determined.

There remain the Fourth Gospel and the Acts.  Our estimate of the Johannine evidence must clearly be very largely affected by the view we take of the historical value of the Gospel as a whole ; though it must be recognised that no part of it falls in so well with the belief that the writer was, or was in immediate touch with, an eye-witness and disciple of Jesus as the last two chapters.  The narratives are detailed, and yet marked by the greatest reserve ; they are marked by inward consistency, and yet this consistency does not appear artificial ; and they imply such a conception of the resurrection as we may well suppose St. Paul to have held.  Canon Streeter has recently gone so far as to conjecture that St. John xxi. rather than St. Matthew xxviii. is our best guide as to the " lost ending " of St. Mark.  Be that as it may, it is difficult to believe that the historian who approaches these chapters without *parti pris* can fail to be arrested by their intrinsic claims to his serious consideration.

Before we pass to a study of what the records tell us, a word should be said with regard to the importance of the Acts of the Apostles.  What the Acts does is to attest beyond all question a fact which must govern our whole estimate of the historical evidence for the resurrection.  It is the fact of the changed lives and characters of the Apostles.  Whatever else we may say of the resurrection, we are compelled by the narrative in the Acts to see in it a historical happening adequate to account for the vast psycho-

---

[1] *Cf.* Loisy's view that it is influenced by reaction against Docetism.

logical and spiritual change thus attested.[1]   What Paley said of
" the Christian miracles " in general is true of the resurrection,
that " many professing to be original witnesses . . . passed their
lives in labours, dangers, and sufferings, voluntarily undergone in
attestation of the account which they delivered, and solely in consequence of their belief of these accounts ; and that they also
submitted, from the same motives, to new rules of conduct."
That is a fact which may not take us very far in the determination
of historical detail ; but it will at least absolve us from giving
serious attention to the views of those who attribute the rise of
belief in Christ's resurrection either to some skilful fraud or to
some trivial mistake.[2]

Further, a very striking symbol of this change in the lives of
the disciples may be seen in the religious observance of the first
day of the week, of which Acts records the beginnings.[3]   It is
clear that the primitive Church in Jerusalem maintained, even
with some ostentation, the customs of the Jewish Church and not
least that of the Sabbath ; but they added to this the regular
observance of the first day of the week as their especial day of
worship, and this gradually came to supersede entirely the observance of the Sabbath.   When one reflects on the tenacity with
which devout people cling to religious customs of long standing,
it is obvious that some unusually strong cause must have operated
to produce so startling an innovation as that involved in the institution of the Christian Sunday.   Such a cause can be found in the
association of the first day of the week with the Lord's resurrection, but in nothing else.   There is no suggestion in antiquity that
this observance had any other root but the commemoration of that
fact [4] ; nor is there any trace of evidence for any kind of apostolic

---

[1] It does not seem to me necessary here to discuss the narratives in the
apocryphal *Gospel according to the Hebrews* and the *Gospel of Peter*.   These
are clearly *Tendenzschriften* belonging to the second century, and cannot be
regarded as independent sources.   The former is interesting, however, as stating
that the appearance to St. James was accompanied by an eucharistic action—
" He took bread and blessed and brake "—analogous to that at Emmaus.

[2] As, for instance, that the women went to the wrong grave, or that the
Lord was not really dead when taken down from the cross.

[3] Acts xx. 7 ; *cf.* i Cor. xvi. 2.

[4] There appears to be no suggestion that the occurrences of Pentecost
recorded in Acts ii. were responsible for the observance of Sunday.   Pentecost
remained for Christians, as it had been for Jews, an annual festival (Acts xx. 16),
and no connection with the weekly Sunday can be traced.

decree initiating the usage. It grew up, that is to say, as the natural and spontaneous expression of the faith that on the first day of the week Jesus rose from the dead ; and it thus affords strong indirect support to that note of time in regard to the resurrection in which all the documents agree.

It has often been observed that the Gospel narratives of the resurrection present a number of discrepancies,[1] which it is exceedingly difficult and indeed probably impossible to harmonise. Some of them are insignificant ; but others, such as the place of the appearances, whether Jerusalem or Galilee or both, and the length of time over which they were spread, are more substantial ; and we need not shrink from admitting that the evidence forbids our giving upon them a decisive verdict. But this is by no means, as is sometimes supposed, to discredit the evidence as a whole. On the contrary, it is rather a testimony to its honesty. When we remember that the facts it handles were *ex hypothesi* such as baffled a complete explanation, and that the first witnesses confessed themselves incredulous and bewildered in face of them, then the existence of discrepancies in the accounts argues a close contiguity with the experiences related ; whereas a compact and coherent narrative would have given us cause to suspect the deliberate artifice of later hands. Precisely similar discrepancies, moreover, meet us in the evidence available for many of the most striking events in history ; and yet we do not for that reason reject them. What we do is to weigh the documents by reference to the position and character of their writers ; to weigh the different statements of each by reference to the access which the author may be supposed to have had in each case to means of observation ; to prefer eyewitnesses or those who have had access to the testimony, whether written or not, of eye-witnesses ; and not to reject evidence simply because it is of later date or lays more emphasis on the supernatural.[2] Our duty towards the evidence is not to harmonise it, but to weigh it, and so doing to form as true an estimate as we can of the happenings to which it relates.

[1] These are fully set forth by Schmiedel, in *E.B.*, art. Resurrection.

[2] *Cf.* Sir Edwyn Hoskyns' essay above, pp. 164 ff. Also Dr. E. A. Abbott's *St. Thomas of Canterbury*, i. pp. 348, 388. Note, for instance, Dr. Abbott's observation that the account of Herbert of Bosham, though biassed against " miracle," is often wrong where others are right.

## 2. *Theories of Visions*

One of the main characteristics of modern attempts to account for the evidence thus briefly surveyed is the emphasis laid on the records of the appearances of Jesus and the interpretation of these by some theory of visions. The kernel of truth, it is urged, which underlies the resurrection narratives, is the fact that the disciples saw visions of their Master soon after the crucifixion, and passed to the inference that He had risen from the dead ; and out of this belief and the experiences behind it grew up the legends of the " miraculous " resurrection. The theories of visions fall broadly into two classes, according as the visions are regarded as " subjective " or " objective." Supporters of the former view, which is well represented by Schmiedel in the *Encyclopædia Biblica*,[1] insist that the disciples' visions were " subjective " in the sense of being simply a product of their mental condition at the time. This theory, however, encounters acute difficulties from the standpoint both of psychology and history. On the psychological side it requires us to ascribe to the disciples morbid and pathological dispositions which their whole subsequent conduct appears to belie ; while historically it involves us in the almost grotesque belief that a world-wide religion of some nineteen centuries' vitality was founded on a series of delusions. It is not surprising that more sober critics, such as Harnack and Meyer in Germany and the English school generally, should have sought for a version of the theory which would not be open to such palpable objections. So arose the theory of " objective " visions, which, ever since Keim propounded his notion of the " telegram from heaven," has had weighty supporters. According to this view the belief in the resurrection sprang from the disciples' visions ; but these visions were caused by the invisible Christ Himself, really present with them. The disciples were inspired by God to see what they saw : Jesus was really alive, and the eye of faith could behold Him.

An initial criticism of this theory of visions, in whichever of these two forms it be presented, is that it involves the use of a distinction between " subjective " and " objective " which has no warrant either from psychology or from philosophy ; and the facts which the theory is advanced to explain are left as much hanging

---

[1] Art. " Resurrection."

in the air as ever. It is arguable that the distinction corresponds closely with that which psychology makes between hallucinations and illusions ; but it has been used, at least by supporters of the "objective" version, to support a conclusion which involves the philosophical judgment of "true" or "false." The truth is that all visions are objective as well as subjective, in that what is seen in them, be they dream or hallucination or mystical insight, is as much an object as in the case of normal perception : the question is whether or not the object which the mind images is real or unreal. In the former case, the vision may be called " true " or " veridical "; in the latter case it may be called " false " ; and in the case of our Lord's resurrection that is the issue which is of primary importance.

It is necessary, therefore, to discard the distinction which has dogged the theory of visions in the literature of Higher Criticism on the resurrection. Yet various considerations should make us pause before we discard the theory itself. We have to remember certain facts which make it difficult to believe that, in the narratives of the Lord's appearances, we are dealing with cases of normal perception by the disciples. These facts are partly of a historical, partly of a doctrinal order. On the historical side we have the fact already alluded to, that none but believers (so far as the Scriptural evidence goes) saw the risen Lord ; the Fourth Gospel makes it clear that His entrances and exits were mysterious ; and the presumption is not unnatural that, if a Herod or a Caiaphas had been present in the upper room, he would not have seen Jesus. This presumption is strengthened by considerations of doctrine. We have St. Paul's clear statement that " flesh and blood cannot inherit the kingdom of God "—a statement which, as Professor Lake points out,[1] appears to rest on his knowledge of Christ's resurrection and to be inconsistent with the belief that His risen body was "material." We have, finally, our Lord's own teaching about the resurrection state, in which " they neither marry nor are given in marriage, but are as the angels in heaven." There is, therefore, very strong ground for saying that the Lord's risen body was not physical in the sense that it possessed metrical properties, and therefore not perceptible to any normal percipient.[2] In such circumstances we are

---

[1] *The Resurrection of Jesus Christ*, ch. i.

[2] It would, I suppose, be possible to argue that the risen Lord, though normally " spiritual," could and did " externalise " Himself for the duration of each appearance, and invest Himself with " mass " for that period. This seems to rest on the belief that the appearances of our Lord afford stronger

justified in saying that the theory of visions deserves on its merits
a more sympathetic consideration than it is apt to receive from
orthodox theologians.    It has a value, that is to say, which is largely
independent of the question of its adequacy to account for the
Church's belief in the resurrection.   The appearances of Jesus,

evidence for His resurrection if they involved normal sense-perception on the
part of the disciples than if they were " spiritually discerned." The following
passage from an article by a modern philosopher, Dr. C. D. Broad (*Hibbert
Journal*, Oct. 1925, pp. 42, 43), will serve as a reminder of how complicated
the matter in fact is :

" Perception may roughly be defined as being in direct cognitive contact
with an existent something which manifests certain qualities to the percipient,
and is instinctively regarded by him as a part or an appearance of a more
extended and more enduring object which has certain other qualities that are
not manifested to the percipient at the moment.   *E.g.* when I say that I see
a penny, I am in direct cognitive contact with something which manifests the
qualities of brownness and approximately circular shape ;  and I instinctively
regard this as a part or an appearance of something which is permanent, which
has an inside as well as an outside, and which has qualities like hardness and
coldness that are not at present being manifested to me.   If this belief be
mistaken, I am not perceiving what would commonly be called a ' penny.'
Now it is notorious that in ordinary sense-perception we are often deluded, and
sometimes wildly deluded.   A simple example is mistaking a mere mirror-
image for a physical object, and a still more striking example is perceiving
snakes or pink rats when one is suffering from *delirium tremens*.   It is quite
certain, then, that there are delusive sense-perceptions.   Now, in the case of
sense-perception there are several tests which we can use to tell whether a perception is delusive or not.   We can check one sense by another, *e.g.* sight by
touch.   We can appeal to the testimony of others and find out whether they see
anything that corresponds to what we see.   Finally, we can make inferences
from what we think we perceive, and find whether they are verified.   We can
say : ' If there are really rats running about my bed my dog will be excited,
bread and cheese will disappear, and so on.'   And then we can see whether
anything of the kind happens.   Now it does not seem to be possible to test the
alleged supersensible perception which some people claim to have of God by
any of these means.   Very few people have had the experience at all ; they are
very difficult to describe, and therefore to compare ; and it is very hard to
point to any verifiable consequences which would follow if, and only if, these
perceptions were not delusive."

On this we may observe that, on the theory here advocated, precisely the
same three tests are applicable to the disciples' perception of our Lord.
(*a*) Sight is checked by hearing, and *vice versa*.   St. Luke implies—though he
does not state—that touch also was used.   But, as Professor Goudge has pointed
out, this sense no less than sight or hearing has its counterpart in mystical
experience.   (*b*) The testimony of others.   So the Emmaus story is checked
by the Eleven ; that of the Eleven by St. Thomas ; that of the women by the
two disciples from Emmaus, etc.   And the collective character of some of the
appearances is here in point.   (*c*) The verification of inferences in practice
corresponds to what the masters of the mystical life speak of as the vocational
effect of a true mystical experience.

in short, require, and will be found to repay, a careful study simply as mystical or vocational experiences of the disciples.

### 3. *Tests and Types of Mystical Experience*

When we place the " appearances " of Jesus in that category, we render them comparable at once with a series of religious phenomena with which Catholic theology has a long familiarity. It is theology, moreover, of a type fully as critical of its subject-matter as that which we are accustomed to associate with modern Protestantism.   Mystical writers, for instance, such as St. Theresa or St. John of the Cross, insist constantly that the extraordinary phenomena of the religious life—ecstasies, visions, locutions and the like—are subject to countless dangers, imitations and delusions. This is no occasional concession to scepticism, but is a fundamental principle of their whole treatment of the subject.   Their phrase-ology differs in many respects from that of our psychologists to-day; but they are no whit less alive to the distinction between the false and the true, the pathological and the spiritual, and to the frequent occurrence of morbid states of mind which closely simulate those of healthy life.   They set themselves, therefore, to diagnose the symptoms of each condition ; to formulate canons applicable to them ; and to prescribe remedies, such as more exercise and fresh air, in cases where there is reason to suspect delusion.   In all cases, moreover, subjects of abnormal experiences are advised to submit them to the criticism, and their lives to the guidance, of some competent director.   The writings of the great mystics are thus characterised by precisely those qualities of vigilance, candour, and love of truth which we find in any scientific tradition of thought to-day ; and in applying their criteria to the records of the risen Lord's appearances, we are not removing these " into the clouds," but are submitting them to tests of a very concrete and searching kind.

Among the many criteria by which the mystical writers are wont to test the truth of visions and locutions, two stand out pre-eminently.   One is that expressed in the saying of Richard of St. Victor : " I will not believe that I see Christ transfigured, unless Moses and Elias are with Him." [1]   He means that no mystical

---

[1] Cited by Miss Evelyn Underhill in *Theology*, x. 10—an article to which I am much indebted.

experiences can be trusted as true, unless they are in concord with
the moral law and with divine revelation. They must be in
relation, that is to say, with the authoritative tradition which forms
the background to the subject's spiritual life. This does not mean
that they are not individual and original ; St. Theresa insists that
divine communications made in this way are commonly sudden in
their occurrence and unexpected in their content. But they are
not fantastic. They have their context. The form, whether
visual or auditory, in which they are clothed, must have palpable
links with the corporate and institutional life to which the subject
belongs, however much abstraction from it or re-association of its
elements there be.[1] We cannot, of course, always trace these
connections in the records of their experiences which prophets and
seers have left to us ; but salient illustrations of the principle come
readily to mind. Thus, Isaiah's vision is plainly coloured by his
knowledge of the mysterious figures which brooded over the
mercy-seat. The "showings" of the Seer of Patmos are steeped
in the imagery of the Book of Ezekiel and of the Jewish apocalypses.
St. Augustine's hearing of the words, *tolle, lege,* was the experience
of one who knew that the Christian faith was contained in
Scriptures. The heavenly beings seen by Joan of Arc were
modelled on the statues familiar to her in her parish church at
Domrémy. Comparison of the Lucan narrative of the Nativity
with some of the stories in Judges will suggest that the visions of
Mary were deeply influenced by her familiarity with the records
of her nation's saints.

The importance of this principle is that it provides a point of
contact between the saints and modern psychology. The " traditional " element in the mystical experience on which the saints set
such store is nothing else than what psychologists denote to-day
as the product of the unconscious or subconscious mind. They
assert that visions, trances, dreams and the like are the precipitate,
so to speak, of activities in which the mind has been engaged below
the surface of consciousness. The phenomenon, moreover, is

---

[1] My friend, the Rev. H. K. Skipton, points out to me what is probably
an interesting example of this in the life of Bunyan. According to *Pilgrim's
Progress*, what eases Christian of his burden is the sight of a crucifix : and
various facts make it likely that this was a crucifix thrown to the ground some
years before Bunyan's day within the precincts of an old monastic house (now
called The Chantreys) beside the Pilgrim's Way, which is the "road" of
Bunyan's book.

by no means restricted to religion. The well-known French mathematician, Henri Poincaré, [1] gives a remarkable example of its occurrence in the development of his own researches ; and similar first-hand evidence is available for Lord Kelvin. In recognising, as the mystical writers do, that the thoughts and images round which the mind was working before the vision or audition is experienced determine in large part the form of the experience, they exhibit a close agreement with the scientific thought of to-day as to the psychological mechanism underlying it. Where they differ is in refusing to regard this admittedly subjective element as the whole story ; the ultimate truth or value of the experience as a whole depends on its harmony with the truest and most valued convictions and experiences of their conscious life ; and by use of this criterion they drew a distinction (which was not a psychological distinction) between veridical and non-veridical visions—the former coming from God, the latter, either by the suggestion of hallucination, or by direct experience, from the devil. And those who believe that truth was really reached in analogous ways by a Poincaré or a Kelvin will not hesitate to say that on that point the saints were right.

A second and more certain test of the validity of such visions and locutions is to be found in their effect. The first fear and confusion are tranquillised into peace and joy ; the soul is humbled, not elated ; the words heard are rich in meaning and implication and are never forgotten ; their truth is whole-heartedly believed, and they are charged with a life-giving authority and power.[2] They are, that is to say, fundamentally vocational.[3] The test provided by the traditional imagery in which such experiences are clothed is by itself inconclusive ; its absence renders them suspicious, but its presence is not a sufficient guarantee of validity. It is when this criterion is reinforced by the further and more telling criterion of the effect of the experience on character and life that its veridical

---

[1] Cited by Canon Streeter in the *Hibbert Journal* for January 1925. It is curious that Canon Streeter does not notice the inconsistency between this citation and his own unproven assertion that this method of arriving at truth is characteristic only of " primitive " ages or peoples.

[2] *Cf.* especially *The Interior Castle*, Mans. vi.

[3] This is so in the case of religious experience. In the case of scientific knowledge a better word would be *illuminative*. It is significant that H. Poincaré mentions " conciseness, suddenness, and immediate certainty " as leading characteristics of this experience.

nature becomes evident. The demonstration that the visions of an Isaiah or an Ezekiel were no product of delusion lies in the activities to which they were called and through which they left an abiding mark upon history ; and the same is true of St. Peter's vision at Joppa, and of St. Paul's on the way to Damascus. The experiences bore precisely those fruits of penitence and peace, of certainty, and above all of clear vocation which the "higher critics" of the mystical life assert with unanimity to be the hall-mark of divine revelation.

Once more, the critics of the mystical life discriminate not only between true and false in the experiences we are considering, but also recognise differences of type among those which are veridical, and classify them accordingly. Three kinds of visions and locutions especially are distinguished, and are called respectively exterior, imaginal,[1] and intellectual : a classification which is probably psychological, corresponding to the degree of visualisation in each case. Exterior visions and locutions are those in which the subject believes himself to see the object with his bodily eyes and to hear the words with his bodily ears. These are regarded as very rare ; and they are marked by an element of error, in that the object seen is not entirely such as in the vision it seems to be. The resurrection appearances are commonly assigned to this category, in that the Lord's body, though real, was glorified and no longer subject to ordinary physical laws.[2] Imaginal visions, on the contrary, are those in which the subject is aware that his physical senses are not employed : he sees with the eye, and hears with the ear, of the soul ; the bodily eyes and ears may be closed. Such experiences are often accompanied by ecstasy, and sometimes by anæsthesia ; the image seen is often an infused light ; and it is gone in a flash, though it leaves a permanent impression. The visions of Isaiah, of St. Stephen, and of "St. John the Divine" are commonly classed here ; a more modern example would be St. Francis's vision at the time when he received the *stigmata*. It is significant that a modern mystic like the Sadhu Sundar Singh, who appears to have been unacquainted with this classification of visions

---

[1] Dr. Thouless has coined this word as a substitute for the word "imaginary" (used by the mystics themselves) as less open to misunderstanding. *Introduction to the Psychology of Religion*, p. 73.

[2] *Cf.* St. Thomas, *Summa Theol.*, III. qu. 54, art. 1–3, where the nature of angelic beings is discussed.

and locutions when describing his own, made precisely the same distinction between the exterior and the imaginal experiences in his own life on purely empirical grounds. The third type of phenomena are those which are called "intellectual," when the subject is aware of a divine presence and communication, but without either sense or imagination appearing to be impressed. These may often be of long duration ; and the mystical writers agree in regarding them as the most valuable, because the least liable to error, of all the three types of experience. It is to this class, in all probability, that we should assign the vision described in the closing pages of Dante's *Paradiso* or that which Pascal records in his " Memoriale," or that again which is recorded by Sir David Shackleton in *South*.[1] Finally, we find records of experiences which, like some of the "showings" vouchsafed to Julian of Norwich, cannot be assigned to any one of these classes simply, but can only be styled " mixed," in that they present characteristics belonging to more than one class.

In dealing, however, with the resurrection appearances of our Lord, there is an important discrimination to be made. Several of the recorded appearances were to a number of people at the same time ; whereas the mystical experiences we have been considering are normally those of individuals alone. This point is important, not for its bearing on the truth or falsehood of the visions and auditions (for any argument that might be based on the psychological theory of collective hallucinations is open to correction at once from the historical fact of collective vocation), but for its bearing upon our estimate of the evidence. The effect is greatly to broaden our basis of judgment. We have no reason to assume that, in the case of these collective appearances, the experiences of all the witnesses were of the same type : indeed it is probable that they differed considerably in the degree of their visualisation, and consequently in the details which they recorded. A cause of this

---

[1] " I know," he writes, after describing the march across South Georgia (chapter x), " that during that long and racking march of thirty-six hours over the unnamed mountains of South Georgia it seemed to me often that we were four, not three. I said nothing to my companions on the point, but afterwards Worsley said to me, ' Boss, I had a curious feeling on the march that there was another person with us.' Crean confessed to the same idea. One feels ' the dearth of human words, the roughness of mortal speech ' in trying to describe things intangible, but a record of our journeys would be incomplete without a reference to a subject very near to our hearts."

kind may explain, for example, the discrepancy between the Lucan and the Johannine accounts of the appearance to the Eleven on the first Easter evening. To some who were present it may really have appeared that the Lord " did eat before them," and St. Luke may have preferred this testimony as a safeguard against Docetism [1] ; while St. John preferred evidence in which the " exterior " elements in the experience were less prominent. We can be certain that these collective experiences gave rise to various streams of oral tradition, and that St. Luke—and probably also the author of the Fourth Gospel—was conversant with these. Each Evangelist selected the version which best fitted his general purpose and his whole conception of the resurrection. But it is a mistake to suppose that the versions are mutually exclusive for the historian. On the contrary, the differences are what we should expect, if the experiences were of the mystical type.

### 4. *Application to the Records of the Appearances*

The application of these principles to the narratives of the resurrection produces results of importance in more ways than one ; and we may summarise them as follows :

1. The conclusion, which seems dictated by general considerations of psychology and history, that the visions of Jesus which the disciples saw and the locutions which they heard were veridical is filled in and confirmed. A new factor is introduced into our estimate of the internal evidence for the Lord's appearances ; and features in the records which historical criticism has tended to fasten upon as pointing to the " subjectiveness " of the experiences are found in no way to prove them valueless or untrue, but rather to point the other way. Thus, it has been urged that the allusions to the breaking of bread at the conclusion of the walk to Emmaus and to the exposition of Scripture in connection with that vision and with others provide the real clues as to what happened ; and that the repetition by the disciples of that solemn rite and of the searchings of prophecy to which Jesus had accustomed them produced an atmosphere of tense devotion, and led to their supposing that they saw and heard Him. But, if the rigid canons of criticism proper to experiences of this kind be applied, the contention loses

[1] Though I think that a simpler reason may be found in the fact that St. Luke was a doctor.

much of its force.   The breaking of bread and the exposition of the Scriptures provide precisely those links with the context of the disciples' previous life which in parallel cases are regarded as a mark of genuineness.[1]   The feedings on the hill-side, the Eucharist at the Last Supper, the many occasions when they had listened to Jesus interpreting the Old Testament in public or in private— these experiences had sunk deep into their minds and been the food of their constant thoughts, until the shock of the cross had seemed to dismiss them as only an idle memory.   And so they must have remained, had not the events of " the third day " stimulated them afresh into consciousness, not now as a medley of bewildering and unrelated ideas, but as a coherent and convincing revelation of truth, the answer to a thousand questions.   A sound psychology will demand a cause for such a mental revolution [2] ; but, when the cause is forthcoming, it will see in the features of the narrative— the breaking of bread and the exposition of Scripture—symptoms of the mind's working which it knows to be wholly natural.[3]

2. Still more significant is the way in which the resurrection appearances answer to tests of vocational effect.   The twice-repeated " Peace be unto you " prefacing the investiture of the disciples with their priestly calling in St. John, the apostolic commission to preach the gospel recorded in St. Matthew or St. Luke, the threefold charge addressed to St. Peter, the words addressed to St. Paul at his conversion—all these represent the impression made on the minds of the Apostles by these experiences.   They belong to every strand available in the documentary evidence ; and their testimony is unanimous that the visions and locutions which the disciples received at this time were vocational.   And they provide, as nothing else can, an adequate explanation for the fact that

[1] Thus, H. Poincaré says that experiences of the type he describes in his own life are not fruitful unless they come as the crown of " days of voluntary efforts " on the subject in hand.

[2] It is not perhaps inconceivable that such a revulsion of mind might have occurred spontaneously, *given sufficient time*.   But it is asking too much to believe that it could have occurred spontaneously within forty-eight hours of the crucifixion.   And no fact is better attested historically than that the change occurred on " the third day."

[3] St. Theresa seems to have come very near to the conception of the sub-conscious mind.   Speaking of imaginal locutions, she says that " whether from the lower or the higher soul, or from outside, these originate from God." She recognises, that is to say, that in these experiences God frequently speaks to the soul along the lines of the mind's natural pre-occupations and ideas.

x

the men of broken faith who forsook their Master in the hour of danger went out into the world a few weeks later fearless and certain, proclaiming Christ as the Saviour and Judge of mankind.

3. This emphasis on the vocational character of the appearances which is so marked a feature of the narratives in the Gospels has a direct bearing on the interpretation of the earliest testimony to the resurrection, that of St. Paul. The fact that in his first letter to the Corinthians St. Paul places the appearance to himself on the way to Damascus in the same category as the other appearances which he records has long been felt by theologians to present a difficult problem ; and criticism has not been slow to suggest that St. Paul regarded his own experiences as the norm of the others and as having equal evidential value with them for the resurrection of Christ. The inference, however, is premature. St. Paul's language undoubtedly requires us to understand that *on some plane, and in some important respects,* his vision and those of the other Apostles were strictly parallel and of equal value. But to assume, as is commonly done, that he regarded them as of equal value on the evidential plane is to jump to unwarrantable conclusions. Careful study of the records of the appearances in the Gospels suggests, on the other hand, that for the Evangelists the vocational elements in these experiences were fully as important as the evidential : in some they are manifestly predominant. The appearances of Jesus are recorded, that is to say, to account not only for the resurrection, but also and equally for the mission of the Apostolate and the Christian Church. They are as much the first chapter of Church history as the last of the story of the Incarnation. What if this be their primary meaning and interest for St. Paul ? Various considerations make it probable that this was, in fact, the case. His title to the Apostolate was, as we know, hotly challenged at Corinth ; and from the beginning circumstances must have made it essential that his position in the Church should be defined according to some recognised principle. The principle chosen was the fact that he had seen the Lord. His vision, that is to say, was accepted by the leaders of the Church as having the same vocational character as that experienced by themselves. And, finally, if we turn again to St. Paul's words, we find them entirely consistent with such a view. Not only does he close the chronicle of the appearances with a discussion of

his own title ; but the chronicle itself is introduced as though it constituted a distinct article of belief[1] in the Gospel which he had received—as distinct from the resurrection as that was from the burial, or as the burial was again from the redemptive death. Linguistic considerations, that is to say, confirm what we have already seen to be probable on other grounds, viz., that the appearances, owing to their vocational character, were regarded by the early Church as having a credal value independent of their testimony to the resurrection. They represent the divine commission of the Apostolate and the Church ; and in that context St. Paul needs to make no discrimination between the various appearances which he records.

4. At the same time, it does not follow that in other respects discrimination should not be made ; and the testimony of the mystical writers suggests that in fact the appearances were not all of the same type, even though all were equally veridical. Thus, St. Paul's conversion-experience bears all the marks of an imaginal vision. We are told that a bright light shone round him ; but in none of the accounts is it said that he saw the figure of Jesus[2] ; while, on the other hand, the locutions were clear and it was Jesus who spoke them. It would, of course, be hazardous to attempt to classify the recorded appearances of Jesus with any precision; but it is at least possible that some of them were of the same kind as St. Paul's. The story of the walk to Emmaus, again, presents some of the characteristics of an intellectual vision ; the emphasis throughout is on what the disciples " knew " rather than on what they saw or heard, and the experience is of long duration. This difference of character, moreover, might perhaps account for the fact that this appearance is ignored by St. Paul. At the same time the evidence points clearly in certain cases to the visions and locutions being exterior. That to Mary Magdalene was evidently of this type, and St. Luke's narrative implies that the appearance to the Twelve on the evening of the first Easter Day was likewise ; for in both

---

[1] Each article is introduced by the conjunction ὅτι, which is well represented by inverted commas in English. Thus St. Paul says his teaching was: " Christ died," "He was buried," "He rose again," "He appeared." The argument is independent of whether or not the " primitive *credo* " ends with verse 5 ; *cf. supra*, p. 292.

[2] His question, " Have not I seen the Lord ? " is none the less fully justified, but as an interpretation rather than as a description of his experience. So, too, Acts ix. 27, xxii. 14.

cases we find the element of mistake which is a characteristic of exterior visions. It is probable, also, that the ascension is best explained in this way. But the evidence in fact does not admit of our speaking with confidence.[1] There is good reason to suppose that the Church at Jerusalem did everything possible to discover and to record what took place on each occasion, and this tendency must always be set off against any tendency to " materialise " experiences which were essentially part of a mystery. But in any circumstances such experiences are difficult to describe with accuracy ; and the Apostles had not at hand those principles of classification which theology was later to develop.

Peculiar significance attaches to the appearance to St. Peter. Not only does St. Paul place it at the head of his list ; but St. Luke alludes to it in a way that conveys the strongest impression of veracity. At the same time, it is nowhere described. Various reasons might be conjectured for this, but none is more probable than that the experience was in fact indescribable in its clarity and power. One is tempted to conjecture that we may have here the clue to the abrupt ending of St. Mark's Gospel. The Pauline and Lucan evidence points to the fact that this incident would normally have followed next in his narrative. St. Mark may have written some account of it, and on further reflection have torn it up ; or he may have come to feel, when he reached this point, that he could indeed go no further. In either case he might feel loth to record any of the other experiences, if he could not record this, the chief and most striking of all. The conjecture is, of course, no more than a guess ; but it at least absolves us from postulating a " lost ending " for which no evidence exists, and gives a reason for the abruptness of the ending that we have.[2]

5. The study of the appearances of the risen Lord as mystical or vocational experiences of the disciples goes far to mitigate the difficulty presented by the discrepancies in the evidence for the

---

[1] Allowance must also be made for the possibility that the experiences were of a " mixed " character ; *cf.* Thouless, *The Lady Julian*, p. 44.

[2] Canon Streeter thinks that the appearance to Peter of which St. Luke and St. Paul speak is identical with that described in St. John xxi. This seems impossible to reconcile with the time assigned to it by St. Luke and (by implication) by St. Paul. Nor is there any difficulty in supposing that there was more than one appearance to St. Peter. The Johannine statement that the appearance by the Lake was the third appearance *to the disciples* seems to call for no such elaborate explanation as Canon Streeter gives it.

ascension. In the Acts St. Luke dates the ascension forty days after the resurrection [1] ; but from his Gospel we should gather that the story of Christ was complete on the evening of the first Easter Day itself ; while St. John gives no account of the ascension but suggests that it was closely coincident with the resurrection, and that His appearances were manifestations of One whose journey to the Father was already advanced beyond the borders of time and space.[2] The discrepancy becomes less formidable, however, in the light of the foregoing discussion. The experience known as the ascension will then be regarded as an " exterior vision " from which the disciples learnt that their Lord had ascended into heaven.[3] There is no real inconsistency in St. Luke. In his Gospel he records those visions and locutions which were especially evidential for the resurrection. In the Acts he singles out for particular mention that experience which more than any other brought home to the disciples the reality and scope of their new vocation. In both cases he is serving the purposes he had set himself as the historian first of Christ and then of Christ's Apostles. St. John, on the other hand, writing as a theologian with his whole attention concentrated upon the Person of the incarnate Son, sees nothing in the incident called the ascension which adds or can add to men's knowledge of Him and of His glory. Whatever be the process of interior personal change through which the Lord passed in His relations with the Father after the resurrection, it was not such as could be measured in time. All that could be measured in time was the education of the disciples, and he records moments in this education and brings out their vocational significance. But the Lord whom they see has already resumed the heavenly life which He had with the Father before the creation, and it is from that mysterious other world that He appears to His Church on earth.

---

[1] It is significant that the Epistle of Barnabas implies that the ascension took place on a Sunday.

[2] *Cf.* especially St. John xx. 17 (" Touch me not," etc.). Few utterances of our Lord are more difficult to interpret. But, if the text be right, I should paraphrase as follows : " The old reserve and detachment which have marked our intercourse still hold good : for I am still with you, but not yet in you, and my journey is not yet finished. But go and tell my brethren that it is ending and I am already ascending, etc." The present tense ἀναβαίνω, rather than ἀναβήσομαι, is significant.

[3] The " element of error " which characterises exterior visions was in this case the belief that our Lord was lifted physically from the earth.

6. Finally, it may be claimed that consideration of the appearances as veridical visions goes some way towards solving the problem of where they took place. The problem does not lie merely in the fact that St. Matthew and the Johannine appendix describe appearances in Galilee, whereas St. Luke restricts them severely to Jerusalem and its environs. That the disciples should have journeyed to Galilee and back again to Jerusalem within the forty days before the ascension is by no means impossible. The real difficulty, however, lies further back, in the meaning of the Lord's promise, " I will go before you into Galilee." It has been observed [1] that these words occur at a crucial point in the Marcan narrative ; and that, if they were literally meant, they represent an anticlimax hard to reconcile with the known principles of our Lord's discourse. It can be shown, moreover, that both to St. Mark and to St. Luke they presented a puzzle, which each unravelled in his own way. The true clue, however, is provided by St. Matthew who, when recording the appearance in Galilee, lays the whole emphasis upon the fact that the disciples received from Jesus the revelation of His plenary authority and their own world-wide commission to the Gentiles. What the Lord had meant by Galilee, in short, was contained in the prophet Isaiah's phrase, " Galilee of the Gentiles " ; it was the symbol of the world waiting to be evangelised. The Lord's allusion, in fact, was precisely to that vocation of the Apostles which, as we have seen, was the main meaning of the appearances and caused them to constitute for St. Paul almost a distinct article of his creed.

This does not of itself go very far towards settling the historical question as to whether there were appearances in Galilee. But it illuminates other evidence which does. We need not suppose that the Johannine appendix represents the " lost ending " of St. Mark in order to justify ourselves in giving credence to the tradition of a Galilean appearance there embodied ; and the Matthæan record of the appearance on the mountain in Galilee has usually been regarded as providing the occasion for the appearance, to which St. Paul refers, " to five hundred brethren at once." I do not

---

[1] By Sir Edwyn Hoskyns, in *Theology*, vii. 14 ff. I can do no more than summarise the arguments and conclusions of that article. The difficulty is also faced by Spitta in his *Streitfragen der Geschichte Jesu* ; *cf.* Montefiore, *The Synoptic Gospels*, p. 1089. *Cf.* also Dr. Wade, *New Testament History*, p. 480.

think that we can get rid of the evidence for the occurrence of appearances in Galilee. But, if the ascension be interpreted as we have interpreted it above, and as apparently St. John interpreted it, the discrepancy with the Lucan tradition ceases to be grave. The broad difference of character between the Jerusalem and the Galilean appearances—the former evidential, the latter vocational —is seen to go back to the mind and purpose of our Lord Himself. St. Luke is concerned with those appearances whose primary meaning lay in their testimony to the Lord's resurrection. St. Matthew, in the majestic conclusion of his Gospel, lays the emphasis rather on the world-wide vocation to which the risen Lord now called His disciples. The Fourth Gospel, as its manner is, combines the two, and brings out in unmistakable fashion the dominant significance of each series. Nor is it difficult to see why the second lesson needed different surroundings from the first. The vast truth of their vocation which the disciples had to realise as implicit in the resurrection was not one that would easily come home to them amid the bustling multitudes of the Jewish capital. For that, as for the realisation of the fact itself, other influences would be needed as well as the words of the risen Lord Himself ; and foremost among these would be all the associations of Galilee— its memories of earlier missions and commissions, and all that the Lord's teaching and ministry there had made it to mean. Only after this lesson had been learnt were the minds of the disciples ripe for understanding the truth declared in the ascension, that the Lord had indeed entered into His glory.[1]

To sum up. The study of the appearances of the risen Lord as mystical experiences of the disciples is justified by the fact that the resurrection was itself a " mystery," and that the manifestations accompanying it were confined to those whose faith Jesus had Himself trained. The details of the evidence, moreover, confirm the view, which on broad psychological and historical grounds is seen to be most probable, that the visions and locutions experienced

---

[1] The view here advocated suggests a change in the traditional interpretation of 1 Cor. xv. 7 (τοῖς ἀποστόλοις πᾶσιν), which is usually referred to the ascension. But there appears to be no reason whatever for this identification, except the desire to "harmonise" the accounts. The E.V. translation of τῷ ἐκτρώματι (1 Cor. xv. 8), "to one born out of due time," probably suggested the idea that St. Paul has in mind the fact that his vision was in the period after the ascension. But the word has no note of time about it, and refers simply to the suddenness and violence of his conversion.

by the disciples—even though in the strict sense "subjective"—were veridical : for it shows them to be traditional in form and vocational in character ; and this vocational character is the common element in virtue of which St. Paul speaks of all the appearances as of the same validity for faith. At the same time there are signs that the experiences in question were not all of the same type, though all alike were veridical; and the differences revealed in the narratives, though they may not be pressed, correspond in many ways with those clearly distinguished types which are familiar to the saints. And, finally, all the appearances, to whichever type they belong, admit readily of the Johannine interpretation of the Lord's risen life, in the sense that they are appearances of the heavenly and glorified Christ. What St. Luke records in the Acts was that particular vision which taught the disciples what they could not have apprehended immediately, that their Lord had indeed departed to the Father. The Galilean appearances were concerned to impart a fuller revelation of the resurrection and of all that it involved for the universal mission of the Church.

Before passing on to consider the adequacy of this theory to compass the whole faith and fact of the resurrection, it is worth while to pause and note how much it involves. Whatever philosophy we profess—whether we call the resurrection mystery or miracle—we have to recognise that in such a matter as this a point must be reached sooner or later where the mind's progress is arrested in a reverent agnosticism. For believers generally that point is reached at a stage further than we have so far travelled ; it is reached, that is to say, when we stand by the empty tomb. But there are many thoughtful believers to-day who cannot go so far, and who halt at the point which our enquiry has now reached. They do not regard the evidence as certifying us of more than the fact that the Lord appeared to His disciples and gave them a clear call to work in His behalf. It is desirable, however, that both orthodox and modernist should realise how much this belief signifies. It signifies accepting as true a number of occurrences or experiences which the saints do not hesitate to describe as "miracles." It involves also accepting them as acts in which God has definitely intervened in human experience to reveal and to teach. These acts are interpreted, moreover, in a way which gives to the occurrences a profoundly spiritual meaning, and which renders irrelevant alike the liberal's question as to how the risen Lord was clothed [1] and the traditionalist's assertion that the earth was lighter by so many pounds when the Lord ascended into heaven.[2]    Finally, they are of that transcendent and supra-normal character which claims and receives the homage of a man's whole surrender and obedience ; so that those who accept in practical faith this theory of veridical visions cannot but commit themselves to that Spirit who prompted them and who built upon them the Church of the Apostles

### 5. *Limitations of this Analogy*

Nevertheless, while all this is true, we must face at the same time the limitations of this faith.    In the first place, in so far as it is a doctrine of Christ, it is a doctrine of His foundation of the Church and of His giving commission to the Apostolate rather than of His resurrection from the dead.    No one who seriously believed this faith could belittle the Church's supernatural calling or doubt its vocation to holiness or question its title to be the Body of Christ. In that sense it exacts a Churchmanship which is unquestionably Catholic.    But it does not reach by itself to the Catholic belief in Christ's resurrection.    It is not in essence the Easter message. For that message is first and foremost a message of the Person rather than of the doings of the Son of God.    It declares something that happened to Him as the climax of His human life and death. Its primary reference is to His experience, not to the experience tion to the disciples lies a prior mystery concerning only Himself which others had of Him.    Behind the mystery of His new rela- and the Father and embodying in one signal event the mighty power of God.    And it is this which is the kernel of the Easter faith.

Secondly, the act of God involved in the theory of visions is an act which determines the future rather than interprets the past. But the gospel with which the primitive Church went out into the world, though it claimed to represent the authoritative word of God and vision of Christ, was first and foremost a gospel of divine redress.    It was the gospel of the cross, because it was at the same time the gospel of the cross's reversal and transvaluation.    It is

---

[1] Cf. *Liberalism in Religion*, by the Dean of St. Paul's.    Dr. Wade, in his admirable (even if unduly modernist) *New Testament History*, says, I think, all that we need say : " The details of the Appearances (dress, speech, wounds, etc.) were mediated through the memory."

[2] Cf. *Some Loose Stones*, by the Rev. R. A. Knox.

possible that the appearances alone might have led the disciples to infer that their Master had survived death ; but what they said was far more than this—they said that He had conquered death. This is a belief which quite outranges any doctrine of immortality. The first Christians believed, as we have seen, that those who died before the Lord's coming were immortal in the sense that they survived death ; but they did not say of them that they conquered death. They reaped indeed the benefits of the conquest ; but the conquest itself was Christ's. And the certainty of their faith on this point calls for some more substantial ground than was provided by the appearances alone. It calls for an act of God in the life of Christ which matched at every point the apparent defeat which He suffered on the cross. Christ's conquest of death must be as complete, as convincing, as all-embracing as death's apparent conquest of Him had been. It must extend to every relation of His Person which death had touched, and show that at no single point was the power of sin and death left in possession of the field.[1]

And assurance of that kind is not sufficiently accounted for by any theory of visions. There is nothing in the theory which conflicts with it, except the claim that it is inadequate. But its inadequacy requires us to review the evidence again ; to restore the appearances, which we have isolated for a particular purpose, to their place in the whole narrative ; and to pick up along with them those other strands of testimony which the documents offer to our investigation.


## IV

### THE RESURRECTION OF CHRIST

#### 1. *Convergent Testimony*

Few facts are more strongly attested by the documentary records of the resurrection than that the disciples' belief in it rested in the first instance upon a number of converging lines

---

[1] Professor Taylor draws my attention to the striking passage on resurrection where Soloviev urges that, *unless* the physical dissolution of life is reversed by resurrection, evil is *obviously* more potent than good. (*Three Dialogues on War, Progress, and the End of History*, English translation, pp. 162 f.)

of evidence, none of which by itself was convincing. This is a feature of the narratives which is not easy to account for, unless it be authentic. It is perhaps intelligible that, if the disciples had reached the conviction that Christ was risen simply on the strength of the appearances, their belief should have come to embody itself in a legend of the grave being empty ; but it is not at all easy to believe that a legend of this kind should have presented us with a picture of the formation of the conviction so natural, inwardly consistent, and free from artifice as that which we have. Such evidence is of a high degree of credibility. It is discordant and uncertain precisely on those details of time and place which men easily forget ; it is harmonious, on the other hand, and coherent on that which they most easily remember—namely, the impact of great experience on the development of their own minds. And when we find this impact varying with different individuals and at different moments in the story, and varying in ways which our own experience of life shows us to be intrinsically probable, we have a right to conclude that our evidence is in close contact with the truth.

Little more need be said here with regard to the appearances. The view which regards them as analogous to the mystical experiences of the saints will seem to some inadequate ; and they will prefer to think of the risen Lord "as one who no longer felt physical obstacles, but who could still submit, if His purpose so demanded, to physical conditions." [1] The present writer does not feel that this doctrine of what one may call occasional externalisation contains any truth which is absent from the theory of veridical visions, while it entails, in his judgment, difficulties of its own, and particularly in regard to the ascension. But the conditions of our Lord's risen life are confessedly outside our experience, and our interpretation of them cannot be other than partial. In either case the question is not so much whether an analogy with mystical visions exists, but how far it can be pressed ; and on that issue there may well be difference of opinion.

Mention has already been made of two other factors besides the

---

[1] Gore, *Belief in God*, p. 269. *Cf.* also Dr. Sparrow Simpson, *The Resurrection and Modern Thought*, p. 418 : " In that glorified body the penetration of matter by spirit was so complete that He could at will re-enter into terrestrial conditions and become perceptible to the senses of human beings upon earth." Yet I am not sure that this fully represents Dr. Sparrow Simpson's view on the whole.

appearances which contributed to the disciples' conviction of the resurrection — the exposition of Scripture and the breaking of bread. Both these occur in St. Luke's narrative of the walk to Emmaus ; but it is significant that he does not say that they led the two disciples to the inference that Jesus was risen. The effect was to cheer and encourage them with the belief that He was not far from them. Other narratives in the Gospels illustrate the occurrence further. Thus, St. Luke records that on one occasion Jesus ate before them, in proof that He was not a ghost. The silence of St. John on this incident, though otherwise he records the appearance, suggests that St. Luke is recording a version of an act which was in reality of a piece with that at Emmaus [1] ; and the narrative in the Johannine appendix points to a similar experience. What would appear probable is that the solemn distribution of food, recalling the mysterious feedings on the hill-sides and still more the rite at the Last Supper, was used by the risen Lord as a means of recognition.

Not less striking is the part played by the exposition of Scripture. " Did not our heart burn within us, while he talked with us by the way, and opened to us the scriptures ? "—there we seem to have a glimpse of a real experience often repeated since in the story of the Church. Both St. Luke and St. John in different ways point to the fact that the understanding of Scripture played an essential part in the formation of the resurrection faith. St. John records as exceptional the fact that the beloved disciple believed in the resurrection on the strength of the empty tomb alone, seeing that he and St. Peter "as yet . . . knew not the scripture, that He must rise again from the dead." St. Luke narrates in connection with the appearance to the Eleven and their commission on the first Easter evening a repetition of the exposition of prophecy which was so signal a feature of the walk to Emmaus. And both Evangelists are recording a feature of the disciples' experience at this time which the severest critic must submit to be intrinsically probable. For it is not the kind of fact which the weavers of legend, eager for miracle, would have any interest in recording. On the contrary, it supplies a link in the evidence which shows the

---

[1] St. John xx. 20 contains an allusion to Jesus showing His hands and His side—language which the writer of the Fourth Gospel might well use, if he had in mind the Eucharistic rite. The incident belongs to the appearance recorded in Luke xxiv. 36–43 and John xx. 19–25.

disciples to have been reasonable men. The fact of the resurrection, that is to say, despite its external attestation, was not faith for them, until it had been integrated with the rest of their religious life. For this life the Scriptures had a peculiar authority, second only to the words of the Lord Himself. Only when they saw that the cross and the resurrection were the fulfilment of prophecy could they fully believe that Christ had risen from the dead.

Once more, this emphasis on the understanding of Scripture has a close bearing on the adequacy of the theory of visions. For, if the visions of Jesus rather than the empty tomb were the decisive factor in the formation of the disciples' faith, we should suspect that the parts of Scripture now unveiled would have reference to them. We should expect St. Paul to say that Jesus " appeared " " according to the Scriptures," as he said this of the death and the resurrection ; and there were many passages in the Psalms and the Prophets which he and the Evangelists could have cited. But neither in St. Paul nor in the Gospels is the exposition of Scripture given any bearing whatever upon the appearances. They lie side by side as collateral evidences to a great fact other than themselves, for which the main evidence was of a different character.

## 2. *The Empty Tomb*

We come, therefore, finally to that evidence which was regarded by the primitive Church and has been regarded ever since, as the principal guarantee for Christ's resurrection—I mean, the empty tomb. It is no exaggeration to say that, so far as the documentary evidence is concerned, no fact recorded in the New Testament is better attested than this. Not only is St. Mark's narrative available here to confirm those of St. Paul and of the later Evangelists ; but the discovery is told with a directness and simplicity which seem to be the echo of the eyewitnesses themselves. It is reasonable that those who reject the entire Gospels as historically valueless should reject this testimony too ; but to accept them generally as good sources of historical information and yet to refuse to follow them on this point argues an *apriorism* and an arbitrariness in dealing with evidence which is an affront to scientific method.

It is not surprising, therefore, that contemporary criticism should concentrate rather on accounting for the grave being empty than on questioning whether or not it was so. Various theories have been advanced on this score. The earliest, viz., that the disciples secured the Lord's body by stealth, is no more credible to-day than it was when the first Evangelist wrote his Gospel. Nor can we attach credence to the view that the Jews themselves removed the body ; for, had they done so, they could have nipped Christianity in the bud by avowing the fact when the resurrection was first preached. Insurmountable difficulties, in fact, attend any theory which attributes the removal of the body either to the devotion of friends or to the malice of enemies. And the same difficulties really attach, though at a stage further on, to the view that " the Romans, fearing a public disturbance, took advantage of the Sabbath quiet to remove the body." [1] For it is incredible that the Lord's disciples and friends should have been the only persons interested in the grave and likely to visit it. Even if we reject the intrinsically probable statement of Matthew that the Jewish leaders asked for and obtained a guard, we may be perfectly certain that they would not leave the grave entirely unvisited and unwatched, at least by day ; and it could not have been long before they too were asking the question as to why it was empty. Had Roman soldiers removed the body, or had such a statement had the slightest foundation in fact, the Jews must have given it currency, and the Romans would have had good cause to encourage the notion. The saying, still current when the first Gospel was written, that the disciples removed the body by stealth represents in fact the bankruptcy of all attempts on the part of the Jews to suggest any other explanation.

The truth is that the empty tomb presents the mind with one of those issues where the decision is made at a deeper level of personality than that which is concerned simply with the weighing of historical evidence. If a man follows the evidence so far as to envisage the empty tomb but then deserts it for pure hypothesis, it is because he is drawn aside by other than historical considerations. It is because he has been overcome by that arrested wonder which underlies all serious agnosticism. And the effect of the empty tomb is either to arrest wonder or to expand it. The case with us who study the evidence is the reverse of what it was with the first witnesses. We first satisfy ourselves as to the appearances of the Lord, and find our wonder expanding as we do so, until it

[1] Canon Streeter, in *Foundations*, p. 134.

comes either to arrest or to yet further expansion at the empty
tomb. The first disciples begin to wonder when they hear of
the empty tomb. Mary's first impulse is one of dismay : "They
have taken away the Lord out of the sepulchre and we know not
where they have laid him." Peter and John run to verify the
tidings ; and, though for the beloved disciple wonder at the state
of the grave ripens swiftly then and there into faith, Peter departs
" wondering in himself at that which was come to pass." The
two disciples walking to Emmaus have heard that the grave is
empty, but can only find in it matter for astonishment. Only
when the Lord has appeared decisively and when Scripture has been
added to interpret their experience—only then does the first wonder
expand into faith and adoration. Nevertheless, for us as for them
the full truth of the resurrection requires each strand of the threefold cord of evidence for its apprehension. It requires the appearances as the basis of a transcendent vocation deriving from
the risen Lord ; it requires Scripture as the bond which links the
resurrection with the cross in one redemptive Gospel ; it requires
the empty tomb as the great pledge that death has indeed been
conquered.

The reality to which the evidence thus points is of an order
beyond our comprehension. Reason can estimate the evidence ;
but when that is done, it must make way for other functions of the
mind—for constructive imagination, for wonder, and for faith.
What is involved is such a change in the body of Jesus as takes it
out of the category of things to which the laws of natural science
apply, and sets it in a relation to experience, both His and ours, to
which we know no parallel. Various terms have been coined to
describe it, such as sublimation or etherealisation ; but these are no
more than symbols of our ignorance and wonder. We do not know
what are the potentialities of matter when indwelt by the soul of
the Son of God, though we can well believe that in such a case it is
exempt from the sentence of corruption. What faith claims is that,
in embodying the manhood of God Incarnate, the whole course
of physical evolution reached its highest destiny, and through the
conquest of death passed over into forms of energy as yet unguessed.
Into the mystery of that mode of being only the heart of the
worshipper can penetrate ; and its only language when it does so is
that of St. Thomas, MY LORD AND MY GOD.

# THE SPIRIT AND THE CHURCH
# IN HISTORY
## BY ERIC MILNER-WHITE

# CONTENTS

# I

## The Distinctiveness of the Church in History due to its Possession of Spirit

The Church is a nation without race, without boundaries, with no common language or courts of law, without army or fleet. Yet it is never treated as of no account. States and men may love or hate, they cannot ignore it. Its bonds of unity, even in outward disunion, constantly prove to be tougher than ties of tongue and kindred ; its boundaries are never at any moment settled, and claim indeed to extend beyond the visible world. Though without arms, it is always at war ; though without codes, courts and police, its moral ideal is in all quarters of the world heroic ; and in practice the heights of moral beauty are its common fruit. For it has a *spirit*.

The spirit, whatever it be, which thus binds and inspires this supernational body calls for serious consideration merely on account of its obvious achievements. First, because it has brought so large and lasting a people into existence. Since that baptismal Day of Pentecost the world has seen many empires of colossal strength shiver and sink, many changes of catastrophic importance to the development of man, much increase of knowledge with consequences subtle, profound, bewildering. Yet this peculiar people has not only survived, but has driven its foundations deeper with every change : it has not merely kept together a remnant living on the tradition of ancient faith and fame, but has increased with every century, gathering in recruits by the brilliant newness of an old appeal. The peoples enter it because it gives life. The empires, armed and coherent, fall ; the Church, by human standards incoherent and weaponless, stands. The mystery of its survival is at least a title to respect ; it is the body which first claims investigation if we would investigate the eternal in human affairs.

Not less mysterious is the influence of this spiritual nation upon the individuals of its obedience. Here almost all analogy to the secular state ceases. And if we turn to other faiths and philosophies, comparison again is difficult, simply because these too have proved mortal. Faiths have perished in their hundreds and philosophies in their thousands. They were influential, but only for a day and days. But the Church lives and grows, commanding a devotion which is both passionate and steady. Its liveliest rival is Mohammedanism ; yet here Christianity has nothing to fear in depth or quality of influence, or in appeal to the higher intellect, or in moral achievement. Its "spirit" is a superior one, or a loftier, fuller, manifestation of the same.

Observe the intensity, steadiness, and range of this influence. Unlike the impulses of patriotism which awake suddenly at crisis, and, when it is over, doze again, the inspiration of the Church presses more or less evenly upon its members throughout all the days of their conversion. It is not evoked from without at any special danger, but works from within, in the daily aspiration of heart and mind, and the efforts of an abiding devotion. Temper is tuned, selfishness purged, suffering transfigured, diverse purpose unified, all the variations of daily experience made to contribute to wealth of character, and the peace of active charity. There appears to be no kind of temperament, no rank of life, no difference of circumstance or intellect or ability or race or civilisation, which this influence cannot grip and bless. And it is true to say that to the individual its onset comes always as a surprise, an ever new thing to man despite its frequency amongst men, a welcome thing despite its disturbing nature—a witness at least to the general sense that it comes from without.

Over and beyond the force with which it wakes the individual and changes his life, it has extended its moral and ethical ideals over the peoples most conspicuous for progress, civilisation, and power ; and all attempts to break from these seem to end in weariness and failure, sometimes, as in the German following of Nietzsche, in world-disaster. The noble pagan of to-day cannot but live, up to a point, by the ethical teaching of Christ's Church, lest he fall below the highest standard he meets. Christian character is an argument impossible to ignore; to be answered, as it is propounded, only in terms of living. The search for a superior ethic has conspicuously failed. The best and most thoughtful non-believers, therefore, submit to Christian influence in the sphere of living where they do not in the sphere of thought. The history of Western civilisation is inextricably bound up with the steady establishment of a less imperfectly Christian ethic, and the East begins to move uneasily to the same stimulus. Apart then from any question of the truth of Christianity, the Christian ideal of actual living has a living influence, and is to some extent effective outside the converted, beyond the Church's nominal adherents. That is to say, the spirit which is the bond and inspiration of the Church itself, does a work through it which is indisputably important to the whole world.

Nobody wishes to pretend that even the best lives of Christians, much less their actual average standard, approach the ideal of the Church Catholic. But the ideal, which is to be " like Christ," " to be conformed to His image," " to abide in Him and He in us," " to be perfect as our Father in heaven is perfect," has never for one instant ceased to be presented to its members ; and the pattern of the Head has produced in every generation not a handful but hundreds of acts and lives of a heroic virtue. The great merciful activities which the sympathy of the Church first found to do, the abolition of slavery, the institution of hospitals,[1] the raising of the status of women, the zeal for education when none other cared, have now passed into the very fabric of Western civilisation. But it is seldom noted that even now the hardest works of mercy are still left to those whose devotion to Christ provides them both with the perseverance for the task and with the readiness to remain unknown and obscure in the doing of it. The worst wreckage of indulgence and sin can still be dealt with only by the Church's Homes of Mercy. The educational and medical care of backward races is left to the Christian missionary. The bulk of such social work as is unpaid and voluntary is done demonstrably by people who " go to church." And though in sentiment most people desire social reform, it is still only the minister of Christ and his little band of helpers who live in the midst of the conditions which others lament.

Then what is the *claim* of the Church ? Does it match these facts ? From so potent and deathless an empire, we should expect high claims ; and find them. This, we are told, is the

---

[1] The Church was not the inventor of the hospital any more than our Lord was the inventor of the name " Father " for God. But Christianity at once transformed human thought and practice by raising the care of the sick to the plane of essential religious and civic duty.

people of the Eternal God, the fellowship of His incarnate Son, inspired and guided by His very Spirit, a holy priesthood, steward of the mysteries and dispenser of the gifts of God's love, of the forgiveness of sins, of a new life in grace and of a communion with God which will develop and deepen world without end.

It is to the examination and explanation of this claim that the rest of this essay must be devoted. The sins of the Church must of course be thrown in against the achievements ; the achievements be regarded more carefully to see if they correspond, and how they correspond, to the claim ; and whether they justify it. We must start with the premise (surely indisputable) that there is a spirit within the Church—a unique and remarkable spirit—which gives it aim, character, force, indestructibility, and essential unity ; but is it *holy* spirit, the Spirit of God ?

## II

### The Development of the Church in History progressively reveals its Spirit as Holy Spirit

The Church of God on any showing existed before the coming of Christ. He indeed was born into it. The Jewish race had long been conscious of itself as what we should now call a Church. This sense was denied to other peoples, whose development, if under the guidance of God, was so unconsciously. The Hebrew people may have been mistaken, but their literature puts their conviction of special privilege beyond all possible doubt. And their history corresponds impressively to the conviction. Never did a folk so feeble, with a history so chequered, and situation and politics so impossibly difficult, give such gifts to the world. They were gifts to the spiritual development of mankind, and to nothing else at all. We cannot even date the Church's birth ; like the mysterious Melchizedec, it is without descent, having neither beginning of days, nor end of life. Whether the call of Abraham be history or legend, it bears undeniable witness to a sense of special vocation and divine guidance, implanted at an early date in this obscure Semitic tribe. No one can mistake that it was this sense, pressing invisibly and perpetually over long spaces of time, which gave the race its peculiar tenacity, and explains its strange line of development. The story of Abraham is a parable of the early stages of a profound religious growth. With the awakening of vocation in man and race it embodies also the discovery of monotheism, the conception of a moral God who demanded faith, the sacrifice of mind and heart, rather than the cruel sacrifices of fear ; who punished the guilty, but whose righteousness the righteous man could approach for lavishness of mercy. In that undated dawn, and in silent ways, a new spirit entered earth and was comprehended ; without doubt, a higher spirit than prevailed elsewhere, a spirit of higher truth.

Thenceforward the Hebrew people had *a sacramental value to the world.* It neither posed nor presumed ; it did not try to teach other peoples, but itself was taught. Like any naughty schoolboy, it hated rather than liked its lessons, and rebelled against its teachers, yet consistently it learned. It thought that it learned for itself, a learning real and long and hard enough ; but time has shown that its learning was a deeper thing, for the whole world, a learning sacramental, almost vicarious, still of fundamental value. Under Moses and Joshua, the sense of divine guidance grew unescapable. Jehovah was their own, as other gods belonged to other races ; but how different He ! At the same time, the acceptance of the primitive law marked a further inflow of spirit, and involved both a clearer definition of God and a new conscience towards Him : His moral demand became the first obligation both of state and individual. The code has never gone wholly out of date in so far as the duty towards God and neighbour has become the foundation of almost universal morality. Again then, a spirit of truth entered, worked within and issued forth from an insignificant race, which claimed a particular character for God, and a particular vocation from Him ; which in the face of constant distress it held fast and finally delivered to mankind.

The vocation was deepened and fostered by the line of Hebrew prophets. There has never been in history a phenomenon more remarkable, nor one which bears so easily the appearance of an irruption of spirit. About the prophets' own interpretation of themselves there is no doubt at all. " Thus saith the Lord,' they cry. They stand between Yahwe and His people, convey His reproofs and encouragements, expound His character and demands, discern His will and intentions. They do not address themselves to the individual, but to the nation. It is to a national conscience, to the Church, that they appeal. And the God Whom they represent is a moral personality, "inexorable in His requirement of a righteousness corresponding to His own." From this standpoint, unparalleled in that age, they could develop their doctrines of sin, of suffering, of responsibility national and individual, of a Messiah to come, of the triumph of the Kingdom of God, carrying them to new spiritual heights, and driving them into the consciousness of the nation-church, so that they became an abiding possession on the earth.

So remarkable a phenomenon indeed is this, both in content and persistence, that questioning minds of the capacity of Bishop Gore's have seen here a foundation powerful enough on which to base their faith in God. Such glory and power belong to the pre-Christian Church of God even in these most modern days. It is therefore fair to say that the Old Testament Church, the elect race, has been to the world sacramental, not only of a mono-theistic creed, but also of the development of man on his spiritual side, in his spiritual character. Salvation came indeed of the Jews ; and every step of their spiritual progress has been sacramental of that world-salvation. Through them, what we may now call Holy Spirit has entered the world in ever greater degree, as a living and abiding force, its own evidence and its own gospel.

—Entered the world and secured permanence *through an organisation, an institution* bounded and disciplined, not primarily by law or doctrine, but by *race*. Holy Spirit came by a people. This is not to say, that the Spirit of God worked only in Israel. He worked and works throughout His own poem of creation. But in Israel His life was concentrated, confined, guarded, fostered in an institution dominated by that vocation only. To Israel He came expressly as Captain of the Lord's host, and pre-eminently through His own host He revealed Himself to the nations of men. If the host had failed . . . but it did not. It ought to have failed by all human chances ; except for this single pertinacity, its history was ignominious ; but the call of God was without repentance ; the most feeble folk persisted by the Spirit that was with it and in it.

John, the last prophet, was followed immediately by the Christ, and a new revelation, too large to be confined any longer to one race, overturned the old barriers and spread north, south, east, and west. It overleapt the barriers not only of race, but even of death, by the rising of Jesus from the dead. The new covenant did not destroy, but fulfilled the old : and what had been racial became universal. It was part of Christ's declared gospel that it should. It was not part of Christ's gospel that His adherents should lose their cohesion. On the contrary, He conceived their new unity as more august and absolute than anything earth had seen or prophets dreamed—akin to and partaking of the very unity of the Godhead. Both in their writings and actions His immediate followers stressed this character of the new ecclesia. St. Paul spent his active life in tearing down the middle wall of partition, and building the new fellowship that should know no distinction of race or class. To his writings the Church is a most glowing inspiration, no mere organisation or propagandist machine, but a new race, a new kingdom, the very Body of Christ. St. Peter's description is not dissimilar nor less lyrical : " Ye are an elect race, a royal priesthood, a holy nation, a people for God's own possession." The sense of the vocation of the holy nation was not less because it now ceased to be identified with Israel after the flesh, but infinitely greater. The stress upon its unity, now that it was changed from a unity of blood to one of spirit, was infinitely exalted. With the new revelation, the task of the elect race was more clearly seen and understood, and the new power which had come into the world for its fulfilment was recognised, palpably felt, personified and named the Holy Ghost. These things only enhanced the distinctiveness of God's people. They peculiarly possessed His Spirit, and were peculiarly knit by it. They felt a divine responsibility, a vocation, as a body. So much is a mere matter of history. It is matter of history also that the consciousness of fellowship and vocation drove them by successive steps into a definite, though loose, outward organisation : it is indeed hard to see what else could have happened, considering the extraordinary nature of the ministries which Christians felt bound to share amongst themselves and to give to the world. The process began with the Founder Himself, who made deliberate choice of twelve apostles. The apostles took their duty of ordering the new society outwardly as seriously as any other of their responsibilities : there is no more sacerdotal writing in existence than the very first chapter of the Acts. The rest of the book continues the tale of the establishment of the new race. The worst difficulty was faced at once and marvellously overcome—the breaking down of the barrier between Jew and Gentile. No power on earth could hold up a Spirit capable of that. Nobody imagines that the original leaders, Peter, James, or Paul, wholly understood what they were doing, or laid the conscious plans of politicians which always prove so vain. But they felt the inspiration of a mighty cause of God, which demanded unremitting propaganda, and which not only required unity in the inspired fellowship, but *made it*. The unity of Christ's fellowship was indeed to be, as He intended, utter ; to be expressed not only by outward organisation and not only by inward love, but in both and all ways. It should have no boundaries which could cramp expansion, such as race, or which could limit the free flow of Christ's spirit, such as a law ; and yet it must draw bold the lines which should define and proclaim its revelation, simple boundaries of belief and discipline and outward order, alike the guarantees of its reality as a fellowship or kingdom, and the visible, audible expression of its sacramental vocation to a non-Christian world.

Since then, nineteen hundred years have rolled by ; time sufficient, surely, to judge how this fellowship, the Church, has performed its function ; and whether we can with any certainty detect the divine guidance and relationship which it claims, and with any reasonableness yield it allegiance.

## III

### The Witness of Historical Achievement to the Claim of the Church

In the first place, the New Race has shown, on a more ambitious field, that remarkable characteristic of the old, indestructibility. It has had a no less stormy passage through time. The armed tribes and empires over the little Hebrew boundaries gave place to the criticism of the whole world, and every known weapon, fair and unfair, of thought and word and deed. No institution on earth has sustained such constant attacks from without and betrayals within—and the Judas works always more havoc than the Caiaphas. Yet so far from showing signs of disappearing with its day, unexpected resources have again and again turned the worst moments of apparent failure into a new era of growth. Indestructibility may not be an argument for faith, but it is for reverence, and for serious study of the principle which secures a life so unique. For this survival has not been that of a fortress standing foursquare and uncaptured ; but that of an army with banners, moving, advancing, ubiquitous ; increasing ever, not in mere numbers—though, without the witness of missionary pertinacity, the case for the Church would be weaker—but in the width and depth of its spiritual message and in the purity of its moral ideal. Just as the Jewish race developed in largeness of faith and hope, so the Christian ; often enough, too, like the Jewish, through its sorrows and failures. The truths on which, historically, it was founded, have proved themselves to be ceaselessly and vigorously dynamic, and capable of boundless expansion and applicability without any loss of either simplicity or definiteness. They do not grow out-of-date. The noblest livers need them. Mohammedanism as a faith is static ; Buddhism and Hinduism as certainly retrograde, despite spasmodic efforts of moral and theological reform in places where they are face to face with Christianity : the situation in India, indeed, vividly resembles the conflict of religions in the later Roman Empire. The Christian explosive shatters every civilisation which it enters, making way for one based on higher sanctions. Before the war of 1914 it had become a popular article of faith that civilisation in itself was progressive. If men are wiser now, they have no yet grasped the truth which gave rise to that easy philosophy that in a Christian civilisation the Christian motive present is regarded broadly, always progressive. Its own swift motion, indeed, creates more difficulties for Christianity than the attacks of all its foes. The army is frequently terrified at the far-marching of its pioneers, and would cling to ancient bivouacs. Yet onward it goes, not by virtue of the courage or generalship of its earthly chiefs, nor yet by the often ill-directed ardour of its warriors ; but by something implicit in its nature, some irresistible yearning towards more perfect achievement and more profound interpretation, some persevering disgust with things that are ; in fact, by the drive of Holy Spirit.

The impressiveness of this impulse gains in force when we turn from its general movement in time to its particular influence on individuals. Inspiration is a common experience beyond any conceivable bound of the Catholic Church or of conscious religion. The poet, the musician, the artist, the thinker know it well. That does not alter the facts that the Church is the very home of spiritual experience ; that its life consists primarily in such purely spiritual energies as prayer ; that it, alone of institutions on earth, proposes to guide, heal, and perfect the soul. However Christians may live in practice, they never cease to be urged to unselfishness, humility, and love as their first glory. The love, labours, and lowliness of the Crucified stand ever before their eyes ; union and communion with Him is their single goal. And in millions, some greatly, some slowly and partially, they respond. The true history of the Church has never been written in human book, and never will be ; for it has taken place not in courts, curias, and councils where power is great and decisions are registered, but in cottages, streets, and places where men work and pray. Its spiritual fervour issues in the preaching and practising of good morals, blazes forth in conversions, mounts to God by a ceaseless series of heroisms, which are often more than martyrdoms, just because they are secret and humble and new every morning.

The Church has no monopoly of such high and holy spirit ; but it exists for it and illustrates it, not at intervals or by chance, but constantly ; and thereby is a sacrament of Holy Spirit, perpetually reserved, daily reconsecrated, in a selfish and material world. Because of the Church, the standards of mankind are doomed ever to be faced by the standards of the saints, and are forced to some measure of imitation, lest inferiority of fruits reveal too clearly inferiority of truth.

The inspiration of the Church has proved strong enough to alter the course of history, more profoundly than is often appreciated, by its production of the Christian character. And that brings us to the phenomenon of Christian missions. There are three sides of this strange and constant energy to emphasise. The first is the obvious one of " foreign " missions. Christianity is not, of course, the only missionary religion, but it is the most missionary, and the only one which seems to appeal to all peoples— white, yellow, brown, and black. Nineteen hundred years have not exhausted the impulse ; on the contrary, it has never been more eager than it is now : the last century has seen more devotion and wealth put into missionary effort than any period in history :

and the success rivals the sacrifice. But, again, not only is Christianity the most missionary of faiths, but it has the most enduring results to its credit. It began with the conversion of Southern Europe, passing on to the North and West. The consequence in every case has been the establishment and rapid growth of what we call civilisation. Civilisation[1] is primarily a growth in love and goodness, in wisdom and truth of outlook : the increase of mercy and opportunities for education alike are inevitable, when the love of Christ, and of the neighbour for whom He died, becomes the most solemn duty of men. In the missionary work which often seems so inexplicable and ill-judged to the modern Englishman, the Church seeks to do for African, Polynesian, and Asiatic what once it did for Saxon and Frank. And the task has an urgency now which is new in history. For the less advanced races suffer bitterly from the impact of the developed civilisation of the West : they are wholly at its mercy even when it wants to be disinterested and benevolent (which is, again, only the case where Christian sanctions are strong): they cannot appropriate its virtues without a long training in morality, and an education, practical and spiritual, in wholly new categories. But its vices are easy to adopt : there is no doubt that without the faith of the West many races would perish by its sins. And as it is only the Christian ethic, however imperfect, of their rulers which saves them from the worst forms of exploitation, so it is only the Christian missionaries, those unmodern moderns who, for love of Christ, marry poverty, loneliness,

---

[1] The writer can give no meaning to the word civilisation which is barren of moral and spiritual content. Of course civilisations may degenerate and fall ; for the very gains and graces of living originally inspired by moral advance, and inevitably attendant upon it, may grow rank and abuse the soil from which they sprang. That moral decay time and again sets back civilisation is only proof of the necessity of moral vigour and ideal to advance it. Herein lies the world-importance of the Church's power of revival, mentioned later in the essay. It is the best, perhaps the only, *guarantee of progress* which mankind possesses. Recent events have only shown the incapacity of intellectual advance as a guarantee, apart from moral. But the " divine discontent " and the unflagging hope of the Church must for ever climb ; the Body which exists to realise the perfection of Christ cannot be content with the moral conscience of any moment of its past, even the fairest. It looks back to no golden age. It does gaze continually on Jesus Christ, and does take courage from the achievement of individual saints,—but only that it may reach forward. This spirit is now *within* civilisation, and its surest hope : there is no precedent for its final failure yet !—what it has done in less than 2000 years is marvellous enough in our eyes.

and exile, who can and do give them the long, patient teaching, and the moral discipline, which is the hope of their future.

The third side of this missionary ardour of the Church has been less noticed, but is not less valuable as witness of the impulse of Holy Spirit. The only weapon of propaganda is *persuasion*. It has taken the Church, indeed, a long time to understand its only allowable method, the Spirit of a God who is Love, and the example of the Christ who never used force. There is no love in haste, and only a curse in force. Men find it hard ever to forgive the use of force by the Church, and their instinct is right. The regimentation of the Church of Rome even now governs disastrously the popular conception of the Catholic Church, since it suggests the atmosphere of compulsion, the use of force, or the loss of freedom in that which claims and means to be the very Body and organ of love and spiritual liberty. But in reality force has played a very small part, less perhaps than no part at all, in the expansion of Christianity. Even the words and teachings of missionaries have accomplished little enough, apart from the lives behind them. Alike the spread, the maintenance and the growth within Christian countries of Christianity has been due to the persuasion of Christ-like lives. The witness therefore of missions to the presence of Spirit within the Church does not rest merely upon the pertinacity of a peculiar and unworldly vocation amongst men, or upon the results to converted nations, or upon the constant expansion of the Body of Christ ; it rests still more upon the amazing phenomenon of lives that are *different*, of men who never teach and preach, it may be, by word of mouth, but who convert, simply by means of the beauty and power of the Spirit that is in them.

## IV

### Modern Periods of Decadence and Revival ; and of Intellectual Stress and Progress

The drive of the Spirit within the Body has in the fields of character and propaganda been constant. But there are other fields in which to the modern mind it does not seem so true. In the first place, some of the Christian centuries or generations in Europe have been not only stagnant but decadent ; and secondly, when new truth, especially scientific truth, has emerged, the fiercest resistance to it seems to have proceeded from the citadels of organised religion. These objections to " institutional religion" weigh heavily to-day ; the modern man has come to confound orthodoxy with obscurantism ; and to regard the Catholic Church, the admitted centre and strength of the Christian world, as a foe to intellectual freedom and to the discovery of truth.

It is not enough to urge that the primary duty of the Church is to conserve its revelation in its completeness and purity for the benefit of all, and to sift and test the spirits carefully and long before they are admitted to the rank of divinity. Admittedly there have been periods when general Christian standards have been low, and the authorities of the Church a byword of reproach. We need do no more than point to the fourteenth and fifteenth centuries before, and the eighteenth century after the Reformation. In the former period, the corruption at the headquarters of the Western Church can hardly be exaggerated, and it infected the whole with malign disease. Yet, paint we never so darkly the papal leadership and morals, the Catholic community never stayed quiet under the scandal. The voice of protest and appeal rose loud. Sometimes it was the voice of states, seeking to safeguard themselves against this bewildering, degenerate power, in claim so supernatural, in practice so mercenary and unholy ; and the methods of reform by general councils, and by emphasis upon the independence of the National Church, declared themselves, as at Basle and in Gallicanism. Sometimes it was the voice of a single prophet of reform, a Wycliffe, a Hus, a Wessel, a Savonarola, an Erasmus. At no time did the humbler and more persuasive speech of saint and mystic falter, of Catherine and Bernardino, both of Siena, of the German mystics and the Dutch schoolmasters, of Thomas à Kempis. Fresh springs of devotion were many, piety deep, in the century before the Reformation ; it was the liveliness of Christian devotion, not only its deadness, which made the revolt. Similarly in the eighteenth century, Christianity was not dead because its officials were cold and worldly, and because it was suffering through its new disunity the devastating experience of provincialism. The peoples waited for their Wesleys and followed them.

To say that the action of the Spirit is constant, is not the same as saying that the professing Christian world receives it equably, levelly, consistently. What is not true of any other movement of human thought is not to be thought true of religions. The facts of history only correspond to the laws of the individual mind, which moves in seasons germinal, creative, and absorptive. Far more important to any just criticism of the Church than its times of stagnation is its power of revival. This indeed has proved constant. The seasons of sloth and sin (real or apparent) have been but the prelude to some amazing outburst of spiritual energy, unpredictable, defying human probabilities, working enormous transformations, vitally changing the prevailing categories of thought. More and more it appears that in these revivals the intellectual and the spiritual combine, unwitting allies ; that is to say, the paths of the Spirit do not move merely in the province of what we call so narrowly the " religious " or still less the " ecclesiastical " ; but, for advance here, instigate and require movement in the whole higher powers of man. Thus the Renaissance and Reformation are not truly two movements, two awakenings, this intellectual and that spiritual, but two sides of one. The godliest deed of those unpleasing fifteenth-century popes was their welcoming of pagan thought. Man's failure is often enough God's opportunity ; so too the failure of His Church the Spirit of God can turn to His praise. Renaissance and Reformation act and counteract, influence and counter-influence, hurt and counter-hurt, mingle, achieve, transform, and yet leave huge tasks for the centuries of rest to work out after the centuries of tumult pass. Similarly, the age through which we are still passing shows the Spirit at work liberating spirit at once through scientific criticism and discovery, and through the emulation (at first hostile, but eventually friendly, and certainly inevitable) of the deeper moral and spiritual forces, which make available the conquests of mind to character and life.

Here indeed we stumble upon a general truth, hitherto too little recognised, we believe, both by believers and by others : that there never is, nor can be, a great spiritual movement apart from the company of an intellectual advance ; nor a great movement of mind without a corresponding burst of spiritual progress. Usually, but not always, the new knowledge or ideas function first ; and intellectual renascence passes into spiritual, as the new comes into contact or conflict with the old in the fields of faith and conduct. The Church, as the guardian, interpreter, and inspirer of the highest faith of man, is bound by its very being to sift and to test ; and it cannot do this quickly, for it tests not only by the processes of thought, but by those also of prayer and of living. The mind fares forth, the prophets cry in the desert, of the people some are inspired but most perplexed, the Church examines with a care involving experience as well as thought ; and so the Spirit's new impulse of spirit gains a home which will hold the new, now reconciled, added, mingled with the old, in trust for all men and all time. To recognise the inevitability of some such cycle is to lessen the chances of conflict and disaster, both by softening the impatience of pioneer and prophet, and also by modifying their unpopularity and terror to those whose outlook is bounded by what has been and what is. Prophet and priest have always feared and hated one another, each blind to the fact that both are ministers of the same Spirit. At the moment it seems to be the peculiar mission of the Church of England to reconcile the antagonism of the intellectual and the churchman, by saying and showing, first, that the Church has no fear of the thinker, but rather welcomes and thanks him ; that his meaning to it ultimately (however one-sided and singly-concentrated on his novelty he may be for the present) is that of a revivalist, the seer of new truth being the minister of new Spirit : and secondly, that, on the other hand, the Church of the Holy Spirit is the final critic of all new ways of thought, the final test of truth, and its trustee for the future ; in that its one interest and ministry is to add to the one treasury of truth the things new to the things old, guarding them first and distributing them freely, not merely to the mind (which the schoolmaster can do) but to the inmost spirit and whole character of man.

This "sacramental conception" of the Church's place and work in the world is growing conscious and apparent, we believe, by that which is its best illustration, the history of the last seventy years. A crisis of mind and spirit, comparable to any in history, only less great than that consequent upon the coming of Christ Himself, declared itself in the second half of the last century. It had been gathering force for several decades, but, in this country at least, came into the open with the publication of " The Origin of Species " and of " Essays and Reviews." The one was a great and permanent book, the other a little and transient. But they served to announce to every man the two lines of new

z

thought, the one the result of the scientific investigation of the natural world, the other consequent upon the scientific historical criticism of the Scriptures. Both affected and upset the received beliefs of the Western world. The inevitable conflict of old and new took place in the religious field : it must always do so, because that is the dearest and most vital place of man's possession ; there he houses the innermost sanctities and sanctions of his being, and loss elsewhere counts nothing in comparison with loss here. Man, being of little faith, fears the diminution of his treasure more than he believes in its increase. That should not be put down to the fault of religion which is the fault of man's nature. For awhile in the seventies and eighties the world grew dark even to those of most faith ; many left the Christian fold, and among the prophets were false ones who proclaimed the death of Christ. The Church as trustee of truth seemed to small visions to be failing just when, as a matter of fact, it was performing its proper function in the most signal manner. Just as the impact of the new thought had been gradual, so too was the Church's examination and appropriation of the new gifts of the Spirit to spirits. Each was a matter of three or four decades, less than a man's lifetime, a short space for so vast a revolution and reconciliation. It would not be true yet to say that the stress is over, because, by the mercy of God, the scientists are still researching, and the critics still upon their documents. Nevertheless, not only have the main principles of reconciliation and appropriation been perceived, but the religious revival which was in progress before the crisis asserted itself has received from it that enrichment which makes the Catholic revival in the Church of England, with all its consequences within and without, one of the loveliest and strongest reformations in Christian history. Christ did not die, nor the Church of Christ fail. So far from that, to compare the Church of 1826 with that of 1926 is almost a comparison of death with life. Not one grain of spiritual treasure which the people of Jesus possessed at the earlier date has been lost ; and the gains, who shall count ? And the witness of one more revival, assured and fearless, in circumstances which it is hard to imagine can ever seem so desperate, has been added to the positive gains of truth and of spirit.

The sacrament of the Church therefore has not only survived, but has strengthened both its claims and function.

If it has done this in England, it has done so throughout Christendom ; for what is true of the triumph of Holy Spirit in one part of the field holds good for all. We do not pretend anything so absurd as that the English Church has—if the military metaphor be allowed—fought and won this battle alone ; the old guard of Rome and the East lay behind ; sharpshooters, pioneers, and allies, protestant, modernist, and independent, played essential if unorganised and sometimes embarrassing, parts in the forefront ; but the brunt fell upon that Communion which, under the standard of the Catholic creeds and the discipline of Apostolic order, had the necessary freedom and mobility to march to the guns and make contact with the armies of science. The work of the Church of England through the scientific and critical revolution has been at least of an importance sufficient to justify at the bar of history her position in temporary separation from its fellow-communions of East and West. She has done for the Catholic Church that which Rome was not free to do, and which the East was too far from the centres of modern thinking to comprehend. It is not merely that Catholicism has not suffered by the new categories ; new knowledge of the world has meant in every direction new understanding of God ; criticism of the two Testaments—the fiercest effort of mind in history—has not only revealed the rocks on which they stand, but has given a re-interpretation of their place and meaning in religion which is well-nigh a new revelation ; the concentration of study upon the figure of Christ has but lit up the unique majesty of His perfection and love. That such is now bound to be the result of the nineteenth-century renaissance in the religious sphere can scarcely be denied. A revolution of mind, in itself glorious and wonderful, has led to glorious revelation of God. The Church has lost nothing but what is good to lose ; it has gained rich reality and outpouring of Holy Spirit.

## V

### The Catholic Church a Sacrament of Holy Spirit to the World

And by the Church we mean deliberately and primarily the Catholic Church. Of course all Christianity everywhere has gained by the passing of error or inadequacy of understanding ;

but these inadequacies were more vital to the Protestant position of seventy years ago than to the Catholic; the Catholic verities at the base of Protestantism have stood the test, and have been more and more liberated from outworn dressings. But far more important is the sight, ever growing in clearness, of the function of Catholicism as the trustee for all Christendom of the religion of Christ; and therefore of the sacramental value of the historic Church for the truths deepest and clearest to the world, those which reveal God to man, and man to himself. Protestantism is greatly valuable not only to the world of men, but to Catholicism itself; yet all the time, in the last resort, it depends upon the Church of which it is a criticism. The Catholic Church of early days is its acknowledged inspiration, the Catholic Church of these days its unacknowledged buttress. It is not with any wish to decry the Protestant bodies that we suggest that, in their general meaning, they stand to the Church which is the formal sacrament of Holy Spirit to mankind as, in the sphere of Christian devotion, the sermon stands to the Eucharist or momentary prayer to age-long liturgy.

The Ecclesia, which is to fulfil so sacramental a function, will necessarily show outward and visible signs of its inward grace. Inevitably that will be displayed outwardly amongst other things by some ordering or articulation representative of its perpetual witness. Order and Succession are not ecclesiastical inventions, burdens grievous to be borne, but the unavoidable clothing of the Church's sacramental meaning. You cannot break up and re-start divine sacraments, or they cease to carry their own evidence of validity. A sacrament cannot be both discontinuous and perpetual. The continuity befitting a sacramental race the Catholic Church shows impressively. Its continuity even with that previous election of the Hebrews is unchallengeable, because at the critical point of process the two eras are perfectly united by the Person of Christ, and the expansion is the command of Him who elects. Continuity, however, is a possession of no great independent value in itself; as a guarantee and servant of the sacramental vocation of the Church it is vital. It carries with it also the requirement that we should read the lengthening tale of the historic Church as modern theologians and historians agree to read that of its pre-Christian beginnings. No one has seriously attempted that; perhaps, for the very reason that the essential meaning of the Church to the world has been too vast and far-reaching for isolation and description. It was not the mistakes and backslidings of the Jewish people which made their meaning to mankind, except in so far as these prepared the way to plainer knowledge of God. Nor is it the mistakes and sins of the Catholic Church which matter first, however much they have hindered the coming of its own proposed kingdom of goodwill amongst men. Its meaning and worth to the world have been just this constancy of ideal and of the high beliefs which inspire it. The histories of doctrine, which have been thoroughly written up to and including the Reformation, show that these " high beliefs " are not static, but ever developing in depth and fruitfulness. Other chapters of history confirm the swift development of mind and spirit in the countries ruled or influenced by Christianity, and in none other ; for even Japan's copy of the Christian West forms no exception. The peculiar phenomenon of Christian missions testifies both to the confidence and unselfish energy of the disciples of Holy Spirit, and also to the power of persuasiveness wielded by lives so inspired through all the ages. Not that we assert for one moment that the Christian countries are Christian, or that the Catholic Church at its best moments has been worthy of the Spirit which it knows, loves, and teaches. But it lives and grows, seeming only to be purified and enriched by the successive attacks of states and thinkers and savants ; inspiring millions to seek virtue and love ; and to find both in weal and woe the knowledge and peace of God. So the main fact and true meaning of this Church, apostolically articulated, unbrokenly continuous, becomes clear. It is the one sacramental institution of all time, sacramental of the gift of Holy Spirit, instituted by God, trustee of the birth, death, resurrection, and eternal love of Jesus Christ the Lord.

The phrase " institutional religion " is to-day unpopular, because men see the blemishes of the institution, and wish it holier, freer, still. So much the better. For the enemy of the Church, and that which cramps it most, is not new knowledge or any criticism, but, always and only, sin. The very request, from within or without, for greater holiness and fulness of the Church will bring its own fulfilment, and makes straight the path of Holy Spirit. Priests and preachers may now cease to demand allegiance to the Catholic Church merely as an obligation, and can call men into loyal fellowship with it as a vocation. There can be nothing higher, holier, and truer than to be part of this sacrament of ageless and unaging celebration, consecrating gifts to the world which grow ever richer and purer. The Catholic Church can cease to fear the splendid labours of mind in particular fields, which by dispelling ignorance and making godly use of the intellectual gifts of God, reveal not only scientific but religious truth. Science will cease to lose so heavily by its departmentalism, and good thought will have freer course to the ends of the earth, when thinkers and scientists refuse any longer to weaken the Church by a distrust and aloofness caused by conflicts, fears, misunderstandings which are now too old. For this sacrament to the world will only be complete when it becomes the world, and the Royal Priesthood is universal.

# THE REFORMATION
## BY A. HAMILTON THOMPSON

# CONTENTS

# I

## CHARACTER AND EFFECTS OF THE ENGLISH REFORMATION

IN one of his poems George Herbert, that most loyal and devout son of the Church of England, writes with enthusiasm of the perfect lineaments of his spiritual mother, and contrasts her studied moderation of aspect and attire with the allurements of the wanton of the hills upon the one hand, and upon the other with the dishevelled array of the wayward inhabitant of the valleys. Between Rome and Protestant Nonconformity with its warring sects, the British Church, double-moated by the grace of God, pursues a middle path and finds in the mean her praise and glory.[1]

Such congratulation, if it came from a source less sincere and pure, might be accused of insular self-complacency. But from the doctrine and rites of the Church of England, as organised under the Elizabethan settlement, Herbert derived the spiritual nourishment which satisfied his soul and quickened his pious imagination. Born in 1593, when Whitgift was prosecuting the struggle between episcopacy and puritanism, he died in 1632, the year before the translation of Laud from London to Canterbury. Amid the strife of rival parties, he preserved that ideal of the historic position of the Church of England as a true branch of the Catholic Church, claiming its right to hold the essentials of Catholic doctrine, and exercising the ministry of the Word and Sacraments through a properly ordained priesthood, which, through all the vicissitudes which that Church has undergone, has never been lost. The example and teaching of Herbert and of those who shared his convictions, within a century from the breach with Rome, remind us that the Reformation, in spite of the efforts of extremists and the uncertainty of individual aims, did not effect a complete severance with the past. So far as England was concerned, it was a work of reconstruction. It had its full share of the errors of judgment which beset the restoration of all ancient fabrics : it suffered from the competition of rival

---

[1] George Herbert, *The British Church.*

architects, some of whom preferred demolition to repair : the compromises which were the result of their disputes led to diversities of opinion which have lasted to our own day and are still hotly in debate. But the historic basis of the fabric was preserved. The renovated structure stood firm upon its old foundations, and the fact was apparent, not only to those whose faith was rooted in tradition, but to those also who had vainly endeavoured to bring it under the domination of novel schemes and systems of reform.

In considering the Reformation and its effects upon the Church of the present day, we must face it as a fact of critical importance in our national history. It brought changes with it which cannot be overlooked or disregarded at will. Contemptuous references to "the so-called Reformation," implying that it was a mere illusion, are out of date. They have never carried weight with serious historians, nor have they improved the credit of those who have indulged in them. It is equally impossible to be satisfied with the view that the Reformation was primarily a political movement to which religious considerations were entirely subordinate. Politicians, it is true, used the movement freely to serve secular ends : its history is so closely connected with politics that it is constantly difficult to distinguish between its religious and secular aspects. But in this respect the Reformation is not peculiar : the arguments founded upon the influence of Tudor monarchs and their ministers on its progress might be applied, *mutatis mutandis,* to the age of Constantine, Justinian, or the Saxon emperors. Or again, the adverse verdict which has been passed upon the Reformation in the light of social and economic changes which accompanied and followed it depends upon a romantic and sentimental conception of the Middle Ages which is at variance with fact. In the breaking-up of the medieval polity the Reformation took a prominent part, but as a consequence, not as a cause of a tendency which was present in every department of life and thought.

## II

### The Break-up of the Medieval Polity

When all is said and done, the religious force which was behind the Reformation remains. Although its energies were frequently diverted into alien channels and to unworthy ends, its motive power was the necessity of ecclesiastical reform. The demand for the reform of the Church in head and members had arisen within the medieval Church itself, during the period which had succeeded the disastrous end of the strife between the papacy and the empire. The theory of a dual control of Christendom by a spiritual and a temporal monarch, each exercising within his own sphere an authority derived from God, and working in harmony towards the same end, the establishment of the kingdom of God on earth, had come into existence as the result of the need of temporal support by the spiritual power. It had failed in practice : the continual attempt of one power to overrule the other contradicted its possibility.

### 1. *Failure of the Conciliar Movement*

The field of strife was narrowed into a contest between a German king, with a shadowy claim upon the imperial crown, and a papacy in complete subservience to a foreign monarch, its ally and captor. When the Schism succeeded the captivity of Avignon, the problem of the rivalry between spiritual and temporal rulers receded into the background. The new problem was the preservation of the unity and spiritual sovereignty of the Church beneath an undivided rule. To the would-be reformers during the conciliar period, their immediate task was the settlement of internal polity and discipline. Re-statement of dogma did not occupy their minds : their business was to prevent the recurrence of schism by restoring the papacy upon a sound basis. Their efforts at reconstruction failed, however, in face of the obduracy of the popes to reform by conciliar methods. Their divided interests and jarring schemes were confronted by the august tradition of the papal monarchy, able to hold its own against an unwieldy opposition with no concerted plan. National ambitions and jealousies crossed the path which led to Catholic unity ; and the dispute between pope and council gradually took the form of a new alternative between an united Church governed by papal mandates and a group of Churches, federated by a nominal recognition of the spiritual authority of the Roman pontiff, but ruled by local law and custom and, as a logical consequence, closely allied with the policy of national governments.

## 2. *Lollardy and Orthodoxy*

England, during this period of dispute, adopted no independent policy of her own. Throughout the great schism she had been faithful to the Roman pope : at this juncture she remained within the Roman obedience. Apart from the natural divergency of her attitude towards the papacy from that of France, the accession of the house of Lancaster to the throne had ensured a *régime* of strict orthodoxy. During the troubled reign of Richard II, Lollardy, with its popular interpretation of Wycliffe's theological and political doctrines, had gained some ground, in spite of the efforts of bishops to repress it. But, even then, it had not attained the proportions of an organised movement. Opponents of clerical government coquetted with it, as long as it seemed to promise an attack upon the temporal endowments of churchmen as the main feature of its programme ; but they were not prepared to connive at heresy, and the development of heretical doctrine forfeited it their support.[1] Archbishop Courtenay dealt promptly with its academic defenders at Oxford and forced them to recantation or flight : its adherents in country districts were persons of little influence and, with some exceptions, of low social standing, who were isolated by the vigilant policy of the bishops. Although cases of heresy are frequent in the ecclesiastical records of the fifteenth century, they represent individual opinions which have a common likeness but no common ground of action. The attempted rebellion of Sir John Oldcastle, the most prominent Lollard of the Lancastrian period, was a complete failure ; and popular disturbances, from the Peasants' revolt in 1381 onwards, though they doubtless found encouragement from sympathisers with Lollardy, were symptoms of social unrest and discontent with which theological opinion had no fundamental connection. If unusual intellectual activity, in an age of mediocrity, led Reginald Pecok, a bishop of the Church, into heresy, his heterodoxy had nothing in common with popular Lollardy. The clergy of his day found in him its most powerful and eloquent defender against detractors, and his subsequent deprivation and imprisonment were due as much to his political sympathies as to his theological vagaries.

[1] For the attitude of John of Gaunt to Wycliffe and his followers, see *Fasciculi Zizaniorum* (Rolls Ser.), pp. 114, 300, 318.

### 3. *England and the Papacy*

In this orthodox atmosphere, however, the spirit of national-ism, though not aggressively active, was not absent from ecclesi-astical affairs. It is impossible to attempt to trace in this context the successive steps by which the conception of the medieval Church in Europe had become indissoluble from that of the supremacy of Rome. The first assertions of that supremacy lie far back in history : the authority of the pope, alike as bishop of the old capital of the world, as exercising a patriarchate founded upon the apostolic origin of his see, and as the successor of the prince of the Apostles, had developed into a spiritual monarchy wielded by a prelate who claimed the title of vicar of Christ and commanded the obedience of kings and princes. It could hardly be said that England was backward in recognising this supreme power. The Norman conquest had been sanctioned by a papal bull ; and, if the Conqueror had decreed that he himself was the sole judge within his realm of the apostolic pretensions of any pope and of the validity of his mandates, what pronouncement could be more reasonable as coming from the faithful supporter of Gregory VII, whose throne was menaced by schism ? William, it is true, made a careful distinction between the civil and ecclesiastical spheres of law, so as to prevent mutual encroach-ment ; but it would be a mistake to interpret this action as wholly in the interests of the control of the Church by the Crown. On the contrary, disobedience to the Church incurred coercion by the secular arm, while unauthorised civil intervention with the Church's affairs was prohibited.[1] The freedom thus granted to the ecclesiastical courts was greatly curtailed by the legislation of Henry II. By the constitutions of Clarendon, the judicial power of the Church over the laity was limited by safeguards, appeals to Rome were carefully restricted by the necessity of reference to the king's approval, the question of the possession of disputed benefices was brought within the final cognisance of the king's court, and the Crown claimed the right of nominating bishops and of controlling the subsequent elections.

The spirit of the constitutions of Clarendon, however, was Caesarism, not nationalism. The papacy, indeed, during the century in which it rose to its highest eminence, was the champion

[1] See the ordinance printed in Stubbs, *Select Charters*, ed. Davis, pp. 99, 100.

of local freedom against secular tyranny. The pope who supported Becket encouraged the nascent independence of the Lombard republics and humbled Barbarossa. During the conflict between John and his barons, the influence of Innocent III and of the Church generally was on the side of the rebels ; and the refusal of John to accept the papal nominee to the see of Canterbury added fresh ground to the quarrel. The submission of John to the pope, with all its humiliating circumstances, was a temporary relief from the struggle, and its immediate consequence was the absolution of England from the interdict. Not until the position was changed, and the pope appeared on the side of John, was the action openly condemned as a national disgrace.[1] It was at any rate with the aid of the archbishop appointed by the pope that the barons eventually forced from the king those concessions which, subjected to a wider application than was actually contemplated by their framers, came to be regarded as the chief guarantee of national liberty ; and, in the forefront of the charter in which they were embodied, the freedom of the *ecclesia Anglicana* was formulated. In so far as this famous clause defines the position of the Church within the realm of England, it may be said to countenance the theory of a national Church. But the tyranny against which the English Church protested was not papal, but regal, the tyranny of a national king. The charter in which the protest occurs was witnessed by a primate who was also a cardinal of the holy Roman Church and by the papal subdeacon who had received John's resignation of his crown to the pope : at the head of the names of those who counselled its re-issue in 1216 and 1217 was that of the apostolic legate Gualo. It would be useless to argue that the Church of the English nation was an Anglican body which claimed to be independent of the Holy See. It was an integral part of a Church which is described in the official language of English bishops as Catholic, Apostolic and Roman.

As time went on, circumstances changed. Even Innocent III was willing to absolve John from his oath to observe the Great Charter. The popes of the thirteenth century interfered freely

---

[1] In 1216 the barons, according to Matthew Paris, spoke bitterly of the relations between John and the Pope : " Haec facit charissimus in Christo filius papae, qui suum vassallum tam liberum et nobile regnum inaudita novitate subiugantem tuetur." The same author credits them with strong expressions against the pope : " Ut quid ad nos extendit Romanorum insatiata cupiditas ? . . . Ecce successores Constantini, et non Petri."

in national politics, siding with kings against their subjects and fostering the growing power of France in the interest of their own domination in Italy, until Boniface VIII, asserting his sovereignty with a boldness which exceeded that of his greatest predecessors,[1] overreached himself and destroyed the autocracy which he sought to vindicate. During this period, and still more during the century which followed, a strong current of anti-papal feeling set in throughout England. Popes who were subjects of a hostile power made intolerable demands upon the compliance of the nation. The system of reservation and provision of bishoprics and rich benefices traversed the rights of cathedral chapters and patrons of churches, and challenged the competence of royal courts of justice. Appeals to the papal Curia, provocative of long and expensive litigation, overrode the jurisdiction of prelates and their delegates. Bishops found their appointments to vacant dignities and prebends forestalled by the appearance of proctors of foreign cardinals and papal officials to prosecute the claims of their principals to fill such vacancies. The payment of first-fruits to the pope and of periodical fees in lieu of personal visits to Rome or Avignon landed bishops in debt and involved them in financial complications with Italian bankers.[2] The papal court was a market in which spiritual privileges were bought and sold, and the pope's collectors in England kept a watchful eye upon all possible sources of revenue. Parliament took advantage of the most successful period of Edward III's war with France to pass the statutes of 1351 and 1353, in which provisors and appellants outside the king's courts were subjected to legal penalties ; and these statutes were more stringently enacted forty years later. Praemunire, however, long remained a dead letter [3] ; and the statutes of Provisors merely had the effect of establishing a *modus vivendi* between pope and king, without benefit to the freedom of the Church as postulated in the Great Charter.

[1] See the declaration in the bull *Unam sanctam* (Extrav. Comm. I. viii. 1) : " Porro subesse Romano Pontifici omni humanae creaturae declaramus . . . omnino esse de necessitate salutis." This may be a logical inference from the claims put forward by earlier popes, but it goes far beyond their actual statements in the unconditional inclusiveness of its terms.

[2] Valuable evidence upon this subject may be gathered from the wealth of financial detail contained in the unpublished register of Archbishop Melton (1317–40) at York, under the heading *Intrinseca de camera*.

[3] For recent commentary upon the statute of 1393 and its working, see W. T. Waugh, *The Great Statute of Praemunire* (*Eng. Hist. Rev.*, xxxvii. 173–205).

No temporal legislation, as a matter of fact, could affect the spiritual supremacy of the pope.  Anti-papal statutes were passed in parliament without the concurrence of the spiritual lords, who shrank from compromising the allegiance which they owed to the visible head of the Church.  So far as the Crown was concerned, a deliberate rejection of the Roman see as the source of ecclesiastical preferment would have been impolitic.

The pope might be restrained from impinging upon the rights of English patrons; but, if English incumbents were to enjoy the advantages of plurality and non-residence, the sanction of the Holy See was necessary.  The parliaments of Edward III and Richard II, in safeguarding the temporal power of the Crown, insisted on the theory that ecclesiastical endowments were the gift of royal and noble benefactors, and that the descendants of such donors inherited claims which could not be set aside by papal interference [1] ; but they asserted no principle which vindicated independence of the spiritual supremacy of Rome for the Church in England.

The fact that, upon so important a point as the patronage and disposal of benefices, the common law of the realm held its own is by no means to be overlooked or minimised.  At the same time, in matters within the competence of ecclesiastical courts, the judges resorted to no national code of law.  The canon law of England was the canon law of the Western Church, and the canon law of the Western Church was papal law, in whose authoritative texts the canons of early councils and the opinions of individual fathers of the Church were reinforced by an enormous mass of papal pronouncements upon every conceivable subject.  Many of these, as a very casual study of the first five books of the Decretals will show, had been delivered with relation to English cases : under Alexander III and Innocent III, England had taken its full share in augmenting the law of the Church as decreed by the popes.  It is true that successive archbishops of Canterbury had issued constitutions in their provincial synods, and that these had their due weight in Church courts.  It might also be possible, as in the case of Pecham's constitution concerning pluralities, that a primate, by inadvertence or excessive zeal, might

---

[1] This theory was expressed in the statute of Carlisle (1307), and repeated in the preambles of the statutes of 1351 and 1390.  See *Statutes of the Realm*, i. 150, 316 ; ii. 90.

contradict the purport of an apostolic decree. The final interpretation, however, depended upon the Roman solution of the problem. Further, even had provincial constitutions possessed a local superiority to the law of the Church as a whole, they formed in themselves no complete body of law. Their volume is relatively insignificant, and, comprehensive as they are, they provide no full or satisfactory answer to the questions which came before ecclesiastical lawyers in their ordinary practice. All that they contributed was a general summary of the law of the Church upon subjects which constantly came within the scope of that practice ; and in this respect their authority was conditioned, like those of the legatine constitutions of Otho and Ottobon, for which English lawyers had at least equal respect, by the terms of documents included in the vast body of canon law. In the fifteenth century Lyndwood, with a masterly command of his sources, provided the authoritative commentary upon the provincial constitutions, and, in so doing, deserved the gratitude of English practitioners. But Lyndwood's book is not a *Corpus juris*. It is merely a guide to the interpretation and amplification of the *dicta* of English primates by reference to canon law and to the Roman civil law on which the foundations of canon law were laid. The appearance of Lyndwood's *Provinciale* did not mean that the English lawyer abandoned Gratian and the Decretals : all that happened was that he was enabled to find his way about them with much less trouble than before, and this is the advantage which Lyndwood still offers to the reader who would derive profit from his pages.[1]

Lyndwood's exposition of the provincial constitutions is almost contemporary with the victory of the papacy over its conciliar opponents. It is unequivocally the work of a lawyer who recognises the papacy as the fountain-head of ecclesiastical law. It belongs to a period at which the idea of an English national Church was as yet unformulated. But, even so, the principle of nationalism was gaining ground. There was a current theory that Henry V, in his joy at the termination of the great schism and his devout gratitude for his successes in France, had promised

---

[1] See the essay on Lyndwood in Maitland, *Roman Canon Law in the Church of England*, 1–50. Maitland's conclusions on these points are inevitable in the light of ecclesiastical documents : see, *e.g.* the elaborate arguments upon points of law in *Hereford Reg. Trefnant (Cant. and York Soc.)*, pp. 73–90, 103–114. In these documents the appeal is entirely to Roman law, civil and canon.

to allow Martin V an unprecedented control over English benefices at the disposal of the Holy See.[1] This was not the policy of the regency which, at Henry's early death, entered upon the administration of the *damnosa haereditas* which he bequeathed to his infant son. The story of the translation of Kempe to the see of York in 1425 illustrates the principle that, where the temporal power chose to press its will upon the pope, his policy was to comply with its demands. An examination of the appointments to English sees from the middle of the fourteenth century onwards indicates that, even where the papal right of translation was exercised to avoid the difficulties which might arise in consequence of the Statutes of Provisors, the will of the Crown was not ignored.

The normal method was for the pope to confirm the nomination made in the name of the Crown. The chapter of the cathedral church received the *congé d'élire* : on the transmission of the election to the pope, the letters of provision were made out which were necessary to the spiritual validity of the appointment. It is possible that, in unimportant sees, cathedral chapters were allowed a free hand. But the fact remains that the Crown, as founder and patron, treated appointments which were nominally elective as presentations to benefices in its gift, with a growing disregard of constitutional formalities. Its nominees were given custody of the temporalities of vacant sees to which they were elected and provided as a matter of course. At his election the nominee of the Crown was already virtually in possession. Moreover, a comparison of such documents as the official headings prefixed to episcopal registers will show that, while bishops reckoned their pontifical years from the date of their consecration or translation, the act by which their temporalities were restored to them was regarded with increasing importance as putting them in full control of their diocesan jurisdiction.[2]

This was the position upon the eve of the Reformation. The supreme authority of the pope in matters spiritual was respected

[1] See *Cal. Papal Letters*, viii. 216–18. The whole series of documents of which the letter of Eugenius IV, containing the statement that Henry V had this intention, is one, is very instructive as illustrating the relations between the Crown and papacy in the case of a disputed appointment to a see.

[2] This may be remarked in the rubrics at the beginning of the registers of the 15th and early 16th century bishops of Hereford. These omit all mention of election. In 1504 Bishop Mayew is stated to have been called to the see by apostolic authority and the nomination of the Crown : in the case of Bishop Bothe (1516), only nomination by the Crown is mentioned.

implicitly. Whether he was the true source of episcopal juris-diction is still a moot point on which canonists disagree : large as are the assumptions which can be and have been made on behalf of the vicar of Christ, there are obvious limits to the powers of a vicar. But, as vicar of Christ, he possessed a jurisdiction which transcended that of any diocesan bishop and was superior to the patriarchal authority of the successor of Peter. He was the " uni-versal ordinary," wielding powers which superseded the mandates of bishops and the decisions of their judges in the ecclesiastical courts. If a bishop was slow in executing a commission entrusted to him in his own diocese by the Holy See, and in a matter which he might reasonably consider to belong to his own province as local ordinary, the pope could transfer execution to a commissioner who could take the business in hand without reference to the dio-cesan. An offender who was unwilling to stand to the judgment of his bishop could evade it by procuring absolution from the collector who acted as the pope's agent in England.[1] At the same time, where the temporal power was concerned, the pope was obliged to walk warily and submit to compromise. As the papacy, from the temporal point of view, fell into the position of an Italian principality, it became involved in the intricacies of national politics which it could no longer direct, and its power of enforcing its will upon kings and their ministers was seriously curtailed. Thus, at the period of the English Reformation, the English Church, although subject to the jurisdiction of Rome, had become definitely national in composition. If, in the early part of the sixteenth century, Italians were promoted to English sees, this was merely a logical result of the understanding between the papacy and the government. Where their mutual interests were concerned, pope and king were ready to accommodate each other ; but, where those interests collided, the advantage lay with the Crown. The Church, in fact, was in service to two masters ; and, in a trial of strength between the two, the allegiance of the Church was necessarily influenced by the temporal sovereign who could bring the most direct pressure to bear upon her.

[1] Instances of both types of case mentioned here may be found in the history of the small chantry college of Irthlingborough (*Assoc. Archit. Soc. Reports* xxxv, 267 *sqq.*). The authority of the " universal ordinary " is stated explicitly in the bull *Sancta* (Extrav. Comm. I. iii. 1) : " Sancta Romana ecclesia quae disponente Domino super omnes alias ordinariae potestatis obtinet principatum a Deo, utpote mater universorum Christi fidelium et magistra."

## III

### THE REFORMATION ON THE CONTINENT

The truth of the matter is that, at the beginning of the sixteenth century, the preservation of the papal jurisdiction depended upon the compliance of the pope with the will of temporal monarchs. At no time was the spiritual influence of the papacy lower. The power which, three centuries earlier, had stood for righteousness against the kings of the earth was reduced to defending its precarious position upon Italian soil by fostering political combinations against the foreign powers which threatened its security in turn. Its hope lay in its ability to maintain the balance between national jealousies. Meanwhile, however, there were ominous signs that, in the pursuit of its Italian policy, its hold upon Christendom was relaxed. In countries whose orthodoxy was beyond question, that orthodoxy was a matter of national conservatism. Spain, of all nations, repressed heresy most sternly and effectively ; yet the attitude of the Spanish kings to the Holy See during the century which followed the union of the crowns of Castile and Aragon was by no means that of submissive children. Their filial obedience, constantly tried, was tempered by the consciousness that their spiritual parent needed to be kept in order by admonitions and even by open threats. In the north of Europe, heresy developed openly. The climax of tendencies which could no longer be kept in abeyance was reached in 1527, when the forces of the Most Catholic king who was also ruler of Germany, a mixed multitude of divided creeds and diverse national sympathies under the leadership of a French renegade, attacked and plundered Rome. The pope lay at the mercy of Charles V. Two centuries and a quarter earlier, Dante, with all his hatred for Boniface VIII and the corruption of the papal monarchy, had seen with horror the lilies enter Anagni and Christ bound and reviled once more in the person of His vicar.[1] In 1527 pious minds might still feel compunction for the captivity of the pope ; but the catastrophe was the result, not of such an effort to re-assert a spiritual dominion over princes as gave the fall of Boniface VIII a certain nobility, but of a long course of diplomacy in which that dominion had been well-nigh forfeited. Henceforward the

*Purg.* xx. 86 *sqq.*

business of the papacy was to regain its spiritual authority, with the help of the nations which were still ready to admit it ; and the problem of the internal reform of the Church became once again a pressing question.

## IV

### THE ANGLICAN SOLUTION

Nevertheless, the disaster had come, and must in any case have come, too late for the revival of a spiritual monarchy, uniting all national Churches into a compact body under one head. On the one hand, revolt against that headship was spreading, and involved rebellion against the whole doctrinal system of which the pope was the chief representative. The attack upon traditional dogma, with its appeal to the freedom of private judgment in matters of faith, assailed the entire mechanism which guarded the faith of the medieval Church. New systems of spiritual polity were invented to suit new theories : a large portion of the Christian world was split into sects, united only in their rejection of the doctrine of the transmission of divine grace through the ministry of a hierarchy which culminated in the person of the vicar of Christ. On the other hand, this manifold division and lack of settled purpose were confronted by the hope that unity still could be maintained under a spiritualised and reformed papacy To hold the political aspirations of the papacy in check was not to hinder its exercise of legitimate authority, but to promote its influence in its own proper sphere and to justify its claim to dominion over the souls of men considered as members of the Christian commonwealth, apart from their position as members of distinct nationalities.

Thus the Reformation upon the continent became a conflict between two ideals of reform. In face of destructive schemes which did away with the old ecclesiastical system and all that it represented, the conception of the reform of the Church from within, long dallied with and postponed, became a practical object. The choice lay between the abandonment of outward unity for a sectarianism guided by individual caprice and the maintenance of the compact symmetry of ecclesiastical order under the quickening influence of a renewed spiritual fervour. To both parties the idea of a hierarchy without the papacy was inconceivable. The necessity of a vicar of Christ as head of the visible Church, as supreme legislator and tribunal of appeal, was the question at the root of their differences. Impugners of the papal jurisdiction attacked the whole system which it had overshadowed and included beneath its working. The defenders of that system set themselves to strengthen and assert the papal authority as the permanent safeguard of its active existence. Between a spiritual autocracy on the one hand and the will-worship of the individual on the other there could be no intermediate path. At best, the alternative to unquestioning surrender of the will and judgment was the adoption of a loose congregationalism, which might assume temporary form under the control of some commanding personality, but had no guarantee of permanence or consistency.

This alternative has long survived the circumstances in which it arose. To the continental protestant of to-day it is as present as ever : it finds expression in the *obiter dicta* of members of our own Church who are more closely in touch with novel readings of theology than with the teaching of history. We are invited to see, in the English Church as the Reformation settlement left it, one of many protestant sects, allied in general sympathy with the reformed systems of the continent, and differing from them only in its retention of the semblance of an antiquated and obsolete machinery. No candid student of the English Reformation will overlook or endeavour to explain away certain features in its development. It began in a formal renunciation of spiritual allegiance to Rome, and in the transference of that allegiance to the Crown as supreme head of a national Church. The political circumstances in which this came about severed England from its connection with the great Catholic powers and made it seek alliances with the princes who had embraced the protestant cause abroad. As a natural consequence, close relations arose between the continental reformers and that party in the Church which regarded the breach with Rome as an opportunity for welcoming novel experiments in doctrine and ecclesiastical government. During the reign of Edward VI this party was in the ascendant : the English liturgy of 1549, which preserved a close continuity with historical models, was superseded three years later by a form of common prayer and worship in which the influence of foreign refugees was allowed to have a disproportionate part. Had that *régime* continued longer, it is not improbable that the Church of England would have been led irrecoverably into a position of mere sectarianism. As it was, this revolutionary progress was checked by the accession of Mary, followed by the temporary return to communion with Rome. But, if conservative sentiment was strongly in favour of strict orthodoxy on the old pattern, it also had a strongly nationalistic bias. Reconciliation with the Holy See was closely associated with an unpopular foreign alliance, and was accompanied by a policy of religious persecution, which, although from one point of view it was no new thing and had the sanction of English law, was nevertheless a tactical error of the gravest kind. In no respect was Mary more to blame than Henry VIII : her motives indeed were purer than his. Persecution, however, of loyal subjects for the sake of religion was a very different thing from persecution exercised, with whatever ruthlessness, against the supporters of a foreign jurisdiction in opposition to the national monarchy ; and the fact remains that, rightly or wrongly, the Marian suppression of heresy affected the minds of Englishmen with a greater and more permanent feeling of repulsion than was caused by the tragedies of the Pilgrimage of Grace and, at a later date, the Rising of the North.

It would be fruitless to speculate what might have happened, had Elizabeth chosen to accept the Roman obedience. However tortuous the policy which she followed at the opening of her reign, there can be no question that in the course which she took she tested national sentiment and gauged it accurately. The Elizabethan settlement was not a glorious thing. It was a compromise which included parties and persons of very diverse views in one religious establishment. Its motive was political : the Church was regarded by the framers of parliamentary legislation as a department of state in which uniformity of practice was an essential condition of stability.[1] The formulae of doctrine which emerged from the settlement were couched in studiously ambiguous terms. Only a special pleader will argue that the Thirty-Nine Articles say one thing and mean another ; but their compilers, where points were in dispute, succeeded in saying two things in one breath

---

[1] The relations between Church and State under Elizabeth have lately been re-examined by Dr. W. P. M. Kennedy, *Elizabethan Episcopal Administration* (Alcuin Club), and his conclusions fully stated in his introduction (vol. i.) to a series of episcopal injunctions and other documents.

with remarkable adroitness. There was no question of concili-
ating a definitely Romanising party in the Church. What was
needed was to provide a *modus vivendi* between the party attached
to episcopal government and the innovators who came back from
exile in centres of foreign protestantism in love with alien methods
of Church polity, a common ground upon which both might
work together as agents of the state, irrespective of mutual
differences.

The idea of the Church as an instrument of national policy
was not new. It was a corollary of the theory of national
monarchies which had superseded the medieval ideal of a world-
wide empire, and during the later Middle Ages, as we have seen,
the civil government had exercised a prepotent influence over the
appointment of bishops. It was a new thing, on the other hand,
to see a temporal ruler controlling a Church within which rival
factions, divided upon fundamental points of doctrine and practice,
strove for the mastery. It is easy, of course, for a certain type of
critic, who regards the Elizabethan settlement merely as a clever
stroke of statecraft, to speak disparagingly of the religious issues
which it involved : such a view neglects the genuine conviction
which lay beneath the controversies of the period, and looks upon
their superficial aspect with hardly concealed scorn. We may
sympathise more entirely with the attitude of the faithful Romanist, who, in that day as now, could not conceive of the Church
without its visible head and postulated that catholicity implied
obedience to the Apostolic Roman see. His Church was busy
with the work of reforming itself. New influences had arisen
in its borders, bent on kindling religious fervour and on strengthening the papal position as the first necessity in their programme
The faith of the medieval Church was being defined and restated
at Trent ; old heresies were being condemned ; dogma was
assuming a settled rigidity. To such a spectator England had
fallen into heresy ; her monarch had incurred excommunication ;
the subjects of the pope were prescribed and hunted down, fined
and imprisoned. The Elizabethan Romanist was ready to risk his
life on behalf of the Holy See, and in so doing he found no foes
more dangerous than the bishops of the Church of England, policing
their dioceses and keeping as strict a watch upon the disaffected
as their predecessors had kept upon the Lollards. He himself
was naturally incapable of discerning in the religious body which

prosecuted him a member of the true Church : it was an apostate communion to which the dignities of the historic Church of the country had been transferred, and its endowments, or such of them as had survived the rapacity of the Crown and the court, had been appropriated. His view survives to-day, not as a mere suspicion or as a weapon of controversy, but as a genuine conviction. The Church of England might congratulate itself on putting an end to the papal usurpation ; but all the while it was usurping the titles, goods and foundations which it had wrested from their ancient holders and had misapplied.

Such a point of view has its logical basis, and outward appearances did much to strengthen it. The traditional liturgy of the Church, round which the fabric of medieval faith had been built and compacted, had gone with all its venerable associations, and was banned as popish and superstitious. In its place there was a form of worship which, if it had not entirely obliterated, at any rate partially obscured its most familiar aspects, and was celebrated with a bareness of ritual in strange contrast with the solemnity of the ancient rite. The process of denuding churches of all ornaments which recalled the past went on under the direction of prelates whose learning and love of antiquity were somewhat inconsistent with their destructive zeal. Yet, amid all these changes, the old machinery of ecclesiastical government remained unimpaired and in perfect working order. Within less than a quarter of a century, four reigns had produced startling fluctuations. Henry VIII had transferred the papal authority over an orthodox Church to the Crown. Under Edward VI the Church had been protestantised. Mary had brought it back into submission to Rome. Elizabeth had deromanised it and subjected it to interests of state. But, through all this, the processes of ecclesiastical law had gone forward in the old way. Apart from the changes of constitution in certain cathedral churches consequent upon the suppression of the monasteries, and from the creation of a few new dioceses, there are few alterations to be traced. The ordinary jurisdiction of bishops remained as in the past. Officials and vicars-general still exercised their delegated authority. In the official records of English dioceses for this period traces of contemporary change are few and far between. Bishops were deprived of their sees and burned for heresy, but the business of diocesan administration, founded upon centuries of long practice, was not interrupted for a single day.[1] The machine whose efficiency in the past had been so largely controlled by papal law could work without the help of the pope.

More than this, in spite of the changes of *personnel* among the bishops themselves, the episcopal succession was not visibly broken. It was preserved throughout the reign of Edward VI at a time when foreign non-episcopal bodies were gaining ground in the country and novel systems had their best chance of success. Without the maintenance of the episcopate, uniformity of religious practice was impossible : the Church, split up into sects, would fall into anarchy and become the prey of civil strife. Episcopacy formed the essential link with the past which ensured order and discipline. It is possible that this, which is not the highest view of the institution, was the most powerful motive which influenced the filling up in 1559 and 1560 of sees vacant by the death or deprivation of Marian bishops. Even so, the consecration of new bishops was not undertaken without the careful provision of valid means to secure the historic continuity of the office. The controversy which has raged round the consecration of Parker has wasted much energy on both sides ; but it has at any rate had the effect of displaying the uneasiness and uncertainty of opinion prevalent among those who have sought to impugn the act.[2] The ground of attack has constantly shifted from one objection to another, until it is reduced to the mere presumption that the act was invalidated by the intention of the consecrators. To this *petitio principii* common sense has only one answer, that, so far as human judgment is capable of defining private intention, the end which the consecrators had in view was the transmission without breach of the apostolic gifts derived in the beginning from the Founder of the Church. Otherwise, their action would have been pointless.

The preservation of episcopal order and jurisdiction, with the far-reaching consequences which it involved, is the distinguishing feature of the English Reformation. It had the inevitable effect of restoring confidence, as time went on, to a Church distressed by internal conflicts of opinion. The hold which foreign pro-

---

[1] Episcopal registers for this period were not always well or fully kept ; but this was due, not to interruption of business, but to negligence in keeping official records posted up to date.

[2] See the searching review of the whole controversy in Dixon, *Hist. Ch. England*, ed. Gee, v. 205 *sqq.*

testantism had obtained upon the English Church weakened throughout the Elizabethan period. Puritan zealots found their cherished doctrines incompatible with episcopacy. In a primate like Whitgift, waging war on behalf of law and order, they saw an authority as dangerous to their ideals as any pope, and an authority backed by all the resources of the civil government. For the stringent measures which the prelates of the sixteenth and seventeenth centuries employed against papists and puritans alike we can have little sympathy in an age of easy toleration. But it is impossible not to recognise that, with all the drawbacks to spirituality involved in the conditions of the Elizabethan settlement, the historic conception of the mission of the Church as the accredited guardian of the appointed means of divine grace held its own and steadily grew in strength. The position of a national Church, free from external interference, which Parker and Whitgift had used their power to uphold, was defined unmistakably by Laud and his supporters. In such men as Lancelot Andrewes, Jeremy Taylor, and George Herbert the power of that Church to attract and to nurture, through its ministry of the Word and Sacraments, the highest type of religious devotion was manifest. Loyal to the Reformation and recognising the protestant attitude of their Church to Rome, they yet proved that such loyalty was consistent with a theology and with forms of worship hallowed by antiquity, and justified the *via media* taken by the English Church as scriptural, primitive and truly Catholic.

It is true that their work was temporarily checked by the puritan revolution. But the religious disorders of the Commonwealth proved the impossibility of the maintenance of civil order without the principle of cohesion provided by the national Church : sectarianism meant confusion and anarchy. The conflict between royalist and republican, between High Churchman and precisian left its permanent mark upon English thought. It perpetuated within the Church itself that opposition of parties which had been inherited from Elizabethan times. On the one hand, orthodox divines upheld episcopacy and its divine origin : on the other, the formalism of episcopal government and the mechanical theories which it seemed to encourage were undervalued by the defenders of less confined views of the operation of divine grace. It must be conceded that the political events of the close of the seventeenth century left behind them an orthodoxy which laid more stress upon bare forms than upon the spiritual meaning of ordinances, and that the Church of the eighteenth century, as a whole, was spiritually at a low ebb. It is a mistake, however, to suppose that the revival of spiritual life which showed itself openly during the second half of the century was wholly promoted by disaffected enthusiasts. It was accompanied, as for example in the Wesleys, by a devout desire to give warmth and reality to the services and doctrines of the Church ; and it was only the distrustfulness and reluctance of ecclesiastical authorities which alienated the would-be reformers and laid the foundations of modern nonconformity. The unreadiness of a privileged institution to set its house in order was still as manifest as it had been three hundred years before.

## V

### The English Church of the Future

Yet the vicissitudes which the Church of England has under-gone since the Reformation have failed to weaken the conviction of her children to-day that she, as a true and living member of the Church of Christ, is in full possession of the means of grace and of the authority for their dispensation. Those means may at times have been underprized, their nature may have been disputed, that authority may have been minimised ; but no careful student of her history can overlook its witness to the constant working of the Spirit of God within her borders. From the days of the Evangelical revival onwards, she has made continual progress as a spiritual force. Under the influence of the Tractarian movement, she recovered a lively sense of her mission and its opportunities which, in spite of opposition and internal controversies, has per-meated her whole organisation at home and abroad, so that even those who still raise the cry of warning against a betrayal of the principles of the Reformation argue almost unconsciously from a point of view complacently familiar with much that an earlier generation denounced. The marked growth of mutual forbear-ance between ecclesiastical parties, though not wholly without its dangers, is due to a heightening of spiritual ideals visible in every department of the Church's activities. The truth has come home to all Churchmen that the life of the individual soul needs for its quickening and sustainment a full sense of loyalty to its corporate responsibilities, that such life finds its true refreshment in that sacramental union with the Head of the Church which binds all faithful souls together in unity and supplies the Church with never-failing strength. And, while this closer cohesion is being effected among members of the Church of England, the need of it is felt as strongly in the religious bodies which stand outside its pale. Contemporary movements in nonconformist communions in England and among protestant bodies abroad are signalised by the desire to abandon a policy of isolation and dissidence, and to seek a common ground of reunion with those who, through all changes and chances, have held to the historic conception of the Church and its ministry.

At the present time, it is possible to look back too apprehensively to the perils which beset the English Church at the Reformation and to the risks which she has subsequently encountered. By identifying ourselves too closely with her past anxieties and controversies, we may lose our sense of perspective. These things cannot be overlooked by the historian, but a sound judgment will regard them as dangers incident to the growth of a living organism which has survived them and gathered from them strength to meet and overcome the trials of the present and the future. Throughout her post-Reformation history, the Church of England has given proof of a steadfastness of purpose and a power of recovery amid such perils which we may well review with thankfulness and confidence. The path on which she entered in the sixteenth century was new and untried, and its beginnings were dark and uncertain ; but no one who watches her progress along it can doubt that she was guided by the Spirit of God, acquiring stores of spiritual energy which have revived her in periods of faintness and have quickened her to fresh and accumulated effort. Under this guidance, she has achieved successes which were beyond the dreams of the medieval Church. She has prosecuted her apostolic mission and planted apostolic faith and order in regions outside the hope and imagination of the most sanguine of Crusaders. Without novel or sensational experiments, adhering closely to traditional lines of doctrine and practice, she has made her influence felt as a permanent element in the life of the Christian Church, fostering in her sons a devotion and a temper of mind which have added no small strength and supplied new impetus to the spiritual activities of the modern world. From the protestantism of her early reformers she has found her way to a positive assertion of her claim to an abiding place in the Catholic community from which she has never separated herself by any action or declaration. The Reformation severed old ties and disunited bodies of professing Christians who owed obedience to the same Lord : it put an abrupt end to an old order of things which had long threatened disruption. The restoration of that visible unity of the Church in its medieval form is hardly possible to-day. But, to those in whose minds the hope of reunion is strong and is not dominated by conceptions, however venerable, belonging to one particular age of human history, the English Church has its part, and perhaps a deciding part, to play in the work of restoring Catholic unity to the Church at large, so that its Lord, at His coming, may present it to Himself a glorious Church, not having spot or wrinkle, or any such thing.

# THE ORIGINS OF THE SACRAMENTS
## BY NORMAN POWELL WILLIAMS

# CONTENTS

# I

## INTRODUCTORY

IT has been said that the radical difference between the Catholic and the Protestant presentations of Christianity consists in the fact that the former is built upon the idea of justification by grace imparted through the sacraments, and the latter upon the idea of justification by faith only. Like most theological epigrams, this sentence purchases its concise and arresting form at the cost of exact veracity. Yet it contains at least a kernel of truth; for it is a matter of common knowledge that the sacraments occupy a central and dominating position in the spiritual life of the Catholic Christian which the specifically Protestant type of devotion does not concede to them. A recent writer has described the part now played by the sacraments in Protestant Christianity as being, on the whole, that of "optional appendages" to religion[1]; and the theory of their nature which this part presupposes may not unfairly be stated in the following terms :—

1. The sacraments are not primarily "means of grace," but rather means whereby the believer publicly declares that he has already received grace. Considered in themselves, they are not *signa efficacia* but *signa mera*.

2. They may, however, become, relatively to given individuals, and in a secondary and improper sense, "means of grace," or "efficacious signs," in so far as their impressive dramatic symbolism works upon the subjective emotions of the worshipper, and serves as an aid to devotional auto-suggestion. This subjective efficacy may be heightened by the reciprocal hetero-suggestion which the members of a devout congregation naturally exercise upon each other when assembled for common participation in a solemn rite. When the collective imagination of the worshipping community is keyed up to a given pitch of exaltation, Christ may be said to be "present"—in the sense that His universal presence is then realised with special vividness—and to fulfil the promise "Where two or three are gathered together

[1] A. E. J. Rawlinson, *Authority and Freedom* (1924), p. 97.

2 B

in my name, there am I in the midst of them " ; though this promise has no special reference to the sacraments, and may come to fruition in meetings for Bible study, praise, or prayer of any kind.

It follows that there can be no such thing as an absolute duty to assist at sacramental ceremonies (except, presumably, for the officials who are commissioned to organise them). An individual citizen, who does not care for military pageantry, clearly requires no justification for habitually absenting himself from the " trooping of the colour " ; and in like manner a Christian, who finds that the symbolic actions known as " sacraments " leave him cold, must be at liberty to discard them from his personal religious practice in favour of other modes of approach to God more congenial to his temperament, without forfeiting the title of " a good Christian." It cannot on this showing be affirmed that the sacraments are " generally necessary," but only that they are *ceteris paribus* helpful, " for salvation."

In clear and unmistakable contrast with this " declaratory," " subjective," and " optional " theory stands that which is characteristic of Catholic Christianity. We may, for the sake of convenience, and without begging any question, describe the former as the " minimising," and the latter as the " maximising " view of the nature of sacraments. For the " maximiser," the sacraments are the most precious things in life, the breath of his nostrils and the staff of his pilgrimage. In his description of them the epithets " declaratory," " subjective," and " optional," as explained above, are replaced by " unitive," " objective," and " generally necessary." He will, indeed, join with the " minimiser " in affirming the universal presence of Christ and of the Holy Spirit in every place and at every time ; but he will add to this the conviction that They are specially present in the sacramental actions, not merely in the sense that the divine power is then imaginatively realised more than at other times, but in the sense that it is objectively accessible and operative in a quite unique degree and after a manner to which Bible-reading and the like offer no analogy, for the purpose of creating, maintaining, or restoring that secret union with God which is the basis of the supernatural life of the soul. And, whilst not eliminating *in toto* the idea of a certain subjective efficacy which may be deemed to flow from the visible, audible, or tangible symbolism, he will maintain that this is always accidental and relatively unimportant, and may on occasion (as in the cases of the baptism of infants and the absolution of unconscious persons *in extremis*) be dispensed with altogether. If it be appropriate to translate the Catholic theory, like its rival, into terms of " suggestion," it may be said that the thoughtful and instructed " maximiser " would not by any means deny that part of the efficacy of the sacraments (except in the two cases just mentioned) may flow from auto-suggestion or from congregational hetero-suggestion, though he would, in the light of his belief in the Communion of Saints, enlarge the conception of the " congregation " so that it would always include both the whole Church militant here in earth and also " angels, archangels, and all the company of heaven." But he would also assert that, in addition to these influences, which represent the working of his own mind and of other finite minds, there is present an element of divine invasion and hetero-suggestion— a power which comes entirely from without and which transforms and quickens the emotional forces evoked by the mere symbolism of the rite from within, as in an estuary the brimming salt flood-tide of the ocean penetrates, suffuses and overwhelms the fresh waters of the river gliding to meet it—a mighty Energy which cannot be rationalised or explained away as the resultant of merely " endopsychic " factors, but proclaims itself, to those who have experienced it, as simply " given," objective, catastrophic, numinous.

This conception contains an implicit challenge, which has been replied to by the counter-cry of " Magic ! " In so far as this counter-cry involves the allegation that sacramental grace is believed by Catholic Christians to operate irrespectively of the moral dispositions and will of the recipient, or to be based upon some supposed power of men to constrain the divine rather than upon the voluntary condescension of the divine to meet human need, its refutation may be found in any text-book of Catholic theology. But in so far as the term " magical " is merely a disparaging synonym for " including an element of objective efficaciousness," it may be candidly admitted that the Catholic Christian must make up his mind to endure this reproach with equanimity. For it belongs to the essence of the Catholic position that the sacraments are in some sense *causal* ; they are *verae causae*, and not merely symptoms, of the reception of grace It would be a task of considerable complexity and difficulty, and it is in any case unnecessary for the purposes of this essay, to find a more precise definition of the mode of this causality which would be equally applicable to each of the specific operations of the several rites commonly known as " sacraments." The task has indeed been attempted by Latin theology, and six centuries of speculation have not proved sufficient for its solution. Nor need English Churchmen feel themselves necessarily bound to defend any one of the hypotheses which have from time to time been produced by outstanding theologians of the West.[1] Though Article XXVII employs the Thomist conception of " instrumental causality " in connection with baptism,[2] it would be unreasonable to assert that we are on that account debarred from holding, if we think fit, the Scotist theory of " occasional causality," which represents the sacraments not so much as *causae per quas*, but rather as *causae sine quibus non*, and conceives the relation between the reception of the outward sign and the bestowal of the inward grace as one of " pre-established harmony," resting upon the appointment of God. Even St. Thomas relapses into vagueness with regard to this subject, when he tells us that " the sacraments of the Church have their virtue specially from the Passion of Christ, the virtue whereof is in a certain manner joined to us (*quodam modo nobis copulatur*) by the receiving of the sacraments."[3] The theologians and official documents of the Eastern Church confine themselves to a general affirmation of a causal relation between the reception of the sacraments and the reception of grace, and do not attempt any narrower determination of this subtle and mysterious question.

Such, in rough outline, are the two main theories of the place of the sacraments in our religion which at present divide the allegiance of Christians ; and though we do not forget the existence of mediating positions and points of view, in practice the choice presents itself as one between two clearly contrasted alternatives.

---

[1] For an account of these (frequently over-subtle) speculations, see *The Catholic Encyclopaedia*, xiii. p. 302.

[2] " Baptism is not only a sign of profession, and mark of difference, whereby Christian men are discerned from others that be not christened : but it is also a sign of Regeneration or new Birth, whereby as by an instrument (*per quod tanquam per instrumentum*) they that receive Baptism rightly are grafted into the Church . . . etc."

[3] *Summa Theol.*, III. lxii. 5.

The individual Christian must necessarily order his devotional life either on the assumption that the sacraments are "generally necessary" means of objective grace, or on the assumption that they are no more than optional pieces of declaratory symbolism. It is self-evident that such a choice must be determined by the mind and the purpose of the Founder of Christianity, if they can be discovered. But the question of our Lord's intentions relatively to the place and the importance of the sacraments turns upon the further question, whether He can be truly said to have "instituted" sacraments or not ? It is universally agreed that our Lord's teaching, explicit and implicit, was confined to the broadest and most fundamental principles of Christian faith and conduct. He never concerned Himself with otiose or non-essential details. He did not act in the spirit of a Rabbinical casuist, nor lay down minute ceremonial ordinances for the purpose of making a "hedge around the Law" ; He is not likely (if we may so say without irreverence) to have devised fresh modes of tithing mint, anise and cummin, or to have invented an improved type of phylactery. If, then, the true view of the sacraments is that they are "optional appendages to the Christian religion," it is not likely that they can be traced to His direct institution ; and, conversely, if they can be traced to His institution, it is certain that they must be a great deal more than "optional appendages." I venture to draw especial attention to this argument, inasmuch as the remainder of this essay presupposes its validity. If our Lord, with all His indifference to mere ceremonial, did actually "institute" the rites known as "sacraments," then those rites must be of the very highest and most central importance in the Christian life ; and it is difficult to see how such an importance can be ascribed to them, unless it is the case that through them God does something for man which man cannot do for himself, that is, unless they are the means or vehicles of supernatural grace. In other words, there would seem to be in logic, as there always has been in Catholic belief, a tenacious mutual connection and cohesion between the ideas of "Dominical institution," "general necessity for salvation," and "objectivity of operation." And if "Dominical institution" can be proved, then the further question which has sometimes been mooted—namely, whether it might be possible to regard the sacraments as Spirit-inspired ecclesiastical developments, which, though not commanded or even contemplated by the historical Jesus, have nevertheless acquired an obligatory character through the witness of the Church's corporate experience to their actual efficacy—manifestly does not arise.

## II

### The Number of the Sacraments

Before, however, proceeding to investigate the strictly historical question of the " Dominical institution" of the sacraments, it is necessary to fix with greater precision the exact denotation of the term " sacraments," as it will be used in this essay.   The term " sacrament " has borne different significations in the history of the Church, varying from the indefinite meaning sanctioned by the usage of patristic times, when it could be applied to almost any solemn rite or part of a rite, to the clear-cut denotation enforced by the sevenfold enumeration of the Schoolmen, or the even more restricted enumeration familiar to us from our own formularies.   Article XXV appears to confine the term " sacrament," in the sense of a rite for which divine institution can be claimed, to Baptism and the Lord's Supper, describing the rest of the mediaeval seven (" those five commonly called sacraments "), in somewhat loose and sweeping phraseology as " such as have grown partly of the corrupt following of the Apostles, partly are states of life allowed in the Scriptures "—neither of which descriptions applies to Confirmation.   From the standpoint of Catholic Christianity as interpreted by the " Vincentian Canon," it would seem that the general distinction drawn by the compilers of the Thirty-Nine Articles between " sacraments of the Gospel," that is, sacraments which belong to the very heart of the Catholic redemptive system—and " those that are commonly called sacraments," that is, other rites or institutions which have been given the name of " sacraments " in order to make up the mystical number of seven—is amply justified.   But it may be questioned whether Article XXV, the language of which, as we have pointed out, has been somewhat carelessly framed, draws the line at precisely the right point, when it places Baptism and the Lord's Supper alone in the former category, and assigns all the rest of the mediaeval seven indiscriminately to the latter.   It is certainly true that Matrimony is not specifically a "sacrament of the

Gospel " ; for our Lord expressly declared, when He repealed the Mosaic permission of divorce, that He was founding nothing new, but merely republishing a natural law which had existed " from the beginning." [1] Nor is it possible, in the light of the historical evidence collected by Father Puller,[2] to describe Unction as a sacrament instituted by Christ ; it is rather a sacrament gradually shaped by the Church, during the first three centuries of our era, out of an indefinite and floating custom of anointing sick people as a means for the " spiritual healing" of physical disease—a custom which would seem to have been employed by the Twelve during our Lord's ministry, presumably with His approval, and is commended by St. James, but concerning which it cannot be shown that our Lord gave any direct command for its continuance. It is doubtless the case that Ordination would be generally held by traditionalist Christians to be a " Dominical sacrament " in the sense of resting upon our Lord's own declared will ; but it can hardly be counted as a *sacramentum evangelicum*, inasmuch as its bearing upon the salvation of its recipients would not be claimed by any Catholic writer to be of the same direct and immediate character as that of Baptism, Confirmation, Penitence, and the Eucharist. These four, in fact, would seem to be sharply distinguished from the other three, either in respect of the origin or of the operation claimed for them or of both ; and it may be said that Article XXV would have represented the underlying mind of historical Christendom more accurately if it had divided the conventional "seven sacraments" into four of the first category and three of the second, rather than into two and five.

The conclusion which follows from the foregoing considerations is, that the " sacraments," with which we are concerned in this essay, and which constitute the core and foundation of Catholic sacramentalism (construed in accordance with the Vincentian Canon, and in independence of scholastic and Tridentine definitions), are *four* in number, namely, Baptism, Confirmation, Penitence, and the Eucharist or Lord's Supper. This enumeration is not very far different from the earliest list produced by ecclesiastical authority during the English Reformation, that

---

[1] Mark x. 5 ff. The statement above remains true, even if the "Matthaean exception " (Mt. v. 32, xix. 9) be regarded as having proceeded from the lips of our Lord.

[2] *The Anointing of the Sick in Scripture and Tradition* (2nd edn. 1910).

contained in the " Institution of a Christian Man," or " Bishops' Book," of 1537 ; but we may claim that our numbering appears to do more justice to Confirmation than the work just mentioned, which relegates the completion of Baptism to the same category as Orders and Extreme Unction.[1]

It is, however, possible to simplify the subject-matter of our inquiry still further ; for Penitence, Baptism, and Confirmation were in primitive Catholicism not three distinct sacraments, but rather parts of, or moments in, one great cleansing, regenerating, and Spirit-imparting rite, which was conceived as both symbolising and effecting the complete transition of the soul from sin and heathenism to full Christian life ; which in the earliest days had no one authoritative name, but seems to have been vaguely and popularly designated as " making the act of faith " (πιστεῦσαι) or " being illuminated " (φωτίζεσθαι) or even as " baptism " *tout court*, but understood as including both the preliminary Penitence and the subsequent Laying on of Hands. This single original rite of entrance to Christianity we will designate by the word " Initiation." It is worth while observing, in order to elucidate certain issues which will appear at a later point in this essay, that the main historical factor which has split this single initiatory rite into three is the rise and universal diffusion of the custom of " infant baptism," an ecclesiastical development of which the New Testament writings contain no mention. What is now known in the West as " Confirmation " is the conclusion of the initiatory rite, cut off and made into a separate sacrament, which is postponed until the arrival of the neophyte at " years of discretion," in order that at least a part of the process by which admission is gained to full membership in the Church of Christ may be experienced by him under conditions of full consciousness and intelligent responsibility.[2] And what is known in both West and East as " Penitence " or " Penance " (*poenitentia*, μετάνοια), which normally, though not invariably,[3] involves an oral con-

---

[1] C. Lloyd, *Formularies of Faith put forth by Authority during the Reign of Henry VIII* (1856 edn.), pp. 128, 129.

[2] This separation of Confirmation from Baptism did not become universal in the West until the sixteenth century ; and it is still unknown in the East, where the Chrism which is believed to be " the seal of the gift of Holy Spirit " is administered immediately after Baptism, even to infants.

[3] For an account of the circumstances under which, according to present Latin discipline, Penance may be administered without any oral confession, see Schieler-Heuser, *Theory and Practice of the Confessional* (1906), p. 645 ff.

fession of sin by the penitent, is the beginning of Initiation, detached from its original context and formed into a substantive rite to serve as a remedy for *post*-baptismal sin, a " second plank after shipwreck " ; and post-baptismal sin is a phenomenon which in the nature of things is more frequent when Baptism is habitually administered to unconscious infancy than when it is received only by adults as the crown and seal of a conscious conversion of the will to God.[1] But Initiation is still very generally performed, in its primitive shape, as a single unitary process including Confession, Washing, and Laying on of Hands, in the mission field, where most catechumens are still persons of adult age, and occasionally in Christian countries, also in the case of adults.

The two fundamental sacraments, therefore, which form the irreducible core or nucleus of the conventional septenary scheme, are Initiation and the Supper of the Lord. It is the historical connection of these with the Founder of Christianity which we now propose to investigate.

## III

### THE EVIDENCE OF THE NEW TESTAMENT

Such an investigation would, two centuries ago, have been a comparatively simple task, as it still would be if the New Testament documents were universally and unquestioningly accepted at their face value. If we leave out of account the inconsiderable " Sacramentarian " and Socinian sects on the Continent, and the Quakers in England, it will be true to say that all theologians of the pre-critical epoch—Roman, Anglican, Reformed, Lutheran—were united in affirming that the Dominical institution of Baptism, at least, is proved—not merely by the regular administration of this rite to converts from the Day of Pentecost onwards, and by the exalted language in which New Testament writers describe its spiritual import, as a mystical participation in the death, burial, and resurrection of the Redeemer,[2] and as the " laver of regeneration " [3]—but by indubitable words of the Lord Himself ; firstly, those in which He foretold to Nicodemus the necessity of the

---

[1] This is not necessarily an argument against the custom of infant baptism ; see below, p. 412, n. 1.

[2] Rom. vi. 3–9.        [3] λουτρὸν παλιγγενεσίας, Tit. iii. 5.

new birth " of water and the Spirit " for all who would enter
the Kingdom of God [1] ; secondly, the solemn charge addressed to
the Twelve by the risen Christ, in which He formally instituted
the sacrament, enjoining His hearers to " make disciples of all
nations, baptizing them in the name of the Father and of the
Son and of the Holy Ghost." [2]    Doubtless there was not the
same unanimity in regard to Confirmation and Penitence ; but
the Dominical institution of the Eucharist, once more, would
have seemed self-evident to all, or nearly all, Christian thinkers,
despite their diversity of opinion as to the right doctrinal interpretation of this supremely sacred rite.   The command " This
do in remembrance of me," embodied once in the *Textus Receptus*
of St. Luke's Gospel [3] and twice in St. Paul's account of the Last
Supper, [4] combined with the declaration " Except ye eat the flesh
of the Son of man and drink his blood, ye have no life in
you . . .," [5] would have appeared so overwhelmingly conclusive
in regard to our Lord's intentions of founding a permanent means
of communion with and commemoration of Himself, that they
would hardly have felt it in need of support from the practice of
the Apostolic Church or the teaching of others of the canonical
books.    And when it is remembered that, for theologians of the
epoch which we have mentioned, these testimonies were set, as
it were, in the adamantine framework of a verbally inspired
volume, thus sharing in its supernatural inerrancy, it will be
seen that for many centuries the question of the Dominical
institution of the greater sacraments was not so much settled as
incapable *a priori* of being discussed.

Those who are acquainted with the present position of the
minute critical and historical investigations, which have been for
the last century and still are being carried out with reference to
the origins of Catholic Christianity, will not need to be reminded
that such a general agreement amongst theological scholars is
now a thing of the past, and that the connection of the sacraments
with the historical Jesus is precisely one of the matters which are
most hotly disputed.    It will be convenient at this point to
sketch briefly the change which has come over the attitude of
Christian scholars towards the Scriptural testimonies just quoted.

[1] John iii. 5.                           [2] Matt. xxviii. 19.
[3] Luke xxii. 19.                        [4] 1 Cor. xi. 24, 25.
[5] John vi. 53.

Not only has the belief in the divinely guaranteed literal inerrancy of the sacred volume vanished, so far as we can see for ever, but the historical reliability of the principal proof-texts, considered merely as human evidence, is called in question. This is specially true of those which, like the Nicodemus passage, occur in the Fourth Gospel. It is no longer possible to assume that the sayings attributed to Christ by the great mystical writer whom we know as "St. John" represent *verbatim* reports of His *ipsissima verba*, reproduced with phonographic accuracy. Even the most conservative estimate of the value of the Fourth Gospel must admit that the discourse-matter embodied in it is to be regarded rather as a unique blend of Dominical teaching and of the Evangelist's own meditations, a blend in which it is now all but impossible to distinguish the two ingredients, than as a bare transcript, without commentary, of some of Christ's actual sayings. Hence we are not at present in a position to rule out the suggestion that the saying about "water and the Spirit" in John iii. may represent not so much what our Lord actually said on any given occasion as what the Evangelist, after a lifetime spent in the fellowship of baptized and spirit-endowed people, was convinced that He meant ; and so long as this possibility remains open, the scientific inquirer will be debarred from using these words (for all the depths of spiritual truth and splendour which he may discern in them) as assured historical evidence for the conscious prevision by our Lord, during His earthly lifetime, of the saving effects which Christian Initiation would have during the long centuries which were to succeed His death.

Similar considerations apply to the cardinal proof-text traditionally adduced on behalf of the Dominical institution of Baptism, Matt. xxviii. 19. It is now generally agreed, amongst Biblical scholars other than those of the Roman Catholic Church, that the Gospel which stands first in our New Testament can only be described as that "according to Matthew" in the sense that it may include sections of a work by him, perhaps the " Logia " stated by Papias to have been compiled in Aramaic by the Apostle Matthew.[1] The same consensus of critical opinion affirms that the final editor of this Gospel, whoever he was, cannot have been an eyewitness of the events which he records (his dependence upon the Marcan narrative is enough to prove this) ; and that

---

[1] Eus. *H.E.* iii. 39.

his editorial principles and methods permitted him a degree of freedom in the way of edifying and haggadic modification or amplification of his sources which is hardly in accordance with the more exacting standards of modern biography, and which (in one or two passages [1]) is utilised in a manner reminiscent of the unrestrained thaumaturgy of the extra-canonical Gospels. If this be so, it is difficult to discover any consideration which decisively excludes the suggestion that " Matthew's " attribution of the baptismal charge to the risen Christ may be dogma couched in a quasi-historical form, rather than history proper : that it represents not so much what Christ actually said as what the Christians of *c.* 80 A.D. were convinced that He ought to, and must, have said.[2] Such a suggestion draws a certain amount of force from the fact that the text Matt. xxviii. 19 contains the Threefold Name in its most clear-cut and technical form, " Father, Son, and Holy Ghost "—a form which occurs nowhere else in the New Testament, and of which the next recorded instance is to be found in the *Didache* [3] (which can hardly be dated earlier than A.D. 100). It is urged that a literal acceptation of " Matthew's " statement, that the use of the Threefold Name was prescribed at the very beginning of Christian history by the supreme authority of the risen Lord, is incompatible with a candid interpretation of the Acts and Epistles, which show that Baptism was for long administered " in the Name of Jesus " only, and that the doctrine of the Trinity itself, as summed up in the scholastically precise formula, " Father, Son, and Holy Ghost," was the comparatively late product of a slow and gradual development, which even in St. Paul's lifetime had not advanced further than the embryonic stage reflected in the primitive benediction " The grace of our Lord Jesus Messiah, and the love of God, and the fellowship of the Holy Ghost, be with you all." [4] But if it is a possible supposition that the final editor of the first Gospel has

---

[1] *E.g.* xvii. 27 (the stater in the fish's mouth) ; xxvii. 52, 53 (the resurrection of the " saints ").

[2] The suggestion, first made by F. C. Conybeare, in the *Zeitschr. f. N.T. Wissensch.*, 1901, p. 275 ff., and afterwards adopted by Prof. Kirsopp Lake in his inaugural lecture before the University of Leyden, that the words " baptizing them in the name of the Father and of the Son and of the Holy Ghost " are a late dogmatic interpolation into the text of St. Matthew, has been effectively dealt with by the late Dr. F. H. Chase, *Journal of Theological Studies*, vi. 483 ff., " The Lord's Command to Baptize," and need not be considered here.

[3] c. 7.                                            [4] 2 Cor. xiii. 14.

(doubtless with the best intentions) read back the developed Trinitarian theology of his own day into the baptismal command, the suspicion is inevitably aroused that the baptismal command itself may be no more than a dogmatic projection upon the background of the past. Such reflections do not, indeed, constitute a decisive disproof of the Matthaean affirmation of the formal institution of Baptism by Christ ; but they are thought by many to remove it from the category of reliable evidence into that of uncertain statements, on which it would be precarious to build a historical case. But if both of the sayings on which the Dominical institution of Baptism is based recede into the limbo of the historically dubious, the institution itself recedes with them : and the field is left open for the hypothesis now widely accepted by the Protestant scholars of the Continent, that the origins of Christian Baptism are to be found, not in any word or declared intention of Jesus, but rather in the Jewish custom of the baptism of proselytes, or in the baptism of John—one or other of which is assumed to have been continued, on their own authority, by the earliest disciples as a natural but purely non-mystical method of symbolising admission to the Christian group, to have been gradually invested, by tradition and usage and other factors which will claim attention presently, with a supernatural awe, and to have been finally ascribed, by a process of *ex post facto* reasoning familiar to all students of ancient religion, to the command of the Saviour Himself.

The evidence for Christ's institution of the Eucharist, as a permanent rite designed to be celebrated after His death and in memory of it, has undergone a similar process of attrition. It is not denied that our Lord at the Last Supper blessed a loaf and a cup, and gave them to His disciples, declaring them to be, in some sense, His body and His blood ; but the question which is debated is that of the intention with which He did so. Was the solemn action, which He then performed, of a purely *ad hoc* nature, consummated once and for all with the view of impressing upon the circle of His intimate friends, and upon them only, the significance of the terrible events which lay before Him ? or did He consciously mean to found a definite liturgical or sacramental ceremony, to be continued by His followers after His visible presence should have been removed from the earth? If we could be certain that His lips actually uttered the command

"This do in remembrance of me " (τοῦτο ποιεῖτε εἰς τὴν ἐμὴν ἀνάμνησιν), the question would be settled.    But this crucial saying, which has hitherto been taken to constitute the main, if not the only Scriptural ground for believing that our Lord intended His action to be repeated, is preserved only in the Gospel of St. Luke (according to the generally received text) and in St. Paul's First Epistle to the Corinthians.    And its occurrence in the text of the third Gospel is now held to be highly questionable, inasmuch as it is omitted, at this point, by the great fifth-century Graeco-Latin Codex D, by four Old Latin MSS.,[1] by Tatian, and the Jerusalemitic Old Syriac—facts which have caused such careful and conservative scholars as Westcott and Hort to excise it from the Lucan account of the Last Supper, as a "Western non-interpolation" which has crept into the text of St. Luke through scribal assimilation to 1 Cor. xi. 24, 25.[2]    The statement, therefore, that Jesus commanded His disciples to repeat in memory of Him the symbolic actions which He performed at the Last Supper must, in the present state of our knowledge, be taken as coming to us on the authority of St. Paul, and of St. Paul only    But the authority of St. Paul, in regard to a matter of historical fact of which he cannot, in the nature of the case, have been an eyewitness, is very far from being unchallenged.    It is not, indeed, disputed that the Apostle of the Gentiles was in all good faith reproducing what he had learnt from the nucleus of original disciples, who had known the Lord in the flesh.    But, as in the case of the Matthaean command to baptize, the possibility that the injunction " This do in remembrance of me " may be due to unconscious aetiological invention spontaneously recurs to the mind.    A comparison of the four versions (given by the three Synoptists and St. Paul) of the words spoken by Christ at the delivery of the Bread and of the Cup reveals the fact that no one version agrees precisely with any other, and textual criticism suggests that St. Luke's autograph may have placed the distribution of the Cup (*without* the words " This is my blood") before that of the Bread.[3]    It is a reasonable inference from the somewhat confused state of the evidence that the Apostolic Church

---

[1] a l ff[2] i.

[2] *The New Testament in Greek* (1881), Appendix, pp. 63, 64.

[3] D a l ff[2] i omit Luke xxii. 19[b]–20, thus making the cup of v. 17 to be the Eucharistic Cup.

was not in possession of a single, uniform, and rigidly stereotyped account of our Lord's sayings and doings at the Last Supper. But if such oral tradition as existed continued to be fluid for some decades after the event to which it refers, it is not by any means impossible that the words "This do" may have imperceptibly crept into that stream of it which was destined to reach St. Paul, as an *ex post facto* legitimation of a custom, originally perhaps based on mere sentiment, of repeating at the common meal of the Christian community, in remembrance of the Master, the significant acts which He had performed at "the last sad supper with His own." If this suspicion is justifiable, the Eucharistic command "Do this . . ." joins the baptismal command "Make disciples of all the nations, baptizing them . . ." in the twilit realm of historical uncertainties. The solitary link connecting the sacramental practice of the Church with the intentions of the Master has been, if not irretrievably snapped, at least attenuated to a degree of fragility at which it can no longer bear the strain which the traditional theory of the Eucharist demands.

It might be objected that, even if the cogency of the foregoing considerations be admitted, they do not prove that our Lord did not institute the sacraments, but only that the existing documentary evidence is insufficient to show that He did. And it might further be suggested that there is at least a possibility of basing the belief in the Dominical institution, not so much upon a couple of proof-texts as upon the universal and immemorial custom of Christendom, which would seem to imply a source not less authoritative than the will of the Saviour Himself. But at this point the non-Catholic critic produces his final, apparently irresistible and overwhelming argument, which (if its validity be admitted) becomes in his hands a logical flail or bludgeon whereby all the attempts of the Catholic apologist to find a basis for traditional sacramentalism in the words and actions of Jesus are mercilessly smitten to the ground. This argument is founded upon the assumption of *the eschatologically limited outlook* of Jesus. During His lifetime (it is contended) Jesus believed that the existing world-order was on the point of dissolution, that the lightnings and terrors of the End might at any moment burst upon mankind, that within a space of time to be measured by months He Himself would be caught up and transfigured in celestial glory, and would return on the clouds of heaven to inaugurate the Messianic millennium upon a supernaturally rejuvenated earth.   Hence He can neither have foreseen nor provided for the long history which the movement kindled by His words was in fact destined to have upon this planet : He can have " founded," or " instituted," nothing—neither Church, nor hierarchy, nor sacraments.   If this position, which Friedrich Heiler describes as " the Copernican achievement of modern theology," [1] really represents the facts, then *cadit quaestio* : it becomes unnecessary even to examine the evidence for " Dominical institution," and the hypothesis of a fortuitous origin of the present Christian sacraments assumes the character of inevitability.   Just as Christian Baptism is (on this showing) to be regarded as the accidental survival of the Jewish proselyte-baptism, utilised by the common sense of the new movement as a symbolic means of admitting new adherents, so the Lord's Supper is the relic of the Jewish *Kiddûsh*, or sanctification of the Sabbath or of a great feast by the blessing of bread and wine on its eve,[2] a ceremony which Jesus had in the circle of His friends and hearers occasionally invested with the additional significance of a ritual rehearsal of the " Messianic banquet," which on the last evening of His life He had employed as an acted parable of His imminent death, and which His followers continued to observe at their club-meal or *Agape*, from habit or feeling rather than from any reasoned theory, as a commemoration or reminder to themselves both of His death and of His future return.   For the first few years of Christianity, therefore, these observances were no more than harmless pieces of sentimental symbolism, with no specifically " sacramental " significance, created or adopted by the Christian community to express its collective emotions on certain solemn occasions.   Many non-Catholic critics would add, that it would have been well if they had remained on this level.

[1] *Der Katholizismus* (1923), p. 3 : " Die Erkenntnis des eschatologischen Charakters seines Evangeliums ist die kopernikanische Tat der modernen Theologie ; mit einem Schlage stürzt sie das katholische Dogmensystem um."

[2] *Cf.* A. Loisy, *Les Évangiles Synoptiques*, ii. p. 542, n. 4.   The *Kiddûsh* may in any case well have been the foundation of the Christian Eucharist ; see G. H. Box, " The Jewish Antecedents of the Eucharist," *Journal of Theological Studies*, iii. 357.

## IV

### THE " MYSTERY RELIGIONS "

The theory just sketched requires as its natural complement an explanation of the manner in which the innocuous customs presupposed by it became transformed into the Catholic sacraments of Initiation and Communion, as known to St. Paul, St. John, St. Ignatius, and St. Justin Martyr, and all or practically all subsequent Christian thinkers and writers down to the sixteenth century of our era. This explanation is found by a consensus of non-Catholic scholarship in the well-known " Mystery-religion " hypothesis, which, though familiar to classical and theological students, may be briefly summarised here, in order that the logical bearings of the complete anti-traditionalist case may be fully exposed.

If we leave out of account the bizarre phenomenon of Caesar-worship, it is true to say that official " paganism," that is, the established religious system or systems with which Christianity found itself confronted when for the first time it spread beyond the borders of Palestine into Northern Syria, Asia Minor, and Europe, consisted of an immense multitude of localised and mutually independent cults, closely associated for the most part with the life of the State and of its provinces and municipalities.[1] Where they did not represent mere survivals of primitive magic and fetichism, these " established " cults were based on a strictly commercial view of the relation between the gods and their worshippers, the god being bound to protect the State or the municipality in return for a given *quantum* of sacrifices, but otherwise being under no obligation to interest himself in the community or its members. It will be clear that so purely contractual a system did not even pretend to satisfy the deeper spiritual needs or aspirations of the individual soul, nor were its ministers conceived to be invested with what we know as " pastoral " functions. A Roman who was oppressed by the enigma of the universe, by the weight of unmerited misfortune, or by the sense of personal guilt, would no more have thought of

---

[1] It is not necessary for the purposes of this brief sketch to take account of private or semi-private worships, such as the cults of the Attic phratries or the *sacra gentilicia* at Rome.

applying to the *flamen Dialis* or to the *quindecemviri sacris faciundis* for ghostly aid and comfort than of confiding in the Prefect of the Praetorian Guards.   Moreover, such reality as the official cults had once possessed had long since been drained out of them, so far as the educated classes were concerned, by the widespread scepticism, which had made it impossible to believe in the substantive and personal reality of the members of the conventional Pantheon.   Even those who, under the influence of the most remarkable Hellenic-Oriental religious teacher of the last two centuries B.C., Posidonius of Apamea,[1] had won their way to a philosophic monotheism, seem to have made no effort to relate their creed to the traditional State religion : Cicero's quotation of Cato's cynical apophthegm, about the difficulty which two *haruspices* must have felt in keeping straight faces when they met in the street, illustrates vividly the utter deadness of the old ceremonies, even for a man whose patriotism, no less than his religious feelings, would naturally have disposed him to make the best of them.[2]

It is not surprising that, during the centuries which immediately preceded and followed the birth of Christ, men who felt the need of a vital and personal religion should have turned away from the desiccated State ceremonies to the warm emotional " Mystery Religions " ; which, in virtue of their private character and their interest in the destiny of the individual soul, may without undue anachronism be styled the " evangelical nonconformity " of the pagan world, and which, in the eyes of the prosaic populations of the West, were endued with a unique glamour by the fact that they came from the wonder-world of the East, the immemorial home of religion.   Of those mystery-cults, some, like those of the Eleusinian Demeter and the " Great Gods " or Kabeiroi of Samothrace, were strictly localised, being capable of celebration only by a priesthood resident at some particular spot, as in the case of the Eumolpidae at Eleusis, though the votaries who had once been initiated might be, and doubtless were, scattered all over the civilised world ; others were of a more avowedly " catholic " or " oecumenical " character in respect of their organisation, which was not tied down to a

---

[1] The latest study of this enigmatic personage appears to be K. Reinhardt, *Poseidonios* (Munich, 1921).

[2] Cic. *De Div.* II. xxiv.

single centre, but covered the whole Empire with a network of shrines and priestly colleges. The most important of these were the four great faiths which respectively clustered around the divine persons of Dionysus the Hunter (Zagreus), Isis the Egyptian queen of heaven, Cybele the sorrowful Mother of Asia Minor, and Mithra the hero-god of Persia, patron of soldiers, whose altars have been found in Roman military stations from the Euphrates to the Solway. To these must be added a host of lesser cults such as those of Atargatis, Adonis, Hermes Trismegistos,[1] and the like. These various faiths were propagated by the *Diasporai* of the nations in which they had originated, much as Judaism was propagated by the *Diaspora* or "dispersion" of Israel : and the syncretistic tendencies of the age enabled them to borrow from each other, and to fuse their usages and even the personalities of their gods, in every kind of proportion. If the *Metamorphoses* of Apuleius may be trusted, the ethical levels of their professional exponents ranged from the most austere virtue to the vilest charlatanism.

The roots from which the Mystery Religions sprang are not difficult to discern. Some, such as the Eleusinian and Egyptian mysteries, were developments of the vegetation-myth common to many primitive peoples, which personifies the vital force of nature, apparently dying in the winter and blossoming into fresh life in the spring, as a god who dies and rises again : others, such as the Orphic mysteries, appear to be built upon survivals of totemic ceremonial. But our knowledge of their fully developed contents, theological and ritual, is exceedingly fragmentary, a fact which is due partly to the faithfulness with which the initiates observed their pledge of secrecy, and partly to the crusade conducted by the victorious Christian Church, after its establishment by Constantine, against the shrines and sacred books of its rivals. Enough, however, remains, both of literary and of archaeological evidence, to furnish us with some conception of their broad underlying ideas.

The basal human need which all alike claimed to satisfy was the craving of the sick soul for "salvation" (*soteria*). The "failure of nerve," [2] which afflicted great masses of the popu-

---

[1] But see below, p. 392, n. 3.

[2] The phrase is borrowed from the heading of c. iv., in *Five Stages of Greek Religion* (Prof. Gilbert Murray, 1925). The whole chapter is an incomparable sketch of the popular emotional background which was common both to Christianity and to the Mystery Religions.

lation during the first century of our era, the widespread pessimism and world-weariness which supervened upon the close of the Roman civil wars, appeared in the consciousness of the individual as a nameless and oppressive fear—a fear of the universe, of the ruthless power of Fate, of the malefic influences of the stars, of annihilation at death, or of the torments of Tartarus.   It was from this fear that the " Mystery Religions" promised deliverance, bestowed by a philanthropic " Lord " (*Kyrios*) or " Saviour " (*Soter*), who himself had known the anguish of death, or at least of poignant sorrow or laborious toil, and who, as it is alleged, promised to transfuse the virtue of his own divine life into the soul of his votary, assuring the latter thereby of pardon, inward peace, and a blessed immortality, through rites of a sacramental character.   As the chief needs of the religious soul are purity and inward strength, it was natural, indeed inevitable, that these rites should have taken the forms of a cleansing bath and of a sacred meal.

We are here upon very uncertain ground, and it is impossible to say whether sacramentalism was strictly universal in these cults or not.   In the rites of Eleusis we hear of a preliminary bath in the sea prescribed for the *mystae*,[1] and the cistern or *lacus* discovered by Sir William Ramsay in the sanctuary at Pisidian Antioch appears to have been used for baptismal purposes.[2] Demosthenes scoffs at the baptism of the Phrygian Cybele, as carried out by Aeschines in his youth, acting as the acolyte of his mother, a strolling priestess [3] ; and, in the romance of Apuleius which gives us the most exhaustive account now surviving of Isiac initiation, the candidate Lucius undergoes a bath and a ceremonial lustration to prepare him for his enlistment in the service of the goddess.[4]   But the most striking parallel (in respect of the spiritual effects claimed for it) to Christian Initiation is to be found in the *taurobolium* or *criobolium*, that is, the bath in the blood of a slain beast, bull or ram, which admitted men to the mysteries of Cybele and Attis, and may have been borrowed from them by the cult of Mithras [5] ;   some sepulchral inscriptions

---

[1] ἅλαδε μύσται; see L. R. Farnell, *Cults of the Greek States*, iii. p. 168.

[2] W. M. Ramsay, *The Teaching of Paul in Terms of the Present Day* (1913), p. 287 ff.

[3] Dem. *de Coron.* 313.                    [4] Apuleius, *Metamorph.* xi. 23.

[5] Cumont, however, thinks that the *taurobolium* was never strictly a part of the Mithraic liturgy (*Textes et monuments figurés relatifs aux mystères de Mithra*, i. p. 334).   For the *criobolium*, see Pauly-Wissowa, *Real-Encycl.*, iv. p. 1718, *s.v.*

testify to the faith of those who had received this horrible rite that they had thereby become "eternally regenerate," *renati in aeternum.*[1] Evidence for sacred meals is tantalisingly sporadic and fragmentary. The most certain instance is to be found in the *omophagia* of the Orphic mysteries, in which the delirious worshippers tore to pieces the sacred ox, believed anciently—though whether in historic times or not, we cannot say—to be the incarnation of Dionysus, and devoured its flesh raw.[2] Sacred meals, including both food and drink, appear to have occurred in the mysteries of Attis,[3] and of the Kabeiroi [4] ; and the rites of Eleusis included the drinking of a mixed cup (the so-called κυκεών) which may or may not have had a sacramental significance.[5] Probably the Mithraic sacred meal of bread and water mixed with *haoma*-juice should be added to the list,[6] though it is possible that this ceremony was a deliberate imitation of, and therefore not a true pagan parallel to, the Christian Eucharist.

This list embodies the principal instances of (apparent) sacramentalism in the pagan mystery-cults. We cannot, however, tell that there may not have been more ; and it is a reasonable presumption that those which we have enumerated would have familiarised the inhabitants of Syria, Asia Minor, and Greece, amongst whom the first expansion of Christianity outside the borders of Palestine took place, with the ideas of cathartic lustrations and sacramental, perhaps even of "theophagic," meals. It is suggested that the specifically Catholic conceptions of Initiation and the Eucharist are the product of a gradual infiltration of such ideas into Christianity from the mystery-faiths described above, a process for the inception of which, it is contended, St. Paul must bear the chief responsibility.[7] The Apostle is not, indeed, accused

---

[1] Other inscriptions, however, imply that the effect of this blood-baptism was only supposed to last for twenty years.

[2] See J. E. Harrison, *Prolegomena to the Study of Greek Religion*, pp. 482–92 ; A. Loisy, *Les mystères païens et le mystère chrétien* (1914), p. 32 ff.

[3] Farnell, *op. cit.* iii. 187.      [4] *Ibid.* iii. 195.      [5] *Ibid.* iii. 186, 195.

[6] F. Cumont, *Les mystères de Mithra* (1913), p. 163.

[7] It should be said that Harnack (*Mission and Expansion of Christianity*, E. tr., 1908, i. p. 230), and two distinguished British scholars, Prof. H. A. A. Kennedy (*St. Paul and the Mystery Religions*, 1913), and Dr. T. R. Glover (*Paul of Tarsus*, 1925, p. 161 ff.), favour or seem to favour a modified form of the "Mystery" theory, which finds the influence of the pagan Mysteries clearly manifested in later Catholicism, but not in the writings of St. Paul, who is thus exempted from the responsibility alluded to above. This position, however, appears ultimately to rest upon the assumption that there is an essential

of having, consciously and with his eyes open, embarked upon a policy of paganising Christianity in order to commend it to the Phrygian and Anatolian populations. The theory is rather that his first converts,[1] on being admitted to the Christian fellowship, and finding that it revered a human Messiah as, in some undefined sense, the "son of God," that it admitted new adherents by means of a ceremonial washing, and that it celebrated a common meal with special and sentimental reference to the death of its hero and prophet, naturally thought of all these matters in terms of the mystery cults with which they were familiar : in other words, that they envisaged Jesus, the Jewish-Christian Messiah, as a *Kyrios*,[2] a mystery-god analogous to Attis, Serapis, Mithras, and the other pagan *Kyrioi* or Redeemers[3] ; that they interpreted the harmless symbol of Baptism as a mysterious and awful sacrament of regeneration, and the "eschatologised *Ķiddûsh*," which concluded the club-feast, as a realistic participation in the body and blood of the *Kyrios*. But, instead of striving with might and main to exclude the infiltration of these alien ideas (the theory goes on) St. Paul weakly acquiesced in them. The Apostle, or his immediate coadjutors and *epigoni*, found that the work of evangelisation was immensely simplified and accelerated if the pagan inquirer could be addressed in the terminology already familiar to him, and if the Gospel could be represented as "the last," and the only true, "word" in Mystery Religions. Stated in this way, Christianity spread with a surprising rapidity ; and St. Paul not merely accepted this transformation as expedient, but actually came to believe in it as true. By a kind of un-

---

incompatibility between the "ethical" and the "objectively sacramentalist" conceptions of Christianity ; and as (for the reasons explained in our introductory section) we repudiate this assumption, we may be permitted for the purpose of this essay to confine ourselves to the more thoroughgoing form of the "Mystery" hypothesis, as set forth by its leading Continental expositors.

    [1] W. Bousset, *Kyrios Christos* (1921), p. 99, suggests that the beginnings of the transformation described above should be placed in the primitive Christian community of Antioch, the first Gentile-Christian Church to come into existence, before St. Paul's missionary journeys.

    [2] See W. Bousset, *Kyrios Christos* (1921), c. iii. pp. 75–104.

    [3] The words of St. Paul in 1 Cor. viii. 5 f. "For even if there are so-called gods, whether in heaven or on earth (as there are many 'gods' and many 'Kyrioi '), yet for us there is one God, the Father . . . and one *Kyrios*, Jesus Messiah . . ." show that the idea of a parallelism between Christ and the Pagan Redeemers existed in St. Paul's mind ; but it will be argued later that parallel conceptions need not be related as cause and effect.

conscious auto-suggestion, he persuaded himself that Baptism and the " Lord's Supper " really were and could do what the Mithraic *taurobolium* and the Dionysiac *omophagia* only pretended to be and to do, and that the Eucharist, at least, had been explicitly instituted by Jesus as a mystery of sacramental might. Christianity thus became Catholicism, and its triumph in the Graeco-Roman world was purchased at the cost of a surrender to the pagan sacramentalism which it should have resisted to the death.

Though considerations of space forbid us to dilate upon the matter now, it is worth while to emphasise the fact that the " Mystery-Religion " theory of the origins of the sacraments (or rather of the origins of the belief in their objective efficacy) does not stand by itself ; it is part and parcel of a wider thesis, namely, what may be called the " Mystery-Religion " theory of the origins of Catholicism in general, including the idea of Christ as a pre-existent Divine being and that conception of God which is ultimately necessitated by a " pre-existence " Christology, namely, the idea of the Trinity. The solidarity of the whole *religionsgeschichtliche* explanation of Catholicism is understood well enough in Germany, though in England there seems to be a tendency to speak and write as though its purview were confined to the sole question of the significance of the sacraments. But such an impartial witness as Heiler will tell us that neither in history nor in logic is it possible to dissociate the idea of Jesus as " Kyrios " from the ideas of Initiation and the Supper as " Mysteries." [1] The educated Catholic, from his own point of view, may be grateful for the implied admission that Catholic Christology and Catholic sacramentalism are interdependent. But, from the point of view of the " Mystery " hypothesis, the Christ of traditional dogma is a generalised blend of Attis, Osiris, and Mithras, wearing as a not too-well-fitting mask the features of Jesus of Nazareth ; and the Christocentric mysticism which is the heart of Catholic devotion is derived from Hellenistic-Oriental paganism, not from anything believed by Israel or taught by Jesus Himself. The silent recollection, with which the Catholic believer, kneeling in some still and empty church, fixes his eyes upon the Rood, becomes but the after-glow of the emotions with which the Mithraic initiate, in some crypt or chapel of the warrior-god, contemplated the Tauroctony, or

[1] Cf. *Der Katholizismus*, pp. 48, 49.

carven *retablo* depicting the slaying of the mystic bull. The lights and the Alleluyas of the Christian Easter are in great measure but the mirage-like reflection of the joy which filled the devotees of Attis, when on the *Hilaria*, the crowning day of the vernal commemoration of his passion, the chief priest whispered to them, as he administered the sacramental balm, " The God has been saved ! " [1]

## V

### CRITIQUE OF THE " MYSTERY " HYPOTHESIS

Such in outline is the great, modern, skilfully articulated and impressively coherent, *alternative* explanation of the genesis of Catholicism which now confronts the traditional belief in the Deity of Christ and in His direct institution of the sacraments. [2] If this alternative explanation can establish itself as the truth, there is an end of historic Christianity as we know it. On the other hand, if it can be shown to rest on arbitrary assumptions and to involve historical or psychological impossibilities, the traditional theory will remain in possession of the field. The scope of this essay is necessarily limited to the question of the sacraments only ; and a few words regarding the method which we propose to follow in examining the " Mystery " theory will conduce to clearness. It will have been observed that the theory, as sketched above, assumes a detailed picture of the state of the " Mystery Religions " during the first generation of Christian history which is by no means universally recognised as an accurate representation of the facts. [3]  Most of our evidence for the character of these cults dates

---

[1] See J. G. Frazer, *Adonis, Attis, Osiris* (1914), i. p. 272.

[2] Signs are, however, not wanting that the " Mystery " theory has reached the zenith of its popularity, and may shortly enter upon a period of decline, even in Germany ; see an article by Robert Eisler, " Das letzte Abendmahl," in *Zeitschr. f. N.T. Wissensch.*, Nov. 1925, in which the author explains that he was once an adherent of the " Mystery " theory, but now considers it " one of the most erroneous conclusions that has ever arisen in the whole history of New Testament study."

[3] A striking instance of the precariousness of the evidence for the " Mystery " theory is provided by the " Hermetic " writings.  R. Reitzenstein, perhaps the best-known Continental student of the subject, regards them as " scriptures " venerated by " Hermetic congregations," so that he is able to use them, in conjunction with magical papyri which mention the name of Hermes, for the purpose of reconstructing a scheme of ideas supposed to have been common to all Mystery Religions in the first century A.D., and to have included the conceptions

from the second and third centuries A.D., and there is no proof that we are entitled to employ it as evidence for the first century. The use of Mithraism in this connection is peculiarly unjustifiable, inasmuch as during St. Paul's lifetime it was all but unknown in Europe, and never took root in lands of Greek speech and culture.[1] It has not been proved that all the apparent analogues of Baptism and the Eucharist to be found in paganism were conceived as sacramental, nor yet that all mystery-cults possessed all of the three cardinal points of the generalised " mystery-scheme " presupposed by the theory, that is (1) a *Kyrios*, (2) a ceremonial washing, and (3) a sacred meal.   But an attempt to reconstruct the stages of development to which the various Mystery Religions had severally attained during the period A.D. 29–70 would require far more space than is at our disposal.   In spite, therefore, of the uncertainties just indicated, we will, for the sake of argument, assume that the advocates of the " Mystery " hypothesis have construed the available evidence correctly, and that their picture of the Mystery Religions in the first century A.D. is free from anachronisms. We can afford to concede them this considerable logical advantage, because, if the strongest form of the " Mystery " theory can be overthrown, it will carry with it in its fall any weaker forms which a searching historical analysis might reveal.

Our criticisms of the " Mystery " hypothesis will, therefore, not be concerned with details ; they will refer solely to its fundamental positions, which may be formulated as follows :

(*a*) That there is no reliable evidence that Christ *did* institute the sacraments.

(*b*) That His " eschatologically limited outlook " proves that He *could* not have instituted them.

(*c*) That the parallelism between Pauline and pagan sacramentalism is only explicable on the supposition that the former is directly derived from the latter.

of the " Spirit," " new birth," and the efficacy of the Redeemer's Name. (See especially *Poimandres*, 1904, pp. 1–36, 219, 226 ff., 366, 368 ; *Die Hellenistischen Mysterienreligionen*, 1910, pp. 33 ff., 112 ff.) The latest editor of these documents, on the other hand, Mr. Walter Scott (*Hermetica*, vols. i, ii., 1925), dismisses the idea of a Hermetic " cult " and " congregations " as a pure invention, and pronounces the *Corpus Hermeticum* to be no more than a fortuitous collection of late Greek-Egyptian philosophical and religious writings, only bound together by the fact that their authors happened to use the figures of Hermes and Tat as conventional *dramatis personae*.

[1] F. Cumont, *Les mystères de Mithra* (1913), p. 31 f.

It will be convenient to consider these points in an order somewhat different from that in which we have stated them.

### 1. *" Parallelism " and " derivation "—the question of* a priori *probability*

The contamination of a higher religion by surviving elements of a lower which it has conquered or is in process of conquering is a phenomenon familiar to the student of the history of religions : the fusion of Yahwism with Canaanitish *baʿal*-worship denounced by the Hebrew prophets, and the transformation of Buddhism into Lamaism, are instances in point.  No one who is intimately acquainted with Catholicism as it exists to-day in Mediterranean countries and amongst peoples of Iberian stock can deny that it contains many details of external observance and of popular piety which are directly borrowed from Graeco-Roman paganism ; a comparison of the model legs, arms, and hands suspended as *ex-votos* before continental shrines of our Lady with the precisely similar objects employed for the same purpose in temples of Isis will bring this fact vividly before the reader's eyes.  *Graecia capta ferum victorem cepit*[1]—the well-known Horatian line applies as much to the struggle of her folk-religion with the victorious faith of Judaea as to the contest of her culture with the barbarian rusticity of Rome.  From the same source are descended the stories of holy wells and trees, winking pictures, sweating statues, flying houses, and other fetichistic and animistic beliefs which flourish rankly in the underworld of the Mediterranean religious consciousness.  It was, perhaps, hardly to be expected that the ark of the Church could traverse the Sargasso Sea of the ancient religions without acquiring some adventitious incrustations of this kind ; and it is not necessary here to distinguish between those which are harmless or even picturesque, and those which definitely retard the speed of the ship.  And it may be observed, in parenthesis, that whatever less desirable effects the Reformation may have had, it conferred at least one permanent benefit upon religion in Northern countries by decisively plucking up the roots of all such heathen survivals, so as to make possible, at any rate in England, a fresh start, and the working out of a presentation of Catholicism which should contain no vital element of which

[1] Hor. *Ep.* II. i, 156.

at least the germs were not to be found in the New Testament. But these toys of the uneducated, " miraculous " stocks and stones, *ex-votos*, and the like, stand on an entirely different footing from the sacraments, which are the subject-matter of our inquiry : partly because such things as thaumaturgical images are in principle no more than separable accidents of any version of Catholicism, and could be relegated *en masse* to the dust-heap without any disturbance of its logical structure, and partly because the beginnings of their infiltration into Christianity can be historically controlled and linked with the vast influx of semi-converted heathen into the Church during the fourth and succeeding centuries ; whereas the sacraments, in substantially their Catholic shape, and the conception of Jesus as *Kyrios* which they presuppose, appear in the pages of the New Testament itself. The fact that direct, if unconscious, borrowing can be proved in the later and less important case of parallelism between Christian and pagan custom does not in itself compel us to assume a similar explanation of the earlier and more important.[1]

Considered in itself, the statement that parallelism proves dependence would seem to be entirely arbitrary. As applied to the relations between Christian and ethnic sacramentalism, it is by no means new : it was asserted as strongly by the early Christian Apologists as by the modern non-Catholic critics, the only difference between these two bodies of writers being that, whereas the critics assume the Christian sacraments to be the reflection of the pagan Mysteries, the Apologists held that the Mysteries were Satanic parodies of the sacraments. But both alike appear to have overlooked a third *prima facie* possibility, which would surely occur to a cultivated Martian or other completely unbiassed investigator, namely, that the connection between the Christian and the pagan rites might be *collateral* (in the sense that both might be independent products of the same psychological factors) and not one of direct dependence or causality. The researches

---

[1] The same consideration applies to the facts (1) that in the fourth and succeeding centuries much " mystery " terminology was applied to the sacraments—*cf*. the title of St. Cyril of Jerusalem's instructions on the sacraments, *Catecheses Mystagogicae*—and (2) that certain details of liturgical observance (*e.g.* the use of milk and honey in connection with Christian initiation—see H. Usener, *Rhein. Mus. für Philol.* lvii. 177) seem to have been borrowed from or at least influenced by the procedure of the pagan mysteries. We are here only concerned with the fundamental essence of Christian sacramentalism as it appears in the New Testament.

of anthropologists seem to show that man everywhere tends to satisfy the same instincts in the same way : the works of Frazer, Crawley, van Gennep, Durkheim, Hubert and Mauss, contain thousands of instances of similar myths, rites, customs, and *tabus* which have sprung up, to all appearance independently, in diverse lands in response to the same social or individual needs, and there is no necessity to postulate a " monophyletic " origin even for so elaborate a system as totemism.   In no other department of scientific thought is it assumed as axiomatic that similar phenomena must be directly related as cause and effect ;  and there seems no reason for making such an assumption within the sphere of the history of religions.[1]   From the most severely impartial point of view, therefore, it must be at least an *a priori* possibility that the Christian lustration and sacred meal came to be interpreted in the same way as their pagan analogues, simply because it was found by experience that they did (for whatever reason) provide a full satisfaction for the same spiritual needs, that is, for those cravings for purity and ghostly strength, which in the pagan world had created the Mystery Religions as a means to their own partial gratification or sublimation.

But a detached Christian investigator—by which phrase I mean an inquirer who had come to admit, in a general sense, the uniqueness and supremacy of the Christian revelation, without having decided which of the existing forms of our religion appeared to be the truest—would, I submit, be prepared somewhat to enlarge the field of this possibility.   He would at least concede that Almighty God, in accordance with the principle of continuity which can be discerned running through His providential govern- ance of history, *may* have willed to do for man, through His final self-revelation, what man had attempted to do for himself through crude and imperfect means of his own devising ;  and that Christianity, as it claims in other respects to sum up and gather into one the various lines of man's secular search for God, may also claim—with pride, and not with apology—to be by divine appointment the supreme and ideal Mystery Religion.   He would see no reason why the " creed of creeds " should not include,

---

[1] We do not forget that some anthropologists, like the late Dr. W. H. R. Rivers, do explicitly assume that all similarities of custom, religious and social, in different nations must be due to the spread of civilisation from a single centre ; but they are far from having converted all their fellow-students to this view.

side by side with an ethic loftier than that of Socrates, and a
theology richer and grander than that of Aristotle, " Mysteries "
more pure and ennobling than those of which Sophocles wrote :

$$ὡς τρισόλβιοι$$
$$κεῖνοι βροτῶν, οἳ ταῦτα δερχθέντες τέλη$$
$$μόλωσ' ἐς "Αιδου.^1$$

And, assuming him to believe both in human free will and in
God's all-pervasive providence, he would admit that the Mystery
Religions may have been an integral element in the vast *praeparatio
evangelica* which began with the emergence of man from the ape ;
that, viewed from the standpoint of human initiative, they may
have been models and symbols, first fashioned by man for himself,
which God, condescending to man's limitations, vouchsafed to
reproduce within the framework of the final religion ; and that,
viewed from the standpoint of divine providence, they may have
been, like the Levitical ordinances, types and foreshadowings of
" good things to come."

The supposed axiom that " parallelism implies dependence "
is, therefore, neither self-evident nor inductively proven, and cannot
be used to invest the hypothesis of " pagan infiltration " with a
degree of *a priori* likelihood superior to that of " Dominical institution." So far as our argument has gone, both hypotheses would
seem to stand on the same level of probability. We may now carry
our analysis a little deeper, with the object of showing that the
" Mystery theory," so far from being more probable than the
traditional view, is actually less so, inasmuch as it involves a gross
psychological impossibility. To make this point clear, let me
remind the reader of the part which, according to this theory, was
played by St. Paul in the genesis of Catholic sacramentalism. As
Augustus found Rome brick and left it marble, so St. Paul is said
to have found Christianity a vague movement of apocalyptic
enthusiasm and to have left it a sacramental *Kyrios*-cult, a more or
less organised Mystery Religion—not as the result of any deliberate
action on his part, but through his too complaisant acquiescence in
the tendency of his converts to construe the Gospel in terms of the
Mysteries with which they were familiar. Now we have seen
that, on the admission of the most typical champions of the Mystery

---

¹ " How thrice-blest among mortals are they, who having beheld these
rites go to the house of Hades " (Soph. *Fr.* 719, ed. Dindorf).

theory, the Catholic ideas regarding Initiation and the Lord's Supper are already present in the First Epistle to the Corinthians, a document which can hardly be dated later than A.D. 55. But the first conversions of pure Gentiles, that is of persons who were neither Samaritans nor Jewish proselytes—and the theory requires a large influx of pure Gentiles to account for the first beginnings of the "infiltration"-process—cannot have happened earlier than A.D. 30-35, between which dates practically all systems of New Testament chronology would place the persecution which arose upon the death of Stephen, scattering the members of the primitive Jerusalemite community through Palestine and Syria, and thereby bringing to pass the momentous circumstance that certain "men of Cyprus and Cyrene" "spake unto the Greeks also the preaching of the Lord Jesus."[1] The radical transformation of the whole idea of Christianity which the Mystery theory assumes must, therefore, have taken not more, and probably rather less, than twenty years for its accomplishment.

Consider for a moment the implications of this supposition. It compels us to suppose that, within a comparatively short space of time, St. Paul's Asian and Hellenic converts unconsciously infected their master and father in Christ with what was, on the hypothesis which we are considering, a profoundly un-Christian point of view; and that this mental infection was so thoroughgoing that the Apostle, whilst still at the zenith of his intellectual and spiritual powers, and still enjoying an unimpaired memory of his past life, came to believe—in diametrical opposition to the truth—that he had "received from the Lord," through the Mother Church of Jerusalem,[2] and had always taught to his disciples, traditions and ideas which in fact he had unwittingly imbibed from them. It necessitates the ascription to him of an incredible degree either of simplicity or of carelessness, in order to account for the alleged fact that—whilst engaged in a campaign against those pagan cults which, in his bitterest moments, he regards, like Justin Martyr, as the work of daemons,[3] and which, in a more tolerant mood, he dismisses contemptuously as the worships of "many (so-called) *Kyrioi*"[4]—he should have unsuspectingly

---

[1] Acts xi. 20.

[2] I here assume the accepted interpretation of ἐγὼ . . . παρέλαβον ἀπὸ τοῦ κυρίου in I Cor. xi. 23 ; see below, p. 400.

[3] Compare I Cor. x. 20 f. and Justin, I *Apol.* 66.

[4] I Cor. viii. 5.

allowed the texture of his devotion and his thought to become saturated by conceptions borrowed from those very " Mysteries " which it was the object of his mission to destroy. If this be incredible, and yet the " Mystery " hypothesis be retained, it can only be on the supposition that St. Paul was dominated by the desire to attract converts at any price, even the price of truth. Only if one or other of these suppositions be accepted—only if we assume that the most heroic of evangelists may pervert his message for the sake of a cheap success, or that the most vigorous of thinkers may so befog himself by self-hypnosis as to lose grip on the realities of his own past life—shall we think it a probable explanation of the genesis of Catholic sacramentalism that " St. Paul, though ready to fight to the death against the Judaising of Christianity, was willing to take the first step, and a long one, towards the Paganising of it."

And only if we attribute a hardly believable blindness to the primitive nucleus of Jewish-Christians, can we suppose—as the " Mystery " theory would compel us to suppose—that, whilst attacking St. Paul with unmeasured ferocity for his liberalism in regard to the imposition of the Law upon Gentile converts, the Judaising faction should nevertheless have acquiesced, with inexplicable placidity, in his far-reaching contamination of the faith of Israel with Gentile ideas of a *Kyrios* and of " sacraments." [1]

### 2. *The evidence for " Dominical Institution " re-examined :* (a) *The Eucharist*

If the foregoing conclusions as to the *a priori* probability of the traditional and the " Mystery " hypotheses are cogent—and I cannot see any way of escape from them—we may now proceed to a re-examination of the *a posteriori* evidence for the " Dominical institution," with the general disposition to trust such evidence, if it can be found. It will be convenient to discuss in the first instance the evidence for Christ's institution of the Eucharist *as a permanent rite*. We may concede at once that the main weight of this hypothesis must rest upon the command which He is believed to have given, "This do in remembrance of me," and

---

[1] If the Judaisers had raised any serious protests against St. Paul's Christology and sacramentalism, some traces of the fact would surely be found in the Acts and Epistles.

that, in the present uncertainty as to the genuine text of Luke xxii. 17–20,[1] the words of St. Paul in 1 Cor. xi. 24, 25 constitute our sole authority for this command.    But, given the conclusions of our last paragraph—and leaving out of account for the moment the " Mystery " critic's trump card, namely, his contention as to the impossibility of our Lord's having made any provision for the future, owing to His " eschatologically limited outlook "— it is reasonable to suggest that St. Paul's authority is *prima facie* good enough.    The Apostle's affirmation is so solemn and significant that it may be quoted at length :

" For I received of the Lord that which I also delivered unto you, how that the Lord Jesus, in the night in which he was betrayed, took bread ; and when he had given thanks, he broke it, and said, This is my body, which is for you : this do in remembrance of me.    In like manner also the cup, after supper, saying, This cup is the new covenant in my blood : this do, as oft as ye drink it, in remembrance of me."

The opening words of this passage, " I received of the Lord that which I also delivered unto you," are almost identical with those which introduce the list of the resurrection appearances in ch. xv. 3 of the same Epistle, " I delivered unto you that which I also received," and presumably bear the same meaning, namely, that the teaching which St. Paul transmitted to the Church of Corinth he had himself received from the Mother Church of Jerusalem.    Such, indeed, is the accepted interpretation of the phrase :  Professor Percy Gardner's suggestion,[2] that the Apostle thereby implies some vision or supernormal " revelation " as the medium whereby he " received" this information "of the Lord," has won very little acceptance.    St. Paul, then, asserts quite definitely and bluntly, not only that Christ instituted the Lord's Supper as a permanent rite, but that he himself had been informed of the fact by the immediate disciples of Christ.    There can be no reason why these latter should have wished to deceive their

---

[1] See above, p. 382.  This admission does not invalidate the phrase in our present Prayer of Consecration, " Who . . . did institute, and in his holy Gospel command us to continue . . .," as some recent proposals for Prayer Book Revision seem rather pedantically to assume ;  the words " in his holy Gospel " need not mean " in one of the four canonical Gospels," but may more appropriately be taken as signifying " in his general message of salvation to the world."

[2] *The Religious Experience of St. Paul* (1911), p. 110 ff.

great recruit and future colleague ; and we have already shown reasons for rejecting the supposition that St. Paul deluded himself into the belief that he had received the Eucharistic tradition from the original Apostles, in much the same way as George IV deluded himself into believing that he had been present at the Battle of Waterloo. The Pauline testimony, then, holds the field so far. It is not temerarious to add that, if it had been only the acts and intentions of Alexander the Great or of Julius Caesar that were in question, testimony from an analogous source would never have been challenged.

The question may be very reasonably raised at this point : "If the words, ' This do in remembrance of me,' are a genuine *logion* of the Lord, how is it that they are absent from the Synoptic Gospels, and presumably from the ultimate sources used by the Synoptists, that is, the Petrine tradition underlying Mark, and what is usually termed LQ, the early and reliable tradition from which Luke drew his Passion-narrative ? " This question deserves a careful reply, all the more so because an adequate treatment of it will involve coming to close grips with the ultimate contention on which the " Mystery " theory rests and apart from which, as we have seen, it does not possess any measure of probability—the contention, namely, that Christ *could* not have instituted any sacraments or made any provision for a future Church, inasmuch as He believed that this present world was on the point of coming to an end. It will conduce to clearness if we formulate our answer first, and state the grounds on which we base it afterwards.

Our answer is in substance as follows. " The silence of the Synoptists, and possibly of the traditions which they employed, as to the command ' This do ' is amply accounted for—and any argument which might be founded on this silence, of a nature hostile to the hypothesis of ' Dominical institution,' is cancelled— by the fact that both Mark (followed by Matthew) and Luke contain another, more enigmatically expressed *logion*, which, though difficult of comprehension at the time of its utterance, was later recognised as being fraught with the same meaning as ' This do,' namely, the expression of the Lord's purpose that His actions should be repeated by His future Church. This *logion* is the verse, ' Verily I say unto you, I will no more drink of the [this, *Mt.*] fruit of the vine, until that day when I drink it new [with you, *Mt.*] in the kingdom of God' (Mk. xiv. 25=Mt. xxvi. 29 [1] =Lk. xxii. 18, with apparently a doublet in v. 16). As the Synoptists record this saying, they might well have thought it unnecessary to record the command ' This do,' even if they had known of it.[2] There is, however, no reason why both sayings should not have been uttered by our Lord at the Last Supper, the Synoptic traditions preserving one and the Pauline tradition the other.[3] " We must now proceed to justify the meaning which we have attributed to the Synoptic saying, " Verily I say unto you, etc."

We can best develop our exegesis of this passage by sketching the interpretation of it which would be given by thoroughgoing upholders of the view opposed to our own. The key to its meaning lies in the phrase " the Kingdom of God." For our Lord's contemporaries, the Kingdom of God meant a new world-order, conceived as a somewhat materialistic millennium, which would immediately succeed the Day of Jehovah with its accompanying cataclysms, in which the present world-order would have been dissolved. In this Kingdom the sovereignty of God would be exercised by the Messiah, reigning over a rejuvenated earth, which would be possessed by the Saints, that is by pious Israelites, in boundless peace, wealth and happiness. We have already sketched the theory that these expectations were shared by our Lord, and that His mental horizon was limited, so far as the existing world-order was concerned, by the belief in the imminence of the End ; from which it would follow that He can have had no idea of providing for the future of His group of disciples under the conditions of this present life by instituting sacraments. This theory, however, provides what is (given its assumptions) a not unreasonable explanation of His action at the Last Supper and of the *logion* now under discussion. It was apparently a common device of the apocalyptists [4] to represent the bliss of the millennial

---

[1] We assume that the Marcan version of this saying is more likely to be original, as being more fresh and vivid in phraseology, than the Lucan. The question as to whether it was spoken *before* the sacred action (Lk.) or *after* it (Mk., Mt.) is irrelevant to the argument.

[2] The presumption is that St. Luke at least *did* know of it, owing to his association with St. Paul.

[3] *Cf.* the two sayings said to have been addressed by our Lord to Judas at the moment of the betrayal—" Comrade, [do] that for which thou art here " (Mt. xxvi. 50), and " Judas, with a kiss dost thou deliver up the Son of man ? " (Lk. xxii. 48)—both of which may well be historical.

[4] *Cf.* 1 Enoch xxv., lxii. 14 ; *Test. Levi*, xviii. 11.

" Kingdom " under the figure of the " Messianic banquet "—
an image ultimately derived from the words of Isaiah xxv. 6,
" In this mountain shall the Lord of hosts make unto all peoples
a feast of fat things, a feast of wines on the lees, of fat things full
of marrow, of wines on the lees well refined." Now it has been
noticed that the acts of blessing and breaking bread in a specially
solemn manner are recorded as having been performed by our Lord
on at least one other occasion during His earthly lifetime, in
connection with the miraculous feeding of a great crowd (or on
two other occasions, if the stories of the Five and Four Thousand
be regarded as based on two separate incidents). Dr. A. Schweitzer
has made the brilliant suggestion [1] that, in order to heighten the
vividness of His teaching about the joys of the coming Kingdom,
Jesus was accustomed from time to time to hold what may be
described as a dramatic or symbolic rehearsal of the " Messianic
banquet," distributing to each of those present a tiny portion of
some common food, bread and fish, or bread and wine ; that the
stories of the " miraculous feedings " represent accounts of such
rehearsals, touched up (when their original significance had been
forgotten) by the addition of the assertion that the participants had
previously been fainting with hunger, but were supernaturally
satisfied by the multiplication of the food ; and that the actions
performed by Him at the Last Supper were meant to be the last
and most solemn of these ceremonial rehearsals, carried out within
the privacy of His own circle of intimate friends, under the
shadow of the impending Passion, by which He believed that He
could force the hand of God and compel the Kingdom to appear.
On this hypothesis, the meaning of the declaration " I will no
more drink of the fruit of the vine " is clear. Roughly paraphrased
it means " This is the last of our ceremonial rehearsals of the
' Messianic banquet,' the last of our symbolic foreshadowings :
the next meal at which we shall meet will be the reality, *the
' Messianic banquet ' itself*, celebrated in the new world-order, in
the unearthly Kingdom of God to be brought down from heaven
by the suffering which lies before Me. *Now* I drink, and invite
you to share, the old wine of this present world, which is ripe to
rottenness and on the point of passing away ; but *then* we shall
drink the new wine of the world to come."

---

[1] *Von Reimarus zu Wrede*, E. T., *The Quest of the Historical Jesus* (1910),
p. 374 ff.

It is impossible within the limits of this essay to examine the "eschatological" theory of the life of Christ in detail ; but it is not too much to say that on the whole such writers as Johannes Weiss and Schweitzer seem to have established, as against the older "Liberal Protestant" view, their main contention, namely, the centrality of the conception of the future "Kingdom" in our Lord's message, and the relatively subordinate position of His ethical teaching, as being merely a "propaedeutic" or preparatory discipline designed to qualify men for entrance into the Kingdom. The acceptance of this general position, however, does not by any means carry with it an acceptance of the more particular assumption which has coloured and determined these writers' whole presentation of the life of Christ, that is, the assumption that our Lord meant by "the Kingdom of God" *no more than what His Jewish contemporaries meant by that phrase*. This latter is the fundamental postulate which lies at the bottom of the hypothesis of His "eschatologically limited outlook," and, consequently, at the bottom of the whole "Mystery" theory. But, I submit, it is a postulate which, though not susceptible of mathematical disproof, is contrary to the inherent rationality of things and renders the general course of human history unintelligible ; for it assumes that the greatest Man of all time possessed little or no originality in the intellectual sphere, that He was the slave and not the master of popular phraseology, and that He did not possess even so much power of foreseeing and providing for the future as is attributed by Mommsen to Julius Caesar.[1]

It is not necessary to invoke the Christology of Nicaea and Chalcedon (which consistent advocates of the "Mystery" theory naturally do not accept), or to dogmatise about the very difficult problem of the limitations of the knowledge exercised by our Lord as man, in order to rebut this assumption ; it is sufficient to appeal to the general probability that the supreme Messenger of God to the world (and we cannot, within the limits of this essay, argue with any one who denies the historical Jesus this position) was not a deluded fanatic, whose prophecies were conspicuously

---

[1] Mommsen (*History of Rome*, E. tr., 1894, V. xi.) credits Caesar with the conscious intention of bringing into existence that unified and homogeneous Italo-Hellenic empire which actually did realise itself under his successors ; why should not a greater than Caesar be credited with the conscious intention of creating that Church and faith which actually did spring from His life and death ?

refuted by the facts, less than a generation after His death. Those who accept this general probability will be prepared to believe that our Lord was perfectly capable of pouring a new and refined content into current popular phrases, and that His prediction (in its Marcan form) " There be some here of them that stand by, which shall in no wise taste of death, till they see the kingdom of God come with power " [1] was fulfilled in very truth at Pentecost, when the Kingdom of God came with power as the Catholic Church and faith, which went forth from the Upper Room, conquering and to conquer. On this hypothesis, the " Kingdom," which is both present and future, both an interior inspiration and an external power, both the product of gradual growth and a catastrophic irruption into the time-series from the eternal world, is nothing other than the new dispensation of faith and grace which actually did spring from Calvary ; it is the " new covenant " consecrated by the blood of the Messiah, the new universal *Ecclesia* or Israel of God. With such an interpretation of the meaning of the " Kingdom " the facts of our Lord's life and teaching, as re-grouped by the " eschatological theory," come into perfect line ; and a new and deeper significance is given to the conception of the " Messianic banquet," as implied in the passages mentioned above.

In the light of this interpretation we may well accept the suggestion that our Lord's action at the Last Supper was not the first action of the kind. It is very probable that the feeding or feedings of great crowds, whether accompanied by miraculous circumstances or not, were meant in the first instance to be symbolic portrayals of the future banquet, which would gladden the hearts of the members of the Messianic Kingdom ; and that the same thought was present to our Lord's mind when He spoke of the Gentiles as " reclining at meat " with the patriarchs, at the mystic feast that was to be.[2] But, if the " Kingdom of God " is the Christian Church and faith, what else can the " Messianic banquet " be than the Eucharist, the *sacrum convivium* which is the centre of its life, and in which the Messiah Himself is believed to be both the Breaker of the bread and the Bread which is broken ?

---

[1] Mark ix. 1 ; the Matthaean version (xvi. 28) misunderstands the point of the saying, and turns it into a prediction of the end of the world and the Parousia of the Son of Man.

[2] Matt. viii. 11 = Luke xiii. 29.

If this is so, the Fourth Evangelist has, at the least, shown a true instinct, and may well be conforming to the historical course of events, when he appends his great Eucharistic discourse at Capernaum to the account of the "miraculous feeding." Whatever the exact purport of the words "This is my body" and "This is my blood"—and I should be trenching on the ground of another writer if I were to discuss this question in detail—it is clear that, on any showing, the communion administered by our Lord at the Last Supper must be regarded as having been *sui generis* and exceptional, because, at the moment when He pronounced these words, His body had not yet been broken, nor His blood shed ; and we may, therefore, without irreverence, conclude that there must have been something, as it were of imperfection, or of a provisional nature, in a communion administered before the accomplishment of that which every Communion is meant to proclaim, namely, the Lord's death.[1] If this is so, then the mysterious *logion*, from which this section of our discussion has started, may be interpreted as meaning : "This is the last of those prophetic actions, whereby I have endeavoured to impress upon you, through type and shadow, the glories of that future 'Messianic banquet,' which will be shared by the elect in the 'Kingdom of God.' The next time that we meet together on such an occasion as this, I shall still be the Host, though present invisibly, and not in tangible form. But the next celebration of this Feast will not be, as this is, a provisional and anticipated transaction of the sacramental mystery ; it will be *the mystery itself*, consummated in the Kingdom of God, that is, in My Church, which in its universalised or Catholic form will be constituted by virtue of the great events which lie before us, My death and resurrection, and the coming of the Holy Ghost."

Interpreted in this way, the saying is not indeed a command to continue the observance of the solemn "drinking of the fruit of the vine" : but it is an affirmation that the observance *would in point of fact be continued* in the future Kingdom : and such an affirmation, made by one who believed Himself to be the King-designate, is the equivalent of a command, in so far as it is an explicit declaration of His purpose and intention. It may therefore be concluded without extravagance that the Synoptic and the

[1] See the Note appended to this essay, " On Mark xiv. 25."

Pauline traditions, taken together, constitute evidence for the " Dominical institution " of the Eucharist (that is, for the performance by Christ of certain actions with the intention that they should be repeated), such as would be considered reasonably adequate for any alleged event belonging to the secular history of the same period and country.

### 3. *The evidence for " Dominical Institution " re-examined :* (b) *Initiation*

The question whether Christian Baptism can be said to have been " instituted " by Christ or not is in some ways a more difficult one. It is clear that in this connection the term cannot be taken as synonymous with " devised " or " invented " ; for the custom had already been practised by Christ's forerunner, John. It will be used, therefore, during the following discussion in the sense of " adopted," " sanctioned," or " enjoined." At this point the earliest Christian documents which we possess, namely the extant letters of St. Paul, fail us ; for though the Apostle of the Gentiles, as we shall see, attributes the highest value to the rite, he does not make any statement, in that part of his correspondence which has survived, as to its exact origin. The only direct statement on the subject contained in the New Testament is the famous verse, Matt. xxviii. 19, in which the risen Christ is represented, not merely as commanding the universal administration of Baptism, but also as prescribing the Trinitarian formula for recitation in connection with the sacramental act. It is impossible, for the reasons mentioned above in Section III,[1] to deny the force of the suggestion that this passage may be a piece of compendious symbolic narrative, that is, of dogmatic theology cast into a quasi-historical form, rather than of history strictly so called ; and we are therefore debarred from using the Matthaean command, " Go ye therefore . . ." as a means of settling the question without further discussion.

On the other hand, there is a reasonable probability that even " Matthew," with all his lack of the minute scrupulousness demanded by the modern scientific historian, would not in regard to a matter of such crucial importance have made so plain and

[1] p. 380 f.

direct an assertion without any sort of *a posteriori* justification. Even though his statement as to the exact occasion on which, and the precise terms in which, the precept was given may not command the fullest confidence, it is possible to hold that it embodies a kernel of truth, and that, on some occasion not known to us, Christ did with His human lips actually enjoin the practice of the custom upon His disciples. In other words, whilst we cannot attribute overwhelming weight to St. Matthew's testimony, it cannot be reasonably denied any weight at all. It is at least good evidence for the belief of the Christian Church some fifty years after the resurrection. The most logical view, therefore, of the function which it may play in our inquiry into the origins of Christian Baptism, will be to regard it as the feather which may decisively weigh down that scale of the historical balance which represents " Dominical institution," if sufficient indirect evidence can be gathered from the rest of the New Testament to invest this hypothesis with considerable likelihood. This text, taken together with the words attributed to our Lord by St. John, about the new birth through water and the Spirit,[1] will be just enough to turn a high degree of probability into reasonable certainty, assuming that such a probability can be established by other means. But if the weight of probability turns out to be in favour of the alternative hypothesis—namely, that which assumes that the disciples spontaneously copied the baptism of John, or the Jewish baptism of proselytes, without any explicit instructions from our Lord so to do—then the Matthaean text, not being more than a feather, will not avail to weigh down the opposite scale.

We will, accordingly, leave the Matthaean evidence for the moment on one side, and examine the *data* furnished by the remainder of the New Testament, in the hope of finding some independent indications as to the origin of Christian Initiation. Such a review must necessarily start from the baptism of John and its Jewish antecedents, but need not go further back into history : the idea of symbolising purification from uncleanness by the act of washing in water is so obvious and natural, and has occurred independently to so many peoples,[2] that it is neither necessary nor indeed possible to determine its ultimate beginnings.

---

[1] John iii. 5.

[2] For detailed information see Hastings, *E.R.E.*, vol. ii., art. " Baptism (Ethnic)."

In the Levitical law, ablutions with water are prescribed as a means of removing ceremonial pollution contracted by the touch of a corpse, or in other ways.[1] These precepts doubtless represent the survival of a primitive stage of religious thought, in which evil is conceived quasi-materialistically as " bad *mana*." From these Levitical lustrations were derived both the baptism of the Essenes,[2] and that by which proselytes after circumcision were made full members of the Jewish Church.[3] In the latter instance the idea was rather that of cleansing the Gentile from the ceremonial defilement with which he was assumed to be infected through a life spent in idolatry, than that of abolishing " original sin," in anything like the Augustinian sense of the term. John the Baptist adopted the custom, but gave it a distinctly ethical and spiritual, as contrasted with its previous quasi-material, significance. This is shown by the fact that John's baptism is described as a " baptism of repentance," [4] and that it was preceded by, or at any rate closely associated with, a confession of sins.[5] Here we discern for the first time two of the essential elements of the great Christian rite of Initiation, namely (*a*) Confession, and (*b*) Baptism. The purpose of John's baptism is said to have been the " forgiveness of sins," [6] and we need not doubt that he and his disciples believed that this was really effected by the act ; the distinction between a declaratory symbol and an efficacious sacrament is too subtle to be grasped by unreflective enthusiasts such as were those who thronged to hear the Baptist's preaching, and is, in any case, alien to ancient modes of thought. This " remission of sins," it would seem, had an eschatological orientation and purpose. Those who received it believed that they had been thereby invested with an invisible spiritual " character," which would be their passport through the terrors of the End, and would ensure their entrance into the calm haven of the Messianic millennium. We are not told that any verbal formula was associated with John's baptism. Despite his eclipse by his mightier Successor, and his early death, his movement seems to have possessed sufficient vitality to persist in the form of a " Johannite " sect, which survived as a kind of parasite on

---

[1] *Cf.* Lev. xv. *passim*, xvii. 15, 16 ; Num. xix.
[2] Jos. *B.J.*, II. viii. 7.
[3] *Jewish Encyclopaedia*, arts. " Baptism " and " Proselyte."
[4] Luke iii. 3 ; Acts xix. 4.     [5] Matt. iii. 6 = Mark i. 5.
[6] Luke iii. 3.

Christianity, administering the " baptism of John," at least down
to A.D. 55.    It will be remembered that one of its most illustrious
members was Apollos, who was eventually led by Aquila and
Priscilla into the larger life of the Christian Church.[1]

It is in contrast with this baptism of John that we perceive
most clearly the *differentia* of Christian Baptism, or baptism " into
the name of the Lord Jesus."    We are told that at Ephesus
St. Paul found certain members of the Johannite sect, who are
given the title of " disciples," [2] and must therefore be presumed
to have been indistinguishable in most respects from full Christians,
but who appear to have manifested none of those supernormal
phenomena generally attributed to the action of the " Spirit,"
and who upon examination confessed that they had not even
heard of His existence.    St. Paul thereupon rebaptizes them " in
the name of the Lord Jesus " ;   and we are told that when this
rebaptism had been completed by the imposition of the Apostle's
hands, the Holy Spirit came upon them, with the result that they
at once manifested the characteristic signs of His presence, namely,
" glossolaly " and prophecy.[3]   This incident is instructive.    It
shows, first of all, that the baptism of John and Christian Baptism
at this date were regarded as entirely different things, not as
imperfect and perfect forms of the same thing.    Secondly, we
gather that, on the external side, the *differentia* of Christian
Baptism is found in the employment of the " name of Jesus " as
part of a spoken formula ;   and, thirdly, that on the spiritual side
its characteristic effect is, not merely the " remission of sins,"
which the Johannine baptism also claimed to bestow, but the
impartation of " holy spirit."   We need not here investigate the
psychological *rationale* of the extraordinary phenomena which
the early Christians attributed to " holy spirit," or the validity of
the conception itself.    We are only concerned to draw attention
to the fact that, whereas Johannine initiation consisted only of
(*a*) repentance, and (*b*) baptism effecting only the " remission of
sins," Christian Initiation consisted of (*a*) repentance, (*b*) baptism,
and (*c*) laying on of hands, which produced *both* the " remission
of sins " *and also* possession of the Holy Spirit.

This ascription to Christian Initiation of a *double* effect,
negative and positive, sin-annulling and Spirit-bestowing, appears

[1] Acts xviii. 26.                        [2] Acts xix. 1.
[3] Acts xix. 1–7.

to run back into the very earliest days of the infant Church. On the Day of Pentecost St. Peter instructs his Jewish hearers as follows : " *Repent* ye, and *be baptized* every one of you *in the name of Jesus Christ*, unto the remission of your sins ; *and ye shall receive the gift of the Holy Ghost.*" [1] In other words, whereas the Johannine practice was a water-baptism only, the Christian rite was both a water-baptism and a Spirit-baptism. At first, it would seem, the illapse of the Spirit was mediated by the baptism alone.[2] Later, when the Apostles began to be confronted by baptisms which did not at once produce the supernormal *charismata* which testified to the Spirit's presence, it was found, as at Samaria,[3] that the imposition of the Apostles' hands was accompanied by the bestowal of what was lacking in the way of spiritual gifts ; and thus, apparently, the impartation of the Spirit became specifically associated with the " laying on of hands " as a distinct, though not as yet a separate, part of the rite. In this way what we now call " Confirmation " came into existence as embodying the positive effects of Initiation, the negative effects being specifically associated with the actual washing ; and in the Epistle to the Hebrews we find the " doctrine of baptisms " and of " the laying on of hands " bracketed together as part of the " foundation," in which it is assumed that adult Christians do not need instruction.[4] The complete continuity between this Apostolic practice and the combined rite of Penance, Baptism, and Confirmation, as we find it in the early patristic period,[5] does not need to be emphasised.

It is clear from the language of the New Testament that the subjects of this initiatory rite were normally adults, who alone were capable of the repentance and confession which formed its initial stage ; though it would be rash to assert that children were never baptized, and the well-known saying of Polycarp, " eighty and six years have I served Christ," [6] seems to show that at least one instance of infant baptism must have taken place before the fall of Jerusalem in A.D. 70. Consonantly with this fact, it appears that " the sins " which are conceived as being washed

[1] Acts ii. 38.
[2] Exceptionally, as in the case of Cornelius and his household, the illapse of the Spirit might actually precede the baptism (Acts x. 44 ff.).
[3] Acts viii. 14.      [4] Heb. vi. 2.
[5] *E.g.* Tertullian, *De Baptismo*, 7, 8, 20.
[6] *Martyrium Polycarpi*, 9.

away by Baptism are what we should call *actual* sins.[1]   Yet, in the exuberant enthusiasm of the Church's youth, it was natural to assume that interior conversion of the soul and exterior initiation into the Christian society were, not merely in theory but in fact, different aspects of the same process, like the concave and convex aspects of a curve.   At first, Baptism seemed to have the effect of transforming its recipient into a "new creation," [2] so effectually that all his sinful impulses and appetites were destroyed, and sin became both a moral and a psychological impossibility for him.   We need not now review the steps of the process whereby it was found, through bitter experience, that this ultra-optimistic estimate of the transforming effects of Initiation was exaggerated, and whereby, in the teeth of embittered opposition, "Penitence" was detached from its place at the beginning of the initiatory rite, and shaped into a subsidiary sacrament for the purpose of imparting a second remission of sins to post-baptismal offenders.   We are only concerned with the ideas which prevailed on these subjects during the lifetime of St. Paul ; and it is sufficient to refer the reader for an extensive treatment of the effects of Christian Initiation to cc. v–viii. of the Epistle to the Romans, in which the Apostle elaborates the primitive ideas of the "remission of sins" and the bestowal of "Holy Spirit" into a magnificent sequence of pictorial conceptions, representing the effects of "faith" and Baptism, that is of the whole change from non-Christianity to Christianity, under the figures of incorporation into the Messiah,[3] the crucifixion of the "old man," [4] the "annihilation of the body of sin," [5] a mystical participation in the death, burial and resurrection of the Redeemer-God, and the reception of the "Spirit of adoption," [6] which entitles the neophytes to repeat the words of the Lord's own prayer, "*Abba*, Father," [7] and which will one day transform them into the "splendour of the freedom of the children of God." [8]   A more prosaic, but no less characteristic,

---

[1] It is impossible here to examine the *rationale* of Paedo-baptism and its connection with the doctrine of "original sin" ; a full discussion of the matter will be found in my forthcoming Bampton Lectures, *The Ideas of the Fall and of Original Sin.*

[2] 2 Cor. v. 17.             [3] Rom. vi. 3 ; *cf.* Gal. iii. 27.
[4] Rom. vi. 6.       [5] vi. 6.         [6] viii. 15.
[7] viii. 15 : for the interpretation of "Abba, Father" as the opening words of the Lord's Prayer, see Th. Zahn, *Römerbrief* (1910), p. 395.
[8] viii. 18 ff.

summary of the various elements in Christian Initiation, both inner and outer, is found in 1 Cor. vi. 11, in which passage the Apostle, after having detailed various abominable types of human sin, adds, with considerable frankness—" And such were some of you [in your pre-Christian lives] ; but ye were *washed*, but ye were *sanctified*, but ye were *justified* [i.e. *absolved*] in the *name of the Lord Jesus* Messiah and in the *Spirit* of our God."

It has been said above that this Pauline conception is clearly continuous, indeed identical, with the doctrine of the earliest Christian writers outside the New Testament, that is, for all practical purposes, with the Catholic doctrine. Can it show a similar continuity with the ideas held in regard to Baptism during the earliest days of Christianity ? *Prima facie* the continuity between St. Peter's teaching as reported in Acts ii. 38 and St. Paul's teaching as expressed in the passages just mentioned appears to be without a break ; the threefold scheme, Penitence, Baptism with water in the Name of the Lord Jesus, Reception of " Holy Spirit," runs all through the New Testament allusions to the subject. We have already adduced considerations to show that St. Paul was not likely to have " paganised," or to have acquiesced in the " paganisation " by his converts of, an originally non-sacramental custom ; and these considerations apply just as much to Initiation as to the Eucharist. It is true that his theology of Initiation represents in one respect an advance upon the primitive ideas embodied in the early chapters of the Acts, in so far as the spiritual effect of Baptism is said to include not merely the impartation of " Holy Spirit" but a transcendental or mystical union with Jesus, the *Kyrios* : this, however, is not so much an addition to the primitive teaching as a clarification of it, which necessarily followed from the ever-growing realisation of the personal distinction between " the Lord " and " the Spirit." The suggestion that the Pauline or deutero-Pauline phrase " having cleansed it " (the Church) " by washing of water with a word " [1] implies a magical conception of Baptism (the " word " being the Name of Jesus used as a spell) and therefore the beginnings of " pagan infiltration," seems purely arbitrary.

We are, then, entitled to conclude, on the basis of this survey of the relevant New Testament passages, that one single conception of " Initiation " runs through the thought and the

[1] Eph. v. 26.

surviving literature of the Christian Church between the Day of
Pentecost (? A.D. 29 or 30) and the destruction of Jerusalem
(A.D. 70). This Christian Initiation, with its *three* members,
Penitence, Washing, Reception of " Spirit," is clearly based upon
the Baptist's initiation, which included *two* members only,
Penitence and Washing. In fact, the Christian rite may be
described as being identical with John's baptism, save for the
addition of two all-important features, one external and the other
internal, namely, the use of a formula containing the name of
Jesus,[1] and the consequent or concomitant impartation of " Holy
Spirit " to the baptized person. By what authority or by whose
will were these additions made ? Three considerations may be
adduced, the cumulative effect of which (I would suggest) is to
establish a very great probability that the historic cause which
transformed the baptism of John into Christian Baptism was the
expressed will of Christ Himself.

(1) The language of 1 Cor. x. 1–4, with its reference to the
Old Testament types of the two great sacraments, shows that
St. Paul bracketed together Baptism and the Eucharist, very much
as a modern Christian might, as rites of equal or all but equal
dignity and awe. (" Our fathers . . . were all baptized unto
Moses in the cloud and in the sea, and did all eat the same spiritual
meat, and did all drink the same spiritual drink." [2]) But there
cannot be any doubt that he bases the whole wonder and mystery
of the Eucharist on the fact of its Dominical institution, and it is
extremely unlikely that he would have coupled with it, as a rite
on the same level, a mere Church-custom which could not
claim a similar august origin. It is, further, inconceivable that
he can have based his exalted conception of Baptism on nothing
at all, or that he naïvely took this rite for granted without raising

---

[1] The early and universal substitution of the Name of the Father, Son,
and Holy Ghost for the " Name of the Lord Jesus " was presumably due to
the influence of Matt. xxviii. 19. In view of the eighteen centuries of prescription which the use of the Three-fold Name can now claim, the modern
Church is doubtless justified in making its employment an absolute condition
of the technical " validity " of the rite as administered at the present day ;
but the Roman Catholic scholar, W. Koch (*Die Taufe im N.T.*, 1921, p. 7)
quotes Pope Nicholas I (*Respons. ad consult. Bulgar., ap.* Denzinger-Bannwart,
*Encheiridion Symb. et Def.*, 335), Cajetan, and Hadrian of Utrecht (later Pope
Hadrian VI) as asserting the standing validity of baptism " in the name of
Jesus " or " of Christ."

[2] See Kirsopp Lake, *Earlier Epistles of St. Paul*, pp. 178, 213.

the question of its *provenance*.  It is equally improbable that, like Tertullian,[1] he connected the saving effects of Baptism with the intrinsic properties of water, or that he relied on the authority of John the Baptist, whose baptism he expressly declares at Ephesus to have been imperfect and provisional.  And it would be anachronistic in the extreme to suppose that his theology of Baptism, as a mystical identification with the death and resurrection of the Messiah, was founded merely on an " induction " from the " observed effects " of a custom which owed its origin and universal diffusion to mere chance.  The earliest Christians were not self-conscious enough to analyse their " experience " in the manner of the modern introspective psychologist, or to base scientific " inductions " upon it.  The fact that St. Paul's extant correspondence does not contain any explicit attribution of the institution of Baptism to Christ does not prove that other letters of his now lost may not have contained such an attribution ; and an argument *a silentio* hostile to " Dominical institution " cannot legitimately be based upon this fact.[2]  We are therefore entitled to claim, on the ground of the great solemnity with which St. Paul speaks of Baptism, implicitly co-ordinating it in respect of majesty and efficaciousness with the Lord's Supper, a very high degree of probability for the supposition that he believed its celebration to be founded on the declared will of Christ.  And if such was St. Paul's conviction, it must also have been the current teaching of the Mother Church of Jerusalem.  He can hardly have claimed for his teaching with regard to Baptism any other authority than that on which he bases his Eucharistic doctrine— " I received of the Lord " (through the mediation of those who had known Him in the flesh) " that which also I delivered unto you . . ."

(2) The narrative of the Day of Pentecost contained in

---

[1] *De Baptismo*, 3–5.

[2] The much-quoted sentence, 1 Cor. i. 17, " Christ sent me not to baptize, but to preach the gospel," if interpreted in the light of its context, merely means that St. Paul's characteristic function, as Apostle of the Gentiles, was preaching, rather than (what we should call) liturgical ministration ; he usually employed others to baptize for him, in order to avoid the possibility of his converts developing an excessive attachment to his own person.  Under circumstances similar to those which prevailed at Corinth, these words would have risen quite naturally to the lips of many Catholic mission preachers, from Savonarola down to Father Dolling ; and it seems purely arbitrary to construe them as a disparagement of Baptism or a denial of its Dominical institution.

Acts ii. represents St. Peter as stating, without a moment's hesitation or reflection, the fully developed theory of Christian Initiation in its three elements, Penitence, Baptism, and the reception of Holy Spirit.[1]  If this narrative can be taken as historically exact, Dominical institution is proved, because there had been obviously no time in which St. Peter could have considered the results of Christian Baptism and formed an inductive conclusion to the effect that it really did impart the Holy Spirit. We do not, however, leave out of sight the fact that the reminiscences of those earliest days transmitted to St. Luke by the Christians of the first generation, may have been unconsciously modified and remoulded in the light of subsequent experience ; and we will not therefore claim this passage as testifying to more than the conviction of the Palestinian Church, some twenty-five years after the resurrection, that Peter did on the Day of Pentecost behave and speak as though he knew beforehand what spiritual effects Christian Baptism would produce, a knowledge which in the nature of the case could only have been derived from the Lord Himself.  This passage therefore indirectly testifies to the belief in Dominical institution, as held by the Mother Church of Christendom less than a generation after the end of Christ's earthly life.

(3) The two foregoing considerations have reference ultimately to the beliefs of the Church of Jerusalem, the fountainhead of all Christian tradition, shortly after the middle of the first century of our era.  But to this may be added a consideration based upon probabilities arising out of admitted facts.  If Christian Baptism does not rest upon the declared will of Jesus Himself it must be regarded as the continuation within Christianity, either of John's eschatological baptism, or of Jewish proselyte-baptism. (There is not the slightest reason for supposing that the first Christians were influenced by the practice of the Essenes.)  Now it is not likely that the disciples of Jesus would, in the absence of express instructions from Him, have continued the custom peculiar to John.  From the point of view of our Lord's followers, John had no importance save as the forerunner of the Messiah (" he that is but little in the kingdom of God is greater than he " [2]) ; and there is no reason why a custom of his should have been supposed to be invested with an authority which did not belong

---

[1] Acts ii. 38.                    [2] Matt. xi. 11—Luke vii. 28.

to its author. This view, moreover, leaves unexplained the immense importance attributed to the use of " the name of the Lord Jesus " by the earliest Christians : it is not likely that the baptism of John was ever administered in the name of John, either by the Baptist himself or by his later disciples. The second hypothesis, that Christian Baptism represents the mere survival of Jewish proselyte-baptism, appears equally unsatisfactory. Proselyte-baptism could *ex hypothesi* only be administered to "sinners of the Gentiles," who were assumed to be polluted with idolatry and stained with all the vices of the Graeco-Roman world ; and to invite orthodox Jews, members of the holy nation, such as were the three thousand baptized on the Day of Pentecost, to submit to this rite would have been to offer them a gratuitous insult, if such an invitation had no better authority behind it than St. Peter's own sense of the fitness of things.

Both these hypotheses, therefore, are quite inadequate to explain the deeply impressive phenomenon of the universal prevalence of Christian Baptism from the earliest days of the movement onwards : and the use of the " Method of Residues " suggests that the true explanation is to be found in some command, or expression of purpose, given by the Lord Himself.

We claim, then, that for the unbiassed explorer of the origins of Christian Initiation these three considerations constitute a group of direction-signs, converging upon the supposition that our Lord, during His earthly life or through one of the resurrection-visions, conveyed to His followers some clear indication of His will in the matter ; and that by themselves they would render " Dominical institution " at least much more probable than any other hypothesis, even if no record of any facts which could be interpreted as such an " institution " had survived. Another finger-post, pointing the same way, is to be seen in the prediction of the Baptist that the Messiah would inaugurate a " Spirit-baptism," which (in St. Mark's version) is explicitly contrasted with the speaker's own " water-baptism." [1] Deeply significant, too, is the fact that Jesus Himself, having submitted to John's " baptism of repentance " in Jordan, experiences forthwith the illapse of the Spirit, which mediates to Him the full realisation of His divine Sonship and therewith some unimaginable consciousness of new birth, as expressed in the mystic locution

[1] Mark i. 8 ; Matt. iii. 11—Luke iii. 16.

"Thou art my Son, to-day have I begotten thee."[1] It does not appear an exaggeration to suggest that by undergoing this momentous experience, in which the interior influx of the Spirit was super-added to the exterior affusion of water, our Lord Himself, in His own Person, transformed the water-baptism of John into Christian Spirit-baptism.

We are now in a position to effect our final evaluation of the evidence. If we place in that scale of the balance which represents "Dominical institution" the cumulative probabilities set out above, adding thereto the feather-weight of the Matthaean testimony; and if we throw into the opposite scale what is in the last resort the only positive argument for "accidental origin," namely, the assumption of our Lord's "eschatologically limited outlook," an assumption which we have already seen to be of a highly arbitrary nature and devoid of any real weight, the reader will be able to judge for himself which scale must be taken to sink and which to "kick the beam." If, in Butler's words, "probability is the very guide of life,"[2] and if, in dealing with events which lie on the further side of a gulf of nearly nineteen centuries, a very high degree of probability may be taken as the practical equivalent of certainty, in sacred as in profane history, the "Dominical institution," in some form, of Christian Initiation may be regarded as reasonably assured.

If a more precise determination of the mode of this "institution" be demanded, the following theory may be tentatively put forward. The Fourth Gospel tells us that, towards the beginning of His ministry, Jesus "came into the land of Judaea, and there . . baptized," at a time when John was still engaged in administering *his* baptism, at Aenon near to Salim (iii. 22, 23). This statement is amplified in iv. 1 by the note that the baptism of Jesus soon outstripped that of John in popularity, and slightly modified in the following verse by the observation that Jesus (like St. Paul at a later date [3]) did not Himself act as the ministrant of baptism, but delegated this function to His disciples. If these statements are historical (and there seems to be no reason why they should not be [4]) a probable outline of events suggests itself;

---

[1] Luke iii. 22 (according to the "Western," and apparently more probable, reading).

[2] *Analogy of Religion*, Introduction.　　　[3] See above, p. 415, n. 2.

[4] It is coming to be universally admitted that the Fourth Gospel contains at least a large infusion of good and reliable tradition, and the details noted above may well belong to such tradition.

namely, (1) our Lord receives baptism from John, and through it the influx of " Spirit " ; (2) He consequently (if we may, without irreverence, employ human language in this regard) conceives the idea of a Messianic baptism, superior to the Forerunner's baptism, which will admit to the " Kingdom " (that is, to the New Dispensation) and impart " Holy Spirit " ; (3) He Himself administers, or provides for the administration of, this baptism during His earthly lifetime, as the means of initiating men into the little group of His adherents, which was the nucleus of the future *Ecclesia* ; (4) this pre-Passional administration of Baptism was, however, necessarily imperfect, just as the one pre-Passional celebration of the Eucharist was imperfect [1] ; though Jesus received the Spirit *for Himself*, at His own baptism, He could not as yet impart Spirit to others, " for Spirit was not yet " [so far as our Lord's adherents were concerned] " because Jesus was not yet glorified," [2] in other words, because He had still to *win* the gift of the Spirit for His new Israel by His suffering and death. Consequently (5) through one or more of the resurrection-appearances He intimates to His followers that the preliminary water-baptism which they have received, whether from John or Himself, will be supplemented and validated by the gift of the Spirit (" ye shall be baptized with the Holy Ghost not many days hence " [3]), and that the complete rite of Initiation is henceforth to be the means of admission into the new People of God.[4]

## VI

### CONCLUSION

If the foregoing considerations are well founded, we are entitled to conclude that the " institution," in the sense previously defined, of the two original and fundamental sacraments, Initiation and Communion, by the Founder of Christianity Himself, may be taken as proved, in the sense that the historical evidence for this hypothesis would be regarded as sufficient by an unbiassed inquirer. The outlines of the traditional theory stand fast, though a certain amount of reconstruction and restatement has

---

[1] See the Note at the end of this essay.      [2] John vii. 39.
[3] Acts i. 5.      [4] Matt. xxviii. 19.

been necessary in regard to detail. It may be reasonably asserted that the affirmation of the Dominical origin of the sacraments rests upon a much wider and more nearly contemporaneous consensus of testimony than do the affirmations of the birth of Herodotus at Halicarnassus or of the martyrdom of St. Peter at Rome ; and yet, of these two latter affirmations the first is not challenged at all, and the second is only disputed by those who on other grounds are strongly opposed to the claims which are made in the name of St. Peter by the present Church of Rome. If, then, the reader is still prepared to admit the cogency of the contention developed in the second section of this essay—namely, (1) that *if* the sacraments were really instituted by Christ they must be of quite overwhelming importance in the Christian life, and (2) that if they are of such overwhelming importance, it can only be because the grounds of their efficacy contain an element which is simply " given " or objective—a task of no small significance will have been accomplished.

But though the argument set forth above would, we believe, be good enough for a student who approached the question without *parti pris*, we do not claim for it mathematical irresistibility. As it will always be possible (*si parva licet componere magnis*) for those who are subconsciously dominated by anti-papal sentiment to deny any sort of connection between St. Peter and Rome, so doubtless it will always be open to those who feel an unconquerable aversion from the idea of objectively efficacious sacraments to reject the case for Dominical institution on one ground or another. To affirm this is not to fall into the vulgarity of imputing a lack of intellectual honesty to those who, like Eduard Meyer, are convinced *a priori* that " The thought, that the congregation . . . enters into a mystical or magical communion with its Lord through the reception of bread and wine . . . can never have been uttered by Jesus Himself " [1] ; it is merely to draw attention to the well-known fact that, in the concrete processes of psychic life, thought and feeling mutually suffuse and interpenetrate one another, and that men's judgments as to what is true, especially in regard to historical questions on which vital practical issues depend, are apt to be insensibly deflected by the unconscious wish that some particular solution may turn out to be true. Whether the influence of such disturbing factors has

[1] E. Meyer, *Ursprung u. Anfänge des Christentums* (1921), i. 179.

been successfully eliminated from our own exposition or not must be left to the reader's decision.

It does not in any case fall within the scope of this essay to deal in detail with the ancient and indurated anti-sacramental *praeiudicium*, which is the real, though hidden, source of the inhibition which restrains many religious persons from so much as considering the possibility that historic Christianity may actually be in possession of the marvellous treasure which it claims. The unexpressed conviction, which to those who hold it appears axiomatic, that a religion of priests, sacraments, liturgies, and ecclesiastical institutions—a religion, that is, which avowedly expresses itself through a phenomenal body or time-garment— must in the nature of things be a lower and inferior kind of religion in comparison with one consisting solely of intellectual concepts or ethical values, eludes dialectical attack by virtue of its emotional origin and its unprovable character. It is not, indeed, difficult to formulate the arguments on which it is nominally founded, as (*a*) that it is degrading to our conception of God to suppose that He can or will produce spiritual effects through the direct instrumentality of material things or external and sensible ceremonies ; (*b*) that sacraments understood in any other than a purely symbolic sense involve a sacerdotalism which is inevitably hostile to individual and civic freedom ; (*c*) that the belief in their objective efficacy is refuted by the sins of many who habitually receive them and the lofty Christian virtues of many who, like the Quakers, reject them. Nor is it harder to set against each of these arguments a group of considerations which would seem in logic to cancel it. To the first, it might be replied that God has never told us that He cannot or will not work spiritual effects through matter or the phenomenal world ; that unless we are prepared to accept a Deistic or Manichaean dualism, He is doing so every day through His immanent Real Presence in the vast multiform sacrament of the visible universe ; that (as Bishop Gore has pointed out) no spiritual operation ascribed to the sacraments of the Church is more sharply super-naturalistic, or bears a more frankly *ex opere operato* character, than the miracle whereby the creation of a new, unique, and individual human personality supervenes upon the consummation of what, considered in itself, is a purely material process. To the second the obvious rejoinder is, that whilst any institution existing amongst men is doubtless capable of perversion, Catholic sacerdotalism, involving as it does that impersonal conception of the part played by the human officiant which is expressed in the doctrine that "the unworthiness of the minister hindereth not the effect of the sacraments," is in principle much less liable to abuse by private ambition than theories of the ministerial function which by placing its essence in preaching and exhortation make its efficaciousness to depend entirely upon the talents, virtues and personal qualities of the individual minister ; and that the history of Calvinistic Geneva and Puritan Massachusetts is sufficient to show that ecclesiastical tyranny has no necessary connection with any one type of sacramental theory. The third is sufficiently countered by two principles which are inherent in the Catholic theology of sacramental grace, namely, *Deus non alligatur mediis*, and *Homo potest sacramentorum gratiae obicem ponere*. But the real vitality of the anti-sacramental *praeiudicium* resides in the emotional energy with which it is charged, and which flows from various underground sources—fear of the Papacy, the xenophobia which makes beliefs held by members of other nations than one's own appear for that reason alone as intrinsically repulsive, the unconscious survival of dualistic modes of thought which sunder God from all contact with matter, hereditary influence, and social suggestion. Those who are subject to this prepossession must always argue back from it to a negation of "Dominical institution" ; it will always appear self-evident to them that Jesus, as the highest spiritual teacher known to our race, cannot have intended to found what they believe to be a religion of the lower grade, and that therefore any evidence that He did so intend must be unreliable.

Historical argument alone can no more dissolve so tough and closely knit a psychic structure than it can create the corresponding, but opposite, conviction, the deep, calm, infinitely satisfying intuition which can only be experienced by those who know the Catholic system from within, and which reveals to them the ineffable harmony and homogeneity of the sacramental principle with the kindred truths of God's immanence in the whole world of created being and of His unique self-expression in the Incarnation. But faith can move mountains, and love wear down seemingly adamantine barriers ; and the believer in the traditional interpretation of the Christian sacraments will rely

upon their inherent power and mysterious compelling attractiveness to be in the long run their most effective missionary.    He
will confidently accept the implied challenge of Dr. Kirsopp Lake's
words, " If the Catholic theory of sacraments prove in the end to
cover all the facts, and to be the only theory which does cover
them, it will in the end be universally accepted " [1] ;  and he will
look for the ultimate fulfilment in a re-united Catholic Christendom of the promise made to the Church of the elder dispensation :
" In those days it shall come to pass, that ten men shall take hold
out of all languages of the nations, even shall take hold of the skirt
of him that is a Jew, saying, We will go with you, for we have
heard that GOD is with you." [2]

## ADDITIONAL NOTE ON MARK XIV. 25

A point connected with this *logion* may be here further explained,
in order to elucidate the view taken in the text as to the significance
of our Lord's actions at the Last Supper :

The implied contrast between the " old wine " which our Lord
had just drunk Himself (this is clearly indicated by the words " I will
not *again* drink . . ."—οὐκέτι οὐ μὴ πίω) and given to His disciples,
and the " fruit of the vine " which He would drink " new " in the
Kingdom of God, suggests that the *imperfect* and *provisional* character
which in the text of the essay has been attributed to the only pre-Passional
" celebration of the Eucharist," may have been so thoroughgoing as to
make it true to describe our Lord's actions on that occasion as constituting,
not a " Eucharist " as we know it now, but a " shadow " Eucharist—
a typical object-lesson, not the mystic and glorious reality which could
only be consummated in the " Kingdom of God " (*i.e.* the new Christian
dispensation) which His death was to inaugurate.    If this is a permissible
view, the Apostles at the Last Supper did not feed upon Christ, as we
do now, in reality, but only in figure ; their first real and sacramental
Communion in the body and blood of Christ can only have been made
after that body and blood had been glorified and freed from spatial
limitations by the resurrection.    This view completely avoids the almost
insoluble difficulty inherent in the traditional interpretation—" How
could our Lord with His own hands give His body and blood to His
disciples (*se dat suis manibus*) whilst evidently standing there before them
in His intact, unbroken body ? "    It must be admitted that there is no
ancient authority for this view : but it appears to be that favoured by
Dr. H. L. Goudge, " 1 Corinthians," p. 105.

---

[1] *Earlier Epistles of St. Paul*, 1911, p. 434.          [2] Zech. viii. 23.

# THE EUCHARIST

BY WILL SPENS

# CONTENTS

# I

## INTRODUCTORY

IT has often been said that one of the greatest needs of our time is a satisfactory glossary of religious terms. As things stand, the Christian apologist finds himself confronted with a dilemma. On the one hand, it is possible for him to try to discard much of the traditional phraseology in which Christian ideas are clothed, and to use only such language as may be supposed to be intelligible to any educated person. The obvious danger of such a policy is that he will, in fact, fail to convey many of the deeper and more difficult ideas for the expression and transmission of which the technical language was developed. His attempt would be like that of a man of science, who should try to give some account of the physical universe without employing any of those terms which scientists have invented. The other alternative is for the apologist to accept frankly the terminology with which the piety and thought of the Church have provided him, and to draw out its significance for the faith of intelligent men to-day. In pursuing this task he may find that some of the old terms are, in fact, no longer useful ; or, again, he may find that they are only useful if they are given a somewhat different meaning from that which they originally connoted. None the less, this policy has certain advantages. It goes far to ensure, for example, that no elements of proved value in the thought of the past are lost by misadventure ; while since the terms which he is discussing are not merely intellectual but also emotional symbols, his thought is kept at every point in close contact with the concrete experience of the worshipping Church. These conditions apply with peculiar force in dealing with a subject like the Eucharist, which is the acknowledged centre of the Church's devotional life, and yet has, for many centuries, given rise to acute theological controversy. Here, if anywhere, it is obviously important that discussion should be synthetic, as well as clear ; and for this purpose it is essential that the second of the two possible policies should be adopted.

In the present case, moreover, this course is clearly more convenient, inasmuch as many of the terms which belong to the current coin of Eucharistic theology have been the subject of careful discussion in the preceding essays and the result of those discussions will be assumed here.   Thus the sixth essay will have made clear the sense in which the word " grace " is used when we speak of the sacrament as a " means of grace."   Again, much has already been said in the essay on the Atonement about the cross as a sacrifice for sin, expressive at once of sin's awfulness and of its forgiveness.   Still more germane, of course, to the present essay, is that which has immediately preceded it, in which it was urged that the sacraments are not merely dramatic but effectual symbols, and that they derive their significance from the fact of our Lord's appointment.   All these words—grace, sacrifice, sacraments, symbol—will occur again in a rather different setting in our consideration of the Eucharist, together with other terms to which reference has not yet been made ;  but the discussion will assume, throughout, the general theological and historical background provided by the rest of this volume.

## II

### Symbol and Sacrament

It would probably not be denied that symbolism of some kind is a necessity of religion as soon as it receives a social and institutional expression.   That this is so would seem to be proved not least by the practice of those Christian bodies which have, in fact, set themselves, so far as possible, to do without it.   Nowhere is this more clear to us than in the case of the Society of Friends, whose emphasis upon the sovereignty of the inward aspect of religion has not prevented them from adopting a symbolism in dress and speech which was, at one time, a picturesque and well-known feature of English life.   Symbols are, in fact, a kind of language which men use when words fail them.   One aspect of this use was expressed by Pope Gregory the Great, when he spoke of images as the " books of the unlettered," [1] implying that words would be beyond their wit to read ;  another aspect is expressed in civic, no less than in religious, ceremonies, as when the unfurling of a flag or the beating of a drum expresses something for which words would be too weak.   Symbolism of this kind occurs frequently in the historical and prophetic books of the Old Testament ;

[1] Gregory, Lib. ix, Ep. cv, *ad Serenum.*

and our Lord's entry into Jerusalem provides a significant example of it in the New. In all such cases, however, the symbolism is dramatic or didactic.

There is, however, another kind of symbolism to which the word effectual may be given, and which is no less a feature of human society ; and it is to this type rather than to the other that the Christian sacraments belong. The distinctive mark of an effectual symbol is that it not merely conveys a message, but effects a result. The accolade is a case in point. More familiar, if less obvious, examples are supplied by token coinage to which an authoritative decision of the State gives certain purchasing value, defined in terms of the sovereign, but quite independent of the coin's intrinsic worth. A little reflection will suggest, in ever-growing number, other illustrations. The essence of such symbolism lies in the association of certain results or opportunities with certain visible signs by a will which is competent to bring about those results or give those opportunities. To the properties which the action or object has in itself are added other properties which may be civic, social, or economic, and it is this second series of properties which is taken for all practical purposes as determining the nature of the symbolic action or object. Those who recognise the authority which appoints the token do not, in fact, use or think of their florins as though they were counters.

From all merely human symbolism, even of this type, the sacraments are, of course, differentiated by the character of the results and opportunities connected with them, and by the fact that these are determined by the will of God Himself ; but none the less the analogy is valuable and real. When we say that the sacraments are effectual signs we mean that certain actions or objects are invested by divine authority with certain spiritual or supernatural properties. The action of washing, for example, in Baptism admits the baptized not merely into the visible fellowship of the Church but into the regenerate order, the Kingdom of God, of which the Church on earth is the expression. In the case of the Eucharist, the bread and the wine are given by Christ's ordinance new properties, which, while they do not annihilate the natural properties of giving sustenance and refreshment, yet so supersede these that we can rightly speak of the objects themselves as wholly changed and transfigured. As Theodoret says, " They remain in their former substance and shape and form, and are still visible and as they were before ; but they are apprehended as what they have become, and are believed and adored as being what they are believed to be." [1]

These considerations, moreover, will enable us to make clear what was involved when Christian theology found itself unable to rest contented with the close parallelism between Baptism and the Eucharist on which the earlier Fathers, notably St. Augustine, used to insist. The form which the development took was the claim that the Eucharist contained not only the two elements which were recognised in Baptism—namely, *sacramentum* and *virtus sacramenti*—but a third element also, which was distinguished as *res sacramenti*. In other words, it was claimed that in the Eucharist there was not only a symbolism of action, but a symbolism of objects as well. And this threefold distinction is a development which is reflected in Anglican formularies, where our Catechism speaks, in the case of the Eucharist, of " sign," " thing signified," and " benefits." If we ask, moreover, the reason which prompted this development we shall be compelled to find it in the words which our Lord is represented as using at the institution of the Eucharist —words which have no parallel in the case of Baptism. To the narratives of that institution we must now turn with a view to discovering what our Lord meant by the effectual symbolism of objects which He then established.

## III

### THE EUCHARISTIC SACRIFICE

If a student of comparative religion, not otherwise acquainted with Christianity, were to enter a church where the Holy Mysteries were being celebrated, and were afterwards asked what kind of service he had been attending, he would undoubtedly say that it was some sacrificial rite ; and he would find his answer endorsed if he were to turn from the service which he had witnessed to the earliest narratives of its institution. It is not only that the descriptions of the rite in the New Testament are marked by certain expressions which have all the appearance of liturgical fixity, nor again that the words used by our Lord, such as the reference to the new covenant, are strongly suggestive of sacrifice. Even more significant is the fact that the records are agreed in placing the rite in a context which is replete with sacrificial associations. On the

[1] Dialogue II, P.G. lxxxiii. 165–168.

one hand, that is to say, it is made clear, particularly by St. Luke, that the Last Supper, and the Eucharist which was its climax, took place under the shadow of the Passover ; and the force of this fact is not diminished, if we adopt the Johannine view as to the date of the crucifixion. On the other hand, all our evidence makes it clear that the rite at the Last Supper was connected by the closest ties with that sacrifice of Christ upon the cross which was so soon to be consummated.

In the light of these facts the natural meaning of our Lord's phrase, " Take, eat, this is my body," and of the corresponding and even more startling phrase as to His blood is surely not difficult to determine : they must have meant that in receiving the bread which He had broken and the cup which He had blessed the apostles were made partakers in a sacrifice, and thereby in the blessings of a sacrifice, in which He was to be the victim. We need not suppose, nor does the evidence suggest, that ritual participation in sacrifices was always regarded as securing and conditioning spiritual consequences. We cannot assign, for example, to the Paschal meal a clear sacramental significance. But this is bound up with the fact that the Jews had apparently ceased to assign to the killing of the Paschal victims any supernatural consequences. In the case, however, of a sacrifice which was regarded as truly propitiatory (and therefore in the case of our Lord's death) it is impossible to believe that devout ritual participation in an appointed manner would not have been supposed both to secure and normally to condition participation in the blessings which flowed from it.

Or, again, if we turn to passages of the New Testament other than the records of the institution, the same conclusion holds good. St. Paul's language, for instance, seems definitely to require this view ; for he was writing for persons familiar in a greater or less degree with Mystery Religions, and it is incredible that he should not have guarded his language far more carefully, had he not regarded the Eucharist as a sacrifice, and believed that devout ritual participation in this sacrifice secured and conditioned participation in spiritual blessings. There is no evidence, moreover, that St. Paul was subject to any criticism on the score of his Eucharistic teaching, and it must therefore be taken as representing what the apostles understood our Lord to have meant. Once more, even the sixth chapter of the Fourth Gospel gives little real support to any different conception of the Eucharist. If by eating His flesh our Lord is taken to have meant merely the reception of His teaching, then His language as recorded could only be pronounced unaccountably misleading and provocative. A real difficulty is removed if the issue was intended to lie not between the Jews' literal interpretation of His words and a final explanation that eating our Lord's flesh meant receiving His teaching, but between that literal interpretation and the sacramental explanation which the Eucharist afforded. On such a view the phrase " the words that I have spoken unto you are spirit and are life " referred to His whole foregoing teaching, including that on the Eucharist. Whatever view be held as to this or as to the historical character of the discourse—and on that question no view is here expressed—it is safe to say that its language could not be what it is unless the Evangelist either himself understood the discourse as having a sacramental and sacrificial reference or was at least endeavouring to account for a current tradition of Dominical teaching in this sense which he could not ignore. Neither the Fourth Gospel nor any other evidence [1] affords any real ground for setting aside that conception. As we have seen, it is implied by the other Evangelists and by St. Paul ; and it may be summed up by saying that the Eucharistic Host and Chalice not only represent our Lord as appropriable in a visible rite as our sacrifice, but also render Him thus appropriable ; an idea which carries with it participation in His life.

Enough has already been said to justify the earlier statement that a stranger present at the Eucharist would naturally describe it as a sacrificial rite. It is necessary, however, in view of current misunderstandings and controversies, to carry the analysis further, and it is the more profitable to do so at this moment in view of recent developments of Eucharistic theology associated with the

[1] *Cf.* the Rev. W. L. Knox's Second Appendix entitled "The Primitive Eucharist " at the end of his *St. Paul and the Church of Jerusalem*. It is not easy to take seriously the attempts which have been made to use the *Didache* as an argument against a sacramental view of the Eucharist. We need only point to the standard of exegesis in the book, which is not merely trivial but on occasion manifestly superficial and untrue. For example, shortly before the often quoted passage on the Eucharist occurs the sentence : " Let not your fasts be with the hypocrites ; for they fast on Mondays and Thursdays, but do you fast on Wednesdays and Fridays " ; while shortly after it occurs the sentence : " Do not test or examine any prophet who is speaking in a spirit ; for every sin shall be forgiven, but this sin shall not be forgiven."

name of Père de la Taille.[1]  The definition of sacrifice from which we shall best approach this task is that which describes it as consisting in two main and necessary elements, one the death of the victim, and the other certain ritual acts, very often concerned with the blood, which invested the death with a supernatural significance or effect.  The word " death " is used rather than " destruction " because, although it is true that not all sacrificial gifts are animate and therefore cannot be said to die when sacrificed, yet the word " death " is in fact more applicable in cases where a living victim is offered.  It does not, that is to say, beg the question of the purpose of the killing of the victim, but leaves the way open for the explanation that at least one purpose of the victim's death is the release and the appropriation of its life.[2] In the case of the sacrifice of the death of Christ the importance of this point is obvious.  The technical term generally used for this element in a sacrifice is immolation or mactation.  The principal objection which has been urged and rightly urged by Anglican theologians against what has been until recently the dominant tradition of Roman Catholic teaching, is that their doctrine of the Eucharistic sacrifice appeared to suggest a further immolation of Christ in every Mass.  This idea is obviously inconsistent with the New Testament, and with its clear belief in the all-sufficing efficacy of the death of Christ.  At the same time the alternative to such a view appeared to be that the Mass could only be called a sacrifice in a sense so subordinate and secondary, and so different from that entertained by Roman or Orthodox theology, as to make the description at best misleading. The importance of a definition of sacrifice on the lines suggested above is that it makes it possible to describe the Eucharist as a sacrifice in a primary sense, without involving or suggesting any repetition of the cross.

---

[1] In view of a considerable similarity between his doctrine of the Eucharistic Sacrifice and my own, it should be said that the position adopted in this essay was worked out independently of Père de la Taille's work, and in fact before I had become acquainted with it.  It can be most fully studied in his *Mysterium Fidei de augustissimo Corporis et Sanguinis Christi Sacrificio atque Sacramento.*

[2] This fact has led Père de la Taille to say that "conversion" would be a better term than " destruction " to use of the sacrificial gift.  In O.T. sacrifices (and in many others) ritual acts concerned with the blood would often appear to involve this conception, the blood representing the life to the worshippers.

For, in the first place, it is asserted on this view that the act of destruction, in virtue of which the Eucharist is a sacrifice, is the one historical death of our Lord on the cross, not some further act of destruction or other corresponding change. But, in the second place, it goes on to discover in sacrifice a second element which is no less characteristic or essential than the victim's death. We can best see the character and the necessity of this element by an illustration. Suppose that Abraham had slain Isaac without ceremony, instead of preparing to slay him on an altar or in accordance with some other convention which clearly expressed his purpose of sacrifice. Would one regard that as fulfilment of a command to sacrifice his son ? Think of any other sacrifice, actual or legendary, and imagine all ritual acts omitted, leaving simply an act of destruction, not performed in a ritual manner. Whatever the purpose of the act, would it fully correspond to what we mean by a sacrifice, save as we have come to apply the term in a metaphorical sense ? In short, is not some ritual act which expressly invests the death with its sacred purpose or significance at least as characteristic an element in sacrifice as is the death itself ?

If, as appears to be the case, this last question must be answered in the affirmative, the explanation is not far to seek. Consider first honorific sacrifices. It is not possible to regard these simply as gifts to the deity worshipped ; the gift is so made as to constitute an act of homage, a formal recognition and acknowledgment of his sovereign claims. There lies the explanation, for example, of the fact that the inherent value of that which is surrendered is, on the whole, less important than that it should have been expressly appointed or that it should possess a natural symbolism ; and there also lies the explanation of the need for such act or acts as will expressly invest the rite with its significance. In consequence, if a formal definition of a sacrifice is to be attempted it would appear necessary so to frame it as to treat this aspect as an essential element, by asserting, for example, that a sacrifice is a series of related actions dictated by belief in some Higher Power and involving (*a*) the giving or giving up of something, in and through a death, to a supernatural Being—or to secure a supernatural end or to secure supernatural aid ; and (*b*) an act or acts dependent on or closely related to the death, and of such a character as formally to invest this with supernatural significance, and thus to render the rite an express acknowledgment of a relation to some Higher Power.

The need for some such definition appears to be no less real in the case of propitiatory sacrifices than in the case of honorific sacrifices. We would hesitate to describe as a propitiatory sacrifice an act of destruction, even if this was conceived as effecting a propitiation, unless the act of destruction was performed in such a manner or accompanied by such further acts as served to express its purpose and significance. If a god was believed to have required the death, say, of the king's son in consequence of tribal sin, and if the king's son was promptly slain without ceremony, we should say that the purpose of his death was the propitiation of the god, but we should not describe what took place as a propitiatory sacrifice. We should so describe it if the manner of his death, or other closely related ritual acts, gave expression to the purpose and significance of the death ; and an explanation of the apparent necessity for such ritual acts may again be found in the fact that they render the rite an express acknowledgment of a relation to God, in this case a relation which has gone wrong. It is precisely in virtue of the presence and significance of such acts that there is not only a purpose of propitiation, but an avowal of that purpose. The rite thus becomes an express acknowledgment of the need for propitiation and, in so far as this propitiation is held to be necessitated by sin, an acknowledgment of the nature of sin and its significance. Nor is acknowledgment before God the whole story. Propitiatory sacrifices are conceived not only as an acknowledgment by man before God, but, in so far as they are thought of as divinely appointed, as an authoritative declaration to man of the significance and effect of sin. In short, such sacrifices have a manward as well as a Godward reference, and the declaration to man as well as the acknowledgment before God implies ritual acts which expressly assign its significance to the act of destruction.

If, then, we are justified in regarding as an essential and important element in sacrifice, no less essential or important than immolation, acts which expressly invest the immolation with its significance, the first condition is secured for a solution of our problem. It may be noted at once that as shown, for example, by the case of the Passover, it is such acts, rather than the killing of the victim, which are necessarily performed by the priest.

On this ground, and for the sake of brevity, in what follows such acts will be referred to as " sacerdotal acts."

It will by now be obvious that the view to which we are approaching is that the Last Supper and the Eucharist are not separate sacrifices from that of Calvary, but supply a necessary element in the sacrifice of Calvary, by expressly investing our Lord's death before God and man with its sacrificial significance. There is nothing, moreover, in sacrificial conceptions to preclude the multiplication of the sacerdotal acts. In the case of our Lord's sacrifice such multiplication was necessary if that sacrifice was to be truly proclaimed, and its benefits duly appropriated, by successive generations. And this necessity is not less but greater in view of the absolute significance we ascribe to our Lord's death in contrast with the " types and shadows " of the older dispensation. For, as has already been pointed out elsewhere in this volume, the essence of Christ's sacrifice on the cross consists in the fact that it is an acknowledgment before God and man of the nature and consequences of sin. It is sin's " covering " or propitiation, which is a necessary antecedent to man's reconciliation with God. What is asserted here is that the Eucharist is that part of the sacrifice of Calvary which, by our Lord's appointment, expressly invests His death with its significance and thus renders it such an acknowledgment. By it He ensured that Christian worship should be centred in the confession of God's infinite holiness and of the awfulness of sin, and that His worshippers of all times and places should only on the basis of that wholly evangelical confession stand secure in His fellowship and grace. It is not an accident that in every ancient liturgy the prayer of Consecration issues from the solemn accents, at once uplifting and humbling, of the *Sanctus*. In other words, while our Lord's death supplies in itself an adequate expression of the nature and consequences of sin, our profiting from the satisfaction thus effected must surely involve our acknowledgment and recognition of this. Such recognition requires expression no less than any other element in religion ; while, if a particular manner of acknowledgment has been appointed, then it is for us to give our recognition this expression rather than to urge, like Naaman, the equal or greater efficacy of possible alternatives.

On the other hand, we cannot regard the Eucharist simply as an acknowledgment by man that our Lord's death exhibits the nature and results of sin, an acknowledgment which is effected by our expressly assigning to that death the significance of an expiatory sacrifice.[1]  At the Eucharist, our Lord's death is invested with this significance in and through a rite which, since it affords participation in the blessings of our Lord's sacrifice, must be held to be performed with divine authority.  Because it is in and through such a rite, and therefore with such authority, that the Church's ministers solemnly invest our Lord's death with an expiatory significance, and thus acknowledge before God and declare to man the nature of sin, they may properly be termed priests.  On the other hand, such a statement of the position is something less than the truth.  This Divine authority is possessed, as we believe, because the Eucharist is celebrated by our Lord's command, whether given at the Last Supper or through the Holy Spirit to the early Church.  In accordance with our conception of Christians not as external to our Lord, but as members of His body, Christian acts performed by His command must be thought of less as performed by His authority, than as performed by Him through the members of His mystical body.  As a result, He is to be conceived as Himself the Priest in the Eucharist, no less than at the Last Supper ; but because His ministers are also our representatives we participate in His sacerdotal act.

On such a view the Eucharist is a sacrifice, not only or primarily because we offer thanksgiving or give money or hallow bread and wine, or even because Christ is there given to be our food, but because by word and act, by the words of institution and in the double consecration and through the act of Communion, His death is proclaimed, before God and man, as an expiatory sacrifice, and because this express investing of a sacrificial death with its significance is no mere declaration, adding nothing beyond declara-

---

[1] The phrase "expiatory sacrifice" is used as best describing a sacrifice which is regarded as propitiatory alike in intention and effect, and as necessitated by sin.  That this significance is assigned to our Lord's death by the Eucharist, and that the early Church regarded the institution as assigning to it this significance, is made clear by the words of institution, as given in the various records and as taken up into the Eucharistic liturgies.  Our Lord's body is described as given for us, His blood as poured out for us, as inaugurating a new covenant, and as poured out unto the remission of sins.  Even apart from the presence of the last of these phrases we should be justified in reading its meaning into any description of our Lord's sacrifice which represents this as propitiatory, since the propitiation thus effected was, from the first and as a matter of course, held to be necessitated through sin.

tion, but is itself an essential element in such a sacrifice, required, not by some trick of definition, but in order to supply an overt acknowledgment and declaration of the nature and consequences of sin. Whether we think of the cross as the one sacrifice or of each Eucharist as a sacrifice, whether we speak of Christ as having been once offered upon the cross or as being offered in every Mass, depends simply on whether we are thinking in terms of one or other of two essential aspects of sacrifice. If we think of sacrifice in terms of the act of destruction, Christ was once offered upon the cross. If we think of sacrifice in terms of the sacerdotal acts which expressly invest an act of destruction with its significance, then Christ is offered in every Mass. Either view is correct from its own angle : and for either view the death is fundamental. Nor does a choice appear possible or desirable between one or other mode of expression. Both must be used in their proper context if we are not to minimise unduly either the cross or the Eucharist.

There is one subordinate point in regard to sacrifice which appears to be of sufficient value and relevance to deserve emphasis. Details in the symbolism of the sacerdotal acts are often highly significant and of real devotional value. It is in this connection that it appears possible to retain and use the truth embodied in conceptions of the Eucharistic sacrifice which emphasise the offering of bread and wine. The fundamental fact in the consecration is that Christ is given to be appropriated as our sacrifice, and that His death is thus expressly invested with a sacrificial significance. But, in subordination to this, we may well dwell on the symbolism of the means by which it is secured : on the consecration of typical gifts of God ; on how much is thereby made of gifts so common or so capable of abuse ; and, by that identification of the worshipper with the thing consecrated, which is so frequent an idea in sacrifice, on the purpose of hallowing ourselves, not to become as many separate and inadequate sacrifices as there are individuals, but to become one with and in Him who is the only perfect sacrifice. If another conception of the Eucharistic sacrifice seems to have been omitted which is too deep-rooted to be thus ignored, it must be replied that the solemn assertion, before God as well as before man, of the expiatory character of our Lord's death is in itself in the strongest possible manner a pleading of that death. Further pleading of that death in the Eucharistic liturgies is valuable as bringing out what is thus involved. It can add nothing to what is involved.

To sum up. The writers of the New Testament, when they speak of the Eucharist, are unanimous in bringing it into the closest connection at once with the Passover and with the cross. They represent our Lord as celebrating this rite, if not for the first time, at least with a new (sacrificial) significance, on the eve of His passion and death. They imply a clear purpose on His part that He should be done to death at the hands of wicked men ; and they show Him forestalling the certainty that His death would appear to His disciples as no more than the judicial murder of a martyr by giving to it, in advance, a significance which, in the light of the resurrection and ascension, would supersede that other interpretation altogether. By what He said and did at the Last Supper, and in our repetition of what He then did, our Lord invested and invests His death with its significance as a sacrifice for sin ; and it was because of this that St. Paul could write, "As often as ye eat this bread and drink this cup ye show forth the Lord's death till he come," and that the writer to the Hebrews could describe the cross as an altar (Heb. xiii. 10). Both alike, the cross and the Eucharist, are integral to the sacrifice of our redemption. The fundamental element—fundamental because of the nature of Him whose life was offered on the cross—is the death of Christ ; and that immolation once made can never be repeated. But equally necessary in its bearing upon the salvation of the world is the rite by which down the long succession of ages our Lord makes His death to be our sacrifice and enables us to appropriate the blessings thus secured.

## IV

### THE REAL PRESENCE

The doctrine of the Real Presence, more perhaps than any other element in Eucharistic teaching, is charged with all the warmth of Christian devotion. The idea of a special presence of God would seem to be in itself one with which religion cannot dispense. It is what gives to many moments of spiritual experience, described in both the Old Testament and the New, their peculiar vividness and freshness of appeal. When Jacob says "Surely the Lord is in this place, and I knew it not " ; or when Moses, at the burning bush, " hid his face, for he was afraid to look upon God " ; or when the psalmist cries " Whither shall I go from thy spirit ? or whither shall I flee from thy presence ? " or, again, " The Lord is in his holy temple, the Lord's throne is in heaven "—in all these cases we are confronted with utterances and actions which belong to the very heart of religion. Jewish faith in particular distinguished three modes of this presence—in Nature, in the Chosen People, and in that central shrine where the invisible glory of the Shekinah brooded over the Mercy-seat ; yet there is nothing to show that their emphasis upon any one of these displaced or weakened their hold upon the others. In all cases, moreover, the context of the term presence suggests that its primary reference is to the experience of grace, and that that reference provides the best key to its definition. In the New Testament we find this element of Jewish faith, as we should expect, transfigured by the fact of the Incarnation and the dispensation of the Spirit. Christ is Himself the personal embodiment of the divine glory and tabernacled amongst men. He promised that when His visible presence was withdrawn He would still be present in the midst of believers gathered in His name ; and the Epistles bear abundant witness to the way in which the earliest Christian communities found this promise fulfilled in their experience of the Holy Spirit and their incorporation into Christ in the Church. The doctrine of the Real Presence asserts that in addition to (but as a consequence of) the more general presence in the Church, the Eucharist affords a presence of our Lord as our sacrifice, and that this presence is of such a character as to give opportunity for full and concrete expression of our worship of the Lamb.

No more than in the case of the Jewish Shekinah are other modes of our Lord's presence depreciated or excluded ; and, indeed, all true Eucharistic theology insists that in the Eucharist our Lord is present as priest as well as victim. The sacramental presence, that is to say, depends upon and derives from Christ's priestly presence in the Church. But that is not to say that the Eucharistic presence has not its own characteristics and claims. In the Eucharist, Christ is present as the Lamb slain from before the foundation of the world ; and the space devoted in each of the Gospels to the narratives of the Passion and crucifixion imply that this is an aspect of our Lord's Being and work which it would be impossible to emphasise too much.

So much will probably be generally admitted ; difficulty arises rather when we come to interpret these ideas in relation to the Eucharistic Gifts. Various terms have been used in Catholic theology to describe this relation. If what has been said in the preceding sections of this essay holds good, we are bound to say that the bread and wine are changed by consecration. They acquire a new property, namely, that their devout reception secures and normally conditions participation in the blessings of Christ's sacrifice, and therefore in His life. Regard being had to their sacrificial context, this is the natural meaning of the description of the consecrated elements, in relation to their consumption, as our Lord's body and blood—His body given for us and His blood shed for us. Outwardly, we have bread and wine ; the inward part and meaning of the sacrament is that these become in this sense the body and blood of our Lord, and as such are received by His people. The act of reception requires appropriation by faith, if reception is to have its proper consequence and complete meaning ; but the opportunity for reception and appropriation is afforded by the sacramental Gifts. The body and blood of our Lord are given after a spiritual and heavenly manner, not by any process separate from, and merely concomitant with, visible administration, but because the bread and wine become in the above sense (without any connotation of materialism) His body and His blood. It is true that this occurs simply in and through their becoming effectual symbols, but wherever the significance of an effectual symbol is certain and considerable we naturally think of it in terms of that significance, as well as in terms of its natural properties. We do not carefully separate in thought the natural properties of a florin and its purchasing value ; rather, we combine the two, and we think of the florin, quite simply, as an object [1] which has certain natural properties and certain purchasing value. We tend to think of the latter as to all intents and purposes a property of the object ; yet it depends simply and solely on the fact that the object is an effectual symbol. The case for a similar view of the Eucharistic symbols is, of course, infinitely stronger. In the first place, the Eucharistic character of the elements turns more directly on the

---

[1] Here, and throughout the essay, the word object is used to connote a complex of persisting opportunities of experience which have a common situation in space. The properties of an object are the component opportunities. Further analysis of "objects" is of course necessary from various points of view ; the above definition appears adequate for the present purpose.

connection between a certain act—to wit, devout reception—and certain results, and the basis of this connection is identical with the basis of those potential sequences between action and effect which constitute the natural properties of a visible thing. The Eucharistic sequences and the natural sequences are both determined by the divine will. In and through consecration those complexes of opportunities of experience which we call bread and wine are changed, not by any change in the original opportunities of experience, but by the addition of new opportunities of experience which are equally ultimate and have far greater significance.

Such considerations justify the tendency to speak of the consecrated elements as Host and Chalice, or as the Blessed Sacrament, or, using our Lord's words, to describe them as His body and blood, not as asserting any material or quasi-material identity with His natural or glorified body and blood, but as asserting that they render Him appropriable as our sacrifice. Any Eucharistic theology which does not begin by treating the words of institution as an immediate assertion of an identity tends also to use such phrases as the sacramental body and blood or the Eucharistic body and blood. Such phrases have a real value. They avoid much misunderstanding, and at the present day and in present circumstances they probably avoid more and more important misunderstandings than they create. On the other hand, they are in turn open to misunderstanding and to criticism which may be summed up in the incongruous phrase employed in this connection, that they teach a multi-corporal Christ. In the only sense in which we can still think of our Lord's glorified body as identical with His natural body, we must, however, think of His sacramental body as identical with that body. The identity between our Lord's glorified body and his natural body must be held to consist in the facts that opportunities of experience which each includes, and normally conditions, are directly determined by that nature which our Lord assumed at His Incarnation ; and that in each case the whole complex of opportunities of experience exists as such in immediate dependence on that nature and affords immediately an expression of it. All this is, however, also the case in regard to the Eucharistic body or blood. And the doctrine thus resulting admits of more than one philosophical expression. In the terms of a value-philosophy, the word " Convaluation "[1] meets the

---

[1] *Cf.* W. Temple, *Christus Veritas*, pp. 247 ff.

case ; though it may be questioned whether " Transvaluation " would not do so even better.  If the doctrine were translated into scholastic terms it would involve the assertion that the substance of the Eucharistic body and blood is the substance of that body and that blood which our Lord assumed at His Incarnation ; and it is in this sense a doctrine of transubstantiation.  But it is not such a doctrine of transubstantiation as is condemned in Anglican formularies, and is neither open to the objections nor presents the difficulties to which those testify.  It does not overthrow the nature of a sacrament but is directly based on assigning to a sacrament that nature which Anglican formularies assign, and is deduced from the traditional Anglican view simply by insistence on the significance and implications of the facts that in the Eucharist we have primarily a symbolism of objects, and that the effectual symbolism of a sacrament is based on, and determined by, the divine will.[1]

It will be obvious that the views which have been advanced have an immediate bearing on the question of Eucharistic adoration. The danger of idolatry (in its narrower sense) lies in the identification of a material object with a divine person.  The position with regard to images is exactly parallel to that with regard to pictures. They may legitimately afford a means for expressing as well as

[1] This is perhaps the most convenient point to notice an important criticism of the line of argument which is being employed.  It is urged that this proves too much : that all that is claimed in regard to the Host or Chalice might be claimed in regard to unconsecrated bread or wine on the ground that these have the " property " that they can be consecrated to become the Eucharistic body and blood, and that this " property," and either complex as including this " property," also depend on our Lord's being and nature.  When, however, an opportunity of experience depends on a special capacity to utilise an object, which capacity is possessed only by certain persons, the opportunity of experience thus presented cannot be regarded as a property of the object, and is rightly referred to the capacity, not to the object.  The possibility of the " Venus of Milo " or of Leonardo's " Last Supper " was not a property of some piece of marble or of certain pigments, although dependent on these.  So with the bread and wine.  The opportunity which the unconsecrated bread and wine afford is not general, so that the same act by any person in the same (regenerate) order would normally have the same effect.  It depends on a special power inherent in the priesthood, even although this power of the priest is, of course, merely the power of an ambassador, and what is involved in his making bread and wine effectual symbols depends not on his will but on the divine will.  A further reply can also be made, in the judgment of the writers, by regard to immediacy of dependence and the nature of the " property " in question, but the above consideration appears adequate for the purpose, and is considerably simpler.

stimulating feelings. Unless it is improper for a man to kiss the picture of one he loves, or place flowers before a picture of a dead wife, or for ardent politicians to decorate the statue of Lord Beaconsfield, it cannot be improper for the Catholic to place flowers or lights before the image of a Saint. Nor is this situation different when the image is an image of our Lord, and, in consequence, of a Person to whom adoration may be paid. But there must be no identification of the object with the person : these must consciously be held apart or idolatry results. In the case of the Sacrament the matter is different. On the view advanced we have objects which are a direct expression of our Lord's being and nature ; which exist in direct dependence on that being and nature as such an expression, and which enable us not only to participate in the blessings of His sacrifice but to be strengthened with His life, thus affording a relation to Him even more intimate than that which His natural body made possible. It is, of course, obvious that even such an object may not be worshipped in itself with that worship which may only be properly paid to a person. Even if our Lord were present in His glorified body, when we knelt before it in our worship of Him, we should not be giving to the Body in itself that worship which may be properly paid only to a divine person, but we should be so far identifying the object with the person that our worship of the person found expression in relation to the object. If the Eucharistic body and blood are no less directly related to Him in that they are no less directly dependent on His being and nature, and if they mediate an even more intimate relation than did His natural body, a similar attitude is justified, and our Eucharistic adoration finds natural and proper expression in acts related to the Sacrament.

It may be worth while, finally, to point out the bearing of these considerations on the devotional use of the Reserved Sacrament. It is desirable to emphasise that from the point of view here advanced the question whether our Lord is present and may be worshipped in the Reserved Sacrament, and the question whether Communion may be given by means of the Reserved Sacrament, are not two questions but one question. When it is asserted that our Lord is present in the Reserved Sacrament, it is not a question of asserting something additional to the fact that Communion may be given by the Reserved Sacrament. If the Reserved Sacrament is in fact capable of giving Communion precisely the arguments as to Eucharistic adoration which have already been advanced apply in the case of the Reserved Sacrament. Further, when this finds expression in devotional practices, what is involved is simply the transposition—in time, though not in thought, and for convenience though not in principle—of elements which are intrinsic parts of the Eucharistic rite. Thus, the devotional use of the Reserved Sacrament is not something independent of Communion and deriving from some separate conception. It is precisely because devout reception unites us to our Lord that the Reserved Sacrament is His body, that He is present in a special manner, and that He can be thus adored.[1]

# V

## CONCLUSION

The foregoing argument will have suggested that the Eucharist is only very imperfectly described in the phrase, so often repeated, that it was given only for the purpose of Communion ; but it will also have been clear that the whole doctrine here advanced is at every point rooted in, and dependent on, the idea of Communion as an integral and culminating part of the rite. If we were to define the purpose of the sacrament, we probably could not do better than use the language of the Catechism, and say that it was instituted " for the continual remembrance of the sacrifice of the death of Christ, and of the benefits which we receive thereby." This essay has been an attempt to draw out the meaning of that pregnant definition. It is, however, by no means the only statement in our formularies which appears to presuppose a Catholic doctrine of the Eucharist. The rubric with regard to reconsecration, for instance, would be unnecessary, if not superstitious, if, instead of the symbolism of the rite being one primarily of objects rather than of action, the acts of individual administration were held to be directly sacramental. The same view is

---

[1] The desirability of the devotional use of the Reserved Sacrament, and the forms which it should take, involve considerations outside the scope of this essay, since practical questions arise as to the risk of inadequate teaching with consequent superstition, and as to such an excess of these devotions as would destroy the proportion of the faith. It may, however, be fairly claimed that objections of these types hold against many other forms of devotion, and that experience in the case of these would appear to show that a remedy is better sought in regulation than in prohibition.

suggested by the rubric as to the consumption of what remains of the consecrated elements ; while more broadly still, the whole structure of the English Communion Office—its requirement of priesthood in the celebrant, its detailed directions as to vesture and ceremony, its preparation of the worshipper by confession and absolution, and not least its truncated Consecration prayer with its abrupt emphasis on the words of institution—points to the symbolism of the rite being conceived as at once sacrificial and effectual.

At the same time, the truth that the Eucharistic sacrifice finds its consummation in Communion is one which cannot be too strongly emphasised. The principle is implicit in the universal fact that no Eucharist is ever celebrated without the priest at least communicating ; and it is an axiom of Catholic teaching that only by devout reception of the Sacrament can the individual worshipper appropriate its benefits. There have been periods in the Church's history, no doubt, when this side of the truth was forgotten ; and it may be admitted that one cause of this has sometimes been an undue stringency of penitential or ceremonial discipline. More serious, however, is a difficulty of an opposite kind, which must be faced before we close. It cannot be denied that to many minds the notion that the partaking of a sacrament should be " generally necessary to salvation " is a great stumbling-block. To such minds the sacramental principle appears to involve a reaction from that pure and spiritual religion which Jesus Christ came to establish. The issue is too large for adequate treatment here, and we must be content with no more than an outline. It will generally be found on examination that this difficulty involves an important underlying assumption—the assumption, namely, that our spiritual experience is, and should be, independent of and separable from our natural experience. But is that true ? Is it not rather the case that spiritual experience, though of course it is more than natural experience, is yet so commonly intertwined with it as to stand to natural experience in the relation of whole to part ? Certainly this is the case in our social relationships. An outstretched hand, for example, may be the expression of an offer of renewed friendship ; and in such a case the offer and its acceptance alike involve this expression as part of the whole experience. In certain circumstances a salute to the national flag is not something separable from our loyalty, but is an integral part of such loyalty and of the experience which this involves. At every turn in our social life acts or opportunities of personal intercourse are ordinarily associated with some outward expression, suitable for its purpose but otherwise arbitrary ; and the facts would appear to suggest that a healthy emotional life requires such an expression in a substantial measure. Within the special field of religious experience the same would appear to be the case. It is easy to say that an excess of sacramentalism is harmful : it is difficult to deny the value of sacramentalism as an element in religion. And sacramentalism found at once a fuller opportunity and a more adequate basis when God became incarnate. By His own acts on earth and through the Church as His mystical body it became possible in a new degree for the Word of God to give expression to opportunities and gifts of grace, and thus to utilise a method of intercourse which men had always employed in their personal relations with each other, and after which they had sought so earnestly, if often so mistakenly, in their relations with God.

There will, of course, always be those whose thought and devotion will tend to lay especial stress upon the " exemplarist " aspects both of the Incarnation and of the cross, and to whom spiritual and moral progress will consist chiefly in the development of the understanding ; and it will usually be found in such cases that the appeal of the Eucharist is not strong. Yet even such people will probably admit that Christ's example, in His life and in His death, is not the whole Christian Gospel, but that this involves an activity of God towards man and in man deriving from the historic and glorified Christ and continuous in the Church ever since. That activity is what we mean by the word " grace." And what the Catholic belief in the Eucharist asserts is that this grace is normally given by means of the Sacrament, which when received in faith—and even for natural nourishment active assimilation is necessary—does in fact renew the believer's union with God. It cannot be too often asserted that it is on the actuality and fruits of that union, and not any conscious feeling of it, that the emphasis is laid in Catholic teaching and practice. It would probably be true to say that " sensible devotion " at the time of Communion is the exception rather than the rule in the case of those who most regularly receive. But " we know whom we have believed," and find in experience that God performs all that

He promises in this rite, so far as our frail faith and feeble penitence allow. More than that we cannot ask ; but less we dare not claim.

## NOTE

The above Essay is based on an article on the Eucharistic Sacrifice in *Theology* (October, 1923); on a pamphlet by the late Mr. Arthur Boutwood (Hakluyt Egerton) and myself, *A Cross Bench View of the Reservation Controversy*, published by the Faith Press; on the Second Appendix to the *Irenicum* of John Forbes by the editor of this volume; and on other material lavishly supplied by him. I am indebted to the publisher of the above article and pamphlet for permission to incorporate certain passages.

# INDEX

*Printed in England at* The Ballantyne Press
Spottiswoode, Ballantyne & Co. Ltd.
*Colchester, London & Eton*